Taking Sides: Clashing Views in Health and Society, 13/e

Eileen L. Daniel

http://create.mheducation.com

ISBN-10: 1259904024 ISBN-13: 9781259904028

Contents

Detailed Table of Contents

Unit 1: The Health Care Industry

Unit 2: Health and Society

Issue: Will Legalizing Marijuana Increase Usage?
Yes: Christian Hopfer, from "Implications of Marijuana Legalization for Adolescent Substance Use," *Substance Abuse* (2014)
No: Christopher Ingraham, from "Now We Know What Happens to Teens When You Make Pot Legal," *Washington Post* (2016)

Physician Christian Hopfer believes that marijuana legalization will increase availability, social acceptance, and possibly lower prices leading to increased usage among adults and teens. Journalist Christopher Ingraham argues that marijuana use among teenagers is essentially unchanged since legalization.

Issue: Is the Use of "Smart" Pills for Cognitive Enhancement Dangerous?
Yes: Alan Schwarz, from "Drowned in a Stream of Prescriptions," *The New York Times* (2013)
No: Phil Taylor, from "Think Positive: The Rise of 'Smart Drugs,' " *PMLive* (2013)

Pulitzer Prize-nominated reporter Alan Schwartz maintains that "smart pills" such as Adderall can significantly improve the lives of children and others with ADHD but that too many young adults who do not have the condition fake the symptoms and get prescriptions for the highly addictive and dangerous drug. Journalist Phil Taylor disagrees and claims that smart drugs are safe and effective in boosting cognition.

Issue: Are There Medical Benefits to Cloning?
Yes: Robin McKie, from "Human Cloning Developments Raise Hopes for New Treatments," *The Guardian* (2013)
No: Brendan Foht, from "The Case against Human Cloning," *BioNews* (2015)

Science editor Robin McKie argues that human cloning can create embryonic stem cells used to treat diseases such as heart failure. Editor of The *New Atlantis: A Journal of Technology and Society* Brendan Foht counters that there are numerous safety and moral issues related to cloning.

Unit 3: Mind-Body Relationships

Issue: Should Addiction to Drugs Be Labeled a Brain Disease?
Yes: Alan I. Leshner, from "Addiction Is a Brain Disease," *The Addiction Recovery Guide* (2016)
No: Steven Slate, from "Addiction Is Not a Brain Disease, It Is a Choice," *The Clean Slate* (2016)

Alan I. Leshner, director of the National Institute on Drug Abuse at the National Institutes of Health, believes that addiction to drugs and alcohol is not a behavioral condition but a treatable disease. Addition Theorist Steven Slate counters that addiction is not a true disease since there is no physical malfunction and the brains of addicts are normal.

Unit 4: Sexuality and Gender Issues

Issue: Is It Necessary for Pregnant Women to Completely Abstain from All Alcoholic Beverages?
Yes: National Organization on Fetal Alcohol Syndrome, from "Is It Completely Safe and Risk-Free to Drink a Little Alcohol While Pregnant, Such as a Glass of Wine?" *nofas.org* (2013)
No: Emily Oster, from "I Wrote That It's OK to Drink While Pregnant. Everyone Freaked Out. Here's Why I'm Right," *slate.com* (2013)

The National Organization on Fetal Alcohol Syndrome provides evidence that even moderate quantities of alcohol can damage a developing fetus and cites new research indicating that even small amounts of alcoholic beverages consumed during pregnancy may be harmful. Economics professor Emily Oster argues that there are almost no studies on the effects of moderate drinking during pregnancy and that small amounts of alcohol are unlikely to have much effect.

to make decisions about sugar consumption themselves and that government should not restrict our access to sugar and sugar-containing food products.

Unit 6: Consumer Health

Issue: Is Weight-Loss Maintenance Possible?
Yes: Barbara Berkeley, from "The Fat Trap: My Response," *refusetoregain.com* (2011)
No: Tara Parker-Pope, from "The Fat Trap," *The New York Times Magazine* (2011)

Physician Barbara Berkeley believes that weight maintenance is not easy but possible as long as people separate themselves from the world of typical American eating. She also claims that some individuals are heavy because they are susceptible to the modern diet or because they use food for comfort. Journalist Tara Parker-Pope disagrees and maintains that there are biological imperatives that cause people to regain all the weight they lose and for those genetically inclined to obesity, it's almost impossible to maintain weight loss.

Issue: Does Obesity Increase the Risk of Premature Death?
Yes: Harvard School of Public Health, from "As Overweight and Obesity Increase, So Does Risk of Dying Prematurely," *Harvard School of Public Health* (2016)
No: Harriet Brown, from "The Weight of the Evidence," *Medical Examiner* (2015)

The editors of the Harvard School of Public Health argue that being overweight or obese is clearly associated with a higher risk of dying prematurely than being normal weight. Writer Harriet Brown maintains that obese individuals with chronic diseases fare better and live longer than those of normal weight.

Issue: Are Energy Drinks with Alcohol Dangerous Enough to Ban?
Yes: Don Troop, from "Four Loko Does Its Job with Efficiency and Economy, Students Say," *The Chronicle of Higher Education* (2010)
No: Jacob Sullum, from "Loco over Four Loko," *Reason* (2011)

Chronicle of Higher Education journalist Don Troop argues that the combination of caffeine and alcohol is extremely dangerous and should not be sold or marketed to college students and young people. Journalist and editor of *Reason* magazine Jacob Sullum disagrees and claims that alcoholic energy drinks should not have been targeted and banned since many other products are far more dangerous.

Issue: Do Diet Sodas Aid in Weight Loss?
Yes: William Hudson, from "Diet Soda Helps Weight Loss, Industry-funded Study Finds," *CNN* (2014)
No: Stephanie Bucklin, from "Why Diet Soda Could Actually Prevent You from Losing Weight," *The Huffington Post* (2016)

CNN Medical Producer William Hudson reports that studies show that diet soda drinkers are likely to lose more weight than water drinkers. Writer Stephanie Bucklin argues that research indicates that diet soda may actually hinder weight loss efforts.

Issue: Do the Benefits of Statin Drugs Outweigh the Risks?
Yes: Jo Willey, from "The Benefits of Statins 'Greatly Outweigh' Small Risks Say Experts," *express.co.uk* (2014)
No: Martha Rosenberg, from "Do You Really Need That Statin?" *huffingtonpost.com* (2012)

Journalist Jo Willey reports that statins' ability to prevent heart attacks and stroke outweighed any risks and that tens of thousands of deaths from cardiovascular disease could be prevented if all eligible adults took the drugs. Investigative reporter Martha Rosenberg interviewed physician Barbara Roberts, who claims that statins treat high cholesterol, which is a weak risk factor for heart disease, and that the side effects of the drugs negate any benefits, especially when taken by otherwise healthy adults with high cholesterol.

Preface

Taking Sides: Clashing Views in Health and Society is composed of debates on controversial issues in health and society. Each issue consists of opposing viewpoints presented in a "yes"/"no" format. Most of the questions that are included here relate to health topics of modern concern, such as universal health insurance, abortion, and drug use and abuse. The authors of these articles take strong stands on specific issues and provide support for their positions. While we may not agree with a particular point of view, each author clearly defines his or her stand on the issues.

This book is divided into six units containing related issues. Each issue is preceded by an introduction, which sets the stage for the debate, gives historical background on the subject, provides learning outcomes, and provides a context for the controversy. Each issue concludes with further exploration of the issue which offers a summary of the debate and some concluding observations and suggests further readings on the subject. The summary also raises further points, since most of the issues have more than two sides. Contributors to this volume are identified, which gives information on the physicians, professors, journalists, theologians, and scientists whose views are debated here.

Taking Sides: Clashing Views in Health and Society is a tool to encourage critical thought on important health issues. Readers should not feel confined to the views expressed in the articles. Some readers may see important points on both sides of an issue and may construct for themselves a new and creative approach, which may incorporate the best of both sides or provide an entirely new vantage point for understanding.

This edition of *Taking Sides: Clashing Views in Health and Society* includes some important changes from the previous edition. For some issues, I have kept the topic from the past edition but have replaced one or both of the selections in order to make the topic more current or more clearly focus the controversy. I also added new topics and selections that reflect current controversies in health and society.

Eileen L. Daniel
SUNY College at Brockport

Editor of This Volume

EILEEN L. DANIEL is a professor in the Department of Public Health and Health Education and a vice provost for Academic Affairs at the State University of New York College at Brockport. She received a B.S. in nutrition and dietetics from the Rochester Institute of Technology, an M.S. in community health education from SUNY College at Brockport, and a Ph.D. in health education from the University of Oregon. A member of the American Dietetics Association, the New York State Dietetics Society, and other professional and community organizations, she has published over 40 articles in professional journals on issues of health, nutrition, and health education. She is the editor of *Annual Editions: Health.*

Acknowledgments

Special thanks to my family. Also, thanks to my colleagues at the State University of New York College at Brockport for all their helpful contributions. I was also assisted in preparing this edition by the valuable suggestions from the Taking Sides: Health and Society Academic Advisory Board. Many of your recommendations were incorporated into this edition. Finally, I appreciate the assistance of the staff at McGraw Hill.

Academic Advisory Board Members

Members of the Academic Advisory Board are instrumental in the final selection of articles for each edition of TAKING SIDES. Their review of articles for content, level, and appropriateness provides critical direction to the editor and staff. We think that you will find their careful consideration well reflected in this volume.

David Anderson
George Mason University

Judith Ary
North Dakota State University

Faye Avard
Mississippi Valley State University

Alice Baldwin-Jones
The City College of New York

Barry Brock
Barry University

Elaine Bryan
Georgia Perimeter College

Cynthia Cassell
University of North Carolina, Charlotte

Jeanne Clerc
Western Illinois University

Susan Crowley
North Idaho College

Evia L. Davis
Langston University

JoAnne Demyun
Eastern University

Karen Dennis
Illinois State University

Diane Dettmore
Fairleigh Dickinson University

Kathi Deresinski
Triton College

Jonathan Deutsch
Goodwin College

Johanna Donnenfield
Scottsdale Community College

Karen Dorman
St. Johns University

Wilton Duncan
ASA College

William Dunscombe
Union County College

Neela Eisner
Cuyahoga Community College

Ifeanyi Emenike
Benedict College

Brad Engeldinger
Sierra College

David Evans
Pennsylvania College of Technology

Susan Farrell
Kingsborough Community College

Jenni Fauchier
Metropolitan Community College

Christine Feeley
Adelphi University

Catherine Felton
Central Piedmont Community College

Paul Finnicum
Arkansas State University

Eunice Flemister
Hostos Community College, CUNY

Deborah Flynn
Southern Conn State University

Mary Flynn
Brown University

Amy Frith
Ithaca College

Bernard Frye
University of Texas, Arlington

Stephen Gambescia
Drexel University

Kathie Garbe
University of North Carolina, Asheville

Deborah Gritzmacher
Clayton State University

Dana Hale
Itawamba Community College

Leslie Hellstrom
Tidewater Community College Leslie

George Hertl
Northwest Mississippi Community College

Martha Highfield
California State University, Northridge

Marc D. Hiller
Universityo New Hampshire

Cathy Hix-Cunningham
Tennessee Technological University

Loreen Huffman
Missouri Southern State University

Kevin Hylton
University of Maryland, Baltimore County

Leslie Jacobson
Brooklyn College

Pera Jambazian
California State University, Los Angeles

Barry Johnson
Davidson County Community College

Marcy Jung
Fort Lewis College

Melissa Karolides
San Diego City College

Leroy Keeney
York College of Pennsylvania

John Kowalczyk
University of Minnesota, Duluth

Sylvette La Touche-Howard
University of Maryland, College Park

Robert Lavery
Montclair State University

Carrie Lee Smith
Millersville University

Hans Leis
Louisiana College

Linda Levin-Messineo
Carlow University

Karen Lew
University of Miami

Michelle Lewis
Fairleigh Dickinson University

Xiangdong Li
New York City College of Technology

Cindy Manjounes
Lindenwood University

Hal Marchand
Western Illinois University

Willis McAleese
Idaho State University

Fredanna M'Cormack
Coastal Carolina University

Michael McDonough
Berkeley College

James McNamara
Alverno College

Julie Merten
University of North Florida

James Metcalf
George Mason University

Eric Miller
Kent State University

Lloyd Mitchell III
Elizabeth City State University

Kara Montgomery
University of South Carolina

Martha Olson
Iowa Lakes Community College

Anna Page
Johnson County Community College

Judy Peel
North Carolina State University

Tina M. Penhollow
Florida Atlantic University

Jane Petrillo
Kennesaw State University

Regina Pierce
Davenport University

Roger Pinches
William Paterson University

Roberta L. Pohlman
Wright State University

M. Paige Powell
University of Alabama, Birmington

Elizabeth Quintana
West Virginia University

Leon Ragonesi
California State University, Dominguez Hills

Ralph Rice
University of Florida At Gainesville

Leigh Rich
Armstrong Atlantic State University

Andrea Salis
Queensborough Community College

Elizabeth Schneider
Keiser University, Ft. Lauderdale

Kathryn Schneider
Pacific Union College

Allan Simmons
Jackson State University

Donna Sims
Fort Valley State University

Kathleen Smyth
College of Marin

Stephen Sowulewski
J. Sargeant Reynolds Community College

Caile Spear
Boise State University

Diane Spokus
Penn State University, University Park

Betsy Stern
Milwaukee Area Technical College

Craig Stillwell
Southern Oregon University

Susan Stockton
University of Central Missouri

Meg Stolt
John Jay College

Winona Taylor
Bowie State University

Michael Teague
University of Iowa

Julie Thurlow
University of Wisconsin, Madison

Theresa Tiso
Stony Brook University

Terry Weideman
Oakland Community College

Introduction

What Is Health?

Traditionally, being healthy meant being absent of illness. If an individual did not have a disease, then he or she was considered healthy. The overall health of a nation or specific population was determined by data measuring illness, disease, and death rates. Today, this rather negative view of assessing individual health, and health in general, is changing. A healthy person is one who is not only free from disease but also fully well.

Being well, or wellness, involves the interrelationship of many dimensions of health: physical, emotional, social, mental, and spiritual. This multifaceted view of health reflects a holistic approach, which includes individuals taking responsibility for their own well-being.

Our health and longevity are affected by the many choices we make everyday: medical reports tell us that if we abstain from smoking, drugs, excessive alcohol, fat, and cholesterol consumption and get regular exercise, our rate of disease and disability will significantly decrease. These reports, while not totally conclusive, have encouraged many people to make positive lifestyle changes. Millions of people have quit smoking, alcohol consumption is down, and more and more individuals are exercising regularly and eating low-fat diets. While these changes are encouraging, many people who have been unable or unwilling to make these changes are left feeling worried and/or guilty over continuing their negative health behaviors.

But disagreement exists among the experts about the exact nature of positive health behaviors, which causes confusion. For example, some scientists claim that overweight Americans should make efforts to lose weight, even if it takes many tries. Many Americans have unsuccessfully tried to lose weight by eating a low-fat diet though the experts debate which is best: a low fat, high carbohydrate diet, or a low carbohydrate diet which includes ample protein and fat. Other debatable issues include whether or not people utilize conventional medicine or seek out alternative therapies.

Health status is also affected by society and government. Societal pressures have helped pass smoking restrictions in public places, mandatory safety belt legislation, and laws permitting condom distribution in public schools. The government plays a role in the health of individuals as well, although it has failed to provide minimal health care for many low-income Americans.

Unfortunately, there are no absolute answers to many questions regarding health and wellness issues. Moral questions, controversial concerns, and individual perceptions of health matters all can create opposing views. As you evaluate the issues in this book, you should keep an open mind toward both sides. You may not change your mind regarding the morality of abortion or the limitation of health care for the elderly or mentally handicapped, but you will still be able to learn from the opposing viewpoint.

The Health-care Industry

In the United States, despite the Affordable Care Act, millions of Americans have no or inadequate health insurance resulting in a resurgence in infectious diseases such as TB and antibiotic-resistant strains of bacterial infections which threaten thousands of Americans all put pressure on the current system along with AIDS, diabetes, and other chronic diseases. Those enrolled in government programs such as Medicaid often find few, if any physicians who will accept them as patients since reimbursements are so low and the paperwork is so cumbersome. On the other hand, Americans continue to live longer and longer, and for most of us, the health care available is among the best in the world. While many Americans agree that there are some situations in which limited health-care dollars should be rationed, it's unclear by whom or how these decisions should be made. Other issues in this section address the issue of the health-care system's role in extending life.

Health and Society

This section introduces current issues related to health from a societal perspective. The controversial issues over the cost of the "war" on cancer, does legalizing marijuana increase its usage, and should cloning research be allowed are addressed. Cloning technology offers the *potential* to cure or treat diseases such as Parkinson's and multiple sclerosis and others. While there are pros and cons to this technology, ethical and moral questions also arise.

Mind Body Issues

Important issues related to the relationship between mind and body are discussed in this section. Millions of

Americans use and abuse drugs that alter their minds and affect their bodies. These drugs range from illegal substances, such as crack cocaine and opiates, to the widely used legal drugs alcohol and tobacco. Increasingly, prescription drugs obtained either legally or not are becoming substances of abuse. Use of these substances can lead to physical and psychological addiction and the related problems of family dysfunction, reduced worker productivity, and crime. Are addictions within the control of individuals who abuse drugs? or are they an actual disease of the brain which needs treatment? The role of spirituality in the prevention and treatment of disease is discussed in this section. Many studies have found that religion and prayer play a role in recovery from sickness. Should health providers encourage spirituality for their patients? Does prayer really help to prevent disease and hasten recovery from illnesses?

Sexuality and Gender Issues

There is much advice given to pregnant women to help insure they have healthy babies. Research indicates that women who avoid drugs, alcohol, and tobacco reduce the risk of complications. If a pregnant woman does not consume any alcohol, her child will not be born with fetal alcohol syndrome. For some women, however, avoiding alcohol during pregnancy is particularly difficult and they question whether or not it's safe to have a moderate amount of alcohol. For years, physicians and other health providers have cautioned that even one drink consumed at the wrong time could negatively affect the outcome of the pregnancy. This obviously created much concern for women especially those who drank before they knew they were pregnant.

Other issues debate the conscience clause relative to health providers and whether or not the benefits outweigh the risks of the cervical cancer vaccine. Should pro-life doctors and pharmacists have the right to refuse to prescribe and/or dispense birth control or morning after pills if their beliefs and conscience do not support the use of these drugs. Also in this section are arguments over whether or not viewing pornography leads to sexual dysfunction.

Public Health Issues

Debate continues over fundamental matters surrounding many health concerns. Topics addressed in this section include issues related to mandatory immunizations, and the ongoing debate over the health impacts of "fracking" While this process of natural gas extraction offers considerable economic benefits, there appears to be a downside related to water pollution and potential human health concerns.

The threat of bioterrorism has resurrected the risk of smallpox, thought to be eradicated in the late 1970s. Should all parents be forced to have their children immunized against smallpox, which carries certain risks? At the turn of the century, millions of American children developed childhood diseases such as tetanus, polio, measles, and pertussis (whooping cough). Many of these children died or became permanently disabled because of these illnesses. Today, vaccines exist to prevent all of these conditions; however, not all children receive their recommended immunizations. Some do not get vaccinated until the schools require them, and others are allowed exemptions. More and more, parents are requesting exemptions for some or all vaccinations based on fears over their safety and/or their effectiveness. The pertussis vaccination seems to generate the biggest fears. Reports of serious injury to children following the whooping cough vaccination usually given in a combination of diphtheria, pertussis, and tetanus) have convinced many parents to forgo immunization. As a result, the rates of measles and pertussis have been climbing after decades of decline. Is it safer to be vaccinated than to risk getting the disease?

Consumer Health Issues

This section introduces questions about particular issues related to consumer choices about health issues or products. As Americans grow increasingly overweight, the most effective means of weight control continues to be debated. Along with that debate is the controversy over whether or not it's possible to lose weight and actually keep it off. The risk associated with the use of alcoholic energy drinks is an increasingly important topic and many college students consume this beverage. . . .

Will the many debates presented in this book ever be resolved? Some issues may resolve themselves because of the availability of resources. An overhaul of the health-care system to provide care for all while keeping costs down seems inevitable, as most Americans agree that the system should be changed. While there's agreement it should be changed, the Affordable Care Act remains controversial even though many Americans now have health insurance. Other controversies may require the test of time for resolution. The debates over the health effects of global warming and the long-term benefits of medical marijuana may also take years to be fully resolved.

Other controversies may never resolve themselves. There may never be a consensus over the right of health providers to be allowed to deny care based on their beliefs, the abortion issue, rationing health care, or whether or not prayer actually affects the outcome of disease. This book will introduce you to many ongoing controversies on a variety of sensitive and complex health-related topics. In order to have a good grasp of one's own viewpoint, it is necessary to be familiar with and understand the points made by the opposition.

Unit 1

UNIT

The Health Care Industry

The United States currently faces many challenging health and health-care concerns including the status of the Affordable Care Act. Unlike other major industrialized nations, the United States doesn't have a single payer plan to fund national health coverage, and several million Americans are without adequate health insurance. There is also controversy over the Affordable Care Act's mandate that employers' health insurance plans cover birth control. Another issue revolves around the health-care resources used to treat the elderly.

Selected, Edited, and with Issue Framing Material by:
Eileen L. Daniel, *SUNY College at Brockport*

ISSUE

Is the Affordable Care Act Successful?

YES: Jared Bernstein, from "The Success of the Affordable Care Act Is a Hugely Inconvenient Truth for Its Opponents," *Washington Post* (2015)

NO: Kevin D. Williamson, from "Obamacare Is Dead," *National Review* (2015)

Learning Outcomes

After reading this issue, you will be able to:

- Discuss the provisions of the Affordable Care Act.
- Assess the impact of the Act on health-care access.
- Discuss the financial implications of the Affordable Care Act.

ISSUE SUMMARY

YES: Senior fellow at the Center on Budget and Policy Priorities, Jared Bernstein believes the Affordable Care Act has met most of its important goals providing coverage to the uninsured.

NO: *National Review* roving correspondent Kevin D. Williamson argues that the Affordable Care Act has not worked since its design was seriously flawed.

The Patient Protection and Affordable Care Act (PPACA), also known as "Obama Care" or the Affordable Care Act, is a federal statute signed into law by President Obama in the spring of 2010. The Act aims to both increase the rate of Americans with health insurance and lower the overall costs of health care. The PPACA includes several components including mandates, subsidies, and tax credits to help and encourage employers and individuals to increase the coverage rate. Additional reforms seek to improve health-care outcomes and streamline the delivery of health care. The Congressional Budget Office predicts that the PPACA will reduce both future deficits and spending for Medicare.

Polls indicate support of health-care reform in general but became more negative in regard to specific plans during legislative debates. The Act that was ultimately signed into law in 2010 remains controversial with opinions falling along party lines. Opinions are clearly divided by age and party affiliation, with a solid majority of seniors and Republicans opposing the bill while a solid majority of Democrats and those younger than 40 are in favor. In a 2010 poll conducted by CNN, 62 percent of respondents said they thought the PPACA would "increase the amount of money they personally spend on health care," 56 percent said the bill "gives the government too much involvement in health care," and only 19 percent said they thought they and their families would be better off with the legislation.

The Act mandates that insurance companies cover all applicants at the same rates regardless of preexisting conditions or gender. In addition, a provision mandates that all insurance policies cover birth control without a co-pay as part of preventive care. The Act requires that all insurance policies cover *all* forms of basic preventive care without a co-pay, including well-woman, well-baby, and well-child visits, as well as other basic prevention care for men and women. This coverage is intended to save costs and promote public health. Basic preventive reproductive and sexual health-care services, including contraception, are therefore also covered without a co-pay. As part of the mandate, all insurance plans must provide coverage without a co-pay for all methods of contraception approved by the Food and Drug Administration. Employees *earn* their salaries and their benefits, and many pay for all or a portion of their health-care premiums out of their salaries. As such, none of this coverage is "free" but is rather covered by the policies they are earning or for which they are paying.

For many Americans, the Affordable Care Act is synonymous with a dysfunctional website. But the former president's health-care law has insured far more people outside the private insurance exchanges—upward of 10 million, beginning with one million children with preexisting conditions who were covered with the law's 2010 passage, and three million young adults who have secured coverage on their parents' health plans. The law never got a public option, but a huge portion of its new enrollees are now on Medicaid, the publicly funded health plan. In the 26 states participating in its expansion, Medicaid now offers comprehensive coverage for anyone earning less than 138 percent of poverty income—US$16,105 for individuals or US$27,310 for a family of three. More than 4.5 million low-income Americans have already gained coverage, and with no enrollment deadline that figure will only grow. Meanwhile, outreach efforts have also brought nearly two million very poor Americans to sign up for Medicaid benefits for which they would already have been eligible.

The law's impact is even greater than these enrollment numbers might indicate. Before the law, insurers previously rejected nearly one in five applicants, today an estimated 120 million Americans with a preexisting health condition cannot be denied coverage. The Affordable Care Act also guarantees zero-co-pay preventive care for policies bought on its exchanges. For some young women with modest incomes who take the Pill, the value of these benefits (up to US$1,200) is greater than the yearly premiums on a very basic plan (roughly US$1,100). Addiction treatment, mental health care, and maternity coverage are all now guaranteed. Even seniors are coming out ahead, having already pocketed an average US$1,265 in savings on prescription drugs bought under Medicare.

While the numbers indicate success, the Act has never been well received by the public. Many people feel there are many downsides to the law including the belief that the law actually forces plans to cover more and more (children must be covered to age 27) that everyone was forced to pay into. In addition, many feel there are too many loopholes which have had negative impacts including employers who have cut back hours or reduced staff to avoid covering their health insurance costs.

Initially, the bill was hyped as a means to both cover the uninsured and help reduce costs for everyone. Many, however, believe that the reality is that the goal of insuring all the uninsured isn't going to be met. The Congressional Budget Office projected that by 2023—more than a decade after implementation—that 31 million people will still be uninsured. Finally, for many Americans, the very fact that the law is run by the government is a reason it is failing. They believe that the government is incapable of ever running anything cost-efficiently or effectively.

Republicans have consistently vowed to repeal the law and replace it with a better plan which was designed early in President Trump's administration. In March, 2017 House Republican leaders pulled legislation to repeal the Affordable Care Act due to lack of political consensus among the party leaders. The Affordable Care Act will remain despite these efforts to repeal it.

YES

Jared Bernstein

The Success of the Affordable Care Act Is a Hugely Inconvenient Truth for Its Opponents

Remember How Much Republicans Wanted to Repeal Obamacare?

The Republican majority in the House of Representatives has voted more than 50 times to repeal the law. Conservatives have twice brought challenges to the Supreme Court Co a court with powerful voices that often lean in their direction Co only to be largely rebuffed both times. The last government shutdown was driven by Republicans who insisted on defunding Obamacare (not to be confused with what may be the next government shutdown, driven by Republicans insisting on defunding Planned Parenthood).

Some suggest that the calls for repealing Obamacare are fading. Sarah Kliff argued that the "near-complete absence of Obama's health overhaul" in last week's Republican presidential debate was "remarkable."

Maybe, but don't count on it. In GOP presidential candidate Jeb Bush's white paper on how he would get to 4 percent growth through supply-side tax cuts, his team of economists stresses that repealing the Affordable Care Act (ACA) will be an "important means of enhancing economic growth." Front-runner Donald Trump said just last week that he was going to replace Obamacare with "DonaldCare," which would be both "absolutely great" and "really spectacular." Repealing health-care reform remains a prominent talking point for Wisconsin Gov. Scott Walker and Sen. Ted Cruz, both GOP presidential candidates.

Well, since we don't know what's in it, I can't comment on DonaldCare.

But I can tell you this about Obamacare: when it comes to meeting one of its most important goals Co providing coverage to the uninsured Co it is working extremely well. It's posting historical gains on this front and, in so doing, both insulating itself from repeal and creating a daunting political challenge for its opponents.

The facts of the case are thoroughly drawn out in this new analysis by my colleagues Matt Broaddus and Edwin Park (B&P) from the Center on Budget and Policy Priorities:

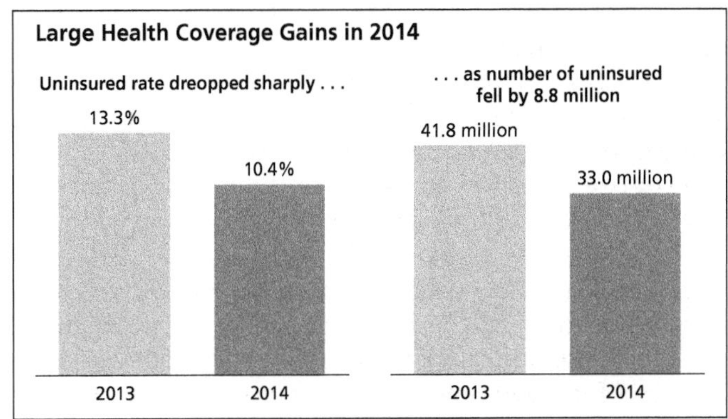

Source: Census Bureau, Current Population Survey.

- As the figure above shows, newly released census data show that the share of those without health coverage fell from 13.3 percent to 10.4 last year.
- That's the largest single-year drop on record based on data going back to 1987.
- In this type of work, the strength of your findings are much bolstered when you see them across multiple sources. As B&P point out, the census findings are "consistent with the historic coverage gains measured in the Centers for Disease Control (CDC) and Prevention's National Health Interview Survey and several private surveys. . . at 9.2 percent, the CDC's estimated uninsured rate for the first quarter of 2015 was the lowest since the CDC began collecting these data in 1997 and more than 40 percent below the peak in 2010."
- The ACA takes a two-pronged attack on covering the uninsured, subsidizing private coverage

through the exchanges and expanding Medicaid in the 25 states (as well as DC) that accepted that part of the deal. Both private and public coverage are making significant gains.

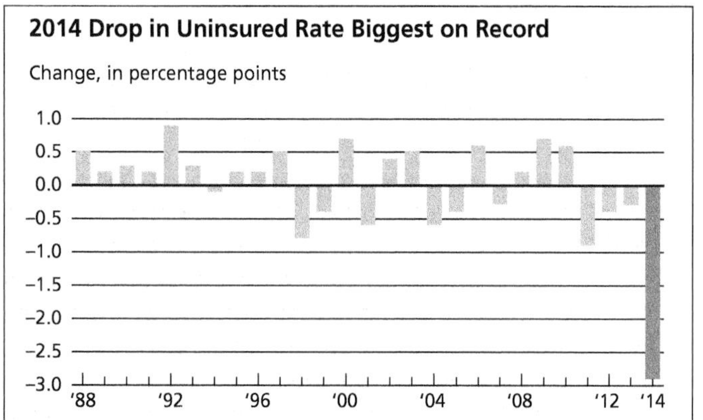

Source: CBPP analysis of Census Bureau, Current Population Survey data. Adjustments are made using Census Bureau guidance to account for survey design changes in 1999 and 2013.

- Speaking of anti-Obamacare ideology and its effect on people, B&P provide this revealing calculation: "If the uninsured rate had fallen in nonexpansion states at the same rate as in expansion states, an additional 2.6 million uninsured Americans would have gained coverage last year."
- Coverage last year grew most quickly among households with income below US$50,000; their uninsured rate fell from about 20 percent to about 15 percent Co in one year! Households above US$50,000 had lower uninsured rates to start with, so we would expect smaller changes, but they, too, went from 9 percent to 7.4 percent.

Such truths are more than inconvenient for sworn enemies of the law. They can bob and weave in their primaries, but once they reach the general election, their Democratic opponent will slam them on these points. And unless they're willing to massively flip Co pretty unimaginable, given the heat generated by the issue for conservatives Co people represented in the numbers and charts above will rightfully fear that their health security is at stake.

I cannot overemphasize the importance of these facts, and, yes, I know better than most that our political discourse too often exists in a fact-free zone. But the success of the ACA strikes at the heart of the dysfunction strategy employed extremely effectively by anti-government conservatives. This is the self-fulfilling-prophecy strategy that campaigns on: "Washington is broken! Send me there and I'll make sure it stays that way!"

Remember, when government messes up, when it shuts down, when it fails to address the things that matter to most people Co economic opportunity, wage stagnation, affordable college Co and, instead, squabbles about Planned Parenthood, the winners are those who can say: "See? We told you. Government's broken!" Never mind that those making that case are the ones doing the breaking.

But with Obamacare, they've been failing, and the more we elevate that case, the closer we get to the road back to Factville.

Jared Bernstein is a senior fellow at the Center on Budget and Policy Priorities.

Kevin D. Williamson

Obamacare Is Dead

It doesn't work because it couldn't work.

Regardless of whether there is a President Cruz or a President Rubio in January 2017, regardless of the existence or size of a Republican majority in Congress, the so-called Patient Protection and Affordable Care Act (ACA) has failed. The grand vision of an efficient pseudomarket in health insurance under enlightened federal management—the heart of Obamacare—is not coming to pass. Obamacare, meaning the operating model that undergirded the law that Congress passed and President Barack Obama signed with great fanfare is dead, and it will not be revived. What remains is fitful chaos.

A brief refresher:

The fundamental problem with ACA is that under it, insurance ceases to be insurance. Insurance is a *prospective* financial product, one that exploits the mathematical predictability of certain life events among very large groups of people—out of 1 million 40- to 60-year-old Americans, x percent will get in car wrecks every year, and y percent will be diagnosed with chronic renal failure—which allows actuaries and the insurance companies that employ them to calculate premiums based on risk, thus funding the reimbursement of certain expenses incurred by the insurance pool's members. Insurance is, by its very nature, always forward-looking, considering events that have yet to come to pass but that may be expected and, to a reasonable extent, predicted with some level of specificity. Under ACA, insurance is retrospective. The ACA mandates that insurance companies cover preexisting conditions, meaning events that already have happened, which renders the basic mathematical architecture of insurance—the calculation of risk among large pools of people—pointless. Insurance ceases to be insurance and instead becomes something else, namely, a very badly constructed cost-sharing program.

Not all cost-sharing programs are bad ideas. Medi-Share, for example, is precisely the sort of voluntary, privately administered mutual-aid program that could—and, I believe, will—end up displacing government-run health-care programs entirely. But Obamacare is a very different kind of beast: it creates a deeply perverse incentive structure by combining compulsory coverage of preexisting conditions with a mandate that is enforced in theory more than in fact. The mandate is necessary to prevent the ruthless exploitation of the preexisting coverage rules: if insurers have to cover you no matter what, then there's no point in buying insurance—thereby sharing in the costs—until you are sick enough to need it.

As James Freeman reports in the *Wall Street Journal*, the ACA's plethora of exemptions—there are at least 30 of them—ensure that a great many people—12 million last year—will simply opt out. "It is easy to avoid or limit exposure to the penalty with some simple tax planning," he writes. In 2016, there were supposed to be 21 million people enrolled in ACA programs; the Obama administration currently predicts that the actual number will be somewhat less than *half* of that. This was entirely predictable; in fact, it was predicted in the pages of National Review, in my book *The End Is Near (and It's Going to Be Awesome)*, and elsewhere.

Many of Obamacare's failures came fast and early. Strike one: "If you like your doctor, you can keep your doctor." Strike two: Obamacare will save "the average family US$2,500 a year on their premiums." Strike three: Obamacare will add "not one dime" to the deficit. We all knew that was coming, just as we knew that people would respond to the very strong incentives not to buy insurance by not buying insurance.

Other failures took longer to become manifest. The architects of Obamacare are deeply distrustful of the role of for-profit companies in the health-care business because, in their nearly pristine ignorance, they falsely believe profits to be net deductions from the sum of the public good rather than measures of the creation of real social value. So they created incentives to set up co-ops, nonprofit enterprises that would administer Obamacare plans in particular states and jurisdictions. It was obvious from the beginning that if Obamacare's perverse incentives created insurance pools that were older and sicker rather than younger and healthier, these co-ops wouldn't be economically viable: you need lots of young, healthy insurance subscribers to offset the costs associated with your older, sicker subscribers. Many of us—myself included—assumed that the federal government under President Obama would simply write these co-ops huge checks to keep them afloat. We were half right: the government is writing them huge checks, but they are failing anyway, so fundamental is their economic unsustainability. Half of the co-ops have gone belly-up already, including large, prominent, splendidly subsidized ones in Kentucky, New York, Louisiana, and South Carolina. Hundreds of thousands of customers have lost their coverage as a result. Hundreds of millions of dollars in taxpayers' money has been poured into these enterprises, to no avail.

Obamacare's partisans were confronted with the economic facts long before the law was even passed, and their answer was: "Never mind the economics, we're the good guys, and you want poor people to die." Democrats argued that Republicans literally wanted to kill poor people, that their plan was for the poor to "die quickly." This is a habitual mode of discourse among progressives: reality doesn't matter; only the purity of Democrats' motives matters. Obamacare is what it is: another damned five-year plan based on wishful thinking and very little else.

The fact is that Obamacare has fallen apart without Republicans' dismantling it. Almost all of its basic promises have failed, it is an economic shambles, and it is a political mess: unsurprisingly, people still don't like it. Less than a third of Americans support the individual mandate, ¾ oppose Obamacare's tax on high-end healthcare programs, and more voters oppose the law categorically than support it. A quarter of voters say the law has hurt them personally. The question isn't why Republicans haven't gotten around to repealing and replacing it—the answer to that question resides at 1600 Pennsylvania Avenue for a while, still—the question is when Democrats will get around to admitting that, purity of their hearts notwithstanding, they and they alone—not one Republican voted for Obamacare—have created a mess that has introduced nothing to American health care except chaos.

The basic principles of meaningful health-care reform are these: let insurance be insurance; understand that ordinary, regular medical procedures, such as physicals and prostate exams, are not insurable events, and account for that in your calculations; the only way to mitigate the effects of scarcity on health care is to make it less scarce by expanding the supply of medical practitioners and facilities; the only way to make insurance more competitive, and therefore more affordable and more responsive to consumers, is to increase the number of players in the markets; the best way to deal with people who are, for example, profoundly disabled, children, or otherwise unable to provide for their own care, is direct, clear-eyed subsidy of their medical expenses, rather than laundering those payments through the insurance market; so long as practicing medicine pays less than filing frivolous lawsuits against doctors, there's going to be a lot of politically induced inefficiency in the system.

Of course markets work for most people, and of course, there are exceptions to that. For 93 percent of the population, the solution to health-care reform is: let markets do their thing. The only real argument is how big a check to write to those looking after the other 7 percent, and how to structure the payments. That's a real fight, too, but it isn't the one we're having. Right now, the Republicans and the Democrats are two political coroners arguing over what time and cause of death to put on the paperwork; rigor mortis set in long ago.

Kevin D. Williamson is a roving correspondent for *National Review.*

EXPLORING THE ISSUE

Is the Affordable Care Act Successful?

Critical Thinking and Reflection

1. Why are so many Americans opposed to the Affordable Care Act when millions have no health insurance?
2. How will the Affordable Care Act be able to significantly increase the number of uninsured Americans? Explain.
3. Describe why many Americans believe the government should not be involved in providing health insurance.

Is There Common Ground?

The government estimated that the Affordable Care Act legislation will lower the number of the uninsured by 32 million, leaving 23 million uninsured residents by 2019 after the bill's mandates have all taken effect. Among the people in this uninsured group will be approximately eight million illegal immigrants, individuals eligible but not enrolled in Medicare, and the mostly young and single men and women not otherwise covered who choose to pay the annual penalty instead of purchasing insurance.

Early experience under the Act was that, as a result of the tax credit for small businesses, some businesses offered health insurance to their employees for the first time. On September 13, 2011, the Census Bureau released a report showing that the number of uninsured 19- to 25-year-olds (now eligible to stay on their parents' policies) had declined by 393,000 or 1.6 percent. A later report from the Government Accountability Office in 2012 found that of the four million small businesses that were offered the tax credit only 170,300 businesses claimed it. Due to the effect of the U.S. Supreme court ruling, states can opt in or out of the expansion of Medicaid.

Also, a component ensuring children could remain included on their parents' plans until age 26 remains a popular, fairly noncontroversial part of the bill. The contraceptive coverage, however, remains contentious. The Affordable Care Act includes a contraceptive coverage mandate that, with the exception of churches and houses of worship, applies to all employers and educational institutions. These regulations made under The Act rely on the recommendations of the Institute of Medicine which concluded that access to contraception is medically necessary "to ensure women's health and well-being."

Additional Resources

Gawanda, A. (2017). Trumpcare. *New Yorker,* 93, 21–22.

Glide, S., & Jackson, A. (2017). The future of the Affordable Care Act and insurance coverage. *American Journal of Public Health,* 107, 538–540.

Hall, C. J. (2017). The Affordable Care Act: Should it stay or should it go? *Health Lawyer,* 29, 2–10.

Obama, B. (2014). The Affordable Care Act: The rollout has been rough. *Vital Speeches of the Day, 80*(1), 25–26.

Williamson, K. (2017). Obamacare unraveled. *New American,* 33, 12–15.

Internet References . . .

Health Care

www.healthcare.gov

Health Care Law and You

www.healthcare.gov/law/

Medicaid

http://medicaid.gov/affordablecareact/affordable-care-act.html

Selected, Edited, and with Issue Framing Material by:
Eileen L. Daniel, *SUNY College at Brockport*

ISSUE

Should the Health Care System Continuously Strive to Extend Life?

YES: Miguel Faria, from "Bioethics and Why I Hope to Live Beyond Age 75 Attaining Wisdom!—A Rebuttal to Dr. Ezekiel Emanuel's 75 Age Limit," *haciendapublishing.com* (2014)

NO: Ezekiel J. Emanuel, from "Why I Hope to Die at 75: An Argument That Society and Families—and You—Will Be Better Off if Nature Takes Its Course Swiftly and Promptly," *The Atlantic* (2014)

Learning Outcomes

After reading this issue, you will be able to:

- Discuss the quality versus quantity of life issues.
- Identify the reasons Americans are living longer.
- Assess the economic impact of extended lifespans.

ISSUE SUMMARY

YES: Physician Miguel Faria contends that lives can be productive and fulfilling and worthwhile past age 75 and that there is a difference between aging and infirmity and illness.

NO: Physician, bioethicist, and vice provost of the University of Pennsylvania Ezekiel J. Emanuel disagrees and claims that society and families would be better off if we died at 75 rather than be incapacitated and unable to live a full life.

In 1980, 11 percent of the U.S. population was over age 65, but they accounted for about 29 percent ($219 billion) of the total American health care expenditures. By the beginning of the new millennium, the percentage of the population over 65 had risen to 12 percent, which consumed 31 percent of total health care expenditures, of $450 billion. It has been projected that by the year 2040, people over 65 will represent 21 percent of the population and they will consume 45 percent of all health care expenditures.

Medical expenses at the end of life appear to be extremely high in relation to other health care costs. Studies have shown that nearly one-third of annual Medicare costs are for the 5 percent of beneficiaries who die that year. Expenses for dying patients increase significantly as death nears, and payments for health care during the last weeks of life make up 40 percent of the medical costs for the entire last year of life. Some studies have shown that up to 50 percent of the medical costs incurred during a person's entire life are spent during their last year!

Many surveys have indicated that most Americans do not want to be kept alive if their illness is incurable and irreversible, for both economic and humanitarian reasons. Many experts believe that if physicians stopped using high technology at the end of life to prevent death, then we would save billions of dollars, which could be used to insure the uninsured and provide basic health care to millions. In England the emphasis of health care is on improving the quality of life through primary care medicine, well-subsidized home care, and institutional programs for the elderly and those with incurable illnesses rather than through life-extending acute care medicine. The British seem to value basic medical care for all rather than expensive technology for the few who might benefit from it. As a result, the British spend a much smaller proportion of their gross national product (6.2 percent) on health services than do Americans (10.8 percent) for a nearly identical health status and life expectancy.

While the economics of extending life is certainly a major issue, the quality of life after a certain age is also a major consideration. Americans are living longer lives leading to a real increase in life expectancy. This is mainly the result of the many scientific and technological discoveries as well as education about our health. Though we are living longer, for many older Americans, their older years are often spent suffering from one or more chronic diseases causing pain and disability. But how does an individual decide which takes precedence, the actual number of years lived or quality of life of those years? While it is a person's own prerogative to decide which they value more, there may be many personal factors that play a role in an individual's decision. No one can make this determination for another person, not even the scientists that have made miraculous breakthroughs in regards to health care. It is a personal decision that is a unique choice for each person to make for themselves.

According to the latest U.S. Census predictions, our country's population of individuals over the age of 65 will increase 1% to 3% per year. If these predictions are accurate, by the year 2030, one in five persons in the United States will be over the age of 65 and this age group will represent 25 percent of the U.S. population. In addition, the United States has a higher number of individuals over 100 than any other nation and approximately 70,000 centenarians exist in our population today. The number of people that are living to be 100 years old is increasing at such a rapid rate that by the year 2050 there will be an estimated 850,000 individuals in the United States over the age of 100.

As a result of these demographic changes, there will be many shifts in health care that will be necessary to care for this growing population. Transportation, home health care, and housing are among the factors that will need to be addressed in order to accommodate those over age 65. Also affected will be Social Security income, Medicare, and Medicaid. These increases in our population can have serious implications on our country as a whole.

For many reasons there is an increase in the average life expectancy of the American population. Life expectancy has risen due to the many advances in public health, science, technology, nutrition, and medicine, and researchers are finding new ways to treat chronic conditions.

Each individual should ask the question of whether they would rather live a longer life that may require the utilization of various forms of medical intervention which may be able to slow or lessen the effects of various diseases. Or would they rather live quality years that are free from all of these various products and inventions of science that may prolong the years that are actually lived, but with the sacrifice of feeling ultimately healthy? This can be a difficult decision for an individual to make, and it may take a person some time to weigh the pros and cons of their unique situation to determine the ultimate choice that is right for them.

Overall, it appears that the best way that a person can ensure that they are living their life with the quality that they desire is to educate himself or herself about the importance of maintaining an overall healthy well-being. This includes taking care of oneself, both physically and mentally. A person should stay up to date with health care professionals when it comes to annual exams and procedures that need to be performed. It is important for each person to listen to their body, and hear what it is telling them. Only a person knows their own body and can tell how they are feeling. It is imperative to know what needs to be done and what changes need to be made to ensure an ultimate healthy well-being. This is where the education that has been provided can take the reins and lead an individual to their optimal health.

YES **Miguel Faria**

Bioethics and Why I Hope to Live Beyond Age 75 Attaining Wisdom!—A Rebuttal to Dr. Ezekiel Emanuel's 75 Age Limit

For several decades, American bioethicists have been providing persuasive arguments for rationing medical care via the theory of the necessary "rational allocation of finite health care resources."(2) More recently, assisted by various sectors of organized medicine, they have developed multiple approaches to justify what they see as the necessary curtailment of services and specialized treatments deemed not medically necessary. The problem persists, though, and the need for rationing health services in increasingly socialized medical systems, including ObamaCare, requires more ingenious approaches, particularly in the U.S., where patients are accustomed to receiving the best medical care that third-party payers are willing to pay for, regardless of whether the payer is the insurance company or the government.(6)

Furthermore, government planners, supported by the ever-accommodating bioethicists, posit that with increasing longevity and augmentation of the population of American elderly, more drastic actions will be required to prevent the bankruptcy of the public financing of medical care. They believe therefore that outright government-imposed euthanasia, not only for the terminally ill but also for the inconvenient infirm and the superfluous elderly, will become necessary.(1,4,8,10)

It is in this context that the individual-based, patient-oriented ethics of Hippocrates, including his fundamental dictum, "First Do No Harm," are seen as an obstacle by the bioethics movement. Obtrusive and in their way, time-honored medical ethics are being eroded and supplanted by the more convenient, collectivist, population-based ethics propounded by today bioethicists. As early as the 1980s, some bioethicists, including Daniel Callahan, then Director of the Hastings Center; Peter Singer, bioethics professor at Stanford University; and John Hardwick of East Tennessee State University, openly insisted that elderly patients who had lived a full life had a "duty to die" for the good of society and the proper utilization of societal health resources.(2) Dr. Callahan pointedly asserted, "Denial of nutrition, may, in the long run, become the only effective way to make certain that a large number of biologically tenacious patients actually die."(11) Likewise, Dr. Hardwick dropped all pretenses regarding their real intentions at about the time of the Clinton health care debate and the tentative formulation of HillaryCare, affirming a "duty to die" was necessary for those citizens whose lives had become not worth living because of chronic disease or advanced age.(7,10) Such openness was not well-received by the American people, and Hardwick's proposals were ignored, or like HillaryCare ostensibly discarded, thrown by the wayside. But appearances can be deceiving. Many proposals of the bioethics movement have quietly and gradually been implemented. Here is an insightful report by Pope Benedict XVI in his address to the Pontifical Academy for Life:

"Some ethicists warn that modern bioethics is in fact a new normative system of ethics that, based on principles of utilitarianism, can never be compatible with Natural Law principles. In the last few decades, bioethics has largely supplanted traditional, Natural Law-based medical ethics in hospitals and ethics boards in most western countries. Under traditional medical ethics, the guiding principle is 'do no harm.' But contemporary bioethics abandons this . . . in an effort to find the utilitarian goal of the 'greatest good for the greatest number.' Under these principles, preserving the life of the human patient is not considered paramount."(12) He is largely correct in his assessment. Moreover, the bioethics movement has recently received more impetus with President Barack Obama's creation of the Presidential Commission for the Study of Bioethical Issues.(9)

But their proposals have not all been fully implemented. To do so, today's bioethicists, although equally determined, are more subtle, and the foremost exponent of the new trend in bioethics is Dr. Ezekiel J. Emanuel.(3) Although 57 years of age and in good health,

Dr. Emanuel says he hopes and wants to live to age 75 and die. He has lived a fulfilled and a good life and it is time to exit. After age 75, Emanuel claims life is a downhill spiral and not worth living. His family disagrees with him and says he is "crazy,"(3) yet the fact remains Dr. Emanuel is a respected bioethicist, the Director of the Clinical Bioethics Department at the U.S. National Institutes of Health, the recipient of numerous awards, but the danger here is he encapsulates the views many bioethicists hold today. He insists that the productivity of creative people reach a peak at age 40 and plateau by age 60. In other words, after age 60, even productive people, create and produce little of value to society.(3) I beg to differ. In a recent conversation with my friend Dr. Russell Blaylock, who has also written on this subject,(1) he opined, "The reason very smart, creative people no longer produce earth-shattering discoveries later in life is because after their great accomplishments, they become department heads, drowning in administrative duties that prevent creative activities." I agree with Dr. Blaylock. Moreover, as we age and mellow and reach retirement, we also achieve satisfaction from a productive life well spent, and begin the contemplation and enjoyment of life that is only possible with the leisure that comes with retirement.

Dr. Emanuel, in stressing the relatively young age in which productive people reach the apex of their creativity, e.g., novelists, poets, and physicists, argues as if becoming poet laureates and Noble Prize winners were the universal aspirations of the average citizen. Most people do not aspire to reach those dizzying heights! The more realistic goals in life, instead, are more mundane, namely, fulfillment and contentment, qualities that are attained by being good citizens, and the satisfaction of leading good and productive lives; men and women performing their occupations and respective jobs, whether menial, artistic or intellectual, and doing them well—in short, being the best we can be in this transitory phase of our existence!

In his article Dr. Emanuel writes that if we live longer than age 75, "we are no longer remembered as vibrant and engaged but as feeble, ineffectual, even pathetic."(3) And as far as suicide or euthanasia, Dr. Emmanuel claims he is against those options, although it escapes him logical reasoning will lead many people to pursue exactly those options when afflicted with depression, physical illness, or merely reaching that lethal age of 75—or even worse. By which I refer to the State compulsorily implementing exactly those policies, purportedly as pragmatic and "sound" health care policies, when in fact they may be implemented for political expediency or budgetary considerations. This is particularly ominous when the State is involved in administering and funding medical care, as in socialized medicine or ObamaCare.(6,7)

In the same vein toward the end of his paper, Dr. Emanuel claims he is not advocating compulsory end of life at age 75 "in order to save resources, ration health care, or address public-policy issues," but that is exactly what he is inferring. In fact, in the next breath, he admits his proposals do have at least two policy implications and that these implications do refer to reducing life expectancy.(3)

Dr. Emanuel complains that Americans are obsessed with performing physical and mental exercises, undertaking diets, taking vitamins and supplements, "all in a valiant effort to cheat death and prolong life as long as possible."(3) In fact, leading healthy lifestyles and sticking to healthy diets are exactly what Americans should be doing, not only to prolong their lives, but even more importantly to improve the quality of their lives, while saving their own health care costs.

"Doing mental puzzles," which people have done to exercise brain function and which Dr. Emanuel derides, (3) may not exactly translate to the highest intellectual exercise. But not so other intellectual pursuits. I refer to reading and studying the classics of history and literature for their own sake; listening to good music in moments of contemplation for mere enjoyment; spending more leisure time with our families—in short enjoying all of those happy activities of leisure and exercising those fundamental virtues, which eluded us in our earlier, more active and hectic years of youth and adulthood. It is in our advancing years that we have the leisure to spend the time in just those intellectual activities that engage the mind and sooth the soul.

Others find happiness and satisfaction in doing what they have always done in life. This is particularly true of those who have answered a professional calling, who obtain intellectual rewards in continuing to practice their professions to the very end or until they are impaired by age or disability. That was the case with my father, a physician. It is the case, I suspect, with Dr. James I. Ausman, editor-in-chief of *Surgical Neurology International*, who at age 76 remains a scholar and an incorrigible multitasker and who seems to gather ever more speed in life as he gets older!

The key to meaningful longevity, then, is to remain active, exercising our intellectual faculties for their own sake, as well as for the preservation of brain plasticity. Dr. Emanuel admits the neural connections that are most utilized are reinforced and preserved, while those connections and synapses not used degenerate and atrophy. However, he is incorrect when he states that we cannot learn as we get older because no new neural connections and re-wirings are possible. Brain plasticity allows us to continue to learn well beyond age 75 for those who remain active, although it is true that in extremely advanced age, learning, creative thoughts, and memory retention become progressively more difficult as degeneration of neural connections and neuronal death take place.

Thus, I am curious as well as perplexed. Has Dr. Emanuel ever had the interest or time to read Thucydides and Herodotus? I wonder if he ever read Plutarch, Livy, Virgil, or any of the poems of Sappho or Elizabeth Barrett Browning? I wonder if he ever read Plato, Aristotle, or understands the meaning of the Aristotelian good life, and the time and activities that are necessary for the attainment of real happiness and wisdom? The ultimate good life is not necessarily found in our hard-working, intensive, utilitarian, and productive years, but in our years of leisure and contemplation that in today's stressful and fast-moving society can be attained only in our advancing years. One can also spend those years continuing to fulfill the duties of citizenship, improving his/her communities, insisting on better government—e.g., preserving and increasing liberty—for one's children and grandchildren, hoping they live in a better world. In this sense, Dr. Emanuel's attitude reflects selfishness and lack of concern for the welfare of others around him or who may come after he's gone! Contrary to Dr. Emanuel's opinion about "faltering and declining" years past age 75, it is idleness, selfishness, and wasteful lives associated with diseases of the soul primarily that are the culprits for moral and intellectual decrepitude, rather than physical decline and reaching a certain capricious chronological age.

I'm not arguing here against individuals exercising their right to medical autonomy, especially those suffering from chronic disease and terminal illness. End-of-life decisions should be left to individual patients, their families, and their physicians. What I'm saying is that lives can be productive and fulfilling, worthy of living past age 75. I'm also cautioning bioethicists from propounding the utilitarian concept of "a duty to die" because a certain lethal age has been reached or chronic illness has become manifest. We cannot separate, nor does Dr. Emanuel distinguish, the process of aging from infirmity and illness. Certainly one leads to the other, and the duty to die at age 75 becomes the duty to die at any age, once a life is deemed not worth living. Death then is prescribed by the government planners and the doctors and bioethicists employed by the State, whether one reaches a certain age or is afflicted by illness.(1,4,8–11)

With the advances in medical care, life expectancy has been prolonged and the quality of life has been made immensely better. Yet, Dr. Emanuel argues: "Since 1960, however, increases in longevity have been achieved mainly by extending the lives of people over 60. Rather than saving more young people, we are stretching out old age." Furthermore, he asserts this is wrong because we are saving the life of older people with a myriad of medical problems and residual disabilities.(3) While I admit this is partly true, many of these people can be returned to normal or near normal life with proper medical and nursing care. Moreover, medical and Judeo-Christian ethics, not to mention the lessons of history, have taught us that we should treat with compassion the sick and the most vulnerable segments of our society. Societies that do not do this descend into cruelty and barbarism. Once again, we must recollect the lessons of fairly recent history. Dr. Leo Alexander, the leading psychiatrist and Chief U.S. Medical Consultant at the Nuremberg War Crimes Trials, in his classic 1949 *New England Journal of Medicine* article described how German physicians became willing accomplices with the Nazis in Ktenology, "the science of killing." This was done, we learn, for the good of German society and the improvement of "the health of the German nation." And in this light, Dr. Alexander asked the critical question: "If only those whose treatment is worthwhile in terms of prognosis are to be treated, what about the other ones? The doubtful patients are the ones whose recovery appears unlikely, but frequently if treated energetically, they surprise the best prognosticators." Once the rational allocation of scarce and finite resources enters the decision-making process in the doctor's role as physician, the next logical step is: "Is it worthwhile to do this or that for this type of patient," or for those who have reached a certain age?(5)

As much as Dr. Emanuel insists he is against euthanasia, his arguments lead inexorably to utilitarian ethics, the idea of lives deemed not worth living, and ultimately to euthanasia. Under the utilitarian ethics of the rational allocation of resources, productive lives whose only merit was considered benefit to society, Hitler issued his first order for active euthanasia in Germany on September 1, 1939. And yet it must be pointed out the road to euthanasia was paved before the Nazis came to power. German physicians in the social democracy of the Weimar Republic, as early as 1931, had openly held discussions about the sterilization of undesirables and euthanasia of the chronically mentally ill. So when the National Socialists (Nazis) came to power, "humanitarian" groups had already been set up, ostensibly for the promotion of health. These misguided groups with arguably "good intentions" had taken the first steps and were very useful serving as cover for the subsequent Nazi mass-killing program. And so it was that years before the onset of World War II and the Final Solution had been implemented, 275,000 non-Jewish citizens were put to death in Germany's "mercy-killing" program. From small beginnings and seemingly "well-intended" proposals, the values of the medical profession as well as an entire society were (and may be again) subverted by deliberately evil or misguided, well-intentioned men working in tandem with the State. Dr. Alexander was correct: "Corrosion begins in microscopic proportions."(5)

In conclusion, the resurgent bioethics movement—stressing "futility of care," conservation of resources, and "the duty to die," while rejecting Hippocrates' dictum of "First Do No Harm" and refusing to stand for what is in the best interest of the individual and the dignity of human life—is transmogrifying the time-honored, individual-based, patient-oriented medical ethics of Hippocrates into a collectivist, population-based ethic derived from the current thinking of the bioethics movement in the United Kingdom and most of Europe, as well as the United States. This resurgent ethic, presently propounded with subtle and dissimulating persuasion, is particularly well exemplified by Dr. Ezekiel Emanuel, today its foremost proponent. This bioethics "duty to die" movement is buttressed by a utilitarian, population-based ethic concerned primarily with the conservation of resources in the administration of socialized medicine by the State, rather than with the individual patient—and represents the first step down the slippery slope of determining who lives and who dies, rationing by death, and euthanasia. Doctors, patients, and the public at large must be made aware of the direction present society is headed.

References

1. Blaylock RL. National Health Insurance (Part II): Any Social Utility in the Elderly? *HaciendaPublishing.com*, September 26, 2009.
2. Callahan D. *Setting Limits: Medical Goals in an Aging Society*. New York: Simon and Schuster, 1988.
3. Emanuel EJ. Why I Hope to Die at 75: An argument that society and families—and you—will be better off if nature takes its course swiftly and promptly. *The Atlantic*, September 17, 2014.
4. Faria MA. Bioethics—The Life and Death Issue. *HaciendaPublishing.com*, October 24, 2012.
5. Faria MA. Euthanasia, Medical Science, and the Road to Genocide. *Medical Sentinel* 1998;3(3):79–83
6. Faria MA. Getting US in line for ObamaCare and medical rationing. *GOPUSA.com*, March 18, 2010.
7. Faria MA. ObamaCare: Another step toward corporate socialized medicine in the *U.S. Surg Neurol Int* 2012;3:71.
8. Faria MA. Slouching Towards a Duty to Die. *Medical Sentinel* 1999;4(6):208–210.
9. Faria MA. The road being paved to neuroethics: A path leading to bioethics or to neuroscience medical ethics? *Surg Neurol Int* 2014;5:146.
10. Smith WJ. *Culture of Death: The Assault on Medical Ethics in America*. San Francisco, CA, Encounter Books, 2000.
11. Wickham ED. *Repackaging Death as Life—The Third Path to Imposed Death*. Presented at the Annual Life Conference Raleigh, North Carolina, October 23, 2010. Citing Bioethicist Daniel Callahan, 1983, "On Feeding the Dying," *Hastings Center Report* 13(5):22.
12. Wickham ED. *Repackaging Death as Life—The Third Path to Imposed Death*. Presented at the Annual Life Conference Raleigh, North Carolina, October 23, 2010. Citing Pope Benedict XVI's 2010 address to the Pontifical Academy for Life.

Miguel Faria is an associate editor-in-chief and a world affairs editor of *Surgical Neurology International*. He is a retired neurosurgeon and neuroscientist, editor and author, medical historian and ethicist, and public health critic.

Ezekiel J. Emanuel

NO

Why I Hope to Die at 75: An Argument That Society and Families—and You—Will Be Better Off if Nature Takes Its Course Swiftly and Promptly

SEVENTY-FIVE.

That's how long I want to live: 75 years.

This preference drives my daughters crazy. It drives my brothers crazy. My loving friends think I am crazy. They think that I can't mean what I say; that I haven't thought clearly about this, because there is so much in the world to see and do. To convince me of my errors, they enumerate the myriad people I know who are over 75 and doing quite well. They are certain that as I get closer to 75, I will push the desired age back to 80, then 85, maybe even 90.

I am sure of my position. Doubtless, death is a loss. It deprives us of experiences and milestones, of time spent with our spouse and children. In short, it deprives us of all the things we value.

But here is a simple truth that many of us seem to resist: living too long is also a loss. It renders many of us, if not disabled, then faltering and declining, a state that may not be worse than death but is nonetheless deprived. It robs us of our creativity and ability to contribute to work, society, the world. It transforms how people experience us, relate to us, and, most important, remember us. We are no longer remembered as vibrant and engaged but as feeble, ineffectual, even pathetic.

By the time I reach 75, I will have lived a complete life. I will have loved and been loved. My children will be grown and in the midst of their own rich lives. I will have seen my grandchildren born and beginning their lives. I will have pursued my life's projects and made whatever contributions, important or not, I am going to make. And hopefully, I will not have too many mental and physical limitations. Dying at 75 will not be a tragedy. Indeed, I plan to have my memorial service before I die. And I don't want any crying or wailing, but a warm gathering filled with fun reminiscences, stories of my awkwardness, and celebrations of a good life. After I die, my survivors can have their own memorial service if they want—that is not my business.

Let me be clear about my wish. I'm neither asking for more time than is likely nor foreshortening my life. Today I am, as far as my physician and I know, very healthy, with no chronic illness. I just climbed Kilimanjaro with two of my nephews. So I am not talking about bargaining with God to live to 75 because I have a terminal illness. Nor am I talking about waking up one morning 18 years from now and ending my life through euthanasia or suicide. Since the 1990s, I have actively opposed legalizing euthanasia and physician-assisted suicide. People who want to die in one of these ways tend to suffer not from unremitting pain but from depression, hopelessness, and fear of losing their dignity and control. The people they leave behind inevitably feel they have somehow failed. The answer to these symptoms is not ending a life but getting help. I have long argued that we should focus on giving all terminally ill people a good, compassionate death—not euthanasia or assisted suicide for a tiny minority.

I am talking about how long I *want* to live and the kind and amount of health care I will consent to after 75. Americans seem to be obsessed with exercising, doing mental puzzles, consuming various juice and protein concoctions, sticking to strict diets, and popping vitamins and supplements, all in a valiant effort to cheat death and prolong life as long as possible. This has become so pervasive that it now defines a cultural type: what I call the American immortal.

I reject this aspiration. I think this manic desperation to endlessly extend life is misguided and potentially destructive. For many reasons, 75 is a pretty good age to aim to stop.

What are those reasons? Let's begin with demography. We are growing old, and our older years are not of high quality. Since the mid-19th century, Americans have been living longer. In 1900, the life expectancy of an average American at birth was approximately 47 years. By 1930, it was 59.7; by 1960, 69.7; by 1990, 75.4. Today, a newborn can expect to live about 79 years. (On average, women live longer than men. In the United States, the gap is about five years. According to the National Vital Statistics Report, life expectancy for American males born in 2011 is 76.3, and for females it is 81.1.)

In the early part of the 20th century, life expectancy increased as vaccines, antibiotics, and better medical care saved more children from premature death and effectively treated infections. Once cured, people who had been sick largely returned to their normal, healthy lives without residual disabilities. Since 1960, however, increases in longevity have been achieved mainly by extending the lives of people over 60. Rather than saving more young people, we are stretching out old age.

The American immortal desperately wants to believe in the "compression of morbidity." Developed in 1980 by James F. Fries, now a professor emeritus of medicine at Stanford, this theory postulates that as we extend our life spans into the 80s and 90s, we will be living healthier lives—more time before we have disabilities, and fewer disabilities overall. The claim is that with longer life, an ever smaller proportion of our lives will be spent in a state of decline.

Compression of morbidity is a quintessentially American idea. It tells us exactly what we want to believe: that we will live longer lives and then abruptly die with hardly any aches, pains, or physical deterioration—the morbidity traditionally associated with growing old. It promises a kind of fountain of youth until the ever-receding time of death. It is this dream—or fantasy—that drives the American immortal and has fueled interest and investment in regenerative medicine and replacement organs.

But as life has gotten longer, has it gotten healthier? Is 70 the new 50?

NOT QUITE. It is true that compared with their counterparts 50 years ago, seniors today are less disabled and more mobile. But over recent decades, increases in longevity seem to have been accompanied by increases in disability—not decreases. For instance, using data from the National Health Interview Survey, Eileen Crimmins, a researcher at the University of Southern California, and a colleague assessed physical functioning in adults, analyzing whether people could walk a quarter of a mile; climb 10 stairs; stand or sit for two hours; and stand up, bend, or kneel without using special equipment. The results show that as people age, there is a progressive erosion of physical functioning. More important, Crimmins found that between 1998 and 2006, the loss of functional mobility in the elderly increased. In 1998, about 28 percent of American men 80 and older had a functional limitation; by 2006, that figure was nearly 42 percent. And for women the result was even worse: more than half of women 80 and older had a functional limitation. Crimmins's conclusion: There was an "increase in the life expectancy with disease and a decrease in the years without disease. The same is true for functioning loss, an increase in expected years unable to function."

This was confirmed by a recent worldwide assessment of "healthy life expectancy" conducted by the Harvard School of Public Health and the Institute for Health Metrics and Evaluation at the University of Washington. The researchers included not just physical but also mental disabilities such as depression and dementia. They found not a compression of morbidity but in fact an expansion—an "increase in the absolute number of years lost to disability as life expectancy rises."

How can this be? My father illustrates the situation well. About a decade ago, just shy of his 77th birthday, he began having pain in his abdomen. Like every good doctor, he kept denying that it was anything important. But after three weeks with no improvement, he was persuaded to see his physician. He had in fact had a heart attack, which led to a cardiac catheterization and ultimately a bypass. Since then, he has not been the same. Once the prototype of a hyperactive Emanuel, suddenly his walking, his talking, his humor got slower. Today he can swim, read the newspaper, needle his kids on the phone, and still live with my mother in their own house. But everything seems sluggish. Although he didn't die from the heart attack, no one would say he is living a vibrant life. When he discussed it with me, my father said, "I have slowed down tremendously. That is a fact. I no longer make rounds at the hospital or teach." Despite this, he also said he was happy.

As Crimmins puts it, over the past 50 years, health care hasn't slowed the aging process so much as it has slowed the dying process. And, as my father demonstrates, the contemporary dying process has been elongated. Death usually results from the complications of chronic illness—heart disease, cancer, emphysema, stroke, Alzheimer's, diabetes.

Take the example of stroke. The good news is that we have made major strides in reducing mortality from strokes. Between 2000 and 2010, the number of deaths from stroke declined by more than 20 percent. The bad news is that many of the roughly 6.8 million Americans who have survived a stroke suffer from paralysis or an inability to speak. And many of the estimated 13 million more Americans who have survived a "silent" stroke suffer from more-subtle brain dysfunction such as aberrations in thought processes, mood regulation, and cognitive functioning. Worse, it is projected that over the next 15 years there will be a 50 percent increase in the number of Americans suffering from stroke-induced disabilities. Unfortunately, the same phenomenon is repeated with many other diseases.

So American immortals may live longer than their parents, but they are likely to be more incapacitated. Does that sound very desirable? Not to me.

The situation becomes of even greater concern when we confront the most dreadful of all possibilities: living with dementia and other acquired mental disabilities. Right now approximately 5 million Americans over 65 have Alzheimer's; one in three Americans 85 and older has Alzheimer's. And the prospect of that changing in the next few decades is not good. Numerous recent trials of drugs that were supposed to stall Alzheimer's—much less reverse or prevent it—have failed so miserably that researchers are rethinking the whole disease paradigm that informed much of the research over the past few decades. Instead of predicting a cure in the foreseeable future, many are warning of a tsunami of dementia—a nearly 300 percent increase in the number of older Americans with dementia by 2050.

Half of people 80 and older with functional limitations. A third of people 85 and older with Alzheimer's. That still leaves many, many elderly people who have escaped physical and mental disability. If we are among the lucky ones, then why stop at 75? Why not live as long as possible?

Even if we aren't demented, our mental functioning deteriorates as we grow older. Age-associated declines in mental-processing speed, working and long-term memory, and problem-solving are well established. Conversely, distractibility increases. We cannot focus and stay with a project as well as we could when we were young. As we move slower with age, we also think slower.

It is not just mental slowing. We literally lose our creativity. About a decade ago, I began working with a prominent health economist who was about to turn 80. Our collaboration was incredibly productive. We published numerous papers that influenced the evolving debates around health-care reform. My colleague is brilliant and continues to be a major contributor, and he celebrated his 90th birthday this year. But he is an outlier—a very rare individual.

American immortals operate on the assumption that they will be precisely such outliers. But the fact is that by 75, creativity, originality, and productivity are pretty much gone for the vast, vast majority of us. Einstein famously said, "A person who has not made his great contribution to science before the age of 30 will never do so." He was extreme in his assessment. And wrong. Dean Keith Simonton, at the University of California at Davis, a luminary among researchers on age and creativity, synthesized numerous studies to demonstrate a typical age-creativity curve: creativity rises rapidly as a career commences, peaks about 20 years into the career, at about age 40 or 45, and then enters a slow, age-related decline. There are some, but not huge, variations among disciplines. Currently, the average age at which Nobel Prize-winning physicists make their discovery—not get the prize—is 48. Theoretical chemists and physicists make their major contribution slightly earlier than empirical researchers do. Similarly, poets tend to peak earlier than novelists do. Simonton's own study of classical composers shows that the typical composer writes his first major work at age 26, peaks at about age 40 with both his best work and maximum output, and then declines, writing his last significant musical composition at 52. (All the composers studied were male.)

This age-creativity relationship is a statistical association, the product of averages; individuals vary from this trajectory. Indeed, everyone in a creative profession thinks they will be, like my collaborator, in the long tail of the curve. There are late bloomers. As my friends who enumerate them do, we hold on to them for hope. It is true, people can continue to be productive past 75—to write and publish, to draw, carve, and sculpt, to compose. But there is no getting around the data. By definition, few of us can be exceptions. Moreover, we need to ask how much of what "Old Thinkers," as Harvey C. Lehman called them in his 1953 *Age and Achievement*, produce is novel rather than reiterative and repetitive of previous ideas. The age-creativity curve—especially the decline—endures across cultures and throughout history, suggesting some deep underlying biological determinism probably related to brain plasticity.

We can only speculate about the biology. The connections between neurons are subject to an intense process of natural selection. The neural connections that are most heavily used are reinforced and retained, while those that are rarely, if ever, used atrophy and disappear over time. Although brain plasticity persists throughout life, we do not get totally rewired. As we age, we forge a very extensive network of connections established through a lifetime of experiences, thoughts, feelings, actions, and memories. We are subject to who we have been. It is difficult, if not impossible, to generate new, creative thoughts, because we don't develop a new set of neural connections that can supersede the existing network. It is much more difficult for older people to learn new languages. All of those mental puzzles are an effort to slow the erosion of the neural connections we have. Once you squeeze the creativity out of the neural networks established over your initial career, they are not likely to develop strong new brain connections to generate innovative ideas—except maybe in those Old Thinkers like my outlier colleague, who happen to be in the minority endowed with superior plasticity.

MAYBE MENTAL FUNCTIONS—processing, memory, problem-solving—slow at 75. Maybe creating something novel is very rare after that age. But isn't this a peculiar obsession? Isn't there more to life than being totally physically fit and continuing to add to one's creative legacy?

One university professor told me that as he has aged (he is 70) he has published less frequently, but he now contributes in other ways. He mentors students, helping them translate their passions into research projects and advising them on the balance of career and family. And people in other fields can do the same: mentor the next generation.

Mentorship is hugely important. It lets us transmit our collective memory and draw on the wisdom of elders. It is too often undervalued, dismissed as a way to occupy seniors who refuse to retire and who keep repeating the same stories. But it also illuminates a key issue with aging: the constricting of our ambitions and expectations.

We accommodate our physical and mental limitations. Our expectations shrink. Aware of our diminishing capacities, we choose ever more restricted activities and projects, to ensure we can fulfill them. Indeed, this constriction happens almost imperceptibly. Over time, and without our conscious choice, we transform our lives. We don't notice that we are aspiring to and doing less and less. And so we remain content, but the canvas is now tiny. The American immortal, once a vital figure in his or her profession and community, is happy to cultivate avocational interests, to take up bird watching, bicycle riding, pottery, and the like. And then, as walking becomes harder and the pain of arthritis limits the fingers' mobility, life comes to center around sitting in the den reading or listening to books on tape and doing crossword puzzles. And then . . .

Maybe this is too dismissive. There is more to life than youthful passions focused on career and creating. There is posterity: children and grandchildren and great-grandchildren.

But here, too, living as long as possible has drawbacks we often won't admit to ourselves. I will leave aside the very real and oppressive financial and caregiving burdens that many, if not most, adults in the so-called sandwich generation are now experiencing, caught between the care of children and parents. Our living too long places real emotional weights on our progeny.

Unless there has been terrible abuse, no child wants his or her parents to die. It is a huge loss at any age. It creates a tremendous, unfillable hole. But parents also cast a big shadow for most children. Whether estranged, disengaged, or deeply loving, they set expectations, render judgments, impose their opinions, interfere, and are generally a looming presence for even adult children. This can be wonderful. It can be annoying. It can be destructive. But it is inescapable as long as the parent is alive. Examples abound in life and literature: Lear, the quintessential Jewish mother, the Tiger Mom. And while children can never fully escape this weight even after a parent dies, there is much less pressure to conform to parental expectations and demands after they are gone.

Living parents also occupy the role of head of the family. They make it hard for grown children to become the patriarch or matriarch. When parents routinely live to 95, children must caretake into their own retirement. That doesn't leave them much time on their own—and it is all old age. When parents live to 75, children have had the joys of a rich relationship with their parents, but also have enough time for their own lives, out of their parents' shadows.

But there is something even more important than parental shadowing: memories. How do we want to be remembered by our children and grandchildren? We wish our children to remember us in our prime. Active, vigorous, engaged, animated, astute, enthusiastic, funny, warm, loving. Not stooped and sluggish, forgetful and repetitive, constantly asking "What did she say?" We want to be remembered as independent, not experienced as burdens.

At age 75 we reach that unique, albeit somewhat arbitrarily chosen, moment when we have lived a rich and complete life, and have hopefully imparted the right memories to our children. Living the American immortal's dream dramatically increases the chances that we will not get our wish—that memories of vitality will be crowded out by the agonies of decline. Yes, with effort our children will be able to recall that great family vacation, that funny scene at Thanksgiving, that embarrassing faux pas at a wedding. But the most-recent years—the years with progressing disabilities and the need to make caregiving arrangements—will inevitably become the predominant and salient memories. The old joys have to be actively conjured up.

Of course, our children won't admit it. They love us and fear the loss that will be created by our death. And a loss it will be. A huge loss. They don't want to confront our mortality, and they certainly don't want to wish for our death. But even if we manage not to become burdens to them, our shadowing them until their old age is also a loss. And leaving them—and our grandchildren—with memories framed not by our vivacity but by our frailty is the ultimate tragedy.

SEVENTY-FIVE. That is all I want to live. But if I am not going to engage in euthanasia or suicide, and I won't, is this all just idle chatter? Don't I lack the courage of my convictions?

No. My view does have important practical implications. One is personal and two involve policy.

Once I have lived to 75, my approach to my health care will completely change. I won't actively end my life. But I won't try to prolong it, either. Today, when the doctor recommends a test or treatment, especially one that will extend our lives, it becomes incumbent upon us to give a good reason why we don't want it. The momentum of medicine and family means we will almost invariably get it.

My attitude flips this default on its head. I take guidance from what Sir William Osler wrote in his classic turn-of-the-century medical textbook, *The Principles and Practice of Medicine:* "Pneumonia may well be called the friend of the aged. Taken off by it in an acute, short, not often painful illness, the old man escapes those 'cold gradations of decay' so distressing to himself and to his friends."

My Osler-inspired philosophy is this: At 75 and beyond, I will need a good reason to even visit the doctor and take any medical test or treatment, no matter how routine and painless. And that good reason is not "It will prolong your life." I will stop getting any regular preventive tests, screenings, or interventions. I will accept only palliative—not curative—treatments if I am suffering pain or other disability.

This means colonoscopies and other cancer-screening tests are out—and before 75. If I were diagnosed with cancer now, at 57, I would probably be treated, unless the prognosis was very poor. But 65 will be my last colonoscopy. No screening for prostate cancer at any age. (When a urologist gave me a PSA test even after I said I wasn't interested and called me with the results, I hung up before he could tell me. He ordered the test for himself, I told him, not for me.) After 75, if I develop cancer, I will refuse treatment. Similarly, no cardiac stress test. No pacemaker and certainly no implantable defibrillator. No heart-valve replacement or bypass surgery. If I develop emphysema or some similar disease that involves frequent exacerbations that would, normally, land me in the hospital, I will accept treatment to ameliorate the discomfort caused by the feeling of suffocation, but will refuse to be hauled off.

What about simple stuff? Flu shots are out. Certainly if there were to be a flu pandemic, a younger person who has yet to live a complete life ought to get the vaccine or any antiviral drugs. A big challenge is antibiotics for pneumonia or skin and urinary infections. Antibiotics are cheap and largely effective in curing infections. It is really hard for us to say no. Indeed, even people who are sure they don't want life-extending treatments find it hard to refuse antibiotics. But, as Osler reminds us, unlike the decays associated with chronic conditions, death from these infections is quick and relatively painless. So, no to antibiotics.

Obviously, a do-not-resuscitate order and a complete advance directive indicating no ventilators, dialysis, surgery, antibiotics, or any other medication—nothing except palliative care even if I am conscious but not mentally competent—have been written and recorded. In short, no life-sustaining interventions. I will die when whatever comes first takes me.

As for the two policy implications, one relates to using life expectancy as a measure of the quality of health care. Japan has the third-highest life expectancy, at 84.4 years (behind Monaco and Macau), while the United States is a disappointing No. 42, at 79.5 years. But we should not care about catching up with—or measure ourselves against—Japan. Once a country has a life expectancy past 75 for both men and women, this measure should be ignored. (The one exception is increasing the life expectancy of some subgroups, such as black males, who have a life expectancy of just 72.1 years. That is dreadful, and should be a major focus of attention.) Instead, we should look much more carefully at children's health measures, where the U.S. lags, and shamefully: in preterm deliveries before 37 weeks (currently one in eight U.S. births), which are correlated with poor outcomes in vision, with cerebral palsy, and with various problems related to brain development; in infant mortality (the U.S. is at 6.17 infant deaths per 1,000 live births, while Japan is at 2.13 and Norway is at 2.48); and in adolescent mortality (where the U.S. has an appalling record—at the bottom among high-income countries).

A second policy implication relates to biomedical research. We need more research on Alzheimer's, the growing disabilities of old age, and chronic conditions—not on prolonging the dying process.

Many people, especially those sympathetic to the American immortal, will recoil and reject my view. They will think of every exception, as if these prove that the central theory is wrong. Like my friends, they will think me crazy, posturing—or worse. They might condemn me as being against the elderly.

Again, let me be clear: I am not saying that those who want to live as long as possible are unethical or wrong. I am certainly not scorning or dismissing people who want to live on despite their physical and mental limitations. I'm not even trying to convince anyone I'm right. Indeed, I often advise people in this age group on how to get the best medical care available in the United States for their ailments. That is their choice, and I want to support them.

And I am not advocating 75 as the official statistic of a complete, good life in order to save resources, ration health care, or address public-policy issues arising from the increases in life expectancy. What I am trying to do is delineate my views for a good life and make my friends and others think about how they want to live as they grow older. I want them to think of an alternative to succumbing to that slow constriction of activities and aspirations imperceptibly imposed by aging. Are we to embrace the "American immortal" or my "75 and no more" view?

I think the rejection of my view is literally natural. After all, evolution has inculcated in us a drive to live as long as possible. We are programmed to struggle to survive. Consequently, most people feel there is something vaguely wrong with saying 75 and no more. We are eternally optimistic Americans who chafe at limits, especially limits imposed on our own lives. We are sure we are exceptional.

I also think my view conjures up spiritual and existential reasons for people to scorn and reject it. Many of us have suppressed, actively or passively, thinking about God, heaven and hell, and whether we return to the worms. We are agnostics or atheists, or just don't think about whether there is a God and why she should care at all about mere mortals. We also avoid constantly thinking about the purpose of our lives and the mark we will leave. Is making money, chasing the dream, all worth it? Indeed, most of us have found a way to live our lives comfortably without acknowledging, much less answering, these big questions on a regular basis. We have gotten into a productive routine that helps us ignore them. And I don't purport to have the answers.

But 75 defines a clear point in time: for me, 2032. It removes the fuzziness of trying to live as long as possible. Its specificity forces us to think about the end of our lives and engage with the deepest existential questions and ponder what we want to leave our children and grandchildren, our community, our fellow Americans, the world. The deadline also forces each of us to ask whether our consumption is worth our contribution. As most of us learned in college during late-night bull sessions, these questions foster deep anxiety and discomfort. The specificity of 75 means we can no longer just continue to ignore them and maintain our easy, socially acceptable agnosticism. For me, 18 more years with which to wade through these questions is preferable to years of trying to hang on to every additional day and forget the psychic pain they bring up, while enduring the physical pain of an elongated dying process.

Seventy-five years is all I want to live. I want to celebrate my life while I am still in my prime. My daughters and dear friends will continue to try to convince me that I am wrong and can live a valuable life much longer. And I retain the right to change my mind and offer a vigorous and reasoned defense of living as long as possible. That, after all, would mean still being creative after 75.

Ezekiel J. Emanuel is a physician, bioethicist, and vice provost of the University of Pennsylvania.

EXPLORING THE ISSUE

Should the Health Care System Continuously Strive to Extend Life?

Critical Thinking and Reflection

1. Does Ezekiel have a valid point about hoping to die by age 75?
2. What are the common causes of pain and disability during the senior years?
3. Should health resources be used to extend life after age 75 at the expense of health care for younger individuals?

Is There Common Ground?

In October 1986 Dr. Thomas Starzl of Pittsburgh, Pennsylvania, transplanted a liver into a 76-year-old woman at a cost of over $200,000. Soon after that, Congress ordered organ transplantation to be covered under Medicare, which ensured that more older persons would receive this benefit. At the same time these events were taking place, a government campaign to contain medical costs was under way, with health care for the elderly targeted.

Not everyone agrees with this means of extending life at all costs. In a recent study, the majority of older people surveyed accept the withholding of life-prolonging medical care from the hopelessly ill but that few would deny treatment on the basis of age alone.

Currently, millions of Americans have either no or inadequate medical insurance and are at risk of being denied basic health care services. At the same time, the federal government pays most of the health care costs of the elderly. While it may not meet the needs of all older people, the amount of medical aid that goes to the elderly is greater than any other demographic group, and the elderly have the highest disposable income.

Most Americans have access to the best and most expensive medical care in the world. As these costs rise, some difficult decisions may have to be made regarding the allocation of these resources. As the population ages and more health care dollars are spent on care during the last years of life, medical services for the elderly or the dying may become a natural target for reduction in order to balance the health care budget.

Additional Resources

Carstensen, L. L. (2015). The new age of much older age. *Time, 185*(6/7), 68–70.

Digangi, P. (2014). Health span vs. life span for baby boomers. *Rdh*, 74–98.

Easterbrook, G. (2014). What happens when we all live to 100? *Atlantic, 314*(3), 60–72.

Hamzelou, J. (2017). Time to stop getting old. *New Scientist, 232*(3107), 22–23.

Sutherland, J. (2017). A new war on the old. *New Statesman, 146*(5350), 19.

Internet References . . .

American Academy of Family Physicians-Geriatrics

www.aafp/org/geriatric/html

American Association of Retired Persons

www.aarp.org

Coalition to Extend Life

www.coalitiontoextendlife.org/

Selected, Edited, and with Issue Framing Material by:
Eileen L. Daniel, *SUNY College at Brockport*

ISSUE

Does the Affordable Care Act Violate Religious Freedom by Requiring Employers' Health Insurance Plans to Cover Birth Control?

YES: Wesley J. Smith, from "What About Religious Freedom: The Other Consequences of Obamacare," *The Weekly Standard* (2012)

NO: Elizabeth Sepper and Alisha Johnson, from "Rhetoric versus Reality: The Contraception Benefit and Religious Freedom," *religionandpolitics.org* (2013)

Learning Outcomes

After reading this issue, you will be able to:

- Discuss the provisions of the Affordable Care Act.
- Assess the impact of the Act on religious liberty.
- Discuss the importance of access to affordable birth control.

ISSUE SUMMARY

YES: Senior fellow in the Discovery Institute's Center on Human Exceptionalism Wesley J. Smith believes birth control cases are just the beginning for far more intrusive violations of religious liberty to come, for example, requiring businesses to provide free abortions to their employees.

NO: Law professor Elizabeth Sepper and research assistant and law student Alisha Johnson counter that the Affordable Care Act strikes a delicate balance by providing broad protection for religiously affiliated employers, while at the same time it protects the freedom of all Americans to live out their own religious and moral convictions.

The Patient Protection and Affordable Care Act (PPACA), also known as "Obama Care" or the Affordable Care Act, is a federal statute signed into law by President Barack Obama in the spring of 2010. The Act aims to both increase the rate of Americans with health insurance and lower the overall costs of health care. The PPACA includes several components including mandates, subsidies, and tax credits to help and encourage employers and individuals to increase the coverage rate. Additional reforms seek to improve health care outcomes and streamline the delivery of health care. The Congressional Budget Office predicts that the PPACA will reduce both future deficits and spending for Medicare.

Polls indicate support of health care reform in general, but became more negative in regards to specific plans during legislative debates. While the Act was ultimately signed into law in 2010, it remains controversial, with opinions falling along party lines. Opinions are clearly divided by age and party affiliation, with a solid majority of seniors and Republicans opposing the bill while a solid majority of Democrats and those younger than 40 in favor. In a 2010 poll conducted by CNN, 62 percent of respondents said they thought the PPACA would "increase the amount of money they personally spend on health care," 56 percent said the bill "gives the government too much involvement in health care," and only 19 percent said they thought they and their families would be better off with the legislation.

The Act mandates that insurance companies cover all applicants at the same rates regardless of preexisting conditions or gender. In addition, a controversial provision mandates that all insurance policies cover birth control without a co-pay as part of preventive care. The Act requires that all insurance policies cover *all* forms of basic preventive care without a co-pay, including well-woman, well-baby, and well-child visits, as well as other basic prevention care for men and women. This coverage is intended to save costs and promote public health. Basic preventive reproductive and sexual health care services, including contraception, are therefore also covered without a co-pay; as part of the mandate, all insurance plans must provide coverage without a co-pay for all methods of contraception approved by the Food and Drug Administration (FDA). Employees *earn* their salaries and their benefits, and many pay for all or a portion of their health care premiums out of their salaries. As such, none of this coverage is "free," but is rather covered by the policies they are earning or for which they are paying.

In January 2013, the Obama administration issued a rule that most employers, including religiously affiliated institutions such as Catholic universities and hospitals, must provide health care coverage that includes contraceptive services for all women employees and their dependents, at no cost to the employee. A narrow exemption exists for some religious employers, limited in most cases to houses of worship. The requirement only affects health care plans created after March 23, 2010. Plans in effect before that date do not have to meet the new rules.

While women's health advocates applauded the new rule, intense pressure from prominent religious organizations, including the U.S. Conference of Catholic Bishops, immediately followed. In response the Obama administration issued a compromise. Objecting nonprofit religious employers will not be required to pay for contraceptive services, instead shifting the cost to the employer's health insurance company. Those opposed to the compromise find the mandate a stark contradiction to the First Amendment to the U.S. Constitution: "Congress shall make no law respecting an establishment of religion." In addition, many Catholic organizations say that shifting the cost of birth control to the insurer does not resolve the moral objection, because they are self-insured, meaning the insurance provider and the organization are one and the same. Opponents also feel the government should have permission to come in and force an organization to violate its religious beliefs. While there is religious opposition, there are some strong proponents of the mandate who maintain that no one is denying anybody's religious rights. Religious activists hold that while protecting religious liberties is an important responsibility of government, blocking a plan designed to serve all people based on the values of one faith system becomes a violation of rights. Those who favor the bill also contend that the bill is about women's right to comprehensive and preventive health care with equal access regardless of cost and it's just good health care.

In the spring of 2013, 18 for-profit companies have filed lawsuits to avoid complying with the birth control benefit in the Affordable Care Act (ACA) based on several claims. One is that providing insurance policies that cover birth control violates the religious freedom of the companies' owners. The owners of these companies share the belief that a woman is pregnant as soon as there is a fertilized egg (the medical definition of pregnancy is successful implantation of an embryo in the uterine wall) and that a fertilized egg has the same rights as a born person. They also claim that the ACA forces them to cover "abortifacients," with most pointing to emergency contraception methods such as Plan B to make their case. Emergency contraception, however, prevents ovulation, and therefore fertilization, and does not work after an egg has been fertilized. These lawsuits, now in various phases of litigation, are posing a critical challenge to the Affordable Care Act. Wesley J. Smith believes birth control cases are just the beginning for far more intrusive violation of religious liberty to come and is concerned over a slippery slope where businesses might be required to provide free abortions to their employees. Attorney and editor Aram A. Schvey argues that access to affordable contraception is a cornerstone of women's independence and equality and that the Affordable Care Act does not violate religious freedom.

Wesley J. Smith

What About Religious Freedom: The Other Consequences of Obamacare

Obamacare won't just ruin health care. It is also a cultural bulldozer. Before the law is even fully in effect, Health and Human Services bureaucrats have begun wielding their sweeping new powers to assault freedom of religion in the name of their preferred social order.

The promulgation of the free birth control rule indicates the regulatory road ahead. The government now requires every covered employer to provide health insurance that offers birth control and sterilization surgeries free of charge—even if such drugs and procedures violate the religious beliefs of the employer. Only houses of worship and monastic communities are exempt. Religious institutions have until August 1, 2013, to comply.

The lawsuits are flying. In August, the Catholic owners of Hercules Industries, a Colorado air conditioning and heating manufacturer, won a preliminary injunction against enforcement of the free birth control rule against their company (*Newland v. Sebelius*). The case hinges on the meaning of the Religious Freedom Restoration Act (RFRA), enacted in 1993 to remedy a Supreme Court decision allowing federal drug laws of "general applicability" to supersede Native American religious ceremonies in which peyote is used. Since many laws not aimed at stifling a specific faith can be construed to do so, the threat to religious liberty was clear. A Democratic Congress passed, and President Clinton signed, RFRA.

RFRA states that the government "shall not substantially burden a person's exercise of religion" unless it can demonstrate that the law "is in furtherance of a compelling governmental interest." The *Newland* trial judge found that forcing Hercules to pay for birth control—the company is self-insured—did indeed constitute a substantial burden on the owners' free exercise of their Catholic faith. Since no compelling government interest was found, the judge protected the company from the rule pending trial. The Department of Justice has appealed.

Alas, in a nearly identical case, *O'Brien v. U.S. Department of Health and Human Services*, U.S. District Judge Carol E. Jackson reached the opposite legal conclusion. Frank O'Brien is the Catholic owner of O'Brien Industrial Holdings, LLC, a mining company in St. Louis. Demonstrating the sincerity and depth of O'Brien's faith, a statue of the Sacred Heart of Jesus greets visitors in the company's lobby, and the mission statement on its website affirms the intent "to make our labor pleasing to the Lord."

Despite acknowledging "the sincerity of plaintiff's beliefs" and "the centrality of plaintiff's condemnation of contraception to their exercise of the Catholic religion," Jackson dismissed O'Brien's case on the basis that forcing his company to buy insurance covering contraception was not a "substantial burden" on his religious freedom.

Here is the philosophical core of the ruling:

> The challenged regulations do not demand that plaintiffs alter tbeir behavior in a manner that will directly and inevitably prevent plaintiffs from acting in accordance with their religious beliefs. Frank O'Brien is not prevented from keeping the Sabbath, from providing a religious upbringing for his children, or from participating in a religious ritual such as communion. Instead plaintiffs remain free to exercise their religion, by not using contraceptives and by discouraging employees from using contraceptives.

Excuse me, but that's a lot like a judge telling a Jewish butcher that his freedom of religion is not violated by a regulation requiring him to carry nonkosher wares in his shop. After all, the government wouldn't be requiring *the butcher* to eat nonkosher meat.

More to the point, Jackson embraced the Department of Justice's reasoning. If this view prevails, it will shrivel the "free exercise of religion" guaranteed by the First Amendment into mere "freedom of worship," limiting RFRA's protections to personal morality, domestic activities, and religious rites behind closed doors. Worse, the court ruled that O'Brien is the aggressor in the matter, *that it is he who is seeking to violate the rights of his employees.* "RFRA is a shield, not a sword," Judge Jackson wrote, "it is not a means to force one's religious practices upon others."

How does O'Brien's desire not to involve himself in any way with contraception force Catholicism upon his employees? He hasn't threatened anyone's job for not following Catholic moral teaching. He hasn't tried to prevent any employee from using birth control. He hasn't compelled employees to go to confession or get baptized. He merely chooses not to be complicit in what he considers sinful activities.

But that analysis presupposes that O'Brien's religious freedom extends to his actions as an employer. It doesn't, sayeth the Obama administration: "By definition, a secular employer does not engage in any 'exercise of religion,'" the Department of Justice argued in the *Newland* case. In other words, according to the Obama administration, the realm of commerce is a religion-free zone.

Some might dismiss these employers' concerns because birth control is hardly controversial outside of orthodox religious circles. But these birth control cases are stalking horses for far more intrusive violations of religious liberty to come, e.g., requiring businesses to provide free abortions to their employees. Consider the Democratic party's 2012 platform:

> The Democratic party strongly and unequivocally supports *Roe v. Wade* and a woman's right to make decisions regarding her pregnancy, including a safe and legal abortion, *regardless of ability to pay.* [Emphasis added.]

If Democrats regain the control of Congress and the presidency they enjoyed in 2009 and 2010, look for the Affordable Care Act to be amended consistent with their platform. After that, it won't take long for HHS to promulgate a free abortion rule along lines similar to the free birth control mandate.

And what could be done about it? According to Judge Jackson's thinking, ensuring free access to abortion would not prevent employers from "keeping the Sabbath." They would not be prohibited from "providing a religious upbringing" for their children or "participating in a religious ritual such as communion." Rather, they would be barred from "forcing their religious practices" on employees by leaving employees to pay for their own terminations. In time, why shouldn't in-vitro fertilization, assisted suicide, and sex change operations be added to the list?

If higher courts accept this radically antireligious view, the only corrective will be to amend RFRA to spell out that its protections extend to the actions of employers. In fact, why not take that step now and short circuit what could be years of litigation defending religious liberty in the public square?

Wesley J. Smith is a senior fellow in the Discovery Institute's Center on Human Exceptionalism.

Elizabeth Sepper and Alisha Johnson

NO

Rhetoric versus Reality: The Contraception Benefit and Religious Freedom

The Catholic bishops argue that the Affordable Care Act's requirement that health plans include contraception violates religious freedom for both religious and secular corporations. Their counsel, Anthony Picarello, has indicated they will not rest until even a Taco Bell franchise owned by a Catholic is exempted from the law. For-profit businesses have joined religiously affiliated non-profits in filing suit to avoid providing their employees coverage for contraception. Most prominently, Hobby Lobby, a for-profit crafts store chain with 13,000 employees, has defied the insurance requirements in the name of free exercise of religion.

To hear these claims, one might think that religious freedom is under attack. But the rhetoric does not match reality. The contraception benefit rule strikes a delicate balance. It provides broad protections for religiously affiliated employers. At the same time, it protects the freedom of all Americans to live out their own religious and moral convictions.

Under the Affordable Care Act, health insurance plans must cover preventive services for women without cost-sharing. This includes all FDA-approved contraceptives from birth control pills to sterilization. This contraception benefit rule addresses pressing problems of gender inequality in healthcare and barriers to obtaining contraception. It recognizes that more than half of women between 18 and 34 cannot afford birth control. Due in large part to the price of contraception, almost half of all pregnancies in the U.S. are unintended. These pregnancies lead to poorer health outcomes for mother and child, and higher costs. Our workforce also suffers, as women abandon their professional and educational goals to have children before they are ready.

In acknowledgement of the varied religious teachings on contraception, the rule, especially with its latest proposed exemptions, provides generous accommodation for religious employers. Those that primarily employ and serve co-adherents, like churches, are entirely exempted from the rule and are not required to provide contraception coverage. Religiously affiliated non-profits, like hospitals, universities, and social service providers, also enjoy broad exemptions. They may exclude contraception from their plans and will not have to contract, arrange, pay, or refer for coverage. But their employees will still have access to contraception through a separate policy provided by the insurance company. Although one might think that the employer ultimately pays for this policy, contraception coverage saves at least as much as it costs and, therefore, is cost-free.

Secular, for-profit corporations, by contrast, must comply with the contraception benefit rule. A wide range of businesses, including food processors and craft stores, have objected to this requirement. They argue that the law forces them to either conduct business in a way that violates their religious beliefs or pay hefty penalties to the government.

But can for-profit companies exercise religion? Companies do not have beliefs or attend services. For-profits are not designed to bring believers together or carry out the mission of a church. They exist to maximize profit; their concern is the bottom line. Our legal system recognizes this difference, and regularly subjects for-profit businesses to regulation while exempting some religious non-profits.

Some say that the shareholders, or owners, of corporations nonetheless have religious beliefs that are burdened by the rule. But our laws do not require exemptions for every claim of religious belief. Instead, under the Religious Freedom Restoration Act, laws are only suspect if they produce substantial burdens on free exercise of religion. Where the law furthers a compelling government interest, as the contraception benefit does, even substantial burdens can be justified.

Here, any burden on the owners' free exercise is insubstantial. It is the corporation, not its owners, that must offer a plan with contraceptive coverage or pay higher taxes. As the Supreme Court has noted, the very purpose of incorporating a business is to create a distinct legal entity with legal rights and obligations separate from the individuals who own it.

Owners of for-profit corporations do not have to purchase or take contraception. They may speak against it and live their lives in accordance with their religious beliefs. Their involvement in the perceived wrongdoing of purchasing or using contraception is highly attenuated.

The employer's alleged burden becomes even weaker when we consider that health insurance, like wages, is compensation that employees earn. When a corporation purchases a health plan that its employees and their families use to buy contraception, it is no more paying for contraception than it does when employees use their wages to buy it. A basic principle of health economics is that there is a tradeoff between wages and insurance. As a recent study in Massachusetts showed, employees pay almost the full cost of their insurance benefits through lower wages.

A serious burden, however, would fall on employees if their employers were excused from compliance with the contraception benefit rule due to their religious objections. Secular, for-profit corporations could then successfully use religion as a shield against any number of laws that promote workers' health and safety. Some businesses might resist coverage of prenatal care for unmarried pregnant women or STD screening, based on the belief that non-marital sex is immoral. Others might challenge vaccinations or depression screening on religious grounds.

As the Supreme Court has observed, bowing to an employer's objection to an insurance scheme for employees ultimately "operates to impose the employer's religious faith on the employees." The contraception benefit rule instead safeguards the religious freedom of each individual. Women, men, and their families will be free to decide whether to use contraception based on their own conscientious beliefs.

Elizabeth Sepper is an associate professor of law at Washington University, St. Louis, MO.

Alisha Johnson is a law student at Washington University.

EXPLORING THE ISSUE

Does the Affordable Care Act Violate Religious Freedom by Requiring Employers' Health Insurance Plans to Cover Birth Control?

Critical Thinking and Reflection

1. Why might affordable birth control be considered the cornerstone of women's independence and equality?
2. Does the Affordable Care Act violate religious freedom? Explain your answer.
3. Describe how providing birth control through the Affordable Care Act might be perceived as a violation of religious liberty.

Is There Common Ground?

The government estimated that the Affordable Care Act legislation will lower the number of the uninsured by 32 million, leaving 23 million uninsured residents by 2019 after the bill's mandates have all taken effect. Among the people in this uninsured group will be approximately 8 million illegal immigrants, individuals eligible but not enrolled in Medicare, and mostly the young and single men and women not otherwise covered who choose to pay the annual penalty instead of purchasing insurance.

Early experience under the Act was that, as a result of the tax credit for small businesses, some businesses offered health insurance to their employees for the first time. On September 13, 2011, the Census Bureau released a report showing that the number of uninsured 19- to 25-year-olds (now eligible to stay on their parents' policies) had declined by 393,000, or 1.6 percent. A later report from the Government Accountability Office in 2012 found that of the 4 million small businesses that were offered the tax credit only 170,300 businesses claimed it. Due to the effect of the U.S. Supreme Court ruling, states can opt in or out of the expansion of Medicaid.

Also, a component ensuring children could remain included on their parents' plans until age 26 remains a popular, fairly noncontroversial part of the bill. The contraceptive coverage, however, remains contentious. The Affordable Care Act includes a contraceptive coverage mandate that, with the exception of churches and houses of worship, applies to all employers and educational institutions. These regulations made under the Act rely on the recommendations of the Institute of Medicine, which concluded that access to contraception is medically necessary "to ensure women's health and well-being."

The initial regulations proved controversial among Christian hospitals, Christian charities, Catholic universities, and other enterprises owned or controlled by religious organizations that oppose contraception on doctrinal grounds. To accommodate those concerns while still guaranteeing access to contraception, the regulations were adjusted to "allow religious organizations to opt out of the requirement to include birth control coverage in their employee insurance plans. In those instances, the insurers themselves will offer contraception coverage to enrollees directly, at no additional cost." Unfortunately, this didn't entirely satisfy religious organizations who still believe their beliefs are being compromised.

Additional Resources

Burlone, S., Edelman, A. B., Caughey, A. B., Trussell, J., Dantas, S., & Rodriguez, M. I. (2013). Extending contraceptive coverage under the Affordable Care Act saves public funds. *Contraception, 87*(2), 143–148.

Church & State. (2015). Priests for Life vows defiance after losing birth control case. *Church & State, 68*(1), 19.

Churchill, S. (2015). Whose religion matters in corporate RFRA claims after *Burwell v. Hobby Lobby stores, Inc.*, 134 S. CT. 2751 (2014)? *Harvard Journal of Law & Public Policy, 38*(1), 437–450.

Richey, W. (2014). Affordable Care Act and birth control: Can corporations assert religious rights? *Christian Science Monitor*, March 23.

Rosenbaum, S. (March/2017). Contraception as a health insurance right. What comes next? *Milbank Quarterly*, *95*, 28–31.

Internet References . . .

Health Care

www.healthcare.gov

Health Care Law and You

www.healthcare.gov/law/

Planned Parenthood

www.plannedparenthood.org

Unit 2

UNIT

Health and Society

Human health is complex, influenced not only by the biology and chemistry of the body but also by societal structures, culture, and politics and economics. Interestingly, public policy and medical ethics have not always kept pace with rapidly growing technology and scientific advances especially if we consider the impact of recent biomedical research. Some developments, for example, those associated with reproductive technologies such as in vitro fertilization and cloning, seem to present us with ethical problems and the need for public policy that are unprecedented. Other relevant issues include the costs associated with treating cancer and the increasing numbers of states legalizing marijuana. Will this lead to less legal issues but more usage, especially among minors? More often, however, the advance of biomedical research has simply added complexity to old problems and created a sense of urgency with regard to their solution.

Selected, Edited, and with Issue Framing Material by:
Eileen L. Daniel, *SUNY College at Brockport*

ISSUE

Is the Cost of Treating Cancer Unsustainable?

YES: Lee N. Newcomer, from "Myths and Realities in Cancer Care: Another Point of View," *Health Affairs* (2014)

NO: Dana P. Goldman and Tomas Philipson, from "Five Myths About Cancer Care in America," *Health Affairs* (2014)

Learning Outcomes

After reading this issue, you will be able to:

- Understand the complex nature of cancer.
- Discuss the reasons why the disease has been so difficult to eradicate.
- Discuss cancer treatments, costs, and their side effects.
- Discuss why the cost of cancer treatments has risen so sharply.

ISSUE SUMMARY

YES: United Healthcare's vice president for oncology, physician Lee N. Newcomer believes that the cost to treat cancer will be unsustainable in the near future and will undermine the progress made in cancer treatment.

NO: Professor of public policy Dana P. Goldman and professor of health economics Tomas Philipson maintain that it's a myth that treatment costs are unsustainable and that restricting patients' treatments is socially wasteful and will likely discourage research innovations.

According to the National Cancer Institute, there will be 18.1 million cancer survivors in 2020, 30 percent more than in 2010, and the cost to treat their disease was $157 billion in 2010 dollars. This is expected to rise as the U.S. population ages and more and more cancers are treated. Cancer is a group of diseases characterized by uncontrolled cellular growth, invasion that intrudes upon and destroys nearby tissues, and may metastasize or spread to other locations in the body via blood or lymph. The malignant characteristics of cancers differentiate them from benign growths or tumors which do not invade or metastasize. Fortunately, most cancers can be treated with drug or chemotherapy, surgery, and/or radiation. The outcome of the disease is based on the type of cancer, for example, lung or breast cancer, and the extent of disease. While cancer affects people of all ages, and a few types of cancer are actually more common in children, most cancer risks increase with age. Cancer rates are increasing as more people live longer and lifestyles change, such as increased smoking occurring in the developing world.

Most cancers have an environmental link, with 90–95 percent of cases attributed to environmental factors and 5–10 percent due to heredity. Typical environmental factors that contribute to cancer deaths include diet and obesity (30–35 percent), smoking and tobacco use (25–30 percent), infectious agents (15–20 percent), and ionizing and nonionizing radiation (up to 10 percent). The remaining may be caused by stress, lack of exercise, and some environmental pollutants. Cancer prevention is related to those active measures that decrease the incidence of the disease. Since the vast majority of cancer risk factors are environmental or lifestyle-related, cancer is largely a preventable disease. Individuals who avoid tobacco, maintain a healthy weight, eat a diet rich in fruits and vegetables, exercise, use alcohol in moderation, take measures to prevent the transmission of sexually transmitted diseases, and avoid exposure to air pollution are likely to significantly reduce their risks of the disease.

Cancer's reputation is a deadly one. In reality about half of patients receiving treatment for invasive cancer will not survive the disease or the treatment. And the cost of these treatments continues to rise and the population in the developed world continues to age. The survival rate, however, can vary significantly by the type of cancer, ranging from basically all patients surviving to almost no patients surviving. Predicting either short-term or long-term survival is challenging and depends on a variety of factors. The most important factors are the type of cancer and the patient's age and overall health. Medically frail patients suffering simultaneously from other illnesses have lower survival rates than otherwise healthy patients. Despite strong social pressure to maintain an upbeat, optimistic attitude or act like a determined "fighter" to "win the battle," research has not shown that personality traits have a connection to survival.

In 1971 then President Richard Nixon signed the National Cancer Act of 1971. The goal of the Act was to find a cure for cancer by increased research to improve the understanding of cancer biology and the development of more effective treatments such as targeted drug therapies, all requiring extensive research costs. The Act is also viewed as the beginning of the war on cancer and the vow to end the disease for good. Despite significant progress in the treatment of certain forms of cancer, the disease in general remains a major cause of death 40 years after this effort began leading to a perceived lack of progress and to new legislation aimed at augmenting the original National Cancer Act of 1971. New research directions, in part based on the results of the Human Genome Project, hold promise for a better understanding of the heredity factors underlying cancer, and the development of new diagnostics, treatments, preventive measures, and early detection ability. The question raised by Lee Newcomer is whether or not the cost to treat cancer will be sustainable in the near future. He asks whether or not these costs will actually undermine the progress made in cancer treatment. Dana Goldman and Tomas Philipson disagree and maintain that restricting patients' treatments based on cost is socially wasteful and will likely discourage research innovations.

YES 

Lee N. Newcomer

Myths and Realities in Cancer Care: Another Point of View

Based on current trends, economists predict that in less than three years a family's typical health insurance premium and out-of-pocket costs will equal 50 percent of the average US-household income.[1] The same study notes that fourteen years later the cost of health care coverage will equal 100 percent of household income. As costs continue to rise, health care providers and researchers must discover methods to reduce the cost of care while advancing the progress that has been made against cancer. In this commentary I take the same five myths that Dana Goldman and Tomas Philipson have sought to debunk[2] and, in reverse order, offer additional considerations that policy makers should take into account.

Myth 5: Supportive Care Is Overused

Goldman and Philipson are correct: It is a myth that supportive care is overused. However, supportive care is undermined by misuse. A study of 1,849 lung and colon cancer patients treated at multiple centers demonstrated underuse of supportive care, with only 17 percent of patients with high-risk chemotherapy regimens receiving granulocyte colony stimulating factors (G-CSFs) to prevent low blood counts.[4] The same study also showed significant overuse. Overall, for these patients, 97 percent of the G-CSFs that were administered were not recommended by evidence-based guidelines.

Palliative care offers one pathway to the discussions of patient goals that are critical for assuring the appropriate use of supportive care. A trial of all lung cancer patients in an academic oncology clinic randomized patients to standard oncology care or to standard oncology care with a palliative care consultation. The palliative care group had better quality-of-life scores, lived 2.7 months longer, used less chemotherapy, and had less aggressive end-of-life care.[4] The palliative care patients established clear goals for their therapy at the beginning of treatment. Without that vital discussion, assigning value to supportive care is either flawed or impossible.

Myth 4: Cancer Treatment at the End of Life Is of Low Value

Goldman and Philipson argue that patients are willing to pay more for hopeful therapy—especially for cancer treatments. The papers supporting this assertion use hypothetical estimates of a patient's willingness to pay. Yet real-world data suggest that patients are less willing to reach into their own pockets for cancer therapies with limited values. An analysis of a large payer data set examined the compliance of oncology patients with specialty pharmacy support-including twenty-four-hour access to oncology pharmacists for side-effect management and compliance encouragement-compared to oncology patients with less comprehensive support from retail pharmacies. Each group paid a $50 copayment for drugs costing about $5,000 per prescription. The mean possession ratio, a measure of compliance based on prescription filled, was 66 percent in the specialty pharmacy group and 58 percent in the retail group.[5] Presumably, the additional support enjoyed by the first group eliminated medical reasons for noncompliance, explaining its 12 percent higher rate of compliance. The remaining 34 percent rate of noncompliance is, therefore, probably the effect of cost. If $50 keeps a patient from purchasing an oncology drug at the end of life, it is hard to believe the melanoma study[6] cited by Goldman and Philipson showing that patients are willing to pay $54,000 for a hypothetical treatment. The difference between these two studies is that one highlights patients' willingness to spend their own money, and the other shows patients' willingness to spend someone else's money.

Myth 3: Treatment Costs Are Unsustainable

As already stated, the US health care system cannot continue to spend at its current trend. The average household cannot be expected to spend its entire income on health care. Because of their high prices, new drugs are attracting the most attention, but cancer therapy involves more than just drugs. Chemotherapy drugs represent 24 percent of total care costs, inpatient and outpatient facility services account for 54 percent, and physician services constitute the remaining 22 percent of total costs for commercially insured cancer patients at UnitedHealthcare.[7] A recent study demonstrated that by finding savings elsewhere, five medical oncology groups could reduce the total cost of cancer care by 34 percent in a cohort of 810 patients, even as they increased cancer drug spending by 179 percent.[7]

Cancer patients are widely portrayed by patient advocates as having an extraordinary financial burden for their illness. Goldman and Philipson, for example, cite examples of patients paying 50 percent of the cost of newer cancer agents.[8] But that is not always the case. Such enormous out-of-pocket expenses are typically associated with low-cost insurance that offers fewer benefits. Patients in these frequently cited examples are almost always taking high-cost oral cancer medications or other specialty medications like them—such as treatment of multiple sclerosis, for example—under low-premium pharmacy plans. Higher-premium plans offer more reasonable patient cost sharing such as the $50 copayment example described earlier. Furthermore, most oncology drugs are given under the medical benefit of an insurance plan, in which drugs are usually subject to the same coverage benefits as the intensive care unit visit mentioned by Goldman and Philipson. Under the medical benefit, out-of-pocket expenses are almost always capped, and once the cap is met, claims are covered completely. Members who purchase insurance with good benefits will pay a higher premium, but their coverage will make their individual cost sustainable.

I agree with many of the points made by Goldman and Philipson debunking Myth 3 that treatment costs are unsustainable. First, treatments that have little or no health benefit should be challenged for reimbursement. Second, cancer patients should not bear more burden than other severely ill patients simply because they have cancer. Hospitals often use this tactic when they purchase oncology practices: On average, according to internal UnitedHealthcare data, medical oncologists in private practice are paid 22 percent more than Medicare rates for providing chemotherapy. However, hospitals that own oncology practices or employ medical oncologists can use their contracting leverage to earn reimbursement for the same service at an average of 146 percent more than Medicare, also according to internal UnitedHealthcare data. It is not right that cancer patients are bearing this heavier burden.

Myth 2: Detection, Not Treatment, Accounts for Most of the Survival Gains

As Goldman and Philipson argue, the number of adult cancers with significant improvement in survival due to treatment breakthroughs is impressive; breast cancer, colon cancer, multiple myeloma, and chronic myelogenous leukemia are good examples. Even more impressive is the progress in pediatric cancer largely as a result of rigorous enrollment of nearly every child into clinical trials. In stark contrast, only about 3 percent of adult cancer patients are enrolled in clinical trials. The US medical care system is missing a great opportunity to quickly learn about new therapies. Enrolling more adults in cancer clinical trials will accelerate the pace of new cancer drug approvals.

Unfortunately, the number of trials being offered is diminishing because of decreased funding and lengthy approval processes. But many organizations have begun to take new approaches. The lung cancer master protocol, the Multiple Myeloma Research Foundation, and the I-SPY adaptive breast cancer trials have shown what is possible when the principles of collaboration, speed, and access are given priority. These programs are proof that the US research system can improve its performance.

Myth 1: The War on Cancer Has Been a Failure

The term "failure" is relative and, I agree with Goldman and Philipson, misguided. When one compares the improvement in survival with heart disease versus cancer—the nation's two largest killers—it is clear that cardiac survival has improved far more than cancer survival.[9] More importantly, both diseases are causing less mortality. To use the metaphor of war, many battles have been won in cancer, but the theater of operations is much larger because there are scores of cancer types. Progress, even at a slower rate, is not failure.

Researchers, patient advocates, and policy makers should, nevertheless, push harder to improve the rate of progress. Finding ways to make cancer care affordable must be an important part of that effort.

Conclusion

A myth is a story, usually without basis in fact, that one tells to explain some practice or event. As Goldman and Philipson have shown, solid facts demonstrate that the cancer community is producing better treatments and outcomes. Yet these advances, though encouraging, can be better. The same cancer community that has achieved such important progress still faces another big challenge: to produce these treatments faster and for less cost.

References

1 Young RA, DeVoe JE. Who will have health insurance in the future? An updated projection. Am Fam Med. 2012;10(12) :156–62.

2 Goldman DP, Philipson T. Five myths about cancer care in America. Health Aff (Millwood). 2014;33(10):1801–04.

3 Temel JS, Greer JA, Muzikansky A, Gallagher ER, Admane S, Jackson VA, et al. Early palliative care for patients with metastatic non-smallcell lung cancer. N Engl J Med. 2010;363(8):733–42.

4 Potosky AL, Malin JL, Kim B, Chrischilles EA, Makgoeng SB, Howlander N, et al. Use of colonystimulating factors with chemotherapy: opportunities for cost savings and improved outcomes. J Natl Cancer Inst. 2011;103(12):979–82.

5 Tschida SJ, Aslam S, Lal LS, Khan TT, Shrank WH, Bhattarai GR, et al. Outcomes of a specialty pharmacy program for oral oncology medications. Am J Pharm Benefits. 2012;4(4):165–74.

6 Lakdawalla DN, Romley JA, Sanchez Y, Maclean JR, Penrod JR, Philipson T. How cancer patients value hope and the implications for cost-effectiveness assessments of high-cost cancer therapies. Health Aff (Millwood). 2012;31(4):676–82.

7 Newcomer LN, Gould B, Page RD, Donelan SA, Perkins M. Changing physician incentives for affordable, quality cancer care: results of an episode payment model. J Oncol Pract. 2014 Jul. [Epub ahead of print].

8 Fenn KM, Evans SB, McCorkle R, DiGiovanna MP, Pustzai L, Sanft T, et al. Impact of financial burden of cancer on survivors' quality of life. J Oncol Pract. 2014 May. [Epub ahead of print].

9 Murphy SL, Xu J, Kochanek KD. Deaths: final data for 2010. National Vital Statistics Reports. 2013;61(4):1–17.

Lee N. Newcomer is an oncology physician and vice president of UnitedHealthcare.

Dana P. Goldman and Tomas Philipson

Five Myths About Cancer Care in America

Much has been made recently about the cost of cancer treatment, often played out in editorials in cancer journals or on the opinion pages of major newspapers.[1,2] Some of the concern reflects beliefs that arose years ago when the illness was not as well understood. In this commentary we present some of the more common myths in America and the much more nuanced reality of today.

Myth 1: The War on Cancer Has Been a Failure

Perhaps no myth is so pervasive and yet so misguided than the one that declares that the war on cancer has been a failure.[3] Today cancer patients live longer, healthier, and happier lives than those in prior decades. Survival rates for all cancers increased by almost four years during the period 1988–2000,[4] creating twenty-three million additional life-years and generating $1.9 trillion in additional value to society, once the health gains are tallied.[5] Survival rates have continued to improve in recent years. A rough comparison of these health benefits with spending on research and development—both private and public—suggests a substantial social return on investment.

Furthermore, progress is being made in dealing with the extreme toxicity of chemotherapy and radiation regimens. Newer therapies often allow better quality of life. For example, long-term breast cancer survivors see an overall improvement in the two years following diagnosis,[6] and delays in chemotherapy have been shown to negatively affect patients' quality of life in some instances.[7] So, while cancer still remains a pernicious disease, there is hope that it can be managed as a chronic illness, with modest side effects.

Myth 2: Detection, Not Treatment, Accounts for Most of the Survival Gains

The public's attention often is drawn to the benefits of early detection. If a tumor is found earlier, it can be treated before metastasis and dramatically improve survival. Celebrities such as Katie Couric and events such as National Breast Cancer Awareness Month encourage screening, and new technologies have made detection more accurate and less invasive.[8] The result has been that screening for some of the most common cancers has increased steadily.[9]

Thus, it comes as a surprise to many that treatment, not detection, has driven the majority of survival gains over the last few decades. During 1988–2000 almost 80 percent of the aforementioned survival gains were attributable to improvements in treatment, with the remaining 20 percent attributable to better detection. By some estimates, early detection accounted for only 3 percent of the increase in all cancer survival.[4]

Furthermore, better detection has no value if effective treatment is not available. A diagnosis of multiple myeloma in the 1960s meant a median survival rate of less than one year,[10] compared to more than six years today.[11] Patients diagnosed with metastatic colorectal cancer could expect an eight-month median overall survival rate two decades ago, compared to thirty months today.[12] These make detection far more valuable. Thus, perhaps ironically, the best way to encourage more screening may be to identify better, earlier-stage treatments.

Myth 3: Treatment Costs Are Unsustainable

As noted earlier, the rising cost of overall cancer treatment—especially the contribution of highprice therapies—has drawn a lot of attention recently.[1] However, this debate avoids a fundamental issue that is broader than cancer care—namely, that the focus should be on the price of health, not the price of health care services.

An analogy with highly active antiretroviral therapy (HAART) to treat HIV is instructive. HAART, which was introduced in the 1990s, dramatically increased longevity for HIV-positive patients,[13] although at a significant financial cost to these patients.[14] Prior to the introduction of HAART, an HIV-positive patient could not buy a longer life at any price. The advent of HAART thus lowered the price of a longer life, although the price of treatment rose.

Ultimately, more than 93 percent of the benefits of developing the new treatment accrued to patients in the form of longer lives, rather than to manufacturers.[15]

Similar declines were seen in the price of health for cancer patients, as measured by the price of each quality-adjusted life-year (QALY). Just over a decade ago, patients suffering from chronic myeloid leukemia faced grim prospects for survival. With the introduction of tyrosinekinase inhibitors (TKIs) in 2002, life expectancy increased by 5.5 QALYs, at a cost of $57,000 per QALY saved.[16] Given that the value of a life-year in the United States falls in the range of $200,000–$300,000,[17] TKIs seem like a good deal. Thus, society secured good value, even at brand-name prices. Next year, one of the first TKIs will lose its patent, and the price could fall dramatically as a generic enters the market.

Of course, not all cancer treatments have had such dramatic improvements on life expectancy, and some drugs may not be worth the cost. However, when the cost of innovative drugs is viewed over their branded and generic lifetime, it seems that a good deal is being obtained for the cancer dollars expended, with substantial increases in survival at reasonable cost.

So why the uproar about cancer in particular? Many health care services have higher costs than oncology drugs—the cost of a stay in the intensive care unit (ICU) is about $20,000[18]—or provide little value for the money, such as magnetic resonance images (MRIs) for sprained ankles.[19] Yet one does not see such handwringing about ICU costs or MRIs because payers and providers have deemed those costs to be acceptable and appropriately allocated.

In fact, the outrage arises because it is the patient, not the insurer, who has to pay. Among specialty drugs, cancer drugs have the highest out-of-pocket spending burden imposed on patients.[20] Patients may be asked to pay 50 percent of the cost of newer cancer drugs out of pocket,[21] compared with a much smaller fraction of the cost of an ICU stay. This financial burden can be "devastating," according to leading oncologists.[2]

Clearly reimbursement for treatments that have little or no health benefit should be challenged. However, blanket policies that shift the cost burden onto a subset of patients with rare or difficult-to-treat cancers—or that lower all prices together—would discourage future innovation and deprive patients of novel therapies.

Myth 4: Cancer Treatment at the End of Life Is of Low Value

This myth arises from a fundamental misconception about the value of care delivered to the terminally ill.[22] More specifically, policy makers assume that the value of a life-year remains constant, regardless of a patient's circumstances. Evidence—and consumer behavior—would suggest otherwise.

An anecdote is helpful. In 2008 the *New York Times* published a story on Avastin, a drug that inhibits the growth of new blood vessels, emphasizing the dilemma posed by its modest improvement in survival rates and high cost. A few days later, reader Jana Jett Loeb wrote a Letter to the Editor, poignantly explaining the value of Avastin to treat her father's glioblastoma off-label: "The hope this drug provides our family is just as important to prolonging my father's life as the drug itself."[23]

As Loeb makes clear, there is additional value in treatments that give people hope, despite modest survival benefit. One study estimated that patients with metastatic disease value treatment at levels twenty-three times higher than the cost of the therapy.[24] It is also known that median survival does not capture the right-tail chance of success often associated with the hope of full remission. As a result, coverage decisions based solely on median survival will neglect the great social value for a minority who live long after the trial ends.

This does not mean that insurers should cover all hopeful therapies in the absence of clinical evidence. However, it does mean that the way in which trial results are evaluated should be reconsidered. A recent study demonstrated that 77 percent of cancer patients with melanoma preferred hopeful therapies, even with uncertainty as to where they would fall on the survival curve, and were willing to pay over $54,000 for a hypothetical treatment with the same median survival but a better chance at long-term survival.[25]

Second, behavior demonstrates that life is more precious when less of it remains. Ordinary people recognize this point, but current quality-of-life metrics do not. While patients often refuse to take their ordinary medications when copayments increase just a few dollars, cancer drugs are different. Patients are willing to pay substantial amounts out-of-pocket, indicating tremendous consumer value.[20,24]

Third, society as a whole places higher value on treatments for those who are sicker. Surveys show that people are reluctant to forgo care for the elderly, even if resources devoted to that care could more effectively improve population health if used elsewhere.[26] The same survey suggests that people would rather society choose interventions that make the lives of a few much better off than interventions that make the lives of many only slightly better off. In the United Kingdom, growing complaints about denials of effective but costly treatments for life-threatening diseases have prompted a compassionate care exception to the cost-effectiveness threshold for patients with poor prognoses.

Finally, recent evidence suggests that healthy people are willing to pay higher premiums for access to treatments analysts often deem of no value. By some estimates, adults in the United States are willing to pay on average an extra $2.60 in insurance premiums for every dollar of cancer drug coverage.[27] Bottom line, the QALY-based approach to decide necessity is inconsistent with patients' and society's value of cancer care.

Myth 5: Supportive Care is Overused

Many of the most effective cancer treatments have significant side effects, including pain, nausea, fatigue, anemia, and susceptibility to infection. Supportive care therapies, such as colony stimulating factors and anti-emetics, address one or more of these side effects. Nevertheless, many view them as a cost with little benefit.[22]

In reality, supportive care enables the administration of more aggressive chemotherapy regimens by avoiding or managing the debilitating effects of the toxicity. Aggressive regimens, facilitated by supportive care, slow disease progression and improve overall survival.

Indeed, some of the best clinical trials include supportive care as part of the protocols.[28] However, the incidence of neutropenia and the use of supportive care therapies are underreported in clinical trial publications, underrepresenting the value to society of supportive care.[29,30] As treatments evolve over time, supportive care regimens will remain an integral part of innovation and patient care.

Conclusion

Cancer has always been the "Emperor of All Maladies."[31] But any illness with such a majestic designation is bound to be surrounded by myths, many of which arose years ago when the illness was much less understood. The reality of cancer today is of a disease far more nuanced, reflecting systematic progress in treating the disease. New paradigms have led to the development of groundbreaking biologic therapies, with a lower risk of adverse events and side effects—but also with a commensurate cost.

It is now known that cancer is actually hundreds of diseases, many of which are rare. Scientific discovery will likely not allow for the development of "common cancer" treatments that will be effective in all cases. Rather, identified cancer subtypes that can be targeted by drugs are ultimately costly to develop, particularly when the treated population is small. Coverage policies that place undue burden on patients may discourage further innovation of treatments targeting rare genetic mutations and tumor subtypes. The call to artificially lower drug prices may address immediate affordability problems but—if done incorrectly—will come at too high a cost for future cancer patients' health.

Notes

1 Experts in Chronic Myeloid Leukemia. The price of drugs for chronic myeloid leukemia (CML) is a reflection of the unsustainable prices of cancer drugs: from the perspective of a large group of CML experts. Blood. 2013;121(22) :4439–42.

2 Bach PB, Saltz LB, Wittes RE. In cancer care, cost matters. New York Times. 2012 Oct 15;Sect. A:25.

3 Faguet GB. The war on cancer: an anatomy of failure, a blueprint for the future. New York (NY): Springer; 2005.

4 Sun E, Jena AB, Lakdawalla D, Reyes C, Philipson TJ, Goldman DP. The contributions of improved therapy and early detection to cancer survival gains, 1988–2000. Forum for Health Economics and Policy. 2010;13 (2): Article 1.

5 Lakdawalla DN, Sun EC, Jena AB, Reyes CM, Goldman DP, Philipson TJ . An economic evaluation of the war on cancer. J Health Econ. 2010;29(3): 333–46.

6 Hsu T, Ennis M, Hood N, Graham M, Goodwin PJ. Quality of life in longterm breast cancer survivors. J Clin Oncol. 2013;31(28):3540–8.

7 Calhoun EA, Chang C-H, Welshman EE, Cella D. The impact of chemotherapy delays on quality of life in patients with cancer. J Support Oncol. 2004;2(2):64–65.

8 Whitlock EP, Lin JS, Liles E, Beil TL, Fu R. Screening for colorectal cancer: a targeted, updated systematic review for the U.S. Preventive Services Task Force. Ann Intern Med. 2008;149(9) :638–58.

9 Clarke TC, Soler-Vila H, Fleming LE, Christ SL, Lee DJ, Arheart KL. Trends in adherence to recommended cancer screening: the US population and working cancer survivors. Front Oncol. 2012 ;2:190.

10 Kumar SK, Rajkumar SV, Dispenzieri A, Lacy MQ, Hayman SR, Buadi FK, et al. Improved survival in multiple myeloma and the impact of novel therapies. Blood. 2008;111(5):2516–20.

11 Kumar SK, Dispenzieri A, Lacy MQ, Gertz MA, Buadi FK, Pandey S, et al. Continued improvement in survival in multiple myeloma: changes in early mortality and outcomes in older patients. Leukemia. 2014;28(5):1122–8.

12 Kopetz S, Chang GJ, Overman MJ, Eng C, Sargent DJ, Larson DW, et al. Improved survival in metastatic colorectal cancer is associated with adoption of hepatic resection and improved chemotherapy. J Clin Oncol. 2009;27(22):3677–83.

13 Sansone GR, Frengley JD. Impact of HAART on causes of death of persons with late-stage AIDS. J Urban Health. 2000;77(2):166–75.

14 Goldman DP, Bhattacharya J, Leibowitz AA, Joyce GF, Shapiro MF, Bozzette SA. The impact of state policy on the costs of HIV infection. Med Care Res Rev. 2001;58(1):31–53; discussion 54–9.

15 Philipson TJ, Jena AB. Surplus appropriation from R&D and health care technology assessment procedures. Cambridge (MA): National Bureau of Economic Research; 2006 Feb. (NBER Working Paper No. 12016).

16 Reed SD, Anstrom KJ, Li Y, Schulman KA. Updated estimates of survival and cost effectiveness for imatinib versus interferon-alpha plus low-dose cytarabine for newly diagnosed chronic-phase chronic myeloid leukaemia. Pharmacoeconomics. 2008;26(5):435–46.

17 Aldy JE, Viscusi WK. Adjusting the value of a statistical life for age and cohort effects. Rev Econ Stat. 2008;90(3):573–81.

18 Dasta JF, McLaughlin TP, Mody SH, Piech CT. Daily cost of an intensive care unit day: the contribution of mechanical ventilation. Crit Care Med. 2005;33(6):1266–71.

19 American Academy of Orthopaedic Surgeons. Sprained ankle [Internet]. Rosemont (IL): AAOS; 2012 Sep [cited 2014 Aug 26] . Available from: http://orthoinfo.aaos.org/topic.cfm?topic=a00150

20 Goldman DP, Joyce GF, Lawless G, Crown WH, Willey V. Benefit design and specialty drug use. Health Aff (Millwood). 2006;25(5):1319–31.

21 Smith TJ, Hillner BE. Bending the cost curve in cancer care. N Engl J Med. 2011;364(21):2060–5.

22 Schnipper LE, Smith TJ, Raghavan D, Blayney DW, Ganz PA, Mulvey TM, et al. American Society of Clinical Oncology identifies five key opportunities to improve care and reduce costs: the top five list for oncology. J Clin Oncol. 2012; 30(1 4):1715–24.

23 Letter to the editor. The high price for a drug, and hope. New York Times. 2008 Jul 12.

24 Seabury SA, Goldman DP, Maclean JR, Penrod JR, Lakdawalla DN. Patients value metastatic cancer therapy more highly than is typically shown through traditional estimates. Health Aff (Millwood). 2012;31(4):691–9.

25 Lakdawalla DN, Romley JA. Sanchez Y, Maclean JR, Penrod JR, Philipson T. How cancer patients value hope and the implications for cost-effectiveness assessments of high-cost cancer therapies. Health Aff (Millwood). 2012;31(4):676–82 .

26 Nord E, Richardson J, Street A, Kuhse H, Singer P. Maximizing health benefits vs egalitarianism: an Australian survey of health issues. Soc Sci Med. 1995;41(10):1429–37.

27 Romley JA, Sanchez Y, Penrod JR, Goldman DP. Survey results show that adults are willing to pay higher insurance premiums for generous coverage of specialty drugs. Health Aff (Millwood). 2012;31(4):683–90.

28 National Cancer Institute. Prospective phase 2 trial of cabazitaxel in patients with temozolomide refractory glioblastoma multiforme [Internet]. Bethesda (MD): National Cancer Institute; 2013 [cited 2014 Aug 26]. Available from: http://www.cancer.gov/clinicaltrials/search/view?cdrid=750138&version=HealthProfessional&protocolsearchid=9363709

29 Dale DC, McCarter GC, Crawford J, Lyman GH. Myelotoxicity and dose intensity of chemotherapy: reporting practices from randomized clinical trials. J Natl Compr Canc Netw. 2003;1(3):440–54.

30 Duff JM, Leather H, Walden EO, LaPlant KD, George TJ Jr. Adequacy of published oncology randomized controlled trials to provide therapeutic details needed for clinical application. J Natl Cancer Inst. 2010;102(10):702–5.

31 Mukherjee S. The emperor of all maladies: a biography of cancer. New York (NY): Simon and Schuster; 2011.

Dana P. Goldman is the Leonard D. Schaeffer Chair and director of the University of Southern California Leonard D. Schaeffer Center for Health Policy and Economics and professor of public policy, pharmacy, and economics at the USC Sol Price School of Public Policy and USC School of Pharmacy.

Tomas Philipson is a professor of health economics at the University of Chicago with posts in the Harris School of Public Policy Studies, Department of Economics, and the University of Chicago Law School.

EXPLORING THE ISSUE

Is the Cost of Treating Cancer Unsustainable?

Critical Thinking and Reflection

1. Why are some cancers so difficult to successfully treat?
2. What are effective ways to reduce the risk of developing cancer?
3. Describe what factors are involved in predicting short- and long-term cancer survival rates.
4. Discuss why increasing costs may undermine the progress made in cancer treatment.

Is There Common Ground?

While many diseases have similar or worse outcomes, cancer is generally more feared than heart disease or diabetes. Cancer is regarded as a disease that must be "battled" and a "war" on cancer has been declared. Fighting or military-like descriptions are often used to address cancer's human effects, and they emphasize the need for the patient to take immediate, decisive actions himself or herself, rather than to delay, to ignore, or to rely on others caring for him or her. This fight is fought with a full array of treatments including surgery, radiation, and chemotherapy. Newer and more targeted therapies are coming, though the cost of this research continues to climb.

Why have costs escalated so much? On some levels, it's the price of success. Cancer deaths have been declining in the United States since the early 1990s. Two out of three people now live at least 5 years after a cancer diagnosis, up from one out of two in the 1970s, according to the American Society of Clinical Oncology doctors who treat the disease. Nine out of 10 women with early-stage breast cancer are alive 5 years after their diagnosis and are likely cured. Modern treatments have fewer side effects and allow patients to have a greater quality of life than chemotherapy did in the past. But they are far more toxic financially.

Of the nation's 10 most expensive medical conditions, cancer has the highest per-person price. The total cost of treating cancer in the United States rose from about $95.5 billion in 2000 to $124.6 billion in 2010, the National Cancer Institute estimated. The true tab is higher—the agency bases its estimates on average costs from 2001 to 2006, before many expensive treatments were available. Cancer costs are projected to reach $158 billion, in 2010 dollars, by the year 2020, because of a growing population of older people who are more likely to develop cancer. That's the societal cost. For individual patients, costs can vary widely even for the same drug. And cost can still be a concern long after initial treatment. Although all cancer patients want and deserve the best possible treatment, the reality of the cost of treatment is an unfortunate part of the disease.

Additional Resources

Cancer treatment costs seldom discussed with Black patients. (2017). *PharmacoEconomics & Outcomes News, 769*

Langton, J. M., Blanch, B., Drew, A. K., Haas, M., Ingham, J. M., & Pearson, S. (2014). Retrospective studies of end-of-life resource utilization and costs in cancer care using health administrative data: A systematic review. *Palliative Medicine, 28*(10), 1167–1196

Makary, M. (2014). The cost of chasing cancer. *Time, 183*(9), 24.

New cancer drugs bring benefits but increase costs. (2015). *PharmacoEconomics & Outcomes News, 722*(1), 20.

Smith, B. D., Jing, J., Ya-Chen Tina, S., Giordano, S. H., Jinhai, H., Jagsi, R., & ... Shirvani, S. M. (2017). Cost and complications of local therapies for early-stage breast cancer. *JNCI: Journal Of The National Cancer Institute, 109*(1), 1–9

Internet References . . .

American Cancer Society

www.cancer.org

American Medical Association (AMA)

www.ama-assn.org

Centers for Disease Control and Prevention

www.cdc.gov/

MedScape: The Online Resource for Better Patient Care

www.medscape.com

U.S. National Institutes of Health (NIH)

www.nih.gov

Selected, Edited, and with Issue Framing Material by:
Eileen L. Daniel, *SUNY College at Brockport*

ISSUE

Will Legalizing Marijuana Increase Usage?

YES: Christian Hopfer, from "Implications of Marijuana Legalization for Adolescent Substance Use," *Substance Abuse* (2014)

NO: Christopher Ingraham, from "Now We Know What Happens to Teens When You Make Pot Legal," *Washington Post* (2016)

Learning Outcomes

After reading this issue, you will be able to:

- Discuss the physical risks associated with marijuana use.
- Assess the cognitive, social, behavioral, and legal issues associated with the use of marijuana.
- Assess the viability of legalization of marijuana.
- Discuss the potential for increased usage if legalized.

ISSUE SUMMARY

YES: Physician Christian Hopfer believes that marijuana legalization will increase availability, social acceptance, and possibly lower prices leading to increased usage among adults and teens.

NO: Journalist Christopher Ingraham argues that marijuana use among teenagers is essentially unchanged since legalization.

At one time, there were no laws in the United States regulating the use or sale of drugs, including marijuana. Rather than by legislation, their use was regulated by religious teaching and social custom. As society grew more complex and more heterogeneous, the need for more formal regulation of drug sales, production, and use developed.

Attempts at regulating patent medications through legislation began in the early 1900s. In 1920, Congress, under pressure from temperance organizations, passed an amendment prohibiting the manufacture and sale of all alcoholic beverages. From 1920 until 1933, the demand for alcohol was met by organized crime, who either manufactured it illicitly or smuggled it into the United States. The government's inability to enforce the law, as well as increasing violence, finally led to the repeal of Prohibition in 1933.

Many years later, in the 1960s, drug usage again began to worry many Americans. Heroin abuse had become epidemic in urban areas, and many middle-class young adults had begun to experiment with marijuana and LSD by the end of the decade. Cocaine also became popular first among the middle class and later among inner-city residents. More recently, crack houses, babies born with drug addictions, and drug-related crimes and shootings are the images of a new epidemic of drug abuse.

Many of those who believe illicit drugs are a major problem in America, however, are usually referring to hard drugs, such as cocaine and heroin. Soft drugs like marijuana, though not legal, are not often perceived as a major threat to the safety and well-being of citizens. Millions of Americans have tried marijuana and did not become addicted. The drug has also been used illegally by those suffering from AIDS, glaucoma, and cancer to alleviate their symptoms and to stimulate their appetites. Should marijuana be legalized as a medicine, or is it too addictive and dangerous? In California, Proposition 215 passed in the November 1996 ballot. A similar measure passed in Arizona and other states have followed. These initiatives convinced voters to relax current laws against marijuana use for recreational, medical, and humane reasons.

Opponents of these recent measures argue that marijuana use has been steadily rising among teenagers and that this may lead to experimentation with hard drugs or at least, increase pot smoking. There is concern that if marijuana is legal via a doctor's prescription or sold in stores, the drug will be more readily available and that will lead to increase usage. There is also concern that the health benefits of smoking marijuana are overrated. For instance, among glaucoma sufferers, in order to achieve benefits from the drug, patients would literally have to be stoned all the time. Unfortunately, the efficacy of marijuana is unclear because, as an illicit drug, studies to adequately test it have been thwarted by drug control agencies.

Although marijuana's effectiveness in treating the symptoms of disease is unclear, is it actually dangerous and addictive especially for teenagers? Scientists contend that the drug can negatively affect cognition and motor function. It can also have an impact on short-term memory and can interfere with perception and learning. Physical health effects include lung damage. Until recently, scientists had little evidence that marijuana was actually addictive. Whereas heavy users did not seem to experience actual withdrawal symptoms, studies with laboratory animals given large doses of tetrahydrocannabinol (THC), the active ingredient in marijuana, suffered withdrawal symptoms similar to those of rodents withdrawing from opiates.

Not all researchers agree, however, that marijuana is dangerous and addictive. The absence of well-designed, long-term studies on the effects of marijuana use further complicates the issue, as does the current potency of the drug. Growers have become more skilled about developing strains of marijuana with high concentrations of THC. Today's varieties may be three to five times more potent than the pot used in the 1960s. Much of the data are unclear, but what is known is that young users of the drug are likely to have problems learning. In addition, some users are at risk for developing dependence.

In the following selections, physician Christian Hopfer states that legalization will likely increase usage especially among young people.

Christopher Ingraham argues that in states where marijuana is legal, usage has not increased.

YES 

Christian Hopfer

Implications of Marijuana Legalization for Adolescent Substance Use

Introduction

The Surgeon General's 1964 report that smoking is harmful was arguably the most important substance abuse intervention in the United States. This report and subsequent efforts by antismoking groups, physicians, and public health agencies resulted in a shift in public perceptions of smoking and was followed by a steady decline of smoking in the United States, resulting in eight million lives being saved since 1964 due to tobacco control polices.[1] Currently, however, a reverse phenomenon for marijuana may be taking place. Claims that marijuana has medicinal properties, widespread state-level legalization of medical marijuana, recent recreational legalization in two states, and advertising of marijuana's purported harmlessness may lead to a substantial increase in adolescent marijuana abuse and dependence.[2] Recent Gallup poll results report that for the first time, a majority of the American population now supports marijuana legalization, suggesting that future policy shifts in the United States are likely to move toward increased marijuana legalization. The purpose of this commentary is to consider the possible implications of such a shift for adolescent substance use and abuse.

History of the Colorado Experience with Marijuana Legalization

Colorado legalized marijuana for medicinal purposes through a physician's recommendation in 2000 and legalized adult recreational marijuana use as of 2014. In the beginning of 2009, when the federal government emphasized that it would not enforce federal bans on marijuana in states that allowed it for medicinal consumption,[4] there were approximately 2,000 patients with a medical marijuana registration in Colorado. Within two years of the change in federal policy, the number of persons holding a medical marijuana registration had increased to an estimated 150,000.[5] Colorado currently has the highest per capita number of medical marijuana license holders, with approximately 3 percent of the population possessing a marijuana license.[6] There has also been a rapid growth in medical marijuana centers, with over 809 dispensaries in Colorado (1/3 of the nation's marijuana dispensaries). Recreational marijuana sales to anyone over 21 began January 1, 2014, and Colorado's marijuana sales taxes (including both recreational and medical) for January, February, and March of 2014, were approximately \$3.5 million, \$4 million, and \$5 million, respectively, reflecting the rapid growth of marijuana sales.[7] Although Colorado has been one of the earliest adopters of marijuana legalization, medical marijuana laws now exist in 21 states and the district of Columbia, allowing for legal access to marijuana *with* a physician's recommendation, and Washington State has legalized recreational adult consumption.[8] Nationwide, many additional states are considering either allowing medicinal marijuana or outright legalization similar to the Colorado and Washington models. Thus, a substantial portion of the United States is experiencing the phenomena of legal adult marijuana use, either through the predominant medicinal route, but also now for recreational consumption in two states.

Historical Experiences with "Nonpenalization" of Marijuana in Holland

Due to the recency of marijuana policy changes in Colorado and in other states, making inferences about their effect on general population and adolescent use patterns is quite difficult. Analyses of the Dutch "coffeeshop" system of "nonpenalization" provide some guidance about the likely effect of such legal changes for Colorado and the United States.[9–12] Based upon previous work analyzing this system, it is worth noting both implications for the United States and areas of probable difference. First, Holland never legalized marijuana but developed a policy of "nonpenalization," which is different from the current US approach, which has resulted in outright legalization in two states. There were two "phases" of cannabis quasi-legalization in Holland: nonpenalization followed by commercialization.[10] During the commercialization phase, there was some evidence of an increase in use among adolescents and some evidence of users increasing their consumption; however, it is important to note that in Holland, cannabis prices remained fairly high, access became more restrictive (buyers currently have to be members of "cannabis clubs"), and that Dutch cannabis policy has shifted in response to perceptions of problematic use patterns developing (e.g., initially youth aged 16 were allowed in the "coffeeshops," but this was then changed to 18). Dutch youth do have a higher mean level of marijuana use than those of youth in other European countries; however, their levels of use are below that of the United States, the United Kingdom, and France, which have all (until recently) not allowed legal cannabis. There was also an increase in adolescent treatment seeking for cannabis problems associated with nonpenalization, although it is unclear whether this was a causal relationship. Growing up within 20 km of a marijuana dispensary was also associated with earlier age of onset of marijuana use.[13] Due to ongoing policy shifts, it is difficult to determine whether Dutch youth were influenced by the "coffeeshop" system and were more likely to try marijuana or use it more frequently than before it existed. The major lessons from the Dutch experience for the United States are that marijuana control policies are likely to evolve; however, full-scale legalization as is now occurring in two states (Colorado and Washington) is a phenomena that is distinct from the Dutch experience. One area of major potential difference is that full legalization and commercialization may substantially reduce the eventual price of marijuana.[9] Adolescents may be particularly influenced by eventual price reductions, as they typically have more limited financial means and may be a primary target of black market sales.

Recent Analyses of United States Data and Case Reports of Adverse Outcomes

A number of articles have analyzed recent US trends in marijuana attitudes and consumption patterns in relation to medical marijuana laws and have come to differing conclusions regarding their effects. A recent report analyzing the effect of medical marijuana laws found that states with such laws have higher marijuana use, although it is unclear whether this effect is causal.[14] Another paper using data from the Youth Behavior Risk Survey up to 2011 found minimal evidence of an effect of changes in medical marijuana laws on marijuana use patterns in the first one to five years after enactment,[15] whereas a different article using data from the National Household Survey on Drug Use that also examined data up to 2011 reported a significant decrease in adolescent perceptions of marijuana risk in Colorado compared with nonmedical marijuana states as well as a significantly higher adolescent marijuana/abuse dependence prevalence after widespread adult medical legalization.[2] A number of reports suggest substantial diversion of medical marijuana to adolescents[16–19] as well as increases of marijuana overdoses in young children[20–22] as well as a significant increase in the proportion of marijuana-positive drivers involved in traffic fatalities in Colorado compared with nonmedical marijuana states.[23] News reports have also recently noted two deaths linked to marijuana edibles, apparently resulting from severe intoxication.[24] In summary, analyses of recent trends in marijuana consumption patterns and their relation to legal marijuana laws provide some evidence that when marijuana is legalized, there is an increase in marijuana use and marijuana-related problem behaviors; however, these findings must still be considered preliminary.

Marijuana as a Possible "Substitute" for Other Substances

Economic theory has focused on the association between alcohol and marijuana use, with some authors suggesting that alcohol and marijuana use are complements,[25] whereas others suggest they are substitutes.[26] For example, Pacula[25] reported that an increased federal tax on beer had "a negative and significant effect on the demand for both alcohol and marijuana, implying that alcohol and marijuana are economic complements." Similarly, creating stricter college alcohol policies has been associated with reductions in marijuana use.[27] In contrast, other groups have shown that restricting the availability of alcohol by increasing the minimum drinking age[26] is associated with increased marijuana use and a decrease in marijuana use and increase in alcohol use around the age of 21 years; when alcohol use becomes legal, consistent with the substitute model.[28] Similarly, Chaloupka and Laixuthai[29] conclude "the successful marijuana-related efforts in the 'War on Drugs,' which can be expected to reduce the supply of marijuana and, hence, increase its price will not only lead to less marijuana consumption, but will have the unintended consequence of raising alcohol consumption." Anderson et al.[30] found that medical marijuana laws were associated with decreased likelihood of past month alcohol consumption and binge drinking. Marijuana and tobacco use are also highly comorbid, and some recent work suggests that changes in marijuana use may impact tobacco use, although the directionality of the relationship also remains unclear. For example, Allsop et al.[31] demonstrated that during voluntary abstinence from marijuana use, tobacco use increased by 14 cigarettes per week. In contrast, Peters and Hughes,[32] studying daily marijuana users during a 13-day period of abstinence, did not demonstrate increases in cigarette or nonmarijuana illicit drug use. Finally, it has recently been suggested that medical marijuana use may be associated with reductions in opioid use.[33,34] Thus, both models have some empirical support but predict opposite marijuana-related effects of legalization and rapid commercialization of marijuana.

Scientific Views on Harms of Adolescent Marijuana Use

A substantial concern about legalization of adult marijuana use is that it will result in an increase in adolescent use, a group that appears to be most vulnerable to its harmful effects. A recent review summarized much of the current knowledge regarding the harmful medical and behavioral effects of marijuana consumption.[35] Adolescent marijuana use has been associated with impairment in a number of areas: impaired cognitive functioning,[36] increased risk of developing marijuana dependence,[37] elevated rates of school dropout,[38] an elevated risk of developing psychotic illnesses,[39,40] and an increased rate of engaging in risky behaviors.[41] Weekly marijuana use under age 18 years has been associated with an eight-point drop in intelligence among those who develop persistent dependence, whereas those with adult onset of comparable levels of use are less affected; importantly, the loss of cognitive capacity may not recover completely after desisting from marijuana use.[42] Some authors have criticized this finding for not accounting for social economic status[43] or personality[44] differences; however, empirical analyses have not found support for this[concern].[45] Schweinsburg et al.[36] reviewed the literature of marijuana's effect on cognition and concluded that adolescents demonstrate persisting deficits related to heavy marijuana use for at least six weeks following discontinuation, particularly in the domains of learning, memory, and working memory. Further, they appear more adversely affected by heavy use than adults. However, the authors noted that "although adolescents who use marijuana heavily demonstrate decrements compared with nonusing teens, it is still unknown whether marijuana use caused or contributed to these effects." Similarly, early use has been associated with poor outcomes in a number of other domains; however, these associations do not necessarily signify causality. Instead, early use may act as a marker of a more generalized tendency to engage in risky behaviors.[46,47] Thus, although many studies of adolescent marijuana use demonstrate harms associated with such use, difficulties in controlling for the effects of third variables or confounders that may influence both marijuana use and adverse outcomes limit the strength of the conclusions that can be drawn about the causal influence of adolescent marijuana use. Finally, all research on the epidemiology of marijuana use conducted to date in the United States has been conducted in an environment where marijuana use is illegal. Results of previous studies examining the patterns of marijuana use and associations with other substances, patterns of development of marijuana use disorders, and associations with other psychopathology may not generalize to conditions of widespread legality, an environment where marijuana use has greater social acceptance, is marketed and available in different forms (e.g., drinks, edibles, and vaporized), and where the marijuana itself may have substantially higher tetrahydrocannabinol contents than marijuana previously consumed.[48]

The issue of scientific clarity regarding the harms of adolescent marijuana use has substantial implications beyond influencing the debate about whether marijuana should be legalized or not. Consider a hypothetical environment where marijuana is legal for adult recreational consumption, widely available, and widely believed to be harmless or even beneficial. How will prevention efforts be conducted if there is not clear scientific, medical, and *public* consensus that marijuana use is harmful? How will treatment be conducted when there is substantial disagreement about the harmfulness of using marijuana? Will primary care physicians screen adolescents for marijuana use as they do for alcohol and tobacco? How will counseling be conducted and what guidelines for physician advice will be promoted? What if an adolescent requests marijuana as a treatment for psychiatric or medical conditions? Legalization implies that law enforcement efforts to control or reduce marijuana use will be limited, leaving public health, medical, and scientific organizations to reduce harm and educate the public. These stakeholders face major challenges in developing clear messages, particularly in an evolving policy climate. If marijuana becomes widely legal in the United States or internationally, the need grows to have current and rigorous scientific evidence about the effects of marijuana consumption, particularly for adolescents. Claims of medicinal benefits need to be addressed clearly, and concerted efforts to develop a coordinated public health policy response to legalization are needed.

Recommendations for a Research Agenda and Practitioners

Marijuana policy continues to evolve; however, legal marijuana use appears likely to become more accepted given recent trends. Tobacco is widely recognized as a legal, but a harmful, substance for both adolescents and adults and is the focus of substantial public health, physician, and scientific efforts to mitigate public harms and consumption. Alcohol is understood to be harmful when consumed in excess, and clear guidelines exist for its consumption by adults. Substantial efforts exist to understand and reduce adolescent drinking. In contrast, marijuana is alternatively a banned substance with no medicinal properties federally, while being allowed for medicinal purposes in many states with essentially no enforcement of federal laws, and now available for recreational consumption in two states. Apparently, partly in response to the growing acceptance of marijuana, the National Institute on Drug Abuse, National Institute on Alcohol Abuse and Alcoholism, the National Cancer Institute, and the National Center on Child Health and Development plan to launch a major national study to examine the effects of substance exposure on developing adolescents.[49] Such a study would certainly help elucidate the effects of marijuana and other substances on the developing adolescent. Additional studies, however, will be needed to examine treatment and prevention messages that can be effective in a more permissive environment, as well as addressing claims of medicinal benefits and coming to a clearer scientific consensus about the strength of such claims. For clinicians in the adolescent substance abuse field who are treating adolescents with cannabis or other substance abuse disorders, a major challenge will be around issues of relapse or use of marijuana in a legal environment. Although this is not a new challenge for any clinician, marijuana may become the new "tobacco" in the sense that patients and their families may view it as not being as serious a substance to worry about and it may act as the first substance that triggers a relapse. Family members own use of marijuana may also become a more serious barrier to adolescents trying to maintain sobriety. Education about the addictive properties and deleterious effects of marijuana for both patients and family members may need to become a more routine part of any adolescent substance abuse treatment.

References

[1] Holford TR, Meza R, Warner KE, et al. Tobacco control and the reduction in smoking-related premature deaths in the United States, 1964–2012. *JAMA*. 2014; 311:164–171.

[2] Schuermeyer J, Salomonsen-Sautel S, Price RK, et al. Temporal trends in marijuana attitudes, availability and use in Colorado compared to non-medical marijuana states: 2003–11. *Drug Alcohol Depend.* 2014; 140:145–155. doi:10.1016/j.drugalcdep.2014.04.016.

[3] Swift A. For the first time Americans favor legalizing marijuana. GallupPoll Web site. Available at: http:www.gallup.com/po!U165539/first-ti.me-americans-favor-legalizingmarijuana.aspx. Published October 22, 2013. Accessed May 22, 2014.

[4] Ogden DW. Memorandum for selected United States attorneys on investigations and prosecutions in states authorizing the medical use of marijuana. The Department of Justice. Available at: http:www.justice.gov/opa/documents/medical-marijuana.pdf. Published October 19, 2009. Accessed May 21, 2014.

[5] Colorado Department of Public Health and Environment. Medical Marijuana Statistics 2011. Available at: http:www.colorado.gov/cs/Satellite/CDPHECHEIS/CBON/1251593017044. Published 2011. Accessed May 22, 2014.

[6] Nussbaum AM, Boyer JA, Kondrad EC. "But my doctor recommended pot": Medical marijuana and the patient-physician relationship. *J Gen Intern Med.* 2011; 26:1364–1367.

[7] Colorado Department of Revenue. Colorado Marijuana Tax Data. Available at: http:www.colorado.gov/cs/Satellite/Revenue-Main/XRM/1251633259746. Published 2014. Accessed May 21, 2014.

[8] Office of National Drug Control Policy. Office of National Drug Control Policy: Marijuana. Available at: http:www.whitehouse.gov/ondcp/marijuana. Published 2014. Accessed May 22, 2014.

[9] Caulkins JP, Kilmer B, MacCoun RJ, Pacula RL, Reuter P. Design considerations for legalizing cannabis: Lessons inspired by analysis of California's Proposition 19. *Addiction.* 2012; 107:865–871.

[10] MacCoun RJ. What can we learn from the Dutch cannabis coffeeshop system? *Addiction.* 2011;106:1899–1910.

[11] MacCoun R, Reuter P. Evaluating alternative cannabis regimes. *Br J Psychiatry.* 2001;178:123–128.

[12] MacCoun R, Reuter P. Interpreting Dutch cannabis policy: Reasoning by analogy in the legalization debate. *Science.* 1997; 278:47–52.

[13] Palali A, Van Ours JC. Distance to cannabis-shops and age of onset of cannabis use. Center Discussion Paper Series No. 2013-048. August 28, 2013. Available at: http:dx..doi.org/10.2139/ssm,2319245. Accessed May 22, 2014.

[14] Cerda M, Wall M, Keyes KM, Galea S, Hasin D. Medical marijuana laws in 50 states: Investigating the relationship between state legalization of medical marijuana and marijuana use, abuse and dependence. *Drug Alcohol Depend.* 2012; 120:22–27.

[15] Lynne-Landsman SD, Livingston MD, Wagenaar AC. Effects of state medical marijuana laws on adolescent marijuana use. *Am J Public Health.* 2013; 103:1500–1506.

[16] Salomonsen-Sautel S, Sakai JT, Thurstone C, Corley R, Hopfer C. Medical marijuana use among adolescents in substance abuse treatment. *J Am Acad Child Adolesc Psychiatry.* 2012; 51:694–702.

[17] Nussbaum A, Thurstone C, Binswanger I. Medical marijuana use and suicide attempt in a patient with major depressive disorder. *Am J Psychiatry.* 2011; 168:778–781.

[18] Thurstone C, Lieberman SA, Schmiege SJ. Medical marijuana diversion and associated problems in adolescent substance treatment. *Drug Alcohol Depend.* 2011; 118:489–492.

[19] Thurstone C, Tomcho M, Salomonsen-Sautel S, Profita T. Diversion of medical marijuana: When sharing is not a virtue. *J Am Acad Child Adolesc Psychiatry.* 2013; 52:653–654.

[20] Wang GS, Roosevelt G, Le Lail MC, et al. Association of unintentional pediatric exposures with decriminalization of marijuana in the United States. *Ann Emerg Med.* 2014; 63:684–689. doi:10.1016/j.annemergmed.2014.01.017.

[21] Wang GS, Roosevelt G, Heard K. Pediatric marijuana exposures in a medical marijuana state. *JAMA Pediatr.* 2013; 167:630–633.

[22] Wang GS, Narang SK, Wells K, Chuang R. A case series of marijuana exposures in pediatric patients less than 5 years of age. *Child Abuse Negl.* 2011; 35:563–565.doi:10.1016/j.chiabu.2011.03.012.

[23] Salomonsen-Sautel S, Min SJ, Sakai JT, Thurstone C, Hopfer C. Trends in fatal motor vehicle crashes before and after marijuana commercialization in Colorado. *Drug Alcohol Depend.* 2014; 140:137–144. doi:10.1016/j.drugalcdep.2014.04.008.

[24] Rittiman B. Denver deaths put focus on marijuana edibles. *USA Today.* April 18, 2014. Available at: http://www.usatoday.com/story/news/nation/2014/04/18/denver-deathmarijuana-edibles/7887025/. Accessed May 27, 2014.

[25] Pacula RL. Does increasing the beer tax reduce marijuana consumption? *J Health Econ.* 1998; 17:557–585.

[26] DiNardo J, Lemieux T. Alcohol, marijuana, and American youth: The unintended consequences of government regulation. *J Health Econ.* 2001; 20:991–1010.

[27] Williams J, Pacula RL, Chaloupka FJ, Wechsler H. Alcohol and marijuana use among college students: Economic complements or substitutes? *Health Econ.* 2004; 13:825–843.

[28] Crost B, Guerrero S. The effect of alcohol availability on marijuana use: Evidence from the minimum legal drinking age. *J Health Econ.* 2012; 31:112–121.

[29] Chaloupka FJ, Laixuthai A. Do youths substitute alcohol and marijuana? Some econometric evidence. *East Econ J* 1997; 23:253–276.

[30] Anderson DM, Hansen B, Rees DI. Medical marijuana laws, traffic fatalities, and alcohol consumption. *J Law Econ.* 2013; 56:333–369.

[31] Allsop DJ, Dunlop AJ, Saddler C, Rivas GR, McGregor IS, Copeland J. Changes in cigarette and alcohol use during cannabis abstinence. *Drug Alcohol Depend.* 2014; 138:54–60.

[32] Peters EN, Hughes JR. Daily marijuana users with past alcohol problems increase alcohol consumption during marijuana abstinence. *Drug Alcohol Depend.* 2010; 106:111–118.

[33] Pacula RL, Sevigny EL. Marijuana liberalization policies: Why we can't learn much from policy still in motion. *J Policy Anal Manage.* 2014; 33:212–221.

[34] Nunberg H, Kilmer B, Pacula RL, Burgdorf JR. An analysis of applicants presenting to a medical marijuana specialty practice in California. *J Drug Policy Anal.* 2011; 4:1. doi:10.2202/1941-2851.1017.

[35] Volkow ND, Baler RD, Compton WM, Weiss SRB. Adverse health effects of marijuana use. *N Engl J Med.* 2014; 370:2219–2227.

[36] Schweinsburg AD, Brown SA, Tapert SF. The influence of marijuana use on neurocognitive functioning in adolescents. *Curr Drug Abuse Rev.* 2008; 1:99–111.

[37] Chen CY, Storr CL, Anthony JC_ Early-onset drug use and risk for drug dependence problems. *Addict Behav.* 2009; 34:319–322.

[38] Lynskey MT, Coffey C, Degenhardt L, Carlin JB, Patton G. A longitudinal study of the effects of adolescent cannabis use on high school completion. *Addiction.* 2003; 98:685–692.

[39] Moore TH, Zammit S, Lingford-Hughes A, et al. Cannabis use and risk of psychotic or affective mental health outcomes: A systematic review. *Lancet.* 2007; 370:319–328.

[40] Zammit S, Moore TH, Lingford-Hughes A, et al. Effects of cannabis use on outcomes of psychotic disorders: Systematic review. *Br J Psychiatry.* 2008; 193:357–363.

[41] Guo J, Chung IJ, Hill KG, Hawkins JD, Catalano RF, Abbott RD. Developmental relationships between adolescent substance use and risky sexual behavior in young adulthood. *J Adolesc Health.* 2002; 31:354–362.

[42] Meier MH, Caspi A, Ambler A, et al. Persistent cannabis users show neuropsychological decline from childhood to midlife. *Proc Natl Acad Sci USA.* 2012; 109:E2657–E2664.

[43] Rogeberg 0. Correlations between cannabis use and IQ change in the Dunedin cohort are consistent with confounding from socioeconomic status. *Proc Natl Acad Sci USA.* 2013; 110:4251–4254.

[44] Daly M. Personality may explain the association between cannabis use and neuropsychological impairment. *Proc Natl Acad Sci USA.* 2013; 110:E979.

[45] Moffitt TE, Meier MH, Caspi A, Poulton R. Reply to Rogeberg and Daly: No evidence that socioeconomic status or personality differences confound the association between cannabis use and IQ decline. *Proc Natl Acad Sci USA.* 2013; 110:E980–E982.

[46] Hopfer C, Salomonsen-Sautel S, Mikulich-Gilbertson S, et al. Conduct disorder and initiation of substance use: A prospective longitudinal study. *J Am Acad Child Adolesc Psychiatry.* 2013; 52:511–518.

[47] Palmer RH, Knapik VS, Rhee SH, et al. Prospective effects of adolescent indicators of behavioral disinhibition on DSM-IV alcohol, tobacco, and illicit drug dependence in young adulthood. *Addict Behav.* 2013; 38:2415–2421.

[48] Mehmedic Z, Chandra S, Slade D, et al. Potency trends of Delta9-THC and other cannabinoids in confiscated cannabis preparations from 1993 to 2008. *J Forensic Sci.* 2010; 55:1209–1217.

[49] National Institutes of Health. Announcement of national longitudinal study of neurodevelopmental consequences of substance use. NOTDA-14-011. May 20, 2014. Available at: http://grants.nih.gov/grants/guide/notice-files/NOTDA-14-011.html. Accessed May 27, 2014.

Christian Hopfer is a physician.

Christopher Ingraham

Now We Know What Happens to Teens When You Make Pot Legal

Rates of marijuana use among Colorado's teenagers are essentially unchanged in the years since the state's voters legalized marijuana in 2012, new survey data from the Colorado Department of Public Health and Environment shows.

In 2015, 21 percent of Colorado youths had used marijuana in the past 30 days. That rate is slightly lower than the national average and down slightly from the 25 percent who used marijuana in 2009, before legalization. The survey was based on a random sample of 17,000 middle and high school students in Colorado.

"The survey shows marijuana use has not increased since legalization, with four of five high school students continuing to say they don't use marijuana, even occasionally," the Colorado health department said in a news release.

The numbers out of Colorado are being closely monitored by policy makers and advocates on both sides of the marijuana legalization divide. Researchers generally agree that marijuana use during adolescence should be strongly discouraged—younger users are more likely to become dependent on the drug, and teens who use marijuana heavily are at higher risk of a number of mental and physical health problems later in life.

Opponents have often claimed that marijuana legalization would lead to more kids smoking pot, with all negative health consequences that would entail. But the scant data available until now haven't borne this out.

. . .

National surveys have shown that teen marijuana use rates are falling across the country. But there haven't been many numbers available specifically for states such as Colorado and Washington where it is legal. Federal data released late last year showed that teen use rates in Colorado and Washington were essentially flat, but they covered only 2014, the first year commercial marijuana was available in those states.

The latest data from Colorado include 2015, reflecting two full years of the legal marijuana market's effect. These numbers give the strongest indication yet that fears of skyrocketing adolescent use have not materialized.

"These statistics clearly debunk the theory that making marijuana legal for adults will result in more teen use," Mason Tvert, director of communications for the Marijuana Policy Project, said in a statement. "Levels of teen use in Colorado have not increased since it ended marijuana prohibition, and they are lower than the national average. Elected officials and voters in states that are considering similar proposals should be wary of claims that it will hurt teens."

Smart approaches to Marijuana, a group opposing legalization, have pointed out that the most recent federal surveys show that teen marijuana use rates in Colorado are among the highest in the country. But this latest survey, conducted by the state of Colorado, shows that teen use rates in that state are about average. Why the discrepancy?

. . .

For starters, this latest survey polled a much larger sample of Colorado students, 17,000, than the federal survey, which polls fewer than 400 Colorado teenagers in a given year. That much larger sample could produce a more accurate estimate than the smaller numbers in the federal drug survey.

There's a simple reason why legalization may not be having much of an effect on teen marijuana use—adolescents already report that marijuana is widely available. Nationally, roughly 80 percent of 12th graders say that pot is easy to get. The kids who want to smoke weed are probably already doing so—and legalization would do little to change that.

Christopher Ingraham is a freelance journalist.

EXPLORING THE ISSUE

Will Legalizing Marijuana Increase Usage?

Critical Thinking and Reflection

1. What are the pros and cons of legalization of marijuana?
2. Would legalization of marijuana increase usage especially among young people?
3. Why is marijuana particularly harmful to adolescents?

Is There Common Ground?

In 1969, according to a Gallup Poll, only 16 percent of American voters supported marijuana legalization, while this number rose to 36 percent by 2005. More recent polling indicates that the number has grown to between 46 percent and 56 percent in 2009. Supporters of the California initiative to legalize the drug estimate that about $15 billion worth of marijuana is sold every year in the state so legalizing it could generate at least $1.3 billion a year in tax revenues.

In Colorado, Washington, Oregon, Maine, and Alaska, attitudes regarding marijuana regulation have changes as these states have legalized the drug for recreational use. According to a 2012 Gallup Poll, about ⅔ of Americans believe the federal government should not intervene in these states. The survey also found an age difference between those that think marijuana should be legal and those that still support prohibition. Most 18- to 29-year-olds favor legalization while less than half of those age 30 to 64 and a third of those older than 65 agree.

Since 2000, the marijuana industry has grown, and officials argue that the legalization of marijuana will be linked to increased usage among children and adolescents because it will make marijuana more available and possibly lessen its perceived risks. However, research conducted in Colorado showed no relationship between legalized marijuana and marijuana use among young people. In the state of Colorado, adolescent use is less than the national average, fewer teens report using marijuana than said they did prior to legalization. Colorado officials believe that underage use will continue to decrease with strict age limits. Risk awareness program surveys conducted in Colorado interviewed over 17,000 students in middle and high school and showed that from 2009 to 2015, the rates in which teenagers smoked marijuana has decreased. In addition, the percentage of teenagers who have smoked marijuana in the past 30 days drop to 21 percent, from 25 percent in Colorado.

A study conducted by Schinke and colleagues attempted to investigate the growing concerns about adolescent use of the drug so the researchers collected and analyzed data on the relationship between marijuana legalization status in the United States and 1,300 adolescents' marijuana use. Their results did not show any relationship between the legalization status of the youths' states of residence and their use of the drug.

Additional Resources

Ashley, B.C. (2017). Factors driving the diffusion of medical marijuana legalization in the United States. *Drug Education, Prevention & Policy,* 24, 75–84.

Dickinson, T. (2015). The war on drugs is burning out. *Rolling Stone,* (1226), 33–37.

Friese, B., & Grube, J. W. (2013). Legalization of medeical marijuana and marijuana use among youths. *Drugs: Education, Prevention & Policy, 20* (1), 33–39.

Monte, A. A., Zane, R. D., & Heard, K. J. (2015). The implications of marijuana legalization in Colorado. *JAMA: Journal of the American Medical Association, 313*(3), 241–242.

Schinke, S. et al. (2017). Is the legalization of marijuana associated with its use by adolescents? *Substance Use & Misuse, 52,* 256–258.

Internet References . . .

Food and Drug Administration (FDA)

www.fda.gov

National Institute on Drug Abuse (NIDA)

www.nida.nih.gov

National Institutes on Health: National Institute on Drug Abuse

http://www.drugabuse.gov/nidahome.html

National Organization for the Reform of Marijuana Laws (NORML)

http://norml.org/

Web of Addictions

http://www.well.com/user/woa

Selected, Edited, and with Issue Framing Material by:
Eileen L. Daniel, *SUNY College at Brockport*

ISSUE

Is the Use of "Smart" Pills for Cognitive Enhancement Dangerous?

YES: Alan Schwarz, from "Drowned in a Stream of Prescriptions," *The New York Times* (2013)

NO: Phil Taylor, from "Think Positive: The Rise of 'Smart Drugs,'" *PMLive* (2013)

Learning Outcomes

After reading this issue, you will be able to:

- Discuss the legitimate uses for drugs such as Ritalin and Adderall.
- Understand the addictive qualities of these drugs.
- Understand how people without ADHD are able to acquire prescriptions for the drugs.
- Understand the consequences of abusing these drugs.
- Assess why illicit use of stimulant drugs has increased dramatically over the past 10 years.

ISSUE SUMMARY

YES: Pulitzer Prize–nominated reporter Alan Schwarz maintains that "smart pills" such as Adderall can significantly improve the lives of children and others with ADHD but that too many young adults who do not have the condition fake the symptoms and get prescriptions for the highly addictive and dangerous drugs.

NO: Journalist Phil Taylor disagrees and claims that smart drugs are safe and effective in boosting cognition.

Medication therapy is a major part of treating attention-deficit hyperactive disorder (ADHD), a common condition that affects children and adolescents and can continue into adulthood for some. Individuals with ADHD generally have difficulty paying attention, focusing, or concentrating. They seem to be unable to follow directions and are easily bored or frustrated with tasks. They are also likely to continuously move and tend to display impulsive behaviors. Overall, these behaviors are generally common in children without ADHD, but they occur more frequently than usual and are more severe in a child with ADHD.

For the past several decades, multiple types of stimulant drugs have been prescribed to treat the symptoms of ADHD. These medications enable individuals with ADHD to better focus their thoughts and overlook distractions and are effective for the majority of patients who take them.

Stimulant medications used to treat ADHD can have side effects, but these tend to happen early in treatment and are usually mild and short-lived, especially when monitored by a physician. The most common side effects include insomnia, weight loss and decreased appetite, and jitteriness. Occasionally, drugs to treat ADHD can cause more serious side effects such as an increased risk of cardiovascular problems. They may also exacerbate psychiatric conditions like depression, psychosis, or anxiety. The ADHD medications are illegal to take without a prescription as they can produce serious side effects and are potentially addictive.

Despite the potential for addiction, prescription stimulant abuse has dramatically increased over the past decade. About 30 percent of stimulant drug use may be diverted to nonmedical usage. College students and young adults take them with the belief that these medications help with mental abilities including studying, memorizing, and test taking. Most people think of ADHD as a difficulty with controlling thought, hence the belief that ADHD medications help with thought control. Interestingly, evidence suggests that when people are given rote learning tasks such as memorizing items on a list, their performance *is* improved by ADHD stimulants. These effects are strongest when people learn the items on the list and have to remember them at least a day after learning. This effect does seem to come from the learning process, because the participants do not need to be on the medication during the test in order to see the effect.

Few research studies, however, have studied memory for complex kinds of information that demand genuine in-depth understanding of the material. So, it is not possible to determine whether ADHD stimulants are simply assisting with learning the kinds of random items that typically appear on memory tests or whether they would also help with the types of complex knowledge important in high school and college classes.

Another area where ADHD stimulants seem to have impact is with *working memory*, the amount of information that people can hold in their mind at the same time. Many research investigations suggest that these medications have limited or no effect on working memory but a few studies show otherwise. Improvement is most likely to be seen in individuals whose normal working memory capacity is the smallest. While the research is inconclusive on the overall advantages of taking stimulant drugs on cognitive enhancement, the risks are clear. Over time, continued use of ADHD medications can make users less effective intellectually due to poor mental functioning mostly caused by insomnia, addiction, or malnutrition. Other side effects which can impair performance include paranoia, aggression, and irritability that can accompany these drugs. Individuals taking the drugs prescribed by physicians are regularly monitored for these side effects as well as disturbances in heart rate, sleep, mood, and appetite. In the following selections, Pulitzer Prize–nominated reporter Alan Schwartz maintains that "smart pills" such as Adderall can significantly improve the lives of children and others with ADHD, but that too many young adults who do not have the condition fake the symptoms and get prescriptions for the highly addictive and dangerous drugs. They take the drugs with the belief that their ability to study, learn, and take tests will be enhanced though the research is mostly not supportive. Journalist Phil Taylor argues that these drugs are safe and effective in boosting cognition.

YES

Alan Schwarz

Drowned in a Stream of Prescriptions

Before his addiction, Richard Fee was a popular college class president and aspiring medical student. "You keep giving Adderall to my son, you're going to kill him," said Rick Fee, Richard's father, to one of his son's doctors.

Virginia Beach—Every morning on her way to work, Kathy Fee holds her breath as she drives past the squat brick building that houses Dominion Psychiatric Associates.

It was there that her son, Richard, visited a doctor and received prescriptions for Adderall, an amphetamine-based medication for attention deficit hyperactivity disorder. It was in the parking lot that she insisted to Richard that he did not have A.D.H.D., not as a child and not now as a 24-year-old college graduate, and that he was getting dangerously addicted to the medication. It was inside the building that her husband, Rick, implored Richard's doctor to stop prescribing him Adderall, warning, "You're going to kill him."

It was where, after becoming violently delusional and spending a week in a psychiatric hospital in 2011, Richard met with his doctor and received prescriptions for 90 more days of Adderall. He hanged himself in his bedroom closet two weeks after they expired.

The story of Richard Fee, an athletic, personable college class president and aspiring medical student, highlights widespread failings in the system through which five million Americans take medication for A.D.H.D., doctors and other experts said.

Medications like Adderall can markedly improve the lives of children and others with the disorder. But the tunnel-like focus the medicines provide has led growing numbers of teenagers and young adults to fake symptoms to obtain steady prescriptions for highly addictive medications that carry serious psychological dangers. These efforts are facilitated by a segment of doctors who skip established diagnostic procedures, renew prescriptions reflexively and spend too little time with patients to accurately monitor side effects.

Richard Fee's experience included it all. Conversations with friends and family members and a review of detailed medical records depict an intelligent and articulate young man lying to doctor after doctor, physicians issuing hasty diagnoses, and psychiatrists continuing to prescribe medication—even increasing dosages—despite evidence of his growing addiction and psychiatric breakdown.

Very few people who misuse stimulants devolve into psychotic or suicidal addicts. But even one of Richard's own physicians, Dr. Charles Parker, characterized his case as a virtual textbook for ways that A.D.H.D. practices can fail patients, particularly young adults. "We have a significant travesty being done in this country with how the diagnosis is being made and the meds are being administered," said Dr. Parker, a psychiatrist in Virginia Beach. "I think it's an abnegation of trust. The public needs to say this is totally unacceptable and walk out."

Young adults are by far the fastest-growing segment of people taking A.D.H.D. medications. Nearly 14 million monthly prescriptions for the condition were written for Americans ages 20 to 39 in 2011, two and a half times the 5.6 million just four years before, according to the data company I.M.S. Health. While this rise is generally attributed to the maturing of adolescents who have A.D.H.D. into young adults—combined with a greater recognition of adult A.D.H.D. in general—many experts caution that savvy college graduates, freed of parental oversight, can legally and easily obtain stimulant prescriptions from obliging doctors.

"Any step along the way, someone could have helped him—they were just handing out drugs," said Richard's father. Emphasizing that he had no intention of bringing legal action against any of the doctors involved, Mr. Fee said: "People have to know that kids are out there getting these drugs and getting addicted to them. And doctors are helping them do it."

". . . when he was in elementary school he fidgeted, daydreamed and got A's. he has been an A-B student until mid college when he became scattered and he wandered while reading. He never had to study. Presently without medication, his mind thinks most of the time, he procrastinated, he multitasks not finishing in a timely manner."

Dr. Waldo M. Ellison
Richard Fee initial evaluation
Feb. 5, 2010

•

Richard began acting strangely soon after moving back home in late 2009, his parents said. He stayed up for days at a time, went from gregarious to grumpy and back, and scrawled compulsively in notebooks. His father, while trying to add Richard to his health insurance policy, learned that he was taking Vyvanse for A.D.H.D.

Richard explained to him that he had been having trouble concentrating while studying for medical school entrance exams the previous year and that he had seen a doctor and received a diagnosis. His father reacted with surprise. Richard had never shown any A.D.H.D. symptoms his entire life, from nursery school through high school, when he was awarded a full academic scholarship to Greensboro College in North Carolina. Mr. Fee also expressed concerns about the safety of his son's taking daily amphetamines for a condition he might not have.

"The doctor wouldn't give me anything that's bad for me," Mr. Fee recalled his son saying that day. "I'm not buying it on the street corner."

Richard's first experience with A.D.H.D. pills, like so many others', had come in college. Friends said he was a typical undergraduate user—when he needed to finish a paper or cram for exams, one Adderall capsule would jolt him with focus and purpose for six to eight hours, repeat as necessary.

So many fellow students had prescriptions or stashes to share, friends of Richard recalled in interviews, that guessing where he got his was futile. He was popular enough on campus—he was sophomore class president and played first base on the baseball team—that they doubted he even had to pay the typical $5 or $10 per pill.

"He would just procrastinate, wait till the last minute and then take a pill to study for tests," said Ryan Sykes, a friend. "It got to the point where he'd say he couldn't get anything done if he didn't have the Adderall."

Various studies have estimated that 8 percent to 35 percent of college students take stimulant pills to enhance school performance. Few students realize that giving or accepting even one Adderall pill from a friend with a prescription is a federal crime. Adderall and its stimulant siblings are classified by the Drug Enforcement Administration as Schedule II drugs, in the same category as cocaine, because of their highly addictive properties.

"It's incredibly nonchalant," Chris Hewitt, a friend of Richard, said of students' attitudes to the drug. "It's: 'Anyone have any Adderall? I want to study tonight,'" said Mr. Hewitt, now an elementary school teacher in Greensboro.

After graduating with honors in 2008 with a degree in biology, Richard planned to apply to medical schools and stayed in Greensboro to study for the entrance exams. He remembered how Adderall had helped him concentrate so well as an undergraduate, friends said, and he made an appointment at the nearby Triad Psychiatric and Counseling Center.

According to records obtained by Richard's parents after his death, a nurse practitioner at Triad detailed his unremarkable medical and psychiatric history before recording his complaints about "organization, memory, attention to detail." She characterized his speech as "clear," his thought process "goal directed" and his concentration "attentive."

Richard filled out an 18-question survey on which he rated various symptoms on a 0-to-3 scale. His total score of 29 led the nurse practitioner to make a diagnosis of "A.D.H.D., inattentive-type"—a type of A.D.H.D. without hyperactivity. She recommended Vyvanse, 30 milligrams a day, for three weeks.

Phone and fax requests to Triad officials for comment were not returned.

Some doctors worry that A.D.H.D. questionnaires, designed to assist and standardize the gathering of a patient's symptoms, are being used as a shortcut to diagnosis. C. Keith Conners, a longtime child psychologist who developed a popular scale similar to the one used with Richard, said in an interview that scales like his "have reinforced this tendency for quick and dirty practice."

Dr. Conners, an emeritus professor of psychiatry and behavioral sciences at Duke University Medical Center, emphasized that a detailed life history must be taken and other sources of information—such as a parent, teacher, or friend—must be pursued to learn the nuances of a patient's difficulties and to rule out other maladies before making a proper diagnosis of A.D.H.D. Other doctors interviewed said they would not prescribe medications on a patient's first visit, specifically to deter the faking of symptoms.

According to his parents, Richard had no psychiatric history, or even suspicion of problems, through college. None of his dozen high school and college acquaintances interviewed for this article said he had ever shown or mentioned behaviors related to A.D.H.D.—certainly not the "losing things" and "difficulty awaiting turn" he reported on the Triad questionnaire—suggesting that he probably faked or at least exaggerated his symptoms to get his diagnosis.

That is neither uncommon nor difficult, said David Berry, a professor and researcher at the University of Kentucky. He is a co-author of a 2010 study that compared two groups of college students—those with diagnoses of A.D.H.D. and others who were asked to fake symptoms—to see whether standard symptom questionnaires could tell them apart. They were indistinguishable.

"With college students," Dr. Berry said in an interview, "it's clear that it doesn't take much information for someone who wants to feign A.D.H.D. to do so."

Richard Fee filled his prescription for Vyvanse within hours at a local Rite Aid. He returned to see the nurse three weeks later and reported excellent concentration: "reading books—read 10!" her notes indicate. She increased his dose to 50 milligrams a day. Three weeks later, after Richard left a message for her asking for the dose to go up to 60, which is on the high end of normal adult doses, she wrote on his chart, "Okay rewrite."

Richard filled that prescription later that afternoon. It was his third month's worth of medication in 43 days.

•

"The patient is a 23-year-old Caucasian male who presents for refill of vyvanse—recently started on this while in NC b/c of lack of motivation/loss of drive. Has moved here and wants refill."

Dr. Robert M. Woodard
Notes on Richard Fee
Nov. 11, 2009

•

Richard scored too low on the MCAT in 2009 to qualify for a top medical school. Although he had started taking Vyvanse for its jolts of focus and purpose, their side effects began to take hold. His sleep patterns increasingly scrambled and his mood darkening, he moved back in with his parents in Virginia Beach and sought a local physician to renew his prescriptions.

A friend recommended a family physician, Dr. Robert M. Woodard. Dr. Woodard heard Richard describe how well Vyvanse was working for his A.D.H.D., made a diagnosis of "other malaise and fatigue" and renewed his prescription for one month. He suggested that Richard thereafter see a trained psychiatrist at Dominion Psychiatric Associates—only a five-minute walk from the Fees' house.

With eight psychiatrists and almost 20 therapists on staff, Dominion Psychiatric is one of the better-known practices in Virginia Beach, residents said. One of its better-known doctors is Dr. Waldo M. Ellison, a practicing psychiatrist since 1974.

In interviews, some patients and parents of patients of Dr. Ellison's described him as very quick to identify A.D.H.D. and prescribe medication for it. Sandy Paxson of nearby Norfolk said she took her 15-year-old son to see Dr. Ellison for anxiety in 2008; within a few minutes, Mrs. Paxson recalled, Dr. Ellison said her son had A.D.H.D. and prescribed him Adderall.

"My son said: 'I love the way this makes me feel. It helps me focus for school, but it's not getting rid of my anxiety, and that's what I need,'" Mrs. Paxson recalled. "So we went back to Dr. Ellison and told him that it wasn't working properly, what else could he give us, and he basically told me that I was wrong. He basically told me that I was incorrect."

Dr. Ellison met with Richard in his office for the first time on Feb. 5, 2010. He took a medical history, heard Richard's complaints regarding concentration, noted how he was drumming his fingers and made a diagnosis of A.D.H.D. with "moderate symptoms or difficulty functioning." Dominion Psychiatric records of that visit do not mention the use of any A.D.H.D. symptom questionnaire to identify particular areas of difficulty or strategies for treatment.

As the 47-minute session ended, Dr. Ellison prescribed a common starting dose of Adderall: 30 milligrams daily for 21 days. Eight days later, while Richard still had 13 pills remaining, his prescription was renewed for 30 more days at 50 milligrams.

Through the remainder of 2010, in appointments with Dr. Ellison that usually lasted under five minutes, Richard returned for refills of Adderall. Records indicate that he received only what was consistently coded as "pharmacologic management"—the official term for quick appraisals of medication effects—and none of the more conventional talk-based therapy that experts generally consider an important component of A.D.H.D. treatment.

His Adderall prescriptions were always for the fast-acting variety, rather than the extended-release formula that is less prone to abuse.

•

"PATIENT DOING WELL WITH THE MEDICATION, IS CALM, FOCUSED AND ON TASK, AND WILL RETURN TO OFFICE IN 3 MONTHS"

Dr. Waldo M. Ellison
Notes on Richard Fee
Dec. 11, 2010

•

Regardless of what he might have told his doctor, Richard Fee was anything but well or calm during his first year back home, his father said.

Blowing through a month's worth of Adderall in a few weeks, Richard stayed up all night reading and scribbling in notebooks, occasionally climbing out of his bedroom window and on to the roof to converse with the moon and stars. When the pills ran out, he would sleep for 48 hours straight and not leave his room for 72. He got so hot during the day that he walked around the house with ice packs around his neck—and in frigid weather, he would cool off by jumping into the 52-degree backyard pool.

As Richard lost a series of jobs and tensions in the house ran higher—particularly when talk turned to his Adderall—Rick and Kathy Fee continued to research the side effects of A.D.H.D. medication. They learned that stimulants are exceptionally successful at mollifying the impulsivity and distractibility that characterize classic A.D.H.D., but that they can cause insomnia, increased blood pressure and elevated body temperature. Food and Drug Administration warnings on packaging also note "high potential for abuse," as well as psychiatric side effects such as aggression, hallucinations and paranoia.

A 2006 study in the journal *Drug and Alcohol Dependence* claimed that about 10 percent of adolescents and young adults who misused A.D.H.D. stimulants became addicted to them. Even proper, doctor-supervised use of the medications can trigger psychotic behavior or suicidal thoughts in about 1 in 400 patients, according to a 2006 study in *The American Journal of Psychiatry*. So while a vast majority of stimulant users will not experience psychosis—and a doctor may never encounter it in decades of careful practice—the sheer volume of prescriptions leads to thousands of cases every year, experts acknowledged.

When Mrs. Fee noticed Richard putting tape over his computer's camera, he told her that people were spying on him. (He put tape on his fingers, too, to avoid leaving fingerprints.) He cut himself out of family pictures, talked to the television and became increasingly violent when agitated.

In late December, Mr. Fee drove to Dominion Psychiatric and asked to see Dr. Ellison, who explained that federal privacy laws forbade any discussion of an adult patient, even with the patient's father. Mr. Fee said he had tried unsuccessfully to detail Richard's bizarre behavior, assuming that Richard had not shared such details with his doctor.

"I can't talk to you," Mr. Fee recalled Dr. Ellison telling him. "I did this one time with another family, sat down and talked with them, and I ended up getting sued. I can't talk with you unless your son comes with you."

Mr. Fee said he had turned to leave but distinctly recalls warning Dr. Ellison, "You keep giving Adderall to my son, you're going to kill him."

Dr. Ellison declined repeated requests for comment on Richard Fee's case. His office records, like those of other doctors involved, were obtained by Mr. Fee under Virginia and federal law, which allow the legal representative of a deceased patient to obtain medical records as if he were the patient himself.

As 2011 began, the Fees persuaded Richard to see a psychologist, Scott W. Sautter, whose records note Richard's delusions, paranoia and "severe and pervasive mental disorder." Dr. Sautter recommended that Adderall either be stopped or be paired with a sleep aid "if not medically contraindicated."

Mr. Fee did not trust his son to share this report with Dr. Ellison, so he drove back to Dominion Psychiatric and, he recalled, was told by a receptionist that he could leave the information with her. Mr. Fee said he had demanded to put it in Dr. Ellison's hands himself and threatened to break down his door in order to do so.

Mr. Fee said that Dr. Ellison had then come out, read the report and, appreciating the gravity of the situation, spoken with him about Richard for 45 minutes. They scheduled an appointment for the entire family.

•

"meeting with parents—concern with 'metaphoric' speaking that appears to be outside the realm of appropriated one to one conversation. Richard says he does it on purpose—to me some of it sounds like pre-psychotic thinking."

Dr. Waldo M. Ellison
Notes on Richard Fee
Feb. 23, 2011

•

Dr. Ellison stopped Richard Fee's prescription—he wrote "no Adderall for now" on his chart and the next day refused Richard's phone request for more. Instead he prescribed Abilify and Seroquel, antipsychotics for schizophrenia that do not provide the bursts of focus and purpose that stimulants do. Richard became enraged, his parents recalled. He tried to back up over his father in the Dominion Psychiatric parking lot and threatened to burn the house down. At home, he took a baseball bat from the garage, smashed flower pots and screamed, "You're taking my medicine!"

Richard disappeared for a few weeks. He returned to the house when he learned of his grandmother's death, the Fees said.

The morning after the funeral, Richard walked down Potters Road to what became a nine-minute visit with Dr. Ellison. He left with two prescriptions: one for Abilify, and another for 50 milligrams a day of Adderall.

According to Mr. Fee, Richard later told him that he had lied to Dr. Ellison—he told the doctor he was feeling great, life was back on track and he had found a job in Greensboro that he would lose without Adderall. Dr. Ellison's notes do not say why he agreed to start Adderall again.

Richard's delusions and mood swings only got worse, his parents said. They would lock their bedroom door when they went to sleep because of his unpredictable rages. "We were scared of our own son," Mr. Fee said. Richard would blow through his monthly prescriptions in 10 to 15 days and then go through hideous withdrawals. A friend said that he would occasionally get Richard some extra pills during the worst of it, but that "it wasn't enough because he would take four or five at a time."

One night during an argument, after Richard became particularly threatening and pushed him over a chair, Mr. Fee called the police. They arrested Richard for domestic violence. The episode persuaded Richard to see another local psychiatrist, Dr. Charles Parker.

Mrs. Fee said she attended Richard's initial consultation on June 3 with Dr. Parker's clinician, Renee Strelitz, and emphasized his abuse of Adderall. Richard "kept giving me dirty looks," Mrs. Fee recalled. She said she had later left a detailed message on Ms. Strelitz's voice mail, urging her and Dr. Parker not to prescribe stimulants under any circumstances when Richard came in the next day.

Dr. Parker met with Richard alone. The doctor noted depression, anxiety and suicidal ideas. He wrote "no meds" with a box around it—an indication, he explained later, that he was aware of the parents' concerns regarding A.D.H.D. stimulants.

Dr. Parker wrote three 30-day prescriptions: Clonidine (a sleep aid), Venlafaxine (an antidepressant) and Adderall, 60 milligrams a day.

In an interview last November, Dr. Parker said he did not recall the details of Richard's case but reviewed his notes and tried to recreate his mind-set during that appointment. He said he must have trusted Richard's assertions that medication was not an issue, and must have figured that his parents were just philosophically anti-medication. Dr. Parker recalled that he had been reassured by Richard's intelligent discussions of the ins and outs of stimulants and his desire to pursue medicine himself.

"He was smart and he was quick and he had A's and B's and wanted to go to medical school—and he had all the deportment of a guy that had the potential to do that," Dr. Parker said. "He didn't seem like he was a drug person at all, but rather a person that was misunderstood, really desirous of becoming a physician. He was very slick and smooth. He convinced me there was a benefit."

Mrs. Fee was outraged. Over the next several days, she recalled, she repeatedly spoke with Ms. Strelitz over the phone to detail Richard's continued abuse of the medication (she found nine pills gone after 48 hours) and hand-delivered Dr. Sautter's appraisal of his recent psychosis. Dr. Parker confirmed that he had received this information.

Richard next saw Dr. Parker on June 27. Mrs. Fee drove him to the clinic and waited in the parking lot. Soon afterward, Richard returned and asked to head to the pharmacy to fill a prescription. Dr. Parker had raised his Adderall to 80 milligrams a day.

Dr. Parker recalled that the appointment had been a 15-minute "med check" that left little time for careful assessment of any Adderall addiction. Once again, Dr. Parker said, he must have believed Richard's assertions that he needed additional medicine more than the family's pleas that it be stopped.

"He was pitching me very well—I was asking him very specific questions, and he was very good at telling me the answers in a very specific way," Dr. Parker recalled. He added later, "I do feel partially responsible for what happened to this kid."

•

"Paranoid and psychotic . . . thinking that the computer is spying on him. He has also been receiving messages from stars at night and he is unable to be talked to in a reasonable fashion . . . The patient denies any mental health problems . . . fairly high risk for suicide."

Dr. John Riedler
Admission note for Richard Fee
Virginia Beach Psychiatric Center
July 8, 2011

•

The 911 operator answered the call and heard a young man screaming on the other end. His parents would not give him his pills. With the man's language scattered and increasingly threatening, the police were sent to the home of Rick and Kathy Fee.

The Fees told officers that Richard was addicted to Adderall, and that after he had received his most recent prescription, they allowed him to fill it through his mother's insurance plan on the condition that they hold it and dispense it appropriately. Richard was now demanding his next day's pills early.

Richard denied his addiction and threats. So the police, noting that Richard was an adult, instructed the Fees to give him the bottle. They said they would comply only if he left the house for good. Officers escorted Richard off the property.

A few hours later Richard called his parents, threatening to stab himself in the head with a knife. The police found him and took him to the Virginia Beach Psychiatric Center.

Described as "paranoid and psychotic" by the admitting physician, Dr. John Riedler, Richard spent one week in the hospital denying that he had any psychiatric or addiction issues. He was placed on two medications: Seroquel and the antidepressant Wellbutrin, no stimulants. In his discharge report, Dr. Riedler noted that Richard had stabilized but remained severely depressed and dependent on both amphetamines and marijuana, which he would smoke in part to counter the buzz of Adderall and the depression from withdrawal.

(Marijuana is known to increase the risk for schizophrenia, psychosis and memory problems, but Richard had smoked pot in high school and college with no such effects, several friends recalled. If that was the case, "in all likelihood the stimulants were the primary issue here," said Dr. Wesley Boyd, a psychiatrist at Children's Hospital Boston and Cambridge Health Alliance who specializes in adolescent substance abuse.)

Unwelcome at home after his discharge from the psychiatric hospital, Richard stayed in cheap motels for a few weeks. His Adderall prescription from Dr. Parker expired on July 26, leaving him eligible for a renewal. He phoned the office of Dr. Ellison, who had not seen him in four months.

•

"moved out of the house—doesn't feel paranoid or delusional. Hasn't been on meds for a while—working with a friend wiring houses for 3 months—doesn't feel he needs the abilify or seroquel for sleep."

Dr. Waldo M. Ellison
Notes on Richard Fee
July 25, 2011

•

The 2:15 p.m. appointment went better than Richard could have hoped. He told Dr. Ellison that the pre-psychotic and metaphoric thinking back in March had receded, and that all that remained was his A.D.H.D. He said nothing of his visits to Dr. Parker, his recent prescriptions or his week in the psychiatric hospital.

At 2:21 p.m., according to Dr. Ellison's records, he prescribed Richard 30 days' worth of Adderall at 50 milligrams a day. He also gave him prescriptions postdated for Aug. 23 and Sept. 21, presumably to allow him to get pills into late October without the need for followup appointments. (Virginia state law forbids the dispensation of 90 days of a controlled substance at one time, but does allow doctors to write two 30-day prescriptions in advance.)

Virginia is one of 43 states with a formal Prescription Drug Monitoring Program, an online database that lets doctors check a patient's one-year prescription history, partly to see if he or she is getting medication elsewhere. Although pharmacies are required to enter all prescriptions for controlled substances into the system, Virginia law does not require doctors to consult it.

Dr. Ellison's notes suggest that he did not check the program before issuing the three prescriptions to Richard, who filled the first within hours.

The next morning, during a scheduled appointment at Dr. Parker's clinic, Ms. Strelitz wrote in her notes: "Richard is progressing. He reported staying off of the Adderall and on no meds currently. Focusing on staying healthy, eating well and exercising."

About a week later, Richard called his father with more good news: a job he had found overseeing storm cleanup crews was going well. He was feeling much better.

But Mr. Fee noticed that the more calm and measured speech that Richard had regained during his hospital stay was gone. He jumped from one subject to the next, sounding anxious and rushed. When the call ended, Mr. Fee recalled, he went straight to his wife.

"Call your insurance company," he said, "and find out if they've filled any prescriptions for Adderall."

•

"spoke to father—richard was in VBPC [Virginia Beach Psychiatric Center] and OD on adderall—NO STIMULANTS—HE WAS ALSO SEEING DR. PARKER"

Dr. Waldo M. Ellison
Interoffice e-mail
Aug. 5, 2011

•

An insurance representative confirmed that Richard had filled a prescription for Adderall on July 25. Mr. Fee confronted Dr. Ellison in the Dominion Psychiatric parking lot.

Mr. Fee told him that Richard had been in the psychiatric hospital, had been suicidal and had been taking Adderall through June and July. Dr. Ellison confirmed that he had written not only another prescription but two others for later in August and September.

"He told me it was normal procedure and not 90 days at one time," Mr. Fee recalled. "I flipped out on him: 'You gave my son 90 days of Adderall? You're going to kill him!'"

Mr. Fee said he and Dr. Ellison had discussed voiding the two outstanding scripts. Mr. Fee said he had been told that it was possible, but that should Richard need emergency medical attention, it could keep him from getting what would otherwise be proper care or medication. Mr. Fee confirmed that with a pharmacist and decided to drive to Richard's apartment and try to persuade him to rip up the prescriptions.

"I know that you've got these other prescriptions to get pills," Mr. Fee recalled telling Richard. "You're doing so good. You've got a job. You're working. Things with us are better. If you get them filled, I'm worried about what will happen."

"You're right," Mr. Fee said Richard had replied. "I tore them up and threw them away."

Mr. Fee spent two more hours with Richard making relative small talk—increasingly gnawed, he recalled later, by the sense that this was no ordinary conversation. As he looked at Richard he saw two images flickering on top of each other—the boy he had raised to love school and baseball, and the desperate addict he feared that boy had become.

Before he left, Mr. Fee made as loving a demand as he could muster.

"Please. Give them to me," Mr. Fee said.

Richard looked his father dead in the eye.

"I destroyed them," he said. "I don't have them. Don't worry."

•

"Richard said that he has stopped Adderall and wants to work on continuing to progress."

Renee Strelitz
Session notes
Sept. 13, 2011

•

Richard generally filled his prescriptions at a CVS on Laskin Road, less than three miles from his parents' home. But on Aug. 23, he went to a different CVS about 11 miles away, closer to Norfolk and farther from the locations that his father might have called to alert them to the situation. For his Sept. 21 prescription he traveled even farther, into Norfolk, to get his pills.

On Oct. 3, Richard visited Dr. Ellison for an appointment lasting 17 minutes. The doctor prescribed two weeks of Strattera, a medication for A.D.H.D. that contains no amphetamines and, therefore, is neither a controlled substance nor particularly prone to abuse. His records make no mention of the Adderall prescription Richard filled on Sept. 21; they do note, however, "Father says that he is crazy and abusive of the Adderall—has made directives with regard to giving Richard anymore stimulants—bringing up charges—I explained this to Richard."

Prescription records indicate that Richard did not fill the Strattera prescription before returning to Dr. Ellison's office two weeks later to ask for more stimulants.

"Patient took only a few days of Strattera 40 mg—it calmed him but not focusing," the doctor's notes read. "I had told him not to look for much initially—He would like a list of MD who could rx adderall."

Dr. Ellison never saw Richard again. Given his patterns of abuse, friends said, Richard probably took his last Adderall pill in early October. Because he abruptly stopped without the slow and delicate reduction of medication that is recommended to minimize major psychological risks, especially for instant-release stimulants, he crashed harder than ever.

Richard's lifelong friend Ryan Sykes was one of the few people in contact with him during his final weeks. He said that despite Richard's addiction to Adderall and the ease with which it could be obtained on college campuses nearby, he had never pursued it outside the doctors' prescriptions.

"He had it in his mind that because it came from a doctor, it was O.K.," Mr. Sykes recalled.

On Nov. 7, after arriving home from a weekend away, Mrs. Fee heard a message on the family answering machine from Richard, asking his parents to call him. She phoned back at 10 that night and left a message herself.

Not hearing back by the next afternoon, Mrs. Fee checked Richard's cellphone records—he was on her plan—and saw no calls or texts. At 9 p.m. the Fees drove to Richard's apartment in Norfolk to check on him. The lights were on; his car was in the driveway. He did not answer. Beginning to panic, Mr. Fee found the kitchen window ajar and climbed in through it.

He searched the apartment and found nothing amiss.

"He isn't here," Mr. Fee said he had told his wife.

"Oh, thank God," she replied. "Maybe he's walking on the beach or something."

They got ready to leave before Mr. Fee stopped.

"Wait a minute," he said. "I didn't check the closet."

•

"Spoke with Richard's mother, Kathy Fee, today. She reported that Richard took his life last November. Family is devasted and having a difficult time. Offerred assistance for family."

Renee Strelitz
Last page of Richard Fee file
June 21, 2012

•

Friends and former baseball teammates flocked to Richard Fee's memorial service in Virginia Beach. Most remembered only the funny and gregarious guy they knew in high school and college; many knew absolutely nothing of his last two years. He left no note explaining his suicide.

At a gathering at the Fees' house afterward, Mr. Fee told them about Richard's addiction to Adderall. Many recalled how they, too, had blithely abused the drug in college—to cram, just as Richard had—and could not help but wonder if they had played the same game of Russian roulette.

"I guarantee you a good number of them had used it for studying—that shock was definitely there in that room," said a Greensboro baseball teammate, Danny Michael, adding that he was among the few who had not. "It's so prevalent and widely used. People had no idea it could be abused to the point of no return."

Almost every one of more than 40 A.D.H.D. experts interviewed for this article said that worst-case scenarios like Richard Fee's can occur with any medication—and that people who do have A.D.H.D., or parents of children with the disorder, should not be dissuaded from considering the proven benefits of stimulant medication when supervised by a responsible physician.

Other experts, however, cautioned that Richard Fee's experience is instructive less in its ending than its evolution—that it underscores aspects of A.D.H.D. treatment that are mishandled every day with countless patients, many of them children.

"You don't have everything that happened with this kid, but his experience is not that unusual," said DeAnsin Parker, a clinical neuropsychologist in New York who specializes in young adults. "Diagnoses are made just this quickly, and medication is filled just this quickly. And the lack of therapy is really sad. Doctors are saying, 'Just take the meds to see if they help,' and if they help, 'You must have A.D.H.D.'"

Dr. Parker added: "Stimulants will help anyone focus better. And a lot of young people like or value that feeling, especially those who are driven and have ambitions. We have to realize that these are potential addicts—drug addicts don't look like they used to."

The Fees decided to go. The event was sponsored by the local chapter of Children and Adults with Attention Deficit Disorder (Chadd), the nation's primary advocacy group for A.D.H.D. patients. They wanted to attend the question-and-answer session afterward with local doctors and community college officials.

The evening opened with the local Chadd coordinator thanking the drug company Shire—the manufacturer of several A.D.H.D. drugs, including Vyvanse and extended-release Adderall—for partly underwriting the event. An hourlong film directed and narrated by two men with A.D.H.D. closed by examining some "myths" about stimulant medications, with several doctors praising their efficacy and safety. One said they were "safer than aspirin," while another added, "It's O.K.—there's nothing that's going to happen."

Sitting in the fourth row, Mr. Fee raised his hand to pose a question to the panel, which was moderated by Jeffrey Katz, a local clinical psychologist and a national board member of Chadd. "What are some of the drawbacks or some of the dangers of a misdiagnosis in somebody," Mr. Fee asked, "and then the subsequent medication that goes along with that?"

Dr. Katz looked straight at the Fees as he answered, "Not much."

Adding that "the medication itself is pretty innocuous," Dr. Katz continued that someone without A.D.H.D. might feel more awake with stimulants but would not consider it "something that they need."

"If you misdiagnose it and you give somebody medication, it's not going to do anything for them," Dr. Katz concluded. "Why would they continue to take it?"

Mr. Fee slowly sat down, trembling. Mrs. Fee placed her hand on his knee as the panel continued.

Alan Schwarz is a Pulitzer Prize-nominated reporter for *The New York Times.*

Phil Taylor

NO

Think Positive: The Rise of "Smart Drugs"

More and More People Are Turning to Nootropics or "Smart Drugs" to Enhance Their Cognitive Ability. But What Do They Do, What Are the Risks and Where Do the Ethical Boundaries Lie?

Imagine popping a pill, and suddenly being able to operate at a higher level of cognitive function, outstripping your peers in academia or the workplace and riding a fast track to success. It may sound too good to be true, but it seems a startling number of people around the world are taking drugs in the hope of achieving just that result.

There is a wealth of data showing that certain drug classes can improve cognitive function in dementia and other mental disorders, and it is an inevitable consequence of this research that some groups have started to look at whether drugs can provide a boost to the mental faculties of healthy people as well.

Brain Boost

The concept is well established in popular culture, with notable examples including the Snap performance enhancer found in Iain Banks' *Culture* series of science fiction books and NZT-48, a drug which transforms Bradley Cooper's feckless writer Eddie Morra into a mental superhuman in 2011 movie *Limitless*.

What is less well-known perhaps is how widespread use of supposedly brain-boosting drugs is right now. The so-called "smart drugs"—also known as cognition enhancers or nootropics—seem to be finding their way into the hands of the public in increasing quantities, at least in academic circles.

In 2008, an informal survey by the journal *Nature* found that around 20 percent of its readers had used drugs to boost their brainpower, mainly for improving concentration. The most common drugs used by the respondents were stimulants such as attention-deficit hyperactivity disorder (ADHD) treatment methamphetamine and modafinil, the active ingredient in Cephalon's narcolepsy treatment Provigil and its generic copies.

More recently, a German study looking at psychoactive drugs in university students found that around 7 percent had used neuro-enhancing drugs, mainly for improving concentration and vigilance.

Outside academic circles, the picture is somewhat different. A recently published report by the Wellcome Trust derived from a survey of 1,400 adults and 460 young people suggests that while use of smart drugs among the general population remains pretty rare, attitudes are fairly tolerant.

Just 2 percent of adults and 1 percent of young people said they had used cognitive enhancers in the past, but around half thought medications normally used to treat conditions like ADHD and Alzheimer's disease are an effective means of improving focus, memory, or concentration in healthy people, and 31 percent said they felt it was acceptable to take them.

Add a sprinkling of media hyperbole—a Google news search reveals dozens of articles in the last few months alone for example—and the stage looks set for smart drugs to move increasingly into mainstream use.

Smart Drugs Are Finding Their Way into the Hands of the Public in Increasing Quantities

Looking at the Evidence

But how robust is the evidence for their benefits? Mitul Mehta of King's College London in the United Kingdom, a specialist in cognitive psychopharmacology, says there are some suggestions from controlled studies that short-term memory can be improved by smart drugs, and a larger body of evidence that they can help people improve focus on a task.

"The evidence they can improve attention is quite clear, while the evidence they can enhance memory is mixed," according to Mehta.

With that in mind, it is perhaps telling that older drugs that were almost synonymous with cognitive enhancement a few years ago—namely, cholinesterase inhibitors, such as donepezil and rivastigmine and the glutamate antagonist memantine—no longer seem to be in vogue.

One reason could be that their benefits on cognition are simply too modest, but it is also possible these drugs are less used because they do not cause positive mood changes, which are reported with both methylphenidate and modafinil, says Mehta, who freely admits this hypothesis is untested.

"There are studies now which show that while stimulants and modafinil have fairly weak effects on cognitive performance, they have clear effects on confidence. That might convince you that you are performing better whilst on a drug even if you are not," he notes.

Assuming Smart Drugs Are Found, Which Are Both Effective and Safe, Should They Be Widely Used?

Beyond the Comfort Zone

A major impediment to research in this area is lack of funding for trials that could answer once and for all whether some of these drugs do actually have an impact on performance. For the pharma industry, developing a drug to improve a healthy person is beyond its comfort zone (consider how hard it has been to get new drugs approved for obesity) and outside the established framework of regulatory approval, medical insurance, and reimbursement for new medicines.

There are, however, a couple of academia-sponsored studies ongoing, including a placebo-controlled 48-person trial of an n-methyl-d-aspartate receptor partial agonist called GLYX-13, which will look at the effect of a single dose of the drug on learning and memory. The trial—sponsored by Northwestern University in the United States—was scheduled to get underway this month and should conclude in 2014. The drug is licensed to pharma company Naurex, which is focusing primarily on developing GLYX-13 as a rapid-acting antidepressant that exerts its effects within hours rather than weeks.

Is It Safe?

At the risk of spoilers, Eddie in *Limitless* soon discovers that there is a serious downside to his neurological performance addiction and away from the drama of Hollywood there are concerns about the long-term effects of the current crop of cognitive enhancers.

In particular, use of stimulants raises the risk of addiction and cardiovascular effects, and some amphetamine-like compounds used as smart drugs are linked to the development of paranoia and even full-blown psychosis. Modafinil meanwhile has also been linked to psychiatric symptoms, hypersensitivity reactions, and severe rashes.

That said, in a recent debate organized by the journal Neuropharmacology, David Nutt, director of the neuropsychopharmacology unit at Imperial College London in the United Kingdom, noted that there is very little evidence that people who use stimulants in this way go on to require treatment for dependency. And with decades of experience with methylphenidate and modafinil, there does not seem to be any major health issues surrounding their use.

Arguably even more worrying is the reality that these drugs are not going to be sourced from legitimate supply channels in the vast majority of cases. Many will be sourced over the Internet, for example, where the risks of buying counterfeit, substandard, and adulterated medicines are well established.

Barbara Sahakian, a professor of neuroscience at Cambridge University, covered the use of cognitive enhancers during a discussion at the Hay Festival in Wales recently, warning that Internet-sourced smart drugs place users at risk of ingesting products that are likely of no benefit and at worst a danger to health.

Moreover, she pointed out that use of methylphenidate by students has been shown to cause sleep disruption in some cases, which actually reduces the capacity to retain information.

Is It Right?

There are also clearly ethical considerations. Assuming smart drugs are found, which are both effective and safe, should they be used widely, for example, to boost productivity in the workplace and make businesses more competitive or just be limited to individuals with a clinical cognitive dysfunction? One could argue, for example, that some critical professions such as surgeons and airline pilots should take them to reduce the risk of mishap.

Sahakian recently gave the following example to illustrate this dilemma. "Imagine two surgeons, one who has been drinking coffee to stay alert and has hand tremors and the other who has been taking cognitive enhancing drugs and has no tremors and is alert. Which would you prefer to operate?"

The other side of the coin is the coercive element that emerges with the use of smart drugs, with students feeling pressurized to take them to keep up with their peers for example. And with no prospect of insurance coverage—meaning cognitive enhancers will have to be paid for out-of-pocket—their emergence raises issues about a two-tier society.

These are all important questions that need to be addressed, and it is encouraging that debate about the use of smart drugs and other human enhancement technologies is getting underway.

A report on the very topic written by experts from the Royal Society, the Royal Academy of Engineering, the British Academy, and the Academy of Medical Sciences and published last year sums the challenge up perfectly: "If any enhancement is seen as valuable, scientists need to work together with social scientists, philosophers, ethicists, policy makers, and the public to discuss the ethical and moral consequences of enhancement, and thus to harness maximum benefit with minimal harm."

Phil Taylor is a journalist.

EXPLORING THE ISSUE

Is the Use of "Smart" Pills for Cognitive Enhancement Dangerous?

Critical Thinking and Reflection

1. Why do so many young people fake symptoms in order to acquire "smart drugs"?
2. Describe the side effects of stimulant drugs such as Ritalin and Adderall. What are the effects that appeal to users?
3. What are the legitimate uses for stimulant drugs such as Ritalin and Adderall?

Is There Common Ground?

On some elite college campuses, up to 25 percent of students admit to nonmedical use of stimulant drugs. "Smart" drugs are also widely used off campus by business executives and others who wish to gain a competitive edge and to better meet deadlines. The drugs are becoming so common, and many people believe they have much to offer individuals and society and should be made more available. The benefits of enhancement drugs include increased alertness and focus and improvement in some types of memory. Among those who do not have attention-deficit hyperactive disorder, research has shown that stimulants consistently and significantly enhance learning of material recalled days later, an obvious advantage when studying for an exam. The drugs may even positively affect certain types of judgment. Improvements in memory and cognitive control have been reported in multiple studies mainly using the drug Ritalin.

While the drugs may offer the benefit of cognitive enhancement, there are questions as to whether their use is both cheating and drug abuse. Will there be pressure among students to take drugs just to keep up with their peers? The obvious parallel to performance enhancing drug use among professional and amateur athletes is often made. One of the biggest concerns, however, is that cognitive enhancement may be wrong not because it is so physically risky or because it creates an unlevel playing field but because it redefines the nature of human achievement itself. The obvious parallel to performance-enhancing drug use among professional and amateur athletes is often made. While ethicists ponder this, the reality is that there are also health risks since the effects of chronic unregulated doses of stimulant drugs can be toxic. The drugs can also cause psychosis, actual cognitive deficits, and addiction.

Additional Resources

Bagot, K. S., & Kaminer, Y. (2014). Efficacy of stimulants for cognitive enhancement in non-attention deficit hyperactivity disorder youth: A systematic review. *Addiction, 109*(4), 547–557.

Hofmann, B. (2017). Toward a method for exposing and elucidating ethical issues with human cognitive enhancement technologies. *Science & Engineering Ethics, 23*, 413–429.

Munro, B.A., et al. (2017). The relationship between nonmedical use of prescription stimulants, executive function and academic outcomes. *Addictive Behaviors, 65*, 250–257.

Sharpe, K. (2014). Medication: The smart-pill oversell. *Nature, 506*(7487), 146–148.

Webb, J. R., Valased, M. R., & North, C. S. (2013). Prevalence of stimulant use in a sample of US medical students. *Annals of Clinical Psychiatry, 25*, 27–32.

Internet References . . .

Food and Drug Administration

www.fda.gov

National Institute on Drug Abuse (NIDA)

www.nida.nih.gov

National Institute of Mental Health (NIMH). Attention Deficit Hyperactivity Disorder (ADHD)

www.nimh.nih.gov/health/publications/index.shtml

Selected, Edited, and with Issue Framing Material by:
Eileen L. Daniel, *SUNY College at Brockport*

ISSUE

Are There Medical Benefits to Cloning?

YES: Robin McKie, from "Human Cloning Developments Raise Hopes for New Treatments," *The Guardian* (2013)

NO: Brendan Foht, from "The Case against Human Cloning," *BioNews* (2015)

Learning Outcomes

After reading this issue, you will be able to:

- Discuss the process of cloning.
- Understand the potential benefits of cloning.
- Assess the difference between adult and embryonic stem cells.

ISSUE SUMMARY

YES: Science editor Robin McKie argues that human cloning can create embryonic stem cells used to treat diseases such as heart failure.

NO: Editor of the *New Atlantis: A Journal of Technology and Society* Brendan Foht counters that there are numerous safety and moral issues related to cloning.

From a biological perspective, cloning is a process which produces similar populations of genetically identical individuals. In the realm of biotechnology, it refers to processes used to create copies of genetic fragments, cells, or organisms. In 1996, the first mammal successfully cloned from an adult cell was a sheep named Dolly. This event was significant because it showed that genetic material from an adult cell (Dolly's biological mother) could be processed to produce an entirely new organism.

While there have been numerous ethical issues raised, there is also the potential to prevent or cure diseases through this process. One application of cloning is to genetically modify animals so that their cells and organs could be transplanted into humans. Since thousands of people die each year because of the lack of available human organs for transplantation, genetically modified animal organs could begin to replace or supplement the need for human organs.

Other illnesses and diseases could be treated by transplanting genetically altered cells. In some neurological diseases such as Alzheimer's and Parkinson's, the symptoms are caused by the death or alternation of certain brain cells. Early research has indicated it's possible to reduce the tremors of Parkinson's disease by transplanting fetal pig brain cells into the brain of a patient. Recently, a team of researchers from Oregon Health and Science University in Portland, OR, reported that they have successfully cloned human embryonic stem (ES) cells by fusing the skin cells of a baby with donated human eggs. Researchers could use this process to create stem cells which have the capability to become any type of cell in our bodies. After being manipulated into the form required to treat a patient with Parkinson's disease (e.g., dopamine neurons in Parkinson's disease), the cells would be delivered to the patient. There would be no concerns of tissue rejection, because the cells would be genetically identical to the patient.

Alzheimer's disease is the most common cause of dementia and there is currently no cure. The first signs of Alzheimer's often include lapses in memory or struggling to find the right words. Over time, symptoms such as confusion, mood swings, or memory loss develop and become increasingly severe. The cause of the disease is still unclear, but researchers have found that people affected by Alzheimer's have an abnormal buildup of certain proteins in the brain. Scientists are unclear whether these changes in the brain lead to the symptoms of Alzheimer's. No stem cell treatments for Alzheimer's disease are currently available. Many different types of neurons in all parts of the brain are affected by the disease, making stem cell treatment very complex. However, researchers have been actively engaged in studying stem cell transplants in rodents and studies have shown some benefits. Much more research is needed before the findings could be applied to developing a therapy for human patients. Many scientists believe that Alzheimer's patients will benefit from stem cells in a different way before the development of potential cell transplantation therapies. By using stem cells derived from Alzheimer patients to grow large numbers of brain cells in the laboratory, scientists can study the disease and search for new drugs.

For individuals with insulin-dependent diabetes, transplanting genetically modified animal pancreas insulin-secreting cells could ultimately produce a cure. Insulin injections or pumps used by diabetics are a treatment, not a cure. Recently, scientists have successfully replaced the damaged DNA of a patient with type 1 diabetes with the healthy genetic material of an infant donor. It is hoped that when these cells are injected back into the diabetic patient, they will begin to produce insulin of their own accord. Using the cloning technique which produced Dolly the sheep in 1996, the procedure would prevent the need for daily insulin injections and effectively "cure" the disease.

Finding drugs for the treatment or prevention of a disease is made easier if there is an animal that mimics the response in the human body for testing the effectiveness of the drug or vaccine. Unfortunately, animals tend to not be susceptible to the same diseases that affect humans such as AIDS. HIV, the virus that causes AIDS, does not either infect or cause the same symptoms in animals as it does in humans. That makes it difficult to test vaccines or other treatments for their potential to treat or prevent the disease. Utilizing cloning technology could produce genetically modified animals which could enhance the development of treatments.

Overall, there are numerous and potential benefits of cloning including the possibility that through cloning technology, scientists will be able to renew activity of damaged cells by growing new cells and replacing them, thus curing disease. In addition, the ability to create humans with identical genetic makeup to act as organ donors for each other, that is, corneal and bone marrow transplants; and infertile couples will be able to have offspring will have either the mother's or father's genetic pattern. However, there are potential downsides to cloning which can include loss of genetic variation; a "black market" of fetuses may arise from certain desirable donors, unknown as well as the infancy and unpredictability of this technology.

While there may be enormous potential in cloning, the ethical issues are considerable. Supporters believe in the development of therapeutic cloning to treat disease. Advocates for reproductive cloning believe that parents who cannot otherwise have children should have access to the technology. Opposition to therapeutic cloning mainly centers around the status of ES cells which is related to the contentious abortion debate. Religious groups are divided, with some opposing the technology and, to the extent embryos are used, destroying a human life while others support therapeutic cloning's potential lifesaving benefits.

Robin McKie

Human Cloning Developments Raise Hopes for New Treatments

People with Conditions Such as Heart Disease or Parkinson's Could Benefit from Tissue Grown with Their Own DNA

Lorraine Barnes suffered a heart attack in 2005 and has lived with the consequences—extreme exhaustion and breathlessness—ever since. "I was separated from my husband and so my children, Charlotte and James, had to grow up overnight because suddenly they were caring for me," she says.

Charlotte agrees: "It turns your world upside down. I worry about my mum day and night, 24/7."

Heart failure leaves Barnes, 49, "drowning and gasping for air," she says. What really preys on her mind, though, is not her present difficulty but her future. "It scares me, as obviously I want to be around to see my children grow up."

There is no cure for heart failure, the aftermath of a heart attack, and the condition is common. Every seven minutes a person has a heart attack in the United Kingdom, and some victims are left so weakened they can hardly walk a few meters.

It's a grim scenario. But the prospects for patients like Barnes last week took a dramatic turn for the better when it was revealed that human cloning has been used for the first time to create embryonic stem (ES) cells from which new tissue—genetically identical to a patient's own cells—could be grown.

Scientists have been working on such techniques (see box) for some time, but their work has been hampered by the difficulties involved in cloning human cells in the laboratory. But the team led by Shoukhrat Mitalipov, of the Oregon Health and Science University in Portland, got around this problem. By adding caffeine to cell cultures, their outputs were transformed. "We were able to produce one ES cell line using just two human eggs, which would make this approach practical for widespread therapeutic use," said Mitalipov.

The development was hailed as a major boost for patients such as Barnes, who might benefit from tissue transplants—and not just heart attack patients but those suffering from diabetes, Parkinson's disease and other conditions.

But the announcement was also greeted with horror. "Scientists have finally delivered the baby that would-be human cloners have been waiting for: a method for reliably creating cloned human embryos," said David King of Human Genetics Alert. "It is imperative we create an international ban on human cloning before any more research like this takes place. It is irresponsible in the extreme to have published this."

Several tabloid newspapers also carried banner headlines warning of the human cloning "danger." Such reactions have a familiar ring. When the cloning of Dolly the sheep was revealed in 1997, there was an outpouring of hysteria about the prospect of multiple Saddam Husseins being created in laboratories.

"At the time the chances of these horrors occurring—when scientists had not even created a single clone of a human cell—were remote," said physiologist Professor Colin Blakemore of Oxford University. "Not that this worried the alarmists. The crucial point is that we should have spent the intervening time thinking about how we should react sensibly to the concept of a human clone when it does become possible. We have not done that and, although the science is still far off, it is getting closer. We need to ask, carefully and calmly: under what circumstances would we tolerate the creation of a human clone?"

At present, such a creation is banned in Britain. No human embryo created by cloning techniques is allowed to develop beyond 14 days. "The research is very tightly regulated and I think there is little chance of a rogue laboratory creating a human clone," said James Lawford Davies, a lawyer who specializes in health sciences. "However, many US states which, ironically, banned therapeutic cloning work because of their strong antiabortion stances have laws that would permit human clones to develop into fetuses."

Experts such as Professor John Harris, director of Manchester University's Institute for Science, Ethics, and Innovation, see positive benefits in reproductive cloning which could have a place in society. He said: "If you take a healthy adult's DNA and use it to create a new person—by cloning—you are essentially using a tried and tested genome, one that has worked well for several decades for the donor. By contrast, a child born naturally has an 8 percent chance of succumbing to a serious genetic abnormality because of the random selection of their DNA. You can avoid that with a clone."

In fact, most arguments against human cloning are foolish, said Harris, adding: "It could be used in medically helpful ways. If a couple find they are carriers of harmful, possibly fatal recessive genetic illnesses, there is a one in four chances they will produce a child who will die of that condition. That is a big risk. An alternative would be to clone one of the parents. If you did that, then you would know you were producing a child who would be unaffected by that illness in later life."

"Or consider the example of a single woman who wants a child. She prefers the idea of using all her own DNA to the idea of accepting 50 percent from a stranger. But because we ban human cloning she would be forced to accept DNA from a stranger and have to mother 'his child.' I think that is ethically questionable. Just after Dolly the sheep was born, UNESCO announced a ban on human cloning. I think that was a mistake."

This point was backed by Blakemore. He said: "Many people react with horror at the thought of a human clone, yet three of every 1,000 babies born today are clones—in the form of identical twins. These twins share not just the same DNA but have grown up in the same uterus and have had the same parenting—features that only intensify their similarities. Society is quite happy about this situation, it appears, but seems to find it odd when talking about cloning."

However, a note of caution was sounded by Ian Wilmut, who led the team that created Dolly the sheep. He said: "The new work may encourage some people to attempt human reproductive cloning but the general experience is that it still results in late fetal loss and the birth of abnormal offspring." It would be cruel to cause this in humans until techniques had been vastly improved, he added.

However, most scientists see Mitalipov's work as encouraging. If nothing else, the prospects for Lorraine Barnes—and countless other patients whose lives could be transformed by transplants—have greatly improved in the long term.

How It Works

The nucleus is removed from a human egg cell and the nucleus from a skin cell is inserted.

An electric shock fuses the skin cell nucleus inside the egg and it begins to divide into new cells. An embryo starts to form.

After a few days, the growth of the embryo is halted and cultures of its constituent stem cells created.

By treating stem cells with different chemicals, they can be transformed into specialized cells such as those that make up heart muscle, brain, pancreas, and other organs. These cells are genetically identical to the original skin cell and can be used to create tissue for transplanting into the skin cell's donor.

Robin McKie is a science editor.

Brendan Foht

The Case against Human Cloning

Compared to the frenzy over human cloning a decade ago, in recent years, the issue has received very little political attention, despite the recent breakthroughs in therapeutic cloning by US scientists (see BioNews 705 and 751). But as the ongoing fights over CRISPR and mitochondrial replacement show, some of the underlying debates about the ethics of genetic engineering and embryo experimentation are still with us.

A new report from the Witherspoon Council on Ethics and the Integrity of Science, a bioethics group consisting of several former members of George W. Bush's President's Council on Bioethics, makes the case for banning both reproductive and therapeutic cloning. The terms "reproductive cloning" and "therapeutic cloning" are not the ones used in the report, which opts instead for the terms "cloning-to-produce-children" and "cloning-for-biomedical-research." As the report argues, the distinction between therapeutic and reproductive cloning is misleading because the creation of a cloned embryo is always a reproductive act—the embryo is a new organism, the progeny of the source from which it was cloned. And therapeutic cloning is never therapeutic for the cloned embryo, which is destroyed, and is not necessarily therapeutic for any particular patients.

Public opinion has always been squarely opposed to cloning-to-produce children, though some academics have defended cloning as an exercise of radical reproductive autonomy. But if there is ever a time when the interests of children should counterbalance the liberty interests of prospective parents, it is in the case of human cloning. The medical risks posed by cloning are well known, and the first experimental uses of cloning would pose unjustifiable risks to the children created.

Beyond the concerns with safety are deeper moral objections to the way cloning would transform procreation into a manufacturing process. This is not, as ethicists like Kerry Lynn Macintosh have suggested, a fallacious argument that cloning would inevitably produce "defective products." Rather, it is an argument that the relationship between the generations will be distorted by the way prospective parents will come to see cloned children as products to be shaped and controlled, accepted or rejected, rather than gifts to be loved unconditionally.

Although some states have prohibited human cloning (with some prohibiting only cloning-to-produce-children while others prohibit all forms of cloning), at the federal-level cloning remains largely unregulated, largely because the controversy over whether to prohibit only cloning-to-produce-children or to pass a comprehensive cloning ban has stymied national legislative action. Some of the cloning laws proposed in the US Congress would have prohibited the transfer of cloned embryos to a woman's uterus. But as Gilbert Meilaender noted in 2002, such laws "create a class of human beings whose destruction is mandated by law." Creating human embryos with the express purpose of destroying them is even more problematic than the incidental destruction of embryos that occurs during IVF or the destruction of "leftover" embryos in other forms of stem cell research, making it very controversial for the US public.

Procuring human egg cells is another serious moral problem for human cloning research. Egg collection procedures pose health risks to women, and the practice of paying women for their eggs could lead to exploitation of those who might feel pressured to subject themselves to risk. Some ethicists have argued that compensation for oocytes is unlikely to provide an undue inducement and that compensation for the "time, inconvenience, and discomfort associated with oocyte retrieval can and should be distinguished from payment for the oocytes themselves." But cloning researchers have found that, in the absence of compensation, they are simply unable to find enough women willing to provide eggs for their research. Clearly, money induces women who would otherwise be unwilling to participate in egg collection procedures, which explains why researchers have sought to reform laws that restrict their ability to pay women for their oocytes.

However, there seems to be a way out of the ethical dilemma posed by cloning-for-biomedical research: the human-induced pluripotent stem (iPS) cells first developed in 2007 provide a promising alternative that does not rely on the destruction of embryos. But cloning research continued after this discovery, and many scientists and ethicists have argued that iPS cells cannot replace cloning and other forms of embryonic stem (ES) cell research, since it is still not clear what types of cells will, in the end, work best for research and therapy.

Of course, pursuing both cloning and other forms of cell reprogramming would be reasonable if there were no ethical problems with either. But even if cloning offers some advantages over iPS cells, the availability of a comparable alternative weakens the case for permitting cloning. A ban on all forms of human cloning would not mean forgoing personalized regenerative medicine, but would, at worst, mean that progress in this field might be slower than it would be without a ban.

Also, the reasons for pursuing both lines of research can be overstated. Using existing ES cell lines, including those created through cloning, scientists could continue to compare the efficacy of the two types of cell lines, while studies of the basic mechanisms of reprogramming can still be conducted using animal models.

The United States has lagged behind other countries in its policies on assisted reproduction technologies (ARTs) for too long. A ban on human cloning is of course not a comprehensive ART policy, and emerging technologies like mitochondrial replacement, next-generation prenatal genetic screening, and genetic modification all deserve more public attention in the United States. But finally crafting a national cloning policy will be an important step toward treating the moral and social issues raised by ART with the seriousness they deserve.

Brendan Foht is an editor of the *New Atlantis: A Journal of Technology and Society.*

EXPLORING THE ISSUE

Are There Medical Benefits to Cloning?

Critical Thinking and Reflection

1. What are the differences between adult and embryonic stem cells?
2. Why are many individuals opposed to cloning?
3. What are the potential benefits to cloning?
4. What are some of the ethical concerns?

Is There Common Ground?

One issue that is often raised when discussing cloning is the possibility of cloning humans to create children. While it's not a part of any legitimate research program, there are small numbers of advocates who argue for the use of closing to produce offspring. Their arguments supporting a future of biotechnologically aided reproduction may gain traction, especially if concerns about safety lessen as the research advances. However, the more serious sources of our opposition to the use of cloning to create children can be challenging to understand, articulate, and support.

The most often cited reason for the opposition to cloning to produce human children is the fear that the well-being and safety of egg donors, women carrying cloned fetuses to term, and the children born via cloning. Current evidence indicates that a large majority of cloned children would be born with medical issues. If the technology improves and reduces these concerns, health would likely become less of an issue. Unfortunately, data from cloned nonhuman animals show a high death rate of fetuses and embryos. As recently as 2010, approximately ⊠ of cloned animal embryos transferred to females resulted in live births. There are reasons to believe that cloned human embryos would suffer the same results. Cloned animals that survive long enough to be born often suffer from health problems including developmental defects and include kidney, liver, and heart disorders as well as a shortened life span.

While there are risks to cloning, if it could be made safe, it could offer ways to enhance the health and wellness of children. Couples affected by genetic diseases could have genetically related children while lessening the risk the child would inherit the condition. Also, prospective parents could protect their children from a number of genetic diseases. Finally, parents could choose a genetically "enhanced" child with desirable characteristics. The debate over cloning to produce human children is a complex issue, and if the science and technology develops, there may more advocates. It remains a controversial subject with a number of serious concerns associated with the process.

Additional Resources

Andrews, B. (2016). Game of Clones. *Mother Jones, 41*, 58.

Begley, S. (2014). The stem cell solution. *The Saturday Evening Post, 286*(6), 52–55.

Smith, W. J. (2017). Brave new world is closer than you think. *Human Life Review, 43*, 47–57.

Wilmut, I. (2016). Dolly & me. *New Scientist, 230*, 40–41.

Internet References . . .

National Bioethics Advisory Commission: Publications

http://www.bioethics.gov/pubs.html

National Human Genome Research Institute

https://www.genome.gov/25020028/cloning-fact-sheet/

U.S. National Institutes of Health (NIH)

www.nih.gov

Unit 3

UNIT

Mind–Body Relationships

Humans have long sought to extend life, eliminate disease, and prevent sickness. In modern times, people depend on technology to develop creative and innovative ways to improve health, extend life, and treat disease. However, as true cures for diseases such as AIDS, addiction, cancer, and heart disease continue to elude scientists and doctors, many people question whether or not modern medicine has reached a plateau in improving health. As a result, over the last decade, an emphasis has been placed on prevention as a way to maintain wellness. Prevention includes maintaining a healthy mind, body, and spirit. In addition, the theme of healing prayer is very common in the history of spirituality.

Selected, Edited, and with Issue Framing Material by:
Eileen L. Daniel, *SUNY College at Brockport*

ISSUE

Should Addiction to Drugs Be Labeled a Brain Disease?

YES: Alan I. Leshner, from "Addiction Is a Brain Disease," *The Addiction Recovery Guide* (2016)

No: Steven Slate, from "Addiction Is Not a Brain Disease, It Is a Choice," *The Clean Slate* (2016)

Learning Outcomes

After reading this issue, you will be able to:

- Discuss the causes of drug addiction.
- Discuss the argument that addiction is a disease and not a behavioral issue.
- Understand the various types of treatment for drug and alcohol addiction.

ISSUE SUMMARY

YES: Alan I. Leshner, director of the National Institute on Drug Abuse at the National Institutes of Health, believes that addiction to drugs and alcohol is not a behavioral condition but a treatable disease.

NO: Addiction theorist Steven Slate counters that addiction is a personal choice and cannot be considered a brain disease.

There are many different theories as to why some individuals become addicted to alcohol or other drugs. Historically, drug and alcohol dependency or addiction has been viewed as either a disease or a moral failing. In more recent years, other theories of addiction have been developed, including behavioral, genetic, sociocultural, and psychological theories. It appears that an individual's genetic makeup can play a major role in developing an addiction. For example, children with an addicted parent are four times more likely than children without an addicted parent to become addicts themselves. Furthermore, over 60 percent of individuals struggling with alcoholism have a family history of alcoholism though it may be a combination of heredity and learned behavior. Many individuals who are suffering from an underlying psychiatric condition, such as anxiety, depression, or mood illnesses, have a higher chance at becoming an addict and vice versa. An addiction can typically start when psychiatric disorders overwhelm individuals with feelings of sadness, anger, and confusion. Troubled with these feelings, individuals may self-medicate with drugs and/or alcohol which can lead to addiction. Also, an individual who lives, works, or studies in an environment prevalent with drug or alcohol usage is also more likely to become addicted to drugs or alcohol. Factors such as peer pressure, societal norms, and access to alcohol and drugs can all play a part in this. Finally, suffering from a traumatic event such as abuse or neglect during childhood, sexual abuse, or the loss of a loved one can strongly factor into an individual's use of alcohol and/or drugs. Overall, while genetic and environmental factors interact with critical developmental stages in a person's life to impact the vulnerability to addiction, adolescents experience a double challenge. Although taking drugs at any age can lead to addiction, the earlier that drug use begins, the more likely it is to progress to more serious abuse. And because adolescents' brains are still developing in the areas that govern decision-making, judgment, and self-control, they are especially prone to risk-taking behaviors, including experimenting with drugs and/or alcohol.

The view that drug addiction and alcoholism are moral failings maintains that abusing drugs is voluntary behavior that the user chooses to do. Users choose to over-indulge in such a way that they create suffering for themselves and others. American history is marked by repeated and failed government efforts to control this abuse by eliminating drug and alcohol use with legal sanctions, such as the enactment of Prohibition in the late 1920s and the punishment of alcoholics and drug users via jail sentences and fines. However, there seem to be several contradictions to this behavioral model of addiction. Addiction may be a complex condition that is caused by multiple factors, including environment, biology, and others. It is not totally clear that addiction is voluntary behavior. And from a historical perspective, punishing alcoholics and drug addicts has been ineffective.

In the United States today, the primary theory for understanding the causes of addiction is the disease model rather than the moral model. Borrowing from the modern mental health movement, addiction as a disease has been promoted by mental health advocates who tried to change the public's perception of severe mental illness. Diseases like bipolar disorder and schizophrenia were defined as the result of brain abnormalities rather than environmental factors or poor parenting. Likewise, addiction was not a moral weakness but a brain disorder that could be treated. In 1995, the National Institute of Drug Addiction (NIDA) supported the idea that drug addiction was a type of brain disorder. Following NIDA's support, the concept of addiction as a brain disease has become more widely accepted.

This model has been advocated by the medical and alcohol treatment communities as well as self-help groups such as Alcoholics Anonymous and Narcotics Anonymous. The disease model implies that addiction is not the result of voluntary behavior or lack of self-control; it is caused by biological factors which are treatable. While there are somewhat different interpretations of this theory, it generally refers to addiction as an organic brain syndrome with biological and genetic origins rather than voluntary and behavioral origins. It appears that an addicted person's impaired ability to discontinue using drugs or alcohol relates to deficits in the role of the prefrontal cortex, the part of the brain involved in executive function. The prefrontal cortex has several important purposes which include self-monitoring, delaying reward, and integrating whatever the intellect indicates is important with what the libido is relaying. The difficulty also has to do with how the brain, when deprived of the drugs to which it is accustomed, reacts to physical and emotional stress. The response is usually exaggerated negative emotion, and even despair. In this setting, the strong association of learned environmental cues (for instance, smelling alcohol beverages at a party or seeing the location where the drug dealer can be found) aggravates the craving for the substance. And the flood of intoxicating brain chemicals called neurotransmitters (chiefly dopamine) during drug use makes the brain relatively insensitive to "typical" sources of pleasure such as a tasty meal or a beautiful sunset.

Alan Leshner believes that taking drugs causes changes in neurons in the central nervous system that compel the individual to use drugs. These neurological changes, which are not reversible, force addicts to continue to take drugs. Steven Slate disagrees. He believes that most addicts are not innocent victims of chronic disease but individuals who are responsible for their choices and recovery.

YES 

Alan I. Leshner

Addiction Is a Brain Disease

A core concept evolving with scientific advances over the past decade is that drug addiction is a brain disease that develops over time as a result of the initially voluntary behavior of using drugs (drugs include alcohol).

The consequence is virtually uncontrollable compulsive drug craving, seeking, and use that interferes with, if not destroys, an individual's functioning in the family and in society. This medical condition demands formal treatment.

- We now know in great detail the brain mechanisms through which drugs acutely modify mood, memory, perception, and emotional states.
- Using drugs repeatedly over time changes brain structure and function in fundamental and long-lasting ways that can persist long after the individual stops using them.
- Addiction comes about through an array of neuroadaptive changes and the lying down and strengthening of new memory connections in various circuits in the brain.

The Highjacked Brain

We do not yet know all the relevant mechanisms, but the evidence suggests that those long-lasting brain changes are responsible for the distortions of cognitive and emotional functioning that characterize addicts, particularly including the compulsion to use drugs that is the essence of addiction.

It is as if drugs have highjacked the brain's natural motivational control circuits, resulting in drug use becoming the sole, or at least the top, motivational priority for the individual.

Thus, the majority of the biomedical community now considers addiction, in its essence, to be a brain disease.

This brain-based view of addiction has generated substantial controversy, particularly among people who seem able to think only in polarized ways.

Many people erroneously still believe that biological and behavioral explanations are alternative or competing ways to understand phenomena, when in fact they are complementary and integrative.

Modern science has taught that it is much too simplistic to set biology in opposition to behavior or to pit willpower against brain chemistry.

Addiction involves inseparable biological and behavioral components. It is the quintessential biobehavioral disorder.

Many people also erroneously still believe that drug addiction is simply a failure of will or of strength of character. Research contradicts that position.

Responsible for Our Recovery

However, the recognition that addiction is a brain disease does not mean that the addict is simply a hapless victim. Addiction begins with the voluntary behavior of using drugs, and addicts must participate in and take some significant responsibility for their recovery.

Thus, having this brain disease does not absolve the addict of responsibility for his or her behavior.

But it does explain why an addict cannot simply stop using drugs by sheer force of will alone.

The Essence of Addiction

The entire concept of addiction has suffered greatly from imprecision and misconception. In fact, if it were possible, it would be best to start all over with some new, more neutral term.

The confusion comes about in part because of a now archaic distinction between whether specific drugs are "physically" or "psychologically" addicting.

The distinction historically revolved around whether or not dramatic physical withdrawal symptoms occur when an individual stops taking a drug; what we in the field now call "physical dependence."

Leshner, Alan I. "Addiction Is a Brain Disease," *The Addiction Recovery Guide*, October 2016. Originally from SCIENCE 278: 45(1997).

However, 20 years of scientific research has taught that focusing on this physical versus psychological distinction is off the mark and a distraction from the real issues.

From both clinical and policy perspectives, it actually does not matter very much what physical withdrawal symptoms occur.

Physical dependence is not that important, because even the dramatic withdrawal symptoms of heroin and alcohol addiction can now be easily managed with appropriate medications.

Even more important, many of the most dangerous and addicting drugs, including methamphetamine and crack cocaine, do not produce very severe physical dependence symptoms upon withdrawal.

What really matters most is whether or not a drug causes what we now know to be the essence of addiction, namely:

The uncontrollable, compulsive drug craving, seeking, and use, even in the face of negative health and social consequences.

This is the crux of how the Institute of Medicine, the American Psychiatric Association, and the American Medical Association define addiction and how we all should use the term.

It is really only this compulsive quality of addiction that matters in the long run to the addict and to his or her family and that should matter to society as a whole.

Thus, the majority of the biomedical community now considers addiction, in its essence, to be a brain disease:

A condition caused by persistent changes in brain structure and function.

This results in compulsive craving that overwhelms all other motivations and is the root cause of the massive health and social problems associated with drug addiction.

The Definition of Addiction

In updating our national discourse on drug abuse, we should keep in mind this simple definition:

Addiction is a brain disease expressed in the form of compulsive behavior.

Both developing and recovering from it depend on biology, behavior, and social context.

It is also important to correct the common misimpression that drug use, abuse, and addiction are points on a single continuum along which one slides back and forth over time, moving from user to addict, then back to occasional user, then back to addict.

Clinical observation and more formal research studies support the view that, once addicted, the individual has moved into a different state of being.

It is as if a threshold has been crossed.

Very few people appear able to successfully return to occasional use after having been truly addicted.

The Altered Brain—A Chronic Illness

Unfortunately, we do not yet have a clear biological or behavioral marker of that transition from voluntary drug use to addiction.

However, a body of scientific evidence is rapidly developing that points to an array of cellular and molecular changes in specific brain circuits. Moreover, many of these brain changes are common to all chemical addictions, and some also are typical of other compulsive behaviors such as pathological overeating.

- Addiction should be understood as a chronic recurring illness.
- Although some addicts do gain full control over their drug use after a single treatment episode, many have relapses.

The complexity of this brain disease is not atypical, because virtually no brain diseases are simply biological in nature and expression. All, including stroke, Alzheimer's disease, schizophrenia, and clinical depression, include some behavioral and social aspects.

What may make addiction seem unique among brain diseases, however, is that it does begin with a clearly voluntary behavior—the initial decision to use drugs. Moreover, not everyone who ever uses drugs goes on to become addicted.

Individuals differ substantially in how easily and quickly they become addicted and in their preferences for particular substances.

Consistent with the biobehavioral nature of addiction, these individual differences result from a combination of environmental and biological, particularly genetic, factors.

In fact, estimates are that between 50 and 70 percent of the variability in susceptibility to becoming addicted can be accounted for by genetic factors. Although genetic characteristics may predispose individuals to be more or less susceptible to becoming addicted, genes do not doom one to become an addict.

Over time, the addict loses substantial control over his or her initially voluntary behavior, and it becomes compulsive. For many people, these behaviors are truly uncontrollable, just like the behavioral expression of any other brain disease.

Schizophrenics cannot control their hallucinations and delusions. Parkinson's patients cannot control their trembling. Clinically depressed patients cannot voluntarily control their moods.

Thus, once one is addicted, the characteristics of the illness—and the treatment approaches—are not that different from most other brain diseases. No mater how one develops an illness, once one has it, one is in the diseased state and needs treatment.

Environmental Cues

Addictive behaviors do have special characteristics related to the social contexts in which they originate.

- All of the environmental cues surrounding initial drug use and development of the addiction actually become "conditioned" to that drug use and are thus critical to the development and expression of addiction.

Environmental cues are paired in time with an individual's initial drug use experiences and, through classical conditioning, take on conditioned stimulus properties.

- When those cues are present at a later time, they elicit anticipation of a drug experience and thus generate tremendous drug craving.

Cue-induced craving is one of the most frequent causes of drug use relapses, even after long periods of abstinence, independently of whether drugs are available.

The salience of environmental or contextual cues helps explain why reentry to one's community can be so difficult for addicts leaving the controlled environments of treatment or correctional settings and why aftercare is so essential to successful recovery.

- The person who became addicted in the home environment is constantly exposed to the cues conditioned to his or her initial drug use, such as the neighborhood where he or she hung out, drug-using buddies, or the lamppost where he or she bought drugs.
- Simple exposure to those cues automatically triggers craving and can lead rapidly to relapses.

This is one reason why someone who apparently overcame drug cravings while in prison or residential treatment could quickly revert to drug use upon returning home.

In fact, one of the major goals of drug addiction treatment is to teach addicts how to deal with the cravings caused by inevitable exposure to these conditioned cues.

Implications

It is no wonder addicts cannot simply quit on their own.

They have an illness that requires biomedical treatment.

- People often assume that because addiction begins with a voluntary behavior and is expressed in the form of excess behavior, people should just be able to quit by force of will alone.
- However, it is essential to understand when dealing with addicts that we are dealing with individuals whose brains have been altered by drug use.

They need drug addiction treatment.

We know that, contrary to common belief, very few addicts actually do just stop on their own.

Observing that there are very few heroin addicts in their 50s or 60s, people frequently ask what happened to those who were heroin addicts 30 years ago, assuming that they must have quit on their own.

However, longitudinal studies find that only a very small fraction actually quit on their own. The rest have either been successfully treated, are currently in maintenance treatment, or (for about half) are dead.

Consider the example of smoking cigarettes: various studies have found that between 3 and 7 percent of people who try to quit on their own each year actually succeed.

Science has at last convinced the public that depression is not just a lot of sadness; that depressed individuals are in a different brain state and thus require treatment to get their symptoms under control. It is time to recognize that this is also the case for addicts.

The Role of Personal Responsibility

The role of personal responsibility is undiminished but clarified.

Does having a brain disease mean that people who are addicted no longer have any responsibility for their behavior or that they are simply victims of their own genetics and brain chemistry? Of course not.

Addiction begins with the voluntary behavior of drug use, and although genetic characteristics may predispose individuals to be more or less susceptible to becoming addicted, genes do not doom one to become an addict.

This is one major reason why efforts to prevent drug use are so vital to any comprehensive strategy to deal with the nation's drug problems. Initial drug use is a voluntary, and therefore preventable, behavior.

Moreover, as with any illness, behavior becomes a critical part of recovery. At a minimum, one must comply with the treatment regimen, which is harder than it sounds.

- Treatment compliance is the biggest cause of relapses for all chronic illnesses, including asthma, diabetes, hypertension, and addiction.
- Moreover, treatment compliance rates are no worse for addiction than for these other illnesses, ranging from 30 to 50 percent.

Thus, for drug addiction as well as for other chronic diseases, the individual's motivation and behavior are clearly important parts of success in treatment and recovery.

Alcohol/ Drug Treatment Programs

Maintaining this comprehensive biobehavioral understanding of addiction also speaks to what needs to be provided in drug treatment programs.

Again, we must be careful not to pit biology against behavior.

The National Institute on Drug Abuse's recently published Principles of Effective Drug Addiction Treatment provides a detailed discussion of how we must treat all aspects of the individual, not just the biological component or the behavioral component.

As with other brain diseases such as schizophrenia and depression, the data show that the best drug addiction treatment approaches attend to the entire individual, combining the use of medications, behavioral therapies, and attention to necessary social services and rehabilitation.

These might include such services as family therapy to enable the patient to return to successful family life, mental health services, education and vocational training, and housing services.

That does not mean, of course, that all individuals need all components of treatment and all rehabilitation services. Another principle of effective addiction treatment is that the array of services included in an individual's treatment plan must be matched to his or her particular set of needs. Moreover, since those needs will surely change over the course of recovery, the array of services provided will need to be continually reassessed and adjusted.

Alan I. Leshner is the director of the National Institute on Drug Abuse at the National Institutes of Health.

Steven Slate 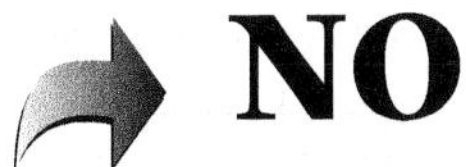 **NO**

Addiction Is Not a Brain Disease, It Is a Choice

They're screaming it from the rooftops: "addiction is a disease, and you can't stop it without medical treatment"! But why are they screaming it so loud, why are they browbeating us about it, why is it always mentioned with a qualifier? You don't hear people constantly referring to cancer as "the disease of cancer"—it's just "cancer," because it's obvious that cancer is a disease, it's been conclusively proven that the symptoms of cancer can't be directly stopped with mere choices—therefore no qualifier is needed. On the other hand, addiction to drugs and alcohol is not obviously a disease, and to call it such we must either overlook the major gaps in the disease argument, or we must completely redefine the term "disease." Here, we will analyze a few key points and show that what we call addiction doesn't pass muster as a real disease.

Real Diseases versus the Disease Concept or Theory of Drug Addiction

In a true disease, some part of the body is in a state of abnormal physiological functioning, and this causes the undesirable symptoms. In the case of cancer, it would be mutated cells which we point to as evidence of a physiological abnormality, in diabetes we can point to low insulin production or cells which fail to use insulin properly as the physiological abnormality which create the harmful symptoms. If a person has either of these diseases, they cannot directly choose to stop their symptoms or directly choose to stop the abnormal physiological functioning which creates the symptoms. They can only choose to stop the physiological abnormality indirectly, by the application of medical treatment, and in the case of diabetes, dietetic measures may also indirectly halt the symptoms as well (but such measures are not a cure so much as a lifestyle adjustment necessitated by permanent physiological malfunction).

In addiction, there is no such physiological malfunction. The best physical evidence put forward by the disease proponents falls totally flat on the measure of representing a physiological malfunction. This evidence is the much touted brain scan.[1] The organization responsible for putting forth these brain scans, the National Institute on Drug Abuse and Addiction (NIDA), defines addiction in this way:

> *Addiction is defined as a chronic relapsing brain disease that is characterized by compulsive drug seeking and use, despite harmful consequences. It is considered a brain disease because drugs change the brain—they change its structure and how it works. These brain changes can be long lasting, and can lead to the harmful behaviors seen in people who abuse drugs.*

The NIDA is stating outright that the reason addiction is considered a disease is because of the brain changes evidenced by the brain scans they show us, and that these changes cause the behavior known as addiction, which they characterize as "compulsive drug seeking and use." There are three major ways in which this case for the disease model falls apart:

- The changes in the brain which they show us are not abnormal at all.
- People change their behavior in spite of the fact that their brain has changed in response to repeated substance use.
- There is no evidence that the behavior of addicts is compulsive (compulsive meaning involuntary; point two addresses this, as well as some other research that will be presented).

This all applies equally to "alcoholism" as well. If you're looking for information on alcoholism, the same theories and logic discussed here are applicable; wherever you see the term addiction used on this site, it includes alcoholism.

Brain Changes In Addicts Are Not Abnormal, and Do Not Prove the Brain Disease Theory

On the first count, the changes in the brain evidenced by brain scans of heavy substance users ("addicts") do not represent a malfunctioning brain. They are quite normal, as research into neuroplasticity has shown us. Whenever we practice doing or thinking anything enough, the brain changes—different regions and neuronal pathways are grown or strengthened, and new connections are made; various areas of the brain become more or less active depending upon how much you use them, and this becomes the norm in your brain—but it changes again as you adjust how much you use those brain regions depending on what you choose to think and do. This is a process which continues throughout life, there is nothing abnormal about it.

. . .

So, when the NIDA's Nora Volkow and others show us changes in the brain of a substance user as compared to a nonsubstance user, *this difference is not as novel as they make it out to be*. They are showing us *routine* neuroplastic changes which every healthily functioning person's brain goes through naturally. The phenomenon of brain changes isn't isolated to "addicts" or anyone else with a so-called brain disease—nonaddicted and nondepressed and non-[insert brain disease of the week here] people experience neural adaptations too. One poignant example was found in the brains of London taxi drivers, as Begley and Jeffrey Schwartz pointed out in *The Mind and The Brain*.[3]

Is Being a Good Taxi Driver a Disease?

A specific area of the brain's hippocampus is associated with creating directional memories and a mental map of the environment. A team of researchers scanned the brains of London taxi drivers and compared their brains to non-taxi drivers. There was a very noticeable difference, not only between the drivers and nondrivers, but also between the more experienced and less experienced drivers.

. . .

So, the longer you drive a cab in London (i.e., the longer you exert the mental and physical effort to quickly find your way around one of the world's toughest to navigate cities), the more your brain physically changes. And the longer you use drugs, the more your brain changes. And indeed, the longer and more intensely you apply yourself to any skill, thought, or activity—the more it will change your brain, and the more visible will be the differences between your brain and that of someone who hasn't been focused on that particular skill. So, if we follow the logic of the NIDA, then London's taxi drivers have a disease, which we'll call taxi-ism, that ***forces them to drive taxis***. But the new diseases wouldn't stop there.

. . .

These brain change don't need to be brought on by exposure to chemicals. Thoughts alone, are enough to rewire the very circuits of the human brain responsible for reward and other positive emotions that substance use and other supposedly "addictive" behaviors ("process addictions" such as sex, gambling, and shopping, etc.) are connected with.

The Stolen Concept of Neuroplasticity in the Brain Disease Model of Addiction

Those who claim that addiction is a brain disease readily admit that the brain changes in evidence are arrived at through repeated choices to use substances and focus on using substances. In this way, they are saying the disease is a product of routine neuroplastic processes. Then, they go on to claim that such brain changes either can't be remedied or can only be remedied by outside means (medical treatment). When we break this down and look at it step by step, we see that the brain disease model rests on an argument similar to the "stolen concept." A stolen concept argument is one in which the argument denies a fact on which it simultaneously rests. For example, the philosophical assertion that "reality is unknowable" rests on, or presumes that the speaker could know a fact of reality, it presumes that one could know that reality is unknowable—which of course one couldn't, if reality truly was unknowable—so the statement "reality is unknowable" invalidates itself. Likewise, the brain disease proponents are essentially saying "neuroplastic processes create a state called addiction which cannot be changed by thoughts and choices"—this however is to some degree self-invalidating, because it depends on neuroplasticity while seeking to invalidate it. If neuroplasticity is involved and is a valid explanation for how to become addicted, then we can't act is if the same process doesn't exist when it's time to focus on getting unaddicted. That is, if the brain can be changed into the addicted state by thoughts and choices, then it can be further changed or changed back by thoughts and choices. Conditions which can be remedied by freely chosen thoughts and behaviors, don't fit into the general understanding of disease. Ultimately, if addiction is a disease, then it's a disease so fundamentally different than any other that it should probably have a completely different name that doesn't imply all the things contained in the term "disease"—such as the idea that the "will" of the afflicted is irrelevant to whether the condition continues.

People Change Their Addictive Behavior In Spite of the Fact That Their Brain Is Changed—and They Do So without Medication or Surgery

In the discussion above, we looked at some analogous cases of brain changes to see just how routine and normal (i.e., not a physiological malfunction) such changes are. Now we're going to look directly at the most popular neuroscientific research which purports to prove that these brain changes actually cause "uncontrolled" substance use ("addiction").

The most popular research is Nora Volkow's brain scans of "meth addicts" presented by the NIDA. The logic is simple. We're presented with the brain scan of a meth addict alongside the brain scan of a nonuser, and we're told that the decreased activity in the brain of the meth user (the *lack of red* in the "Drug Abuser" brain scan presented) is the cause of their "compulsive" methamphetamine use. Here's how the NIDA explains the significance of these images in their booklet—Drugs, Brains, and Behavior: The Science of Addiction:

> *Just as we turn down the volume on a radio that is too loud, the brain adjusts to the overwhelming surges in dopamine (and other neurotransmitters) by producing less dopamine or by reducing the number of receptors that can receive signals. As a result, dopamine's impact on the reward circuit of a drug abuser's brain can become abnormally low, and the ability to experience any pleasure is reduced. This is why the abuser eventually feels flat, lifeless, and depressed, and is unable to enjoy things that previously brought them pleasure.* ***Now, they need to take drugs just to try and bring their dopamine function back up to normal.***

. . .

When these studies were done, nobody was directly treating the brain of methamphetamine addicts. They were not giving them medication for it (there is no equivalent of methadone for speed users), and they weren't sticking scalpels into the brains of these meth addicts, nor were they giving them shock treatment. So what did they do?

These methamphetamine addicts were court ordered into a treatment program (whose methodology wasn't disclosed in the research) which likely consisted of a general mixture of group and individual counseling with 12-step meeting attendance. I can't stress the significance of this enough: their brains were not medically treated. They talked to counselors. They faced a choice between jail and abstinence. *They CHOSE abstinence (for at least 14 months!)—even while their brains had been changed in a way that we're told robs them of the ability to choose to quit "even in the face of negative consequences."*[4]

Even with changed brains, people are capable of choosing to change their substance use habits. They choose to stop using drugs, and as the brain scans above demonstrate, their brain activity follows this choice. If the brain changes caused the substance using behavior, that is, if it was the other way around, then a true medical intervention should have been needed—the brain would've needed to have changed first via external force (medicine or surgery) before abstinence was initiated. They literally wouldn't have been able to stop for 14 months without a real physical/biological medical intervention. But they did . . .

Substance Use Is Not Compulsive, It Is a Choice

. . .

If the theory is that neural adaptations alone cause uncontrolled behavior, then this proposition can easily be shown to be false. I demonstrated above that in the midst of having fully "changed" or "addicted" brains, people do indeed stop using substances, so essentially, it is case closed. But the depths to which the brain disease theory of addiction can be negated go even further, because the basic theory of addiction as representing uncontrolled substance use has never been explained. Explanation of the mechanism by which substance use happens without the individual's consent is conspicuously missing—yet such explanation is a necessary part of such a theory, as Lindesmith writes (again in Addiction & Opiates):

> *. . . besides identifying the two types of phenomenon that are allegedly interrelated, there must be a description of the processes or events that link them. In other words, besides affirming that something causes*

something else, it is necessary to indicate how the cause operates to produce the alleged effect.

There doesn't seem to be any explanation or evidence that substance use is involuntary. In fact, the evidence, such as that presented above, shows the opposite. Nevertheless, when the case for the disease is presented, the idea that drug use is involuntary is taken for granted as true. No evidence is ever actually presented to support this premise, so there isn't much to be knocked down here, except to make the point I made above—is a piano player fundamentally incapable of resisting playing the piano? They may love to play the piano, and want to do it often, they may even be obsessive about it, but it would be hard to say that at the sight of a piano they are involuntarily driven by their brain to push aside whatever else they need to do in order to play that piano.

There is another approach to the second claim though. We can look at the people who have subjectively claimed that their substance use is involuntary and see if the offer of incentives results in changed behavior. Gene Heyman covered this in his landmark book, Addiction: A Disorder of Choice.[2] He recounts studies in which cocaine abusers were given traditional addiction counseling and also offered vouchers which they could trade in for modest rewards such as movie tickets or sports equipment—if they proved through urine tests that they were abstaining from drug use. In the early stages of the study, 70 percent of those in the voucher program remained abstinent, while only 20 percent stayed abstinent in the control group which didn't receive the incentive of the vouchers. This demonstrates that substance use is not in fact compulsive or involuntary, but that it is a matter of choice, because these "addicts" when presented with a clear and immediately rewarding alternative to substance use and incentive not to use, chose it. Furthermore, follow up studies showed that this led to long-term changes. A full year after the program, the voucher group had double the success rate of those who received only counseling (80 to 40 percent, respectively). This ties back in to our first point that what you practice, you become good at. The cocaine abusers in the voucher group practiced replacing substance use with other activities, such as using the sports equipment or movie passes they gained as a direct consequence of abstaining from drug use—thus they made it a habit to find other ways of amusing themselves, this probably led to brain changes, and the new habits became the norm.

Long story short, there is no evidence presented to prove that substance use is compulsive. The only thing ever offered is subjective reports from drug users themselves that they "can't stop," and proclamations from treatment professionals that the behavior is compulsive due to brain changes. But if the promise of a ticket to the movies is enough to double the success rate of conventional addiction counseling, then it's hard to say that substance users can't control themselves. The reality is that they can control themselves, but they just happen to see substance use as the best option for happiness available to them at the times when they're abusing substances. When they can see other options for happiness as more attractive (i.e., as promising a greater reward than substance use), attainable to them, and as taking an amount of effort they're willing to expend—then they will absolutely choose those options instead of substance use, and will not struggle to "stay sober," prevent relapse, practice self-control or self-regulation, or any other colloquialism for making a different choice. They will simply choose differently.

But wait . . . there's more! Contrary to the claims that alcoholics and drug addicts literally lose control of their substance use, a great number of experiments have found that they are really in full control of themselves. Priming dose experiments have found that alcoholics are not triggered into uncontrollable craving after taking a drink. Priming dose experiments of cocaine, crack, and methamphetamine users found that after being given a hit of their drug of choice (primed with a dose), they are capable of choosing a delayed reward rather than another hit of the drug.

Three Most Relevant Reasons Addiction Is Not a Disease

So to sum up, there are at least two significant reasons why the current brain disease theory of addiction is false.

- A disease involves physiological malfunction, the "proof" of brain changes shows no malfunction of the brain. These changes are indeed a normal part of how the brain works—not only in substance use, but in anything that we practice doing or thinking intensively. Brain changes occur as a matter of everyday life; the brain can be changed by the choice to think or behave differently; and the type of changes we're talking about are not permanent.
- The very evidence used to demonstrate that addicts' behavior is caused by brain changes also demonstrates that they change their behavior while their brain is changed, without a real medical intervention such as medication targeting the brain or surgical intervention in the brain—and

that their brain changes back to normal AFTER they VOLITIONALLY change their behavior for a prolonged period of time

- Drug use in "addicts" is not compulsive. If it was truly compulsive, then offering a drug user tickets to the movies would not make a difference in whether they use or not—because this is an offer of a choice. Research shows that the offer of this choice leads to cessation of substance abuse. Furthermore, to clarify the point, if you offered a cancer patient movie tickets as a reward for ceasing to have a tumor—it would make no difference, it would not change his probability of recovery.

Addiction is NOT a disease, and it matters. This has huge implications for anyone struggling with a substance use habit.

References

1. NIDA, Drugs Brains and Behavior: The Science of Addiction, sciofaddiction.pdf.
2. Gene Heyman, Addiction: A Disorder of Choice, Harvard University Press, 2009.
3. Sharon Begley and Jeffrey Schwartz, The Mind And The Brain, Harper Collins, 2002.
4. Links to the 2 methamphetamine abuser studies by Nora Volkow: http://www.jneurosci.org/cgi/content/full/21/23/9414

   http://ajp.psychiatryonline.org/cgi/reprint/158/3/377

. . .

Steven Slate is an addiction theorist.

EXPLORING THE ISSUE

Should Addiction to Drugs Be Labeled a Brain Disease?

Critical Thinking and Reflection

1. What are the root causes of drug and alcohol addiction?
2. What are the benefits to labeling addiction a brain disease?
3. Why could it be harmful to label addiction a brain disease?
4. Describe the types of treatment for alcohol and drug addiction.

Is There Common Ground?

One of the most valuable aspects of labeling addiction a disease is that it removes alcohol and drugs from the moral realm. It proposed that addiction sufferers should be treated and helped, rather than scorned and punished. Though the moral model of addiction has by no means disappeared in the United States, today more resources are directed toward rehabilitation than punishment. Increasingly, it is being recognized and understood that fines, victim-blaming, and imprisonment do little to curb alcohol and drug addiction in society.

An article, "New insights into the genetics of *addiction*" (*Nature Reviews Genetics*, April, 2009), indicates that genetics contributes significantly to susceptibility to this disorder, but identification of vulnerable genes has lagged. In "It's Time for Addiction Science to Supersede Stigma" (*Science News*, 11/8/09), the author discusses advances made in the scientific community in studying *addictions* and says that people should regard drug addicts the same they regard other people with *brain diseases*. To do this, it should be recognized that *addictions* are a form of *brain disease*, and rather than blaming people for becoming addicted, energy should be spent on finding solutions.

Critics argue, however, that this belief either underemphasizes or ignores the impact of self-control, learned behaviors, and many other factors which lead to alcohol and drug abuse. Furthermore, most treatment programs in the United States are based on the concept of addiction as a brain disease, and most are considered to be generally ineffective when judged by their high relapse rates. Many researchers claim that advances in neuroscience is changing the way mental health issues such as addiction is understood and addressed as a brain disease. While calling addiction a brain disease and medical condition legitimizes it, many scientists do not completely support this model.

It appears that the causes of addiction are complex and that brain, mind, and behavioral specialists are rethinking the whole notion of addiction. With input from neuroscience, biology, pharmacology, psychology, and genetics, they're questioning assumptions and identifying some common characteristics among addicts which will, it is hoped, improve treatment outcomes and even prevent people from using drugs in the first place.

Additional Resources

Alavi, S., Ferdosi, M., Jannatifard, F., Eslami, M., Alaghemandan, H., & Setare, M. (2012). Behavioral addiction versus substance addiction: Correspondence of psychiatric and psychological views. *International Journal Of Preventive Medicine, 3*(4), 290–294.

Campbell, M. (2015). Ten ethical failings in addiction treatment. *Alcoholism & Drug Abuse Weekly, 27*(10), 5–6.

Clark, K.J. (2016). Addiction is a chronic brain disease. *American Journal of Managed Care,* 14.

Elam, M. (2015). How the brain disease paradigm remoralizes addictive behaviour. *Science as Culture, 24*(1), 46–64.

Internet References . . .

American Psychological Association (APA)

Offers information on a variety of mental health topics with multiple links.

www.apa.org

National Institutes of Health: National Institute on Drug Abuse

Offers information on drug abuse directed at a variety of constituents: professionals, researchers, teachers, parents, students, and young adults.

http://www.drugabuse.gov/nidahome.html

Web of Addictions

The Web of Addictions site is dedicated to providing accurate information about alcohol and other drug addictions. The site was developed to provide data about drugs of abuse and to provide a resource for teachers, students, and others who needed factual information about abused drugs.

http://www.well.com/user/woa

Unit 4

UNIT

Sexuality and Gender Issues

Few issues could be of greater controversy than those concerning gender and sexuality. Recent generations of Americans have rejected "traditional" sexual roles and values which have resulted in more opportunities and great equality for women. On the other hand, societal changes have seen a significant increase in babies born out of wedlock, the spread of sexually transmitted diseases, Internet pornography, and a rise in legal abortions. Many of these issues such as abortion, birth control, and right to life versus pro-choice remain controversial and may never be fully resolved. This section addresses many of the concerns associated with sexuality, gender, and health.

Selected, Edited, and with Issue Framing Material by:
Eileen L. Daniel, *SUNY College at Brockport*

ISSUE

Is It Necessary for Pregnant Women to Completely Abstain from All Alcoholic Beverages?

YES: National Organization on Fetal Alcohol Syndrome, from "Is It Completely Safe and Risk-Free to Drink a Little Alcohol While Pregnant, Such as a Glass of Wine?" *nofas.org* (2013)

NO: Emily Oster, from "I Wrote That It's OK to Drink While Pregnant. Everyone Freaked Out. Here's Why I'm Right," *slate.com* (2013)

Learning Outcomes

After reading this issue, you will be able to:

- Discuss the risks associated with alcohol consumption during pregnancy.
- Discuss the characteristics of fetal alcohol syndrome.
- Assess the argument that limited amounts of alcohol during pregnancy may not be harmful to the child.

ISSUE SUMMARY

YES: The National Organization on Fetal Alcohol Syndrome provides evidence that even moderate quantities of alcohol can damage a developing fetus and cites new research indicating that even small amounts of alcoholic beverages consumed during pregnancy may be harmful.

NO: Economics professor Emily Oster argues that there are almost no studies on the effects of moderate drinking during pregnancy and that small amounts of alcohol are unlikely to have much effect.

In 1973, a paper was published in the British medical journal *The Lancet.* It described a pattern of birth defects that occurred among children born of alcoholic women and was called "fetal alcohol syndrome" or FAS ("Recognition of the Fetal Alcohol Syndrome in Early Infancy," *Lancet,* vol. 2, 1973). Since that time, thousands of studies have supported the relationship between heavy alcohol consumption during pregnancy and resulting birth defects. One controversial point related to FAS, however, is the amount of alcohol that must be consumed to cause danger to the developing baby. It seems that some threshold must exist though it's unclear what that is.

In their 1973 study, Jones and Smith correlated FAS only among children born to alcohol-abusing women. While the researchers were successful in bringing the syndrome to international attention, it also created apprehension that any amount of alcohol consumption during pregnancy could cause danger to the child. Many doctors and researchers believe that even minute levels of alcohol intake during pregnancy can cause FAS, resulting in a panic that may have exaggerated the dangers of *any* consumption.

Fortunately, FAS is relatively uncommon, though the United States has one of the highest rates in the developed world. This may be related to the pattern of alcohol consumption in this country. In many European countries, alcohol is often consumed daily, whereas in the United States alcohol intake is more confined to weekends. This results in higher blood alcohol levels on those days. In addition, there are other variables that increase the risk of FAS that cannot be linked solely to the amount of alcohol consumed. For example, women who binge drink are much more likely to bear children with the pattern of birth defects linked to FAS than women who consume the same total amount of alcohol over a period of time. In addition to binge drinking, a pregnant woman's health is another significant factor. Women who bear children with FAS often have liver disease and nutritional deficiencies including anemia, infections, and other conditions that exacerbate alcohol's effects on the fetus. Older mothers and those who have given birth to several children are also at greater risk to have children with FAS. While binge drinking, other health issues, and age are important risk factors, the two most significant conditions along with alcohol consumption are low income and cigarette smoking. Low income is related to poor diet, smoking and other drug use, and exposure to pollutants such as lead. Smoking is also a factor in FAS because it contains toxins that reduce blood flow and level of oxygen available to the fetus.

While it appears that heavy alcohol consumption, particularly binge drinking, combined with smoking, poor diet, low income, and concomitant health problems increase the risk of FAS, is there an absolutely safe level of consumption during pregnancy? Two recent studies suggest that alcohol use during pregnancy may be more dangerous for the child than previously thought. In one study, researchers found symptoms of FAS in children whose mothers drank two drinks per day at certain stages of pregnancy. The children born of these women were found to be unusually small and/or had learning or behavioral problems. The researchers also found other defects associated with FAS at a higher rate than expected ("Epidemiology of FASD in a Province in Italy: Prevalence and Characteristics of Children in a Random Sample of Schools," *Alcoholism: Clinical and Experimental Research,* September 2006). A second study confirmed that FAS is not the only concern associated with alcohol consumption during pregnancy. It's also a risk factor for alcohol abuse among the children born of these women ("In Utero Alcohol Exposure and Prediction of Alcohol Disorders in Early Adulthood: A Birth Cohort Study," *Archives of General Psychiatry*, September 2006).

It's apparent that heavy use of alcohol during pregnancy increases the risk of FAS. What is unclear is the risk associated with any amount of alcohol. A 25-year study of babies born to mothers who were social drinkers found that even low intakes of alcohol had measurable effects on their babies. The study concluded that no minimum level of drinking was absolutely safe. See "When Two Drinks Are Too Many," *Psychology Today*, May/June 2004. More recently, in 2015, the American Academy of Pediatrics issued a statement identifying prenatal exposure to alcohol as the leading preventable cause of birth defects as well as cognitive problems later in life.

The following two selections address whether it is safe for pregnant women to drink during pregnancy. The National Organization on Fetal Alcohol Syndrome argues that even a small amount of alcohol can damage a developing fetus and cites new research that indicates that moderate consumption of alcoholic beverages during pregnancy may be harmful and that it's safer to avoid drinking.

Economics professor Emily Oster counters that there are almost no studies on the effects of moderate drinking during pregnancy and that small amounts of alcohol consumed during pregnancy are unlikely to have much harmful effect.

National Organization on Fetal Alcohol Syndrome

Is It Completely Safe and Risk-Free to Drink a Little Alcohol While Pregnant, Such as a Glass of Wine?

No. According to the CDC and the U.S. Surgeon General, "There is no known safe amount of alcohol to drink while pregnant. There is also no safe time during pregnancy to drink and no safe kind of alcohol." According to the American Academy of Pediatrics: "There is no safe amount of alcohol when a woman is pregnant. Research evidence is that even drinking small amounts of alcohol while pregnant can lead to miscarriage, stillbirth, prematurity, or sudden infant death syndrome."

When you drink alcohol, so does your developing baby. Any amount of alcohol, even in one glass of wine, passes through the placenta from the mother to the growing baby. Developing babies lack the ability to process, or metabolize, alcohol through the liver or other organs. They absorb all of the alcohol and have the same blood alcohol concentration as the mother. It makes no difference if the alcoholic drink consumed is a distilled spirit or liquor such as vodka, beer, or wine.

Alcohol is a teratogen, a toxic substance to a developing baby, and can interfere with healthy development causing brain damage and other birth defects. Most babies negatively affected by alcohol exposure have no physical birth defects. These children have subtle behavioral and learning problems that are often undiagnosed or misdiagnosed as Autism or Attention Deficit Disorder instead of one of the Fetal Alcohol Spectrum Disorders.

If you know a woman who is having difficulty abstaining from alcohol, the NOFAS mentoring network, The Circle of Hope, helps and supports women who have used alcohol or illicit drugs while pregnant.

Medical Studies

Several research studies available through the Collaborative Initiative on FASD (CIFASD):

The University of Queensland, 2013. This study finds "women who regularly drink as little as two glasses of wine per drinking session while pregnant can adversely impact their child's results at school."

Alcoholism: Clinical and Experimental Research, 2012. The study concludes, "Reduced birth length and weight, microcephaly, smooth philtrum, and thin vermillion border are associated with specific gestational timing of prenatal alcohol exposure and are dose-related without evidence of a threshold. Women should continue to be advised to abstain from alcohol consumption from conception throughout pregnancy."

International Journal of Epidemiology, 2012. This study states, "Even low amounts of alcohol consumption during early pregnancy increased the risk of spontaneous abortion substantially."

Alcohol Research & Health, 2011. This study found that drinking at low to moderate levels during pregnancy is associated with miscarriage, stillbirth, preterm delivery, and sudden infant death syndrome (SIDS).

Alcohol, Health, and Research World, 1997. This study states, "even a small amount of alcohol may affect child development."

Common Myths

Myth: My doctor said it's fine to have a glass of wine or two while pregnant.

Your doctor might not be informed about the risk of prenatal alcohol exposure or could be uncomfortable talking with you about the risks to your embryo or fetus associated with prenatal alcohol use. Unfortunately, many doctors are not properly educated about the risks associated with prenatal alcohol exposure. The American Congress of Obstetricians and Gynecologists (ACOG) advises women to not consume any alcohol while pregnant. Some doctors tell women that it's okay to drink a little wine because they are not comfortable talking with women who might not be interested in abstaining from alcohol or have difficulty doing so.

Myth: My friends or family members drank a bit and their kids are fine.

Every pregnancy is different. Not everyone who drinks while pregnant will have a child with measurable problems at birth, adolescence, or even adulthood, just like not every cigarette smoker will develop lung cancer. The fact remains that alcohol is toxic to the developing baby. Why take the risk?

Also, some children may have subtle damage from being exposed to alcohol that is not evident until school-age or later, such as problems with learning and behavior. In many of these cases, the problems are most often not linked to the prenatal alcohol exposure, inhibiting an accurate diagnoses and delaying appropriate intervention. According to Dr. Susan Astley Ph.D. and Dr. Therese Grant Ph.D., "Children exposed to and damaged by prenatal alcohol exposure look deceptively good in the preschool years. The full impact of their alcohol exposure will not be evident until their adolescent years."

Myth: There is no evidence of any effects from just one drink.

Dr. Michael Charness of Harvard Medical School gives just one example: "We've been able to show very striking effects of alcohol on the L1 cell adhesion molecule, a critical molecule for development, at concentrations of alcohol that a woman would have in her blood after just one drink."

Myth: A little bit of wine helps to reduce stress and can be healthy while pregnant.

The potential benefits of alcohol use during pregnancy to the *mother* are separate from and are outweighed by the potential risk to the mother's developing child. The scientific and medical research is very clear: No published biomedical research has found any risk-free benefit of prenatal alcohol exposure for the embryo or fetus. Hundreds of papers have conclusively demonstrated that alcohol use has the potential to cause both physical and functional damage to a growing baby.

The good news is that the vast majority of women in the U.S. stop drinking alcohol when they are pregnant. Those who continue drinking may do so because they do not understand the risks of continued drinking or because alcohol is a part of their lifestyle that they do not want to or cannot give up. Women commonly cite the need to relax as one of the reasons they drink during pregnancy even if they understand the risks. Pregnant women should ask their doctor about the diet and exercise that is appropriate for them, and to relax they might listen to soothing music, pamper themselves, take a bath, read, eliminate guilt, try deep breathing or meditation, schedule time for themselves with no responsibilities or distractions, and don't hesitate to ask their friends and family for help if they feel overwhelmed or uncomfortable.

Myth: On a holiday or special occasion, it's perfectly fine to at least have a few celebratory sips.

The human body functions the same, whether it's a holiday or not. Alcohol does not somehow lose its toxicity in utero because it happens to be New Year's Eve, or because wine is consumed instead of whiskey, or because the drinker has an advanced academic degree and a high socioeconomic status. The risk of prenatal alcohol exposure is not a risk to the health of the expectant mother; it is a risk to the development of her offspring.

The guidance to abstain from alcohol when pregnant is not intended to interfere with a woman's lifestyle choice to consume alcohol or in any way judge a woman for choosing to enjoy her favorite alcoholic beverage; it is intended to eliminate the chance her baby will have even the slightest reduction in their intellectual and physical abilities.

Myth: One glass of wine is not enough for the developing baby to even be exposed to the alcohol.

Any alcohol consumed by a pregnant woman is passed to the developing baby, even if it's a small amount. There is no threshold of prenatal alcohol consumption below which the baby is not exposed.

Myth: Drinking wine is better than using heroin or cocaine while pregnant.

Alcohol, including wine, causes far more damage to the developing baby than any other drug. The Institute of Medicine says, "Of all the substances of abuse (including cocaine, heroin, and marijuana), alcohol produces by far the most serious neurobehavioral effects in the fetus." No type of alcohol or illicit drugs consumed during pregnancy are completely without risk.

Myth: You have to be an alcoholic to drink enough to cause real damage.

The medical research is clear: Drinking at a level *below* the threshold for alcoholism can still cause damage to the growing baby. There are many women who are not alcoholics that have children with measurable effects of alcohol exposure. Damage can be caused by a pregnant woman's lack of awareness of the risks—not only as a result of her alcoholism.

Myth: Alcohol can only cause physical deformities. If the baby looks normal, it must be fine.

The vast majority (over 85%) of children with damage from prenatal alcohol exposure have *no* physical birth defects, only cognitive and/or behavioral consequences. There is such a wide range of effects that most subtle behavioral and cognitive difficulties are rarely diagnosed as alcohol-related.

Myth: It is alarming and even condescending for a doctor or anyone else to advise a woman to abstain from alcohol during pregnancy.

In the United States 50% of pregnancies are unplanned, so it is possible that the first time a woman is told that alcohol can harm her pregnancy is after she is already pregnant and has been drinking. It is important for physicians to advise the woman of the risks of alcohol use during pregnancy, be nonjudgmental, and provide guidance for an appropriate intervention if necessary. If a woman has been drinking alcohol during her pregnancy, the earlier she stops the greater the chance that her child will not have alcohol-related birth defects.

All women should be reminded of the risk of prenatal alcohol exposure. If a woman is informed of the risk and decides to drink, that is her decision—NOFAS is opposed to any rules, regulations, or statutes that seek to punish or sanction women for drinking alcohol during pregnancy. Practitioners should always inform their patients about the risks of known exposures.

It is important for pregnant women to be reminded that proper nutrition, good general health, and early and regular prenatal doctor visits might help reduce the effects of light drinking during pregnancy. It is believed that some women have a genetic predisposition that increases the vulnerability of their embryo or fetus to alcohol exposure, and, consequently, some women have a genetic make-up that reduces their vulnerability for having an alcohol-effected birth. However, the scientific community does not know for sure whether or not these genetic and epigenetic factors (changes in how genes are expressed without altering the underlying DNA sequence) contribute to the vulnerable pregnancies for certain women.

The Simple Approach

Thousands of pieces of research have shown alcohol to be a neurotoxin in utero. That means alcohol is a *toxic substance* to the developing baby just like carbon monoxide and lead. Alcohol causes the death of developing brain cells in the embryo or fetus. Common sense advises not exposing a developing baby to *any* amount of a toxic substance.

Medical experts on light drinking during pregnancy— watch on Youtube

Official Recommendations

United States Surgeon General Advisory

The most comprehensive review of alcohol and pregnancy research to date has been conducted by the Office of the Surgeon General within the Office of the Assistant Secretary for Health in the Office of the Secretary, U.S. Department of Health and Human Services. The Surgeon General first advised women to abstain from alcohol during pregnancy in 1981, and issued a new advisory in 2005.

The advisory states in part, "Based on the current, best science available we now know the following:

- No amount of alcohol consumption can be considered safe during pregnancy;
- Alcohol can damage the embryo or fetus at any stage of pregnancy;
- Damage can occur in the earliest weeks of pregnancy, even before a woman knows she is pregnant;
- The cognitive effects and behavioral problems resulting from prenatal alcohol exposure are lifelong."

"For these reasons:

- A pregnant woman should not drink alcohol during pregnancy;
- A pregnant woman who has already consumed alcohol during pregnancy should stop in order to minimize further risk;
- A woman who is considering becoming pregnant should abstain from alcohol."

About half of all pregnancies are unplanned. As a result, many women consume alcohol without knowing that they are pregnant. The Surgeon General's advisory also suggests that women of childbearing age should consult their physician about how best to reduce the risk of prenatal alcohol exposure.

Recommendations

Centers for Disease Control and Prevention
There is no known safe amount of alcohol to drink while pregnant. There is also no safe time during pregnancy to drink and no safe kind of alcohol.

National Institute on Alcohol Abuse and Alcoholism
No amount of alcohol is safe for pregnant women to drink.

American Academy of Pediatrics
The American Academy of Pediatrics recommends women who are pregnant or planning a pregnancy avoid drinking any alcohol.

American College of Obstetricians and Gynecologists
ACOG reiterates its long-standing position that no amount of alcohol consumption can be considered safe during pregnancy.

March of Dimes
Drinking alcohol when you're pregnant can be very harmful to your baby. It can cause your baby to have a range of lifelong health conditions.

National Arc
There is no absolute safe amount of alcohol that a woman can drink during pregnancy. Risk of FASD increase as the amount of alcohol consumed increases.

Baby Center
All public health officials in the United States recommend that pregnant women, as well as women who are trying to conceive, play it safe by steering clear of alcohol entirely.

Statements from Medical Experts

Dr. Kenneth Jones—First Named "Fetal Alcohol Syndrome" in 1973

"When talking about the prenatal effects of alcohol we usually think exclusively about the dose, the strength, and the timing of alcohol exposure. However, perhaps even more important are factors involving the mother—her genetic background and nutritional status to name just two. Based on those maternal factors, what may be a completely safe amount of alcohol for one woman to drink during her pregnancy may be a serious problem for another woman's developing fetus. Without knowing those genetic and nutritional factors that are critically involved with the way a woman metabolizes alcohol, it is not possible to make any generalizations about a 'safe' amount of alcohol during pregnancy. What may be 'safe' for one woman may be 'devastating' for another woman's unborn baby."

Dr. Michael Charness—Harvard Medical School

"Moderate levels of alcohol have been shown to disrupt the activity of a number of molecules that are critical for normal brain development. One such example, the L1 cell adhesion molecule, guides the migration of brain cells and the formation of connections between brain cells. Children with mutations in the L1 gene have developmental disabilities and brain malformations, and, importantly, the function of the L1 molecule is also disrupted by concentrations of alcohol that a woman would have in her blood after a single drink. These kinds of experiments support the view that women who are pregnant or trying to conceive would be safer to abstain from alcohol than to engage in even occasional light drinking.

Absence of proof is not proof of absence. The absence of evidence for developmental abnormalities in women who drink small amounts occasionally during pregnancy does not prove that light drinking is safe. Clinical studies do not have the power to detect small effects of alcohol on brain development, and even significant effects might be missed if the wrong test is used or if testing is conducted at the wrong developmental period. More practically, it is impossible to assure a mother who drinks lightly during pregnancy that her drinking did not result in a small drop in the IQ of her child. Light drinking is not essential to the health or well being of a pregnant woman, so why take a chance?"

If You Already Drank While Pregnant

If you have just found out you are pregnant and you have been drinking alcohol, stop drinking now and talk with your doctor. Any time during pregnancy that you stop drinking you increase the chance that your baby will not be affected by alcohol.

If you are finding it difficult to stop drinking, help is available. Visit your doctor to talk about your drinking, or find a professional in your area using the Substance Abuse and Treatment Facility Locator. You can also contact NOFAS or at (800) 66-NOFAS.

Alcohol and Pregnancy Science

Alcohol, like the chemical element mercury, is a confirmed teratogen (a substance that interferes with normal prenatal development). Alcohol can cause central nervous system (brain and spinal cord) malformations with associated neurobehavioral dysfunction. By comparison, lead is a neurotoxin but not a teratogen in that it produces neurobehavioral dysfunction in the absence of brain and spinal cord malformations.

Science definitively recognizes that when a pregnant woman consumes alcohol, the alcohol crosses the placenta into the blood supply of the developing embryo or fetus. An embryo or fetus has neither the developed organ systems nor enzymes able to metabolize alcohol.

The first paper in the medical literature describing a constellation of birth defects linked to prenatal alcohol exposure was published in France in 1968 by Dr. Paul Lemoine.

The first paper in U.S. medical literature appeared in 1973 authored by Drs. David Smith and Ken Lyons Jones. As of 2012, nearly 4,000 papers have been published confirming the toxicity of alcohol to the embryo or fetus, the underlying mechanisms of alcohol-induced damage to the embryo or fetus, and the physical and functional birth defects related to prenatal alcohol exposure.

No published study has suggested that alcohol is not a teratogen or demonstrated that prenatal alcohol use has any potential benefit to human development.

The basic and biomedical research demonstrates that alcohol damages the developing brain through multiple actions at different cellular sites interfering with normal development by disrupting cell migration, cell functions, and causing cell death.

Alcohol can cause damage to multiple regions of the brain, specifically to the corpus collosum (connects brain hemispheres), cerebellum (consciousness and voluntary processes), basal ganglia (movement and cognition), hippocampus (emotional behavior and memory), hypothalamus (sensory input), among other neural regions.

Ethanol is the principal psychoactive constituent in alcoholic beverages. In utero it has been found to:

- Interfere with normal proliferation of nerve cells;
- Increase the formation of free radicals—cell damaging molecular fragments;
- Alter cells ability to regulate cell growth, division and survival;
- Impair the development and function of astocytes, cells that guide the migration of nerve cells to their proper places;
- Interfere with the normal adhesion of cells to one another;
- Alter the formation of axons, nerve cell extensions that conduct impulses away from the cell body;
- Alter the pathways of biochemical or electrical signals within cells;
- Alter the expression of genes, including genes that regulate cell development.

Human development occurs in an orderly process of biochemical and structural transition during which new constituents are being formed and spatially arranged throughout gestation. At any time in the span of development these ongoing processes can be subtly or severely disturbed or abruptly halted resulting in abnormal development or fetal death.

Therefore, at any time alcohol is present it has the potential to harm development. For example, the hallmark facial dysmorphology associated with Fetal Alcohol Syndrome will only occur if alcohol is present during the specific window of development.

Of all the substances of abuse, including marijuana, cocaine and heroin, alcohol produces by far the most serious neurobehavioral effects on the embryo or fetus.

Women at Risk

Factors known to contribute to the risk of having a child with alcohol-related birth defects include biological susceptibility, poor nutrition, poor general health, and a lack of prenatal care.

Some light and moderate drinkers have offspring with identifiable birth defects while some women who consume alcohol throughout pregnancy have offspring without any apparent or quantifiable birth defects. Research is currently exploring both the genetic and protective factors involved in the manifestation of alcohol-related birth defects.

An examination of sociodemographic factors indicated that generally more older women (~30 or 35 years old and older) drink during pregnancy, but younger women (~24 years old or younger) face higher risks of binge drinking or drinking in the few months prior to recognizing they are pregnant. With regard to race and ethnicity, White women report a higher prevalence of alcohol use than Black or Hispanic women, although Hispanic women may increase use as they become more acculturated in the United States. Differences in prevalence based on geographic location appeared potentially important, with binge drinking more prevalent in the North-central sections of the United States and less so in the Southeast. Higher education and higher income were linked specifically to higher rates of alcohol use during pregnancy in some studies.

Key Facts on Alcohol and Pregnancy

There is no safe amount or type of alcohol to consume during pregnancy. Any amount of alcohol, even if it's just one glass of wine, passes from the mother to the baby. It makes no difference if the alcohol is wine, beer, or liquor or distilled spirits (vodka, rum, tequila, etc.)

A developing baby can't process alcohol. Developing babies lack the ability to process alcohol with their liver, which is not fully formed. They absorb all of the alcohol and have the same blood alcohol concentration as the mother.

Alcohol causes more harm than heroin or cocaine during pregnancy. The Institute of Medicine says, "Of all the substances of abuse (including cocaine, heroin, and marijuana), alcohol produces by far the most serious neurobehavioral effects in the fetus." No type of alcohol or illicit drugs consumed during pregnancy are completely without risk.

Alcohol used during pregnancy can result in FASD. An estimated 40,000 newborns each year are believed to have an FASD, Fetal Alcohol Spectrum Disorders, with damage ranging from major to subtle.

1 in 100 newborns in the U.S. might have FASD, nearly the same rate as Autism. FASD is more prevalent than Down Syndrome, Cerebral Palsy, SIDS, Cystic Fibrosis, and Spina Bifida combined. Alcohol use during pregnancy is the leading preventable cause of birth defects, developmental disabilities, and learning disabilities.

National Organization on Fetal Alcohol Syndrome (NOFAS) is a nonprofit public health charitable organization focused on the issue of fetal alcohol syndrome and fetal alcohol spectrum disorders (FASD).

Emily Oster

I Wrote That It's OK to Drink While Pregnant. Everyone Freaked Out. Here's Why I'm Right.

When I was pregnant, I wondered, as many women do: Can I have a drink? It is well-known that drinking to excess during pregnancy is dangerous, and perhaps less well known but still true, that even one or two episodes of binge drinking can be harmful. But what about an occasional glass of wine with dinner?

Expert opinions on this differ. *What to Expect When You're Expecting* says no alcohol. *Panic-Free Pregnancy* says an occasional drink is fine. A 2010 survey asked obstetricians, "How much alcohol can a pregnant woman consume without risk of adverse pregnancy outcomes?" Sixty percent of the OBs said none, but the other 40 percent said some alcohol was fine. The American Congress of Obstetricians and Gynecologists (ACOG) says no amount of alcohol has been shown to be safe, but the U.K. equivalent (the Royal College of Obstetricians and Gynecologists) says that while not drinking is the safest option, "Small amounts of alcohol during pregnancy have not been shown to be harmful."

My obstetrician said a few drinks a week was fine. But as with everything else, amid this disagreement, I needed to go to the data myself.

I reviewed many, many studies, but I focused in on ones that compare women who drank lightly or occasionally during pregnancy to those who abstained. The best of these studies are ones that separate women into several groups—for example: no alcohol, a few drinks a week, one drink a day, more than one drink a day—and that limit the focus to women who say they never had a binge drinking episode. With these parameters, we can really hone in on the question of interest: What is the impact of having an occasional drink, assuming that you never overdo it?

I summarize two studies in detail in my book: one looking at alcohol consumption by pregnant women and behavior problems for the resulting children up to age 14 and one looking at alcohol in pregnancy and test performance at age 14. Both show no difference between the children of women who abstain and those who drink up to a drink a day. I summarize two others in less detail: one looking at IQ scores at age 8 and a more recent one looking at IQ scores at age 5. These also demonstrate no impact of light drinking on test scores.

I argue that based on this data, many women may feel comfortable with an occasional glass of wine—even up to one a day—in later trimesters. (More caution in the first trimester—no more than two drinks a week—because of some evidence of miscarriage risk.)

Although this discussion takes up only a small share of the book, it has garnered the loudest reaction, much of it outrage. NOFAS, a fetal alcohol syndrome advocacy group, issued a press release even before the book came out saying I was harmful and irresponsible. Amazon reviews of the book—at least some of them by people who explicitly said they would never read it—attacked me and anyone who had a drink during pregnancy as an alcoholic. One commented on my daughter: "Emily Oster claims that her 2-year old daughter is perfectly healthy, yet the full impact of the alcohol exposure on her child will not be evident until the adolescent years."

The president of ACOG has vehemently disagreed with me, saying in a radio interview about occasional drinking that alcohol in pregnancy is more dangerous than heroin or cocaine. Of course, there has been occasional public agreement from OBs (and much more private agreement).

Some of the arguments made in response to the book are tangential. Commenters wish that there was more in the book about the dangers of fetal alcohol syndrome, more discussion of the risks of binge drinking. I spend only a page on this, since it is not the question I believe most readers of the book are asking.

Some of them are philosophical. People ask, "Why take the risk?" since there is no benefit to the baby. But this ignores the fact that we are always making choices that could carry some risk and have no benefit to the baby. Driving in a car carries some risk to your baby, and your fetus does not benefit from that vacation you took. Or they ask, "Is it so hard to give up drinking for nine months?" The answer is, of course, no, but because you might enjoy the occasional beer, it seems worth at least asking the question about the risks.

Then there is the criticism that I cherry-picked studies to fit the story. This certainly isn't the case; the fact that the book doesn't summarize all 23,000 studies in PubMed on alcohol in pregnancy reflects the desire to identify the most reliable and largest and present those. Still, it's reasonable to ask whether there are studies that I missed that tell a different story.

One fact that has been cited to me a number of times, including by the ACOG president, is: "One in 7 children with fetal alcohol syndrome had a mother who drank one to eight drinks per week in the first trimester." The implication is that even light drinking early on (which would be much closer to one than eight drinks) is dangerous. But this claim doesn't come from a study; it comes from a statement made in a letter to the editor, and it's therefore impossible to evaluate critically. One to eight drinks a week could mean eight drinks on one night, for instance, and that is known to be dangerous.

Another study that has been mentioned prominently relates prenatal alcohol exposure to behavior problems in young adulthood. Although some have suggested that this paper identifies impacts of having one drink per day, the analysis actually relates behavior problems to a measure of average daily intake—which includes people having more than that, sometimes a lot more. It's true that some people evaluated in this study drink lightly, but others do not, and by lumping them together it is very difficult to draw conclusions about the light drinkers.

There is a much more technically complex study that I certainly would have included in the book if it had come out in time. It shows that light maternal drinking is associated with small IQ decreases for people with some particular genetic variants. Light maternal drinking is also associated with small IQ increases in people with some other genetic variants. This suggests that further studies may be useful in evaluating genetic risks, although it doesn't provide a lot of guidance at this time.

The bottom line is that the criticism fails to identify studies that have the features we would want: a population that is never binge drinking and a data analysis that looks separately at women who drink lightly and those who drink more. In the book I discuss one study like this, which does argue there are impacts on behavior at one drink per day, but the study fails to adjust for differences across groups, like whether the father lives at home or if there was prenatal cocaine use, among other things.

Like alcohol, Tylenol, caffeine, and anti-nausea drugs like Zofran are substances that—in moderation—are thought to be safe during pregnancy. But they are also substances that in excessive doses could be dangerous. Some women decide that they will therefore avoid them altogether because they cannot be sure. And many women, seeing the evidence in the book on alcohol, will still choose to avoid it.

But others will see the data, like the data on caffeine or Tylenol, and choose to have an occasional drink, as I did. The value of the data is not that it leads us all to the same choice, just that it introduces a concrete way to make that choice.

Emily Oster is an associate professor of economics at Brown University.

EXPLORING THE ISSUE

Is It Necessary for Pregnant Women to Completely Abstain from All Alcoholic Beverages?

Critical Thinking and Reflection

1. What are the short- and long-term effects of fetal alcohol syndrome?
2. Will consuming small amounts of alcohol necessarily cause damage to a developing fetus? Explain.
3. Why is it so difficult to determine a safe level of alcohol consumption during pregnancy?

Is There Common Ground?

Since its medical recognition in 1973, fetal alcohol syndrome (FAS) has progressed from a little known condition to a major public health issue. The condition has been characterized by exaggerated and unproved claims; particularly the cause and impact of the condition. The second article discusses the fact that there is likely a safe threshold for alcohol consumption during pregnancy and that FAS typically occurs among women who consume the highest amount of alcohol and/or binge drink. Binge drinking among women of childbearing age is common in the United States, which has one of the world's highest rates of FAS. In a recent study, researchers determined that one in six women in the United States continues to drink during pregnancy and one in seven consumes more than seven drinks per week; three percent drinks more than 14 drinks per week. Thirteen percent of U.S. women aged 18–44 binge drink. The estimated number of childbearing-age women who engaged in binge drinking rose from 6.2 million in 2001 to 7.1 million in 2003, an increase of 0.9 million.

Fortunately, most women who use alcohol reduce their intake dramatically once they realize they are pregnant. A recent article, however, found that the weighted prevalence of alcohol-exposed pregnancy risk among U.S. women aged 15-44 years was 7.3%. During a 1-month period, approximately 3.3 million women in the United States were at risk for an alcohol-exposed pregnancy (Green, et al., 2016). .But doctors still don't know that risk or harm, if any, results from light to moderate alcohol intake during pregnancy which is why they caution pregnant women to abstain. For ethical reasons, there have been few if any studies conducted on pregnant women to determine if small to moderate intakes of alcohol is harmful. And to confuse the issue, some effects of alcohol consumption during pregnancy may not be apparent until a child starts school or even later in life. Child developmental and behavioral characteristics were examined from the 9-month data point of the Early Childhood Longitudinal Studies-Birth Cohort, a prospective nationally representative study. Several findings showed clear patterns between the amount of prenatal alcohol consumed and sensory regulation, mental, and motor development outcomes. Undesirable social engagement and child interaction were found to be statistically significant at the prenatal alcohol level of one to three drinks per week. Children exposed to four or more drinks per week showed statistically significant and clinically passive behavior on three sensory regulation variables("Maternal Alcohol Consumption During Pregnancy and Infant Social, Mental, and Motor Development". *HYPERLINK "javascript:__doLinkPostBack('','mdb%7E%7Ea9h%7C%7Cjdb%7E%7Ea9hjnh%7C%7Css%7E%7EJN%20%22Journal%20of%20Early%20Intervention%22%7C%7Csl%7E%7Ejh','');" \o "Search for Journal of Early Intervention" Journal of Early Intervention*; March, 2010). Clearly, excessive alcohol consumption during pregnancy has negative effects on fetal growth and development. Less consistent relationships have been shown for the correlation between light-to-moderate maternal alcohol consumption during pregnancy with health outcomes in the offspring. Researchers in the study "Associations of light and moderate maternal alcohol consumption with fetal growth characteristics in different periods of pregnancy: The Generation R Study" examined the associations of light-to-moderate maternal alcohol consumption with various fetal growth characteristics measured in different periods of pregnancy and found various levels of impairment among the children of women who consumed alcohol during their pregnancies (*International Journal of Epidemiology*, Jun,2010).

Although individual differences in reaction to alcohol prevents determining a "safe level" of drinking for all pregnant women, encouraging total abstinence from alcohol during pregnancy is prudent though not necessarily based on research. The changes in fetal activity associated with one or two drinks clearly indicate that the fetus reacts to low levels of alcohol. But these changes don't necessarily mean the fetus is damaged. Until relationships are considerably stronger than the evidence now indicates, the research does not support the consensus that low levels of alcohol intake pose a danger to the developing baby. Even though scientists can't prove small amounts of alcohol are harmful, they can't prove they aren't. On the other hand, setting a realistic threshold may be more effective than encouraging women to completing forgo alcohol. Setting a definite limit, two or less drinks per day for example, may be more realistic to those women who continue to drink during pregnancy. Prevention efforts have not been particularly effective among women who drink at levels that pose the greatest risk to their fetus. They may be able to reduce rather than eliminate all alcohol which could result is a reduced risk for FAS.

Additional Resources

Bellieni C. V., & Gambino, A. M. (2017). Are parents liable for their babies' prenatally acquired injuries?. *Ethics & Medicine: An International Journal Of Bioethics, 33*(1), 55–59.

Green, P. P., McKnight-Eily, L. R., Tan, C. H., Mejia, R., & Denny, C. H. (2016). Vital signs: Alcohol-exposed pregnancies–United States, 2011–2013. *MMWR: Morbidity & Mortality Weekly Report, 65*(4), 91–97.

Landgren, M. (2017, March). How much is too much? The implications of recognizing alcohol as a teratogen. *Acta Paediatrica*. pp. 353–355

Powers, J., McDermott, L., Loxton, D., & Chojenta, C. (2013). A prospective study of prevalence and predictors of concurrent alcohol and tobacco use during pregnancy. *Maternal & Child Health Journal, 17*(1), 76–84.

Sullum, J. (2012). Drink up, moms! *Reason, 44*(5), 13–14.

Internet References . . .

March of Dimes Foundation

www.marchofdimes.com

National Clearinghouse for Alcohol and Drug Information

www.health.org

National Organization on Fetal Alcohol Syndrome: NOFAS

www.nofas.org

Selected, Edited, and with Issue Framing Material by:
Eileen L. Daniel, *SUNY College at Brockport*

ISSUE

Should Pro-Life Health Providers Be Allowed to Deny Prescriptions on the Basis of Conscience?

YES: John A. Menges, from "Public Hearing on HB4346 Before the House State Government Administration Committee," Illinois House State Government Administration Committee (2006)

NO: J. Paul Kelleher, from "Emergency Contraception and Conscientious Objection," *Journal of Applied Philosophy* (2010)

Learning Outcomes

After reading this issue, you will be able to:

- Discuss why some pharmacists refuse to dispense certain medications.
- Understand the mechanisms of the morning-after pill.
- Assess the legality of a pharmacist refusing to filling prescriptions.

ISSUE SUMMARY

YES: Pharmacist John A. Menges believes that it is his right to refuse to dispense any medication that is designed to end a human life.

NO: Professor J. Paul Kelleher argues that the rights of women trumps the rights of medical professionals to refuse services based on religious conviction.

A trend has been making news recently. The pharmacists' refusal clause also known as the conscience clause allows pharmacists to refuse to fill certain prescriptions because of their own moral objections to the medication. These medications are mostly birth control pills and the "morning-after pill" which can be used as emergency contraception (EC). Though nearly all states offer some type of legal protection for health-care providers who refuse to provide certain women's health-care services, only three states—Arkansas, Mississippi, and South Dakota—specifically protect pharmacists who refuse to dispense birth control and emergency contraceptive pills. While only a limited number of states have passed refusal clause legislation specific to pharmacists, more and more states are considering adding it. Most states do have "conscience clauses," which describe a right of refusal for physicians, and in some cases for other providers and for health-care organizations such as religious hospitals. Most of these state laws, as well as similar conscience clauses in federal statutes, professional codes of ethics, and institutional policies, were enacted after the passage of Roe v. Wade in 1973 to permit physicians to opt out of performing or participating in legalized abortions. Today, most medical students opt out of learning how to perform abortions, as they are permitted to do under the American Medical Association's code of ethics. A physician who does not perform abortions—an anesthesiologist, for example—may still be called upon, and can refuse, to participate in the procedure. Some conscience clauses explicitly cover abortion, contraception, sterilization, and the withholding or withdrawing of life-sustaining treatments. Some of these clauses cover local conditions: in Oregon, a conscience clause describes a physician's right of refusal concerning physician-assisted suicide, which is legal in that state. Others are general: they simply acknowledge a right of refusal on conscience grounds. Conscience clauses played a prominent role in the US Food and Drug Administration debate over expanded access to Plan B, including over-the-counter access for women aged 18 and older. (Because this medication is stocked behind the counter, pharmacists are involved in dispensing Plan B even if the patient is an adult. People aged 17 or younger must have a prescription to obtain Plan B from a pharmacy.) Some retail pharmacists claimed a right to both refuse to provide the emergency contraceptive and refuse to refer the consumer to another pharmacist on staff or to another pharmacy. These practices challenged the profession's own guidelines, which recommend a "step away" procedure that allows an individual pharmacist to refuse to provide a service but does not permit this pharmacist to block access to this service. During this controversy, several states adopted conscience clause statutes specifically protecting pharmacists, while others passed legislation aimed at ensuring that individual providers did not hamper consumer access to a medically appropriate drug. In a related type of professional refusal with implications for health care, some judges have sought "blanket recusals" from hearing any case involving abortion petitions by minors.

In the past several years, there have been reports of pharmacists who refused to fill prescriptions for birth control and emergency contraceptive pills. In some of these instances, the pharmacists who refused service were fired, but in others, no legal action was taken. As a result, some women have left their drug stores without getting their pills and not sure where to go to have their prescriptions filled.

While doctors may refuse to perform abortions or other procedures which they morally object to, should pharmacists have the same right? They are members of the health-care team and should be treated as medical professionals. Society does not demand that professionals abandon their morals as a condition of their employment. On the other hand, there are a number of reasons against a pharmacist's right to object. First and foremost is the right of a patient to receive timely medical treatment. Pharmacists may refuse to fill prescriptions for EC because they believe that drug ends a life. Although the patient may disapprove of abortion, she may not share the pharmacist's beliefs about birth control. If she becomes pregnant, she may then consider abortion, an issue she could have avoided if allowed to fill the morning-after pill. Other concerns include the time sensitive nature of the morning-after pill which must be taken within 72 hr of intercourse to effectively prevent pregnancy. Women who are refused the medication by one pharmacist may not be able to get the drug from another. This is especially true if she lives in an area with only one pharmacy. Also, low-income women may not have the time or resources to locate a pharmacy which would fill the prescription.

Other potential abuses could also arise. For instance, some pharmacists may object to filling drugs to treat AIDS if they believe HIV-positive individuals have engaged in behaviors they consider immoral such as IV drug use or homosexual relations. A pharmacist who does not believe in extramarital sex might refuse to fill a prescription for Viagra for an unmarried man. Could a pharmacist's objections here be considered invasive? Further, because a pharmacist does not have access to a patient's medical records or history, refusing to fill a prescription could be medically harmful.

While arguments could be made for both sides, it appears that there needs to be a compromise between the needs of a patient and the moral beliefs of a pharmacist. In the following selections, physician John A. Menges argues that health providers' consciences must be respected. J. Paul Kelleher counters that a provider's conscience can be in conflict with legitimate medical needs of a patient.

John A. Menges

Public Hearing on HB4346 Before the House State Government Administration Committee

[I am] one of the 4 fired Walgreens pharmacists. I was fired for not signing a policy saying that I would indeed fill a prescription if presented with it. I did not see a prescription! Walgreens does not respect a pharmacist's right to choose. I was one of Walgreens' best pharmacists prior to this issue. I had no problem with telling someone when a pharmacist would be available to fill a prescription. I can not fill the prescriptions myself but I try to the best of my ability to not take a side because I want to be able to tell people that this drug can end a life if a woman does have questions. By taking the position I take I find women asking questions. I believe many women wouldn't use this drug if they knew how it can work. If a woman is going to make a real choice as the other side says then the woman needs to have access to both "pro-choice" pharmacist and pro-life pharmacist like myself, so her choice is an informed choice. I pray that by trying to take a neutral position on this issue that some women will listen and some children will live.

The one thing I could not be neutral on is the issue of dispensing. When my three supervisors fired me, I told them "It feels very good knowing that my Faith and Religion is more important to me than a paycheck."

The following is a testimony I gave on a House bill earlier this year [2006].

Testimony

I would like to thank Rep. Granberg for introducing this bill and all members of this committee for giving me the opportunity to speak to you today.

My name is JOHN A. MENGES and I am a licensed pharmacist in the state of Illinois. I am one of the four pharmacists who lost my job with Walgreens for failing to sign an Emergency Contraceptive Policy that violated my religious beliefs. To make things clear to all members of this committee during the 8 months I worked following the Governor's mandate I was not presented with a prescription to fill. During the 3 years I worked at Walgreens I can only recall being presented with prescriptions for this medication 3 times and during that time I estimate that I filled over 71,000 prescriptions.

I am here today because I can not dispense any drug designed to end a human life. Before I enter any discussion of these drugs I would like to try to clarify some terminology. For me human life begins when fertilization occurs. Fertilization is the point at which the sperm penetrates the egg. Life for me is the issue. The redefining of the terms "pregnancy" and "conception" in 1965 by the American College of Obstetricians and Gynecologists only confuse this life issue more. Prior to 1965 "pregnancy" and "conception" began at fertilization when life begins. Now "pregnancy" and "conception" begins at implantation of the embryo in the uterus. This still doesn't negate the fact that embryologists world-wide agree unanimously that human life begins at fertilization. This does explain why the morning after pill is classified as a contraceptive by the FDA and not as an abortafacient and I hope this clarifies why many say this drug doesn't end a pregnancy. Understanding the terminology enables one to realize how confusing the words fertilization, pregnancy, and conception have become. With this very simple explanation of the terminology I want to remind you that the beginning of human life at the point of fertilization is the issue for me. I hold human life at this stage in development with the same respect I hold for any human life.

The drugs I was referring to as I tried to explain some definitions are classified as "emergency contraceptives" by the FDA. Presently "Plan B" also known as the "morning after pill" is the only drug approved to be used for emergency contraception but most oral contraceptives can be dosed to work as emergency contraception. Emergency contraceptive doses are doses that are higher

Menges, John A. "Public Hearing on HB4346 Before the House State Government Administration Committee," Illinois House State Government Administration Committee, February 2006.

than doses of regular birth control. To simplify my discussion of emergency contraceptives I will limit my discussion to "Plan B." Plan B consists of two Progestin tablets containing 0.75 mg of levonorgestrel. The first tablet is to be taken within 72 hours of intercourse and the second tablet 12 hours after the first dose. Without getting into too much detail here the problem I have is the significant post-fertilization mechanism of action by which these drugs work. The mechanisms of action stated in the manufacturers prescribing information include preventing ovulation, altering tubal transport of sperm and/or ova, or inhibiting implantation by altering the endometrium. The time during a woman's menstrual cycle plays an important role in what mechanism of action is at work. The menstrual cycle can last anywhere from 21 to 40 days. Ovulation usually occurs 14 to 15 days before the end of the cycle. If emergency contraception is given early in the cycle it is more likely to prevent ovulation. But during this time ovulation and pregnancy are less likely to occur anyway. As the time for ovulation nears the chance for emergency contraception to prevent ovulation will lessen to the effect that ovulation can occur in some instances after emergency contraception has been taken. Once ovulation has occurred and fertilization has taken place any mechanism that prevents this implantation is the ending of human life.

So what am I doing as a pharmacist if I can't dispense a drug approved by the FDA? Believe me I asked myself this question when the first emergency contraceptive was approved by the FDA in 1998. I was a pharmacy manager in a supermarket pharmacy at the time. My number one priority as pharmacy manager is the same as it is today and that is customer service to my patients. I have always made it known to my employees, supervisors, and patients that I work first for the patient. My employer was a direct beneficiary of this as I always made them look good. The day the first emergency contraceptive was approved I talked with the staff pharmacist who worked with me about his thoughts. Neither of us could dispense emergency contraceptives as it went against everything we believed in. The question I and many pharmacists had to answer was which patient do we serve? Do we serve the women requesting emergency contraceptive or the human life she could be carrying? I could not make a decision to participate in ending any human life so my decision was to refer women and answer any questions they might have if and when the situation arose.

So here I am almost 8 years after the first emergency contraceptives were approved and I can only recall 5 times that I have been faced with prescriptions. Three of those prescriptions I saw while employed with Walgreens. Not that a person can derive any statistical conclusions from 5 prescriptions but I didn't have incident with any of those encounters. In fact I have been thanked for my willingness to talk about emergency contraceptives as many pharmacists avoid the issue. This leads me to the moral issue I read about in different editorials. My choice to step aside and not fill these prescriptions in no way is a reflection of me trying to push my morals on others. It is my upholding my moral beliefs for myself. Our government allows women to make this choice and my actions have never prevented any women from exercising her choice. I have a choice too and my choice is not to dispense any medication that will end a human life. Those are morals that I have to live up to. The people who think I try to push my morals on others need to ask themselves why I dispense medication to patients who have just had an abortion for pain and bleeding. I give these patients the same respect I give every patient. The answers are simple as I went into pharmacy to help people not hurt people. I don't ask questions as to why people need my help because morals don't play a role in my helping people. I went into pharmacy to care for people and help them improve their lives. I love the profession of pharmacy because of all the good I am able to do as a pharmacist. Pharmacy goes beyond the counseling, recommendations and referrals I give. It is much more than my filling prescriptions fast and accurately. It is the respect I give every patient. I listen to my patients and help them when I can. I will never intentionally do any harm to any patient.

On November 28th of last year I lost my job because of my conscience objective to filling a medication that ends human life. My employer fired me for not signing policy asking me to violate my conscience. During the 8 months following the Governor's mandate I was not presented with a prescription to fill. Even though I believe I am currently covered under The Health Care Right of Conscience Act, I would like to ask every member of the house to vote YES on HB 4346. I am one of a small minority of pharmacists in this state who can't fill these medications. By voting YES on HB 4346 you will protect other pharmacists from having to endure what I, my wife, and my 2 children have had to endure these past months. It is difficult to explain my feelings. It hurts.

Without saying anymore I would like to answer any questions members might have. Thank You.

John A. Menges is a licensed pharmacist.

J. Paul Kelleher

Emergency Contraception and Conscientious Objection

Introduction

Emergency contraception (EC)—also known as the morning-after pill—is marketed and sold, under various brand names, in over 100 countries around the world. In some countries, customers can purchase the drug without a prescription. In others, a prescription must be presented to a licensed pharmacist.[1] In virtually all of these countries, pharmacists are the last link in the chain of delivery.

Although the issue has been most prominent in the United States, where family planning products and services are perennial sources of controversy, pharmacists' central role in dispensing EC raises the question of whether they should be granted the legal right to refuse to fill legally prescribed or salable pharmaceuticals when doing so is at odds with their religious or moral convictions. With the arrival in Europe of at least one new and apparently very effective form of EC that is currently under study and consideration for over-the-counter status, pharmacists there may soon have new and more consequential opportunities to impede customer access by refusing to dispense the medication.[2]

In this essay, I shall defend an unconventional answer to the question of whether pharmacists should be granted the right to refuse to dispense EC. The standard answer in the bioethics literature is a qualified yes. This conventional view—sometimes referred to as the moderate view—holds that, at least where pharmacies are plentiful, pharmacists should be granted the legal right to refuse to comply with customers' requests, so long as they refer the customer to another pharmacy where there is a professional willing to dispense the prescribed drugs, and so long as this does not impose an "undue" or "unreasonable" burden on the customer. When redirecting a customer to another pharmacy would be a mere annoyance or slight inconvenience, an objecting pharmacist may protect his or her moral integrity by significantly restricting his or her participation in what is believed to be an immoral or evil act.

Of course, this moderate solution will continue to be strongly rejected by various stakeholders. For example, the pharmacists who claim a right to refuse either wish to avoid complicity in what they view to be serious disregard for human life or else disapprove of nonprocreative sex in general. So these professionals are unlikely to accept a solution that keeps them firmly in the causal chain leading from a woman's desire not to be pregnant to her not being so. Conversely, many women seeking EC will deny the existence of a publicly acceptable rationale for treating them any differently from how other customers are treated; why, they will ask, should the prevailing laws of the land protect *these* refusals, when most would find it absurd to protect a vegan hardware store clerk's refusal to sell fertilizer to a pig farmer, or the refusal of a bookstore clerk to sell travel books to a divorced father known by the clerk to be derelict in his much-needed child support payments? What, if anything, distinguishes these kinds of refusals from those protected by the conventional solution? What could make EC special?

The analysis that follows aims to produce guidance for the formulation of just public policy. It is not, therefore, intended as an exploration of professional duty or virtue. This is in part because there appears to be little support in the bioethics literature of the position I shall defend, namely, that strong antirefusal public policy is a requirement of justice in a liberal democracy. Two extant views do, however, come close to my preferred approach. Julian Savulescu argues that "when conscientious objection compromises the quality, efficiency, or equitable delivery of a [medical] service, it should not be tolerated. The primary goal of a health service is to protect the health of its recipients."[3] But he also grants a prerogative on the part of public policy makers to determine "what kind of health system to deliver."[4] So while *individual* medical professionals should be "punished through removal of license to practice" when their acts of conscience contravene established medical practice, this is because the "place for expression and consideration of different values is at the level of policy relating to public medicine."[5] Thus, even the success of Savulescu's argument would leave open a central question at issue in the debate of conscientious objection in medicine.

The other strongly antirefusal position defended in recent years is that of Robert F. Card. Card, however, deliberately limits himself to a concern with "professional ethical obligations." He therefore remains agnostic on the question of whether his arguments support any particular legal or regulatory measures. Since Card is correct that "not every moral obligation is (or ought to be) codified into law," there is good reason to ask whether his or any other arguments can support public policy mandating that a pharmacist must choose between dispensing EC and removal from his or her position.[6]

While questions concerning the nature of professional duty and virtue are undoubtedly important, I want to go further. For in their roles as citizen legislators, participants in a democracy choose to protect and promote their legitimate interests in various ways. Sometimes this involves creating laws that define inviolable spheres, such as those that protect private property. Sometimes it involves state-sanctioned measures intended to generate investment, spur innovation, and induce participation in a certain enterprise or economic sector. If the relevant fundamental interests are sufficiently important, regulations and requirements will be established alongside educational subsidies, tax breaks, and competition-limiting licensing requirements, in order to ensure congruence between the populace's needs and the operation of the resulting sector. It is therefore important to ask whether there is a sound case in favor of the state's imposing a certain regulatory framework on a profession that serves vital citizen interests. This is true even if there is such a thing as demanding and determinate professional obligations of the sort Card defends. In the end, I will argue that the conventional answer to our public policy question is mistaken; that is, when all publicly relevant interests are given their due, it is *not* acceptable to allow refusals in the big city, where pharmacies abound, but forbid them in the rural countryside, where they are scarce. Rather, there ought to be strong public policy requiring all pharmacists to dispense EC to customers who request it, regardless of the pharmacist's moral or religious objections.

Background

Because it has seen the lion's share of actual pharmacist refusals to dispense EC, I shall use the United States as a case study for what may become increasingly common worldwide. Currently, there is just one product specifically marketed in the United States as EC. This is Barr Laboratories' *Plan B.*[7] After a protracted and politically heated approval process, Plan B was approved by the US Food and Drug Administration (FDA) in August 2006 for over-the-counter sale to women and men 18 years of age or older.[8] Further litigation by reproductive rights advocates led to a March 2009 court order enjoining the FDA to extend over-the-counter access to 17-year-olds.[9] Plan B is now sold over-the-counter at pharmacies by pharmacists and clerks who must verify a prospective buyer's age by inspecting an approved form of identification. (This of course raises further ethical issues concerning access for those who might not have the proper identification, but I shall leave those issues aside in this essay.)[10]

As I have already noted, Plan B and other forms of EC are kinds of "morning-after pill." They should not be confused with *Mifeprex,* also known as RU-486 or "the abortion pill." Mifeprex contains mifepristone and misoprostol and is used to terminate an established pregnancy (defined by the medical community as postimplantation embryonic life). Plan B, by contrast, consists of 1.5 mg of the progestin levonorgestrel (LNG), a synthetic hormone. Studies have shown conclusively that Plan B neither interrupts an established pregnancy nor increases the frequency of fetal abnormalities.[11]

While Plan B does not interfere with established pregnancies, there has been some discord over its specific mechanisms of action. The scientific consensus is that the primary mechanism is that of preventing or postponing ovulation, although many who have moral or religious concerns about EC claim that it can prevent implantation of the fertilized egg into the uterus, thereby preventing pregnancy by depriving the zygote[12] of the environment it needs to survive. Recent clinical data have shown that LNG affects the uterine environment only when it has already acted to inhibit ovulation. So when the uterine environment is affected, it is already highly unlikely that a fertilized egg will encounter that environment.[13]

The effectiveness of EC is expressed as the reduction in a woman's expected chance of becoming pregnant (if she and her partner had used no other form of contraception). So we should read the claim on Plan B's label that it is 89 percent effective like this: "if 100 women had unprotected intercourse once during the second or third week of their cycle and were not treated with ECPs [i.e., emergency contractive pills], about eight would become pregnant. Following treatment with ECPs, only one or two women would become pregnant, a 75 to 89 percent reduction."[14]

While the most recent studies of EC suggest that it can remain effective if started between 73 and 120 hr after intercourse, the effectiveness declines significantly as time passes. Waiting 12 hr to take Plan B decreases its effectiveness rate by 50 percent, with further decreases occurring linearly with time.[15] So health-care providers encourage women to take EC as soon as possible after unprotected intercourse to increase their chances of preventing an unintended pregnancy.

Conscience, Cogency, and Neutrality

A common and necessary first step in any discussion of whether states ought to protect a pharmacist who refuses to dispense certain medications is to address the possibility of damning similarities to white service providers who refuse to serve black customers. Reflection on these racist refusals quickly reveals that there is no unqualified right to act on one's conscience. Still, many more questions are generated by this revealing example than are closed by it. For example, are we entitled to dismiss claims grounded in racist convictions because such convictions are at bottom utterly false and morally odious? Or must the state refrain from evaluating the ultimate validity of the racist's attitudes, and base its stance instead on independent facts about the potential harm to very weighty interests of those whose lives would be affected were racists permitted to act as their conscience dictates? And even if the state is permitted to impose laws based on the premise that racist beliefs are utterly false, could just laws ever be predicated on the premise that a certain religious or moral belief is false?

I believe that, in general, ordinary moral thinking and academic scholarship come down on the same sides on these questions: they hold, first, that the state may legitimately declare racist beliefs false and may properly invoke this stance in a sound justification of antidiscrimination legislation; second, they hold that a just state must refuse even to take up the question of whether any specific religion, religion as such, or even irreligion is true or false. This is the general outlook embodied in the familiar ideal of the separation of church and state. True, this ideal remains nebulous at the margins. Still, it plausibly entails that the state should remain neutral both among religions and between religion and irreligion. It therefore seems to commit its proponents to the view that highly contested metaphysical convictions should play no substantive role in the justification of public policy. Of course, not everyone is a proponent. But separation of church and state is a widely held position in favor of which much can be said.

Unfortunately, accepting this position would again seem to make resolving the issue of pharmacists and EC all the more difficult. For in the case of racist professionals, the patent falsity of the underlying beliefs could be combined with facts about the potential harm to minorities' interests to yield a determinate and cogent policy solution. Since minorities are full-fledged citizens, and since false racist convictions have no standing and so no claim to accommodation, many race-related policy choices have clear answers. But if the state is debarred from basing its policy decisions in other areas on its best judgment regarding the truth or falsity of the moral or religious belief underlying a claim of conscience, then it is unclear how relevant the analogy involving the racist professional is, let alone how reasonable it is to hope for a determinate solution to the EC issue. How can we know what kinds of accommodation to accord religious and metaphysical convictions if we must remain neutral on the question of their cogency?

One answer that has been offered seeks to replace the cogency of the proposition believed with the sincerity of the believer. In their essay on pharmacists' refusals to fill EC prescriptions, Eva and Hugh LaFollette argue first against an unqualified right to conscientious refusal and then go on to state conditions under which a *qualified* right might exist. Drawing parallels with the procedure for winning exemption from military conscription owing to one's conscientious objection to war, the LaFollettes say that a pharmacist claiming an exemption should establish "the plausibility, sincerity and centrality of [his or her] beliefs."[16] Assume for now that proving sincerity and centrality are indeed conditions for winning such an exemption. What about plausibility? Consider a religiously motivated refusal. At first blush, the plausibility condition seems to put the state in precisely the position that the conventional church/state doctrine sought to avoid. When a conscientious objection is religiously based, do the LaFollettes really wish to have the state evaluate an exemption claim by ruling on the plausibility of its religious foundations? In fact, they do not. When they flesh out what they mean by "plausibility," it is clear they mean something more like "plausible-sounding to the agent":

> Not all conscience is created equal; not all conscience should be treated equally. Conscience differs in several relevant ways . . . [One is] Plausibility: Can she explain and offer a plausible justification for her belief *or is she just parroting the views of others?*[17]

Here, the test of plausibility appears to concern the agent's ability to cite what she takes to be reasons supporting *her own* view. Whether they are good reasons appears irrelevant. Later, the condition of plausibility is linked to "giv[ing] a clear rationale for [one's] beliefs."[18] This suggests that the LaFollettes, like most citizens and philosophers, do not want legislatures and tribunals judging the substantive merits of highly contentious beliefs when conflicts between conscience and medicine arise. A careful accounting of the agent's belief system seems to be enough for them.

In contrast, the LaFollettes are plausibly more permissive with regard to certain other beliefs, claiming that "If someone said that she was conscientiously opposed to feeding their children or stopping at traffic lights, then, barring some powerful explanation, we would not think that they are forwarding moral beliefs, no matter how sincerely uttered."[19] Here, the LaFollettes appear in step with the views of ordinary folk: some beliefs (such as racist beliefs) can be dismissed out of hand, while others, regardless of their truth or falsity, cannot be dismissed, and this is sometimes owing to the complex reasons behind the church/state separation doctrine and its extension to various other nonreligious metaphysical views.

Consider now one line of questioning that the LaFollettes envisage being pressed by a government tribunal charged with testing the sincerity of refusals. In the case of pharmacists who refuse to dispense EC on the ground that it implicates them in killing another human, the LaFollettes suggest that the tribunal be guided by the principle that "barring a convincing argument, these pharmacists should also oppose capital punishment and modern warfare, because 90 percent of the casualties are civilians."[20] Putting the issue of the practicality of such tribunals aside for now, we must ask: where would this intellectual cross-examination end? What would constitute a "convincing argument"? After all, plausibility does not entail truth. And if tribunals can go this far in demanding a thoughtful and consistent rationale for pharmacists' views on EC and just war, why can they not pose the problem of evil to those who base their objections on explicitly religious grounds, refusing to grant exemptions for those who cannot marshal a convincing argument for the existence of a benevolent God in a world full of unthinkable and seemingly unnecessary suffering?

I believe that these problems reveal serious flaws in the moderate view to which the LaFollettes appear sympathetic. In contrast, a strong antirefusal position would avoid the need for tribunals, and thus the need to define the limitations to their lines of questioning. Of course, most proponents of the antirefusal stance nevertheless wish to protect religious liberty, so any vindication of a strong antirefusal view will have to explain why it does not unduly restrict that liberty. I address this issue a bit later. I shall first turn to a few other arguments that have been put forward as elements of a successful resolution to this debate. Showing why these arguments fail will clear the way for my preferred approach, which favors a strong antirefusal position.

Doing, Allowing, and the Need for Substantive Moral Analysis

Consider Robert F. Card's claim that the moderate view is fatally unstable. Recall what this view says: pharmacists have the right to refuse when, and only when, they are willing to refer the customer to another willing professional, and when this does not impose an undue or unreasonable burden on the customer. Card, quite correctly, notes that replacing a duty to dispense with a duty to refer "does not remove the pharmacist from the causal chain of events that leads to the use of EC, an act that is considered morally wrong by such objecting pharmacists."[21] Since it is this causal complicity that troubles these pharmacists, replacing the one duty with the other will not allay their worries.

This is certainly a difficult obstacle for the moderate position to overcome. Card claims that taking up this challenge will require the moderate to defend "an intrinsic moral distinction between 'doing' and 'allowing,'" since "a staunch defender of pharmacists" right to conscientious objection . . . sees no ethical difference between dispensing the medication herself and allowing another willing pharmacist to do so."[22] Card then claims that proponents of the moderate position have failed to justify the distinction between doing and allowing, and so therefore seem forced to choose between the two options that do not presuppose the validity of that distinction, namely, allowing all refusals and allowing none of them. But surely this account of the troubled pharmacist's mind-set is inaccurate. For it seems clear that objecting pharmacists themselves embrace the moral difference between doing and allowing. If they did not, they would take themselves to have the same and as much reason to interfere with another pharmacist's dispensing EC as they do to refrain from dispensing it themselves. Yet the pharmacist who quits her job because she is forced to dispense EC does not then take herself to have *as good and as strong* a reason to interfere with third party transactions. Of course, she is likely to think she has *some* reason either to do this or else to act politically to effect a change in policy that constrains third parties. But these will not be precisely the same reasons that led her to quit her job, if only because in staying in her job, the person dispensing EC would have been *her*. The purported equivalence between doing and allowing would entail that anti-EC pharmacists are, by their own lights, morally required to dispense EC if this would lead to the frustration of two additional requests by two other customers at two other pharmacies. (This could happen if, contrary to fact, the amount of EC dispensed is determined by clients' weight and if all pharmacies drew from the same, limited stock. Then, dispensing EC to an obese woman could deplete the available supply, thereby ensuring that two other customers' requests go unmet.) Many objecting pharmacists would, however, show differential concern to avoid their own involvement in wrongdoing, as when they choose to feed and clothe their own children instead of sending the money to an organization that could use the same amount of money to feed and clothe two (or more) other neglected children.

So proving that there is a morally significant distinction between doing and allowing cannot be the key to vindicating the moderate view, since the objecting pharmacist's complaint presupposes the validity of that distinction. Her complaint is precisely that by referring, she is *doing* something immoral, not merely *allowing* it to happen. Those who wish to require objecting pharmacists to refer but not to dispense must, therefore, identify the morally significant difference that could justify granting an exemption from actively filling the latter causal role but not from actively filling the former.

Perhaps, the difference derives from the fact that, sometimes, rationales that favor adopting distal causal roles over more proximate ones stem from purely psychological considerations. Consider a political activist who cannot stomach joining one of the two (in his view) viciously compromised major parties, but who realizes that one is much better than the other on the issues that matter most to him. He may decide that while he just cannot stomach campaigning vocally for the better party's presidential nominee, he can bring himself to hold his nose and write a sizable check to the nominee's campaign. Morally speaking, it may be that there is no significant difference between these two types of contribution. But it may be morally relevant that one type is preferred because of its smaller psychological footprint.

This line of thought is unlikely to sway an objecting pharmacist. Since what is at issue is causal complicity in a perceived seriously wrongful act, contemplation of the result at the end of the causal chain will likely cast a dark pall on all intermediate causes, not simply those closest to the dreaded effect. So proponents of the conventional view cannot appeal to the possibility of a psychological difference in holding that it is wrong to force pharmacists to dispense all drugs directly, but permissible to force them to issue referrals for all drugs they refuse to dispense. But then if the moral distinction is not grounded in psychological facts, what could be its source?

One possible answer is that unlike the case of the political activist, there is an objective moral difference between facilitation and direct involvement. This answer, however, threatens to tie the moderate's hands, and for familiar reasons. In order to determine the moral similarities and differences between two courses of action, and thus in order to determine which is worse, it seems we must have a substantive assessment of the moral nature of each. Yet there is no moral content-neutral way to determine the relative badness or wrongness of two alternatives. But then which perspective shall we take up for the purposes of this evaluation? From the perspective of many objecting pharmacists, the moral gravity of each is determined by explicitly religious or otherwise socially contested metaphysical propositions. From the perspective of state officials wishing to remain agnostic on the merits of religious or metaphysical outlooks, the result will be a wholly different evaluative comparison. And yet there seems to be no escaping the need to rely on *some* substantive moral analysis of the various needs and interests centrally affected by any policy decision in this area. A detailed causal description does not suffice.

For further confirmation of this methodological need, assume for the moment that the state may legitimately recognize pharmaceutically induced zygote-interference as a morally bad consequence. Then, a defender of both the moderate view and the strong antirefusal view might argue that if (1) EC only rarely has this effect, (2) many attempts to purchase EC are by women who simply want it on hand should they need it, and (3) some woman who do take the pills would not have become pregnant anyway, then there is a *de minimis* probability that dispensing EC inserts a pharmacist into a causal chain ending with what is *ex hypothesis* a morally bad outcome.[23] As Card is quick to point out, virtually *every* human action has this probability, and it would be absurd to hold that every one of these actions should not be performed because of such remote possibilities.

Still, it does not follow from the fact that the odds of a bad result are minuscule that an action having those odds is (even *pro tanto*) permissible. Even if a gun was outfitted with a million (or more) chambers and just one bullet, it would still be wrong to point it into a crowd and pull the trigger. Clearly, if anything separates this case from the case of implantation-blocking EC, it is the fact that relevant, legitimate, and morally powerful interests conspire to render pulling the trigger impermissible, while rendering dispensing or taking EC permissible. Just as one increases others' risk of injury and death by legitimately driving one's car, so too might one permissibly increase the risk to a zygote by dispensing a legal medication to a reasonable and autonomous third party while on the job. Whether this is in fact permissible, and whether it is permissible legally to require such dispensation, depends evidently on how the totality of legitimate and relevant interests interact to yield a certain moral conclusion about this particular policy. Thus, even if Card's reduction against the argument invoking a real probability of harm does very little work on its own, reflection on it points us again to the need carefully to assess the substantive interests relevant to the state's decision on this issue.

Monopoly and Compensation

Although the moderate view does not fall to Card's arguments, it has also proven difficult to vindicate. Let us, then, consider another standard move that proponents of the moderate position make in defense of their view. This line often begins with an argument *supporting* a *prima facie* right to refuse. Then, the argument proceeds via the claim that, in many cases, pharmacists' *prima facie* right fails to rise to all things considered right because "the pharmacist is in a privileged position vis-à-vis potential clients."[24] As Elizabeth Fenton and Loren Lomasky put it:

> The institutional structure within which pharmacy is practiced has advantaged one party, and that advantage is secured to some extent at the expense of the other . . . [W]e claim that some limitation of pharmacists' right to choose their clients is justifiable compensation to that clientele for having their own domain of choice limited [through licensing and other regulations that restrict the options of clients by limiting pharmacists' competition].[25]

Since pharmacists benefit from the monopoly-, cartel-, or guild-like status conferred on their profession by the state, and since this scheme itself limits the freedom of clients to enter into pharmacy-related interactions with others, it is reasonable to restrict the right of pharmacists to choose with whom they interact—and this is a matter of compensatory justice.

Fenton and Lomasky are quick to point out that the compensation is owed not by the pharmacy profession to its clients, as if the former were being punished for a wrong they had perpetrated on the latter. Rather, compensation is owed *by the state* to patrons of pharmacies as a means of ensuring that the "distribution of burdens and benefits [of regulatory policy is rendered] more acceptable."[26] This means that the moderate's position follows not from an ideal of reciprocity between the two groups, but from an ideal of *evenhandedness* on the part of policy makers and, ultimately, the populace of a representative democracy. Unfortunately, this solution runs afoul of a problem familiar from attempts in ethics and political philosophy to work out the demands of reciprocity. This is the difficult problem of articulating a criterion of equitability in benefits.

It is true that pharmacists receive a "shield from competition" from the state. But on the other side of the coin is the fact that clients receive the benefit of "protection from unqualified practitioners and [their] own uninformed or impulsive predilections."[27] What, then, is the basis for saying that the benefits and burdens of pharmacy laws and regulations are unjust or inequitable? By way of analogy, imagine the following discussion and ultimate agreement between two acquaintances. "Hello Bill, it's John. Look, I need some help moving Wednesday. I know you're on a deadline with your freelance writing, but it might be worth your while. I've been told that I can hire help for US$200 per day, but I'd prefer to spend the day with a friend." "Sounds OK to me, John. I suppose I can just work longer on my article on Thursday. There is one catch, however. My wife is pregnant. If she happens to go into labor, I'll need to leave. You'll probably want to prorate my compensation, but I have to insist on a guaranteed US$200 for the day." "OK, that's fine. I really want you to help, and I'll take my chances that your kid can wait until Thursday! See you Wednesday."

Are these terms equitable, or not? Each receives a benefit that is important to him, and which seems worth the cost incurred (lost money for one and lost time for freelance work for the other). Yet one acquires a freedom that the other does not: Bill has a qualified right to refuse to work, whereas John has no right to refuse to pay. Is this unfair? One might argue that it is on the ground that Bill took advantage of John. In order to avoid exploitation, Bill should have agreed to lesser pay for less than full work. But this is unpersuasive. The existence of perfectly decent alternative options for John forecloses the possibility that Bill exploited him. In going in for the deal, John took a chance, one that was evidently worth it to him to take. I can see nothing, then, that suggests these terms are not equitable.

The point here is not that this imaginary scenario and the choice over EC policy are exactly parallel. They are not. For one thing, I am primarily concerned with the issue of justified state legislation, not with the sort of private bargaining central to the story. This might suggest that there is no analogue in the EC case to the element in the story that leads to the seemingly fair arrangement between Bill and John. In the latter case, the imbalance is voluntarily agreed to; in the former, it is imposed and backed by the coercive force of the state. But to conclude that this difference impugns the "liberty imbalance"[28] in the EC case would be to ignore the very argument that moderates like Fenton and Lomasky offer in favor of the *prima facie* right of pharmacists to refuse. Let me explain.

While it may be true that bargaining of the sort seen in the interaction between Bill and John should play a very small role in the context of democratic legislation, there are nevertheless *structural* similarities between the two domains that are instructive and morally revealing. In the bargaining case, few would think that benefits and burdens were inequitable if Bill had simply accepted the job for US$200, sans neonatal exemption. For as I have noted, we can point to nothing in this bargain that could taint the resulting agreement. But then, it is difficult to find a reason to impugn the *further bargaining* that leads to Bill's escape clause. Likewise, Fenton and Lomasky offer little defense of their claim that the path of democratic governance that leads to the establishment of a guild of pharmaceutical gatekeepers is a path to inequitable benefits. Far from identifying a problematic imbalance, their account of the genesis of the pharmacy profession shows only that different groups get different things out of the arrangement. In this, things are rather similar to the case of Bill and John. Just as the legitimacy-conferring qualities of a situation of fair bargaining are preserved even when Bill insists on and wins his exemption, so too might a policy permitting pharmacists to refuse be the result of *further workings of a reasonably just and morally insightful system of democratic governance*. This would be the case if that system gives moral arguments a fair hearing and if the *prima facie* right to refuse is as well-founded as Lomasky and Fenton assume. We would then have no clear reason to conclude that the "extra" freedom won by Bill through bargaining is any more legitimate than the extra freedom granted to pharmacists by the combination of democratic regulation of pharmaceuticals and the recognition of a strongly supported *prima facie* right to refuse.

I am therefore not persuaded that the liberty imbalance introduced by democratic governance calls for any *compensation* whatsoever. If there are further constraints that should be incorporated into a system of pharmaceutical regulation that already benefits each stakeholder group far above what they would have received without regulation, these will not emerge from the sort of moral bookkeeping Fenton and Lomasky employ. For one thing, it is inherently problematic—and perhaps impossible—to weigh vastly different benefits on the same scale. Yet even when there *are* clear departures from equality in benefits, these may be unimpeachable, as in when they are the result of either fair bargaining or legitimate democratic governance. So a story highlighting the protection from competition accorded to pharmacists fails to establish even a *prima facie* right to compensation on behalf of their customers. This means that the proper response to an evident liberty imbalance must be guided by further substantive moral analysis and not merely by the tallying up of each side of the moralist's ledger.

Voluntarily Incurred Obligations

Building on their claims that pharmacists have a "liberty right"[29] of conscientious refusal and that pharmaceutical regulation generates a liberty imbalance that favors pharmacists and calls for compensation, Fenton and Lomasky proceed to argue that "a nuanced response to moral disagreement" will often lead to a geographically relative policy permitting (to use their examples) refusals in New York City but forbidding them in rural Kansas. This hybrid line "may be as good as any way to respond to all the interests at stake."[30] It is now time to assess those substantive interests, since this is what I have repeatedly said is the crux of the issue. I am not convinced that pharmacists possess anything approaching a liberty right to refuse to dispense legally available medicines. Nor do I believe that previous attempts to solve this issue have treated women's interests with the respect and concern they warrant.

I have already noted some of the difficulties involved in determining when a right to conscientious objection is genuine. Where is a moderate to draw the line between allowable rationales for refusals and rationales that miss the mark? How does the proponent of the strong pro-refusal line justify burdening women in order to accommodate moral, metaphysical, or religious convictions that many others do not share and which are in any case already ignored or overridden by public policy that makes the drugs legal in the first place?

While Fenton and Lomasky seem content (at least for the sake of their argument) to accommodate conscientious objections founded upon "even eccentric moral stances,"[31] we have encountered reasons to require much more discrimination than they provide guidance for. Just as no rights to refuse are possessed by real estate agents who do not want to sell a house to an interracial couple, no matter how strongly rooted in, say, an eccentric religious faith, no right exists simply because a service provider disagrees with the personal moral choices a client might make in his daily life. A feminist pharmacist may not refuse to dispense a nonemergency product (for a skin rash, say) simply because the customer runs a legal pornographic website which she (rightly) believes to be immorally degrading toward women. Yet even in the midst of secure convictions such as this, it is not an easy task to uncover the necessary publicly acceptable standard that rationales for refusals must meet. Such difficulties are evident in Kent Greenawalt's attempt to articulate one sort of moderate view. In the course of his argument, Greenawalt grants that it may well be permissible to allow a nurse anesthetist to refuse on religious grounds to assist in a reproductive sterilization. Yet he also holds that a nurse who refuses to assist in elective plastic surgery on the ground that "attempts to revise the aging process [are] a sin against God's creation" would, for the purposes of public policy, possess "less than a conscientious objection."[32] But what could make the difference in these cases? It cannot lie in the fervency with which the beliefs are held, as we can easily imagine that each nurse's convictions are held with equal zeal. Nor can the difference be found in the extent to which the view is embraced by other members of society. For why should numbers justify here, if they do not justify the state's establishment of the religion favored by the majority? And as we have seen, some of the reasons counting against the establishment of a state religion also count against granting rights to refuse that hinge essentially on substantive evaluations of the plausibility of the religious outlook from which they emerge. So is Greenawalt claiming that a right to free religious expression *as such*—in contrast with a right to the free exercise of *this* or *that* religion—entails a right to refuse assistance with sterilizations but not assistance with plastic surgery? It is difficult to see how these divergent determinations could be common implications of a single and coherent civil libertarian outlook embodying neither a preference for this or that religion, nor a preference for religion or irreligion as such.

Once we realize that not just any claim to conscience is publicly acceptable and that not every restriction of a citizen's set of options is unjust, we will see that it is insufficient simply to assert, as Greenawalt does, that "there is a powerful reason not to force people to choose between offending their consciences and foregoing a major vocational option."[33] For just as there may be no publicly acceptable rationale for according moral weight to a given invocation of conscience, there may be nothing wrong with "forcing" citizens to make Greenawalt's choice. By way of analogy, there seems nothing in principle wrong with requiring at least one parent in a household to choose between spending more quality time with his or her children and working eight hours a day, five days a week, for a living wage or salary. But if we are willing to "force" parents to make *this* choice between a decent wage and more time with their children, then in saying that a pharmacist should not have to make *her* choice between dispensing EC and a life as a nonpharmacist, we would be saying that a life as a nonpharmacist is a greater deprivation than 4,680 fewer nonfatigued hours spent with one's child (using the arbitrary measure of one extra hour per weekday until the child is 18 years old). I conjecture that very few are willing to say this.[34]

Since we are in urgent need of a way to rule on different claims to conscience without having to rule on the truth or falsity of this or that fundamental worldview, we seek bases for refusals that can appeal to arguments that could be offered by those who differ in their beliefs concerning many fundamental religious and metaphysical issues. Public policy that utilizes only secular grounds available to all has been plausibly held to provide a firm basis for civic respect, respect for those of differing faiths (or no faith at all), the protection of religious freedom, and the protection of religious minorities. Of course, such protections will be justified only if it is permissible for the state to recognize the importance that religion has in the lives of many conscientious citizens of goodwill. And this is indeed something a liberal state should acknowledge. But we must not confuse this acknowledgment with the claim that any given religion should survive or thrive, since this is precisely what is denied by many other conscientious citizens. This suggests that the only acceptable rationale available is the importance of protecting the free exercise of religion or conscience *as such*, given the importance this has in the lives of so many of our fellow citizens. Yet in that case, we will need an argument showing that society deprives a pharmacist of adequate freedom to express her religious convictions, or to act on her conscience, if a job she *voluntarily* pursues or holds—to the exclusion of many other viable career paths—requires her to dispense EC. This seems a difficult case to make.

Women's Interests and the Case Against Refusals

We must now address the burdens that would be imposed upon women who wish to procure EC from objecting pharmacists. Fenton and Lomasky suggest that the very project of identifying the relevant burdens faced by women may be problematic given that such pharmacists insist "that it is the nascent human life that is in dire jeopardy, not the prospective mother."[35] Yet this line of thought is misguided because it encourages evenhandedness between conflicting parties simply because each party's conviction has a mirror image emanating from the other's worldview. When the political admissibility of a worldview is itself questionable, mirror images might not in fact deadlock political deliberation. I have already explained why the pharmacist's claims should not be given the unscrutinized weight in liberal political argument that they so often receive in the moderate's framework. On the other side, however, we have women's clearly relevant interests in reproductive autonomy and in having access to a safe medication that can obviate the need to undergo an invasive surgical procedure. These are likely to be the very considerations that justified the state's regulatory approval of the drug in the first place. Other such considerations likely include the plausible and widely held—yet hardly dispositive—conviction that even if EC did work by interfering with zygote implantation, that which is interfered with is not yet a person, but instead a microscopic mass of cells without significant moral status.[36] EC is legal because it safely permits women to exercise autonomy over their reproductive future and to avoid the need for abortions by ingesting medication that interferes with microscopic entities inside their own bodies. For all these reasons, EC would be a great advance in women's reproductive freedom and autonomy, *even if* it worked only by blocking implantation. Since it works primarily by blocking *fertilization*, its appeal should be all the stronger among those who are duly sensitive to the interests of women.

Reproductive autonomy is not only an important moral value, it is also widely seen as a deeply personal one. Decisions to conceive are often made between partners who often keep them as closely guarded secrets for months, sometimes years. Similarly, attempts to prevent a pregnancy, especially after intercourse, are very often not shared with anyone. So when there is a possibility that a trip to the pharmacy will result in a refusal or public confrontation, many women will find it too emotionally difficult to go through with. Others who request the drug but are denied will suffer further panic and dread as the likelihood that EC will work decreases rapidly as time passes. We therefore cannot say, as many moderates wish to, that when a reasonably prompt referral is possible, refusals are matters of mere inconvenience to a client. For some women, the prospect of denial will lead them to *never become a client* in the first place; for others, each moment that passes will raise the chances of an unintended pregnancy. This may or may not be the stuff of emergencies, but these are not negligible costs of convenience, either. And in a context in which claims to conscience are given the scrutiny they deserve, they will often be decisive.

Conclusion

The era of women's reproductive autonomy is but a miserably small fraction of human history. And despite continuing advances in the right direction, the persistent threat of rape and sexual assault appears impossible to eliminate.[37] In this essay, I have tried to show that the debate over EC and conscience has seen far too many bald invocations of the demands of conscience or religious freedom and far too little consideration of the freedom of women to exercise control over their reproductive future in a liberal society that remains properly agnostic on highly contestable metaphysical and religious convictions. Because cogent, publicly acceptable rationales for the strong antirefusal position pose no significant threat to a fully adequate scheme of religious liberty or freedoms of conscience, and because the moderate and pro-refusal views do threaten women's reproductive autonomy, pharmacists should be forced to choose between dispensing EC and finding another way to make a living.[38]

Notes

1. The Associated Press, "New morning-after pill ellaOne works up to five days," (January 29, 2010).
2. Faculty of Sexual and Reproductive Healthcare, Royal College of Obstetricians and Gynecologists, "New product review: Ulipristal acetate (ellaOne)," www.ffprhc.org.uk/admin/uploads/ellaOneNewProductReview1009.pdf (October 2009).
3. Julian Savulescu, "Conscientious objection in medicine," *British Medical Journal* 332, 7536 (2006): 294–297, p. 296.
4. Savulescu, op. cit., p. 297.
5. Savulescu, op. cit., p. 296.
6. Robert F. Card, "Conscientious objection and emergency contraception," *The American Journal of Bioethics* 7, 6 (2007): 8–14, p. 9.
7. While sale of generic forms of the original two-pill version of Plan B began in August 2009, the Food and Drug Administration recently approved for sale Barr Laboratories' one-dose version called *Plan B One-Step*. See "FDA approves new Plan B labeling," *Wall Street Journal* (July 14, 2009).
8. No research evidence was offered for the age restriction, suggesting it was a move in concert with the initial rejection, which later investigation revealed to be based in part on FDA's Deputy Operations Commissioner's personal concerns about "extreme promiscuous behaviors such as the medication taking on an 'urban legend' status that would lead adolescents to form sex-based cults centered around the use of Plan B". See L. L. Wynn, Joanna N. Erdman, Angel M. Foster, & James Trussell, "Harm reduction or women's rights?" *Studies in Family Planning* 38, 4 (2007): 253–267, p. 254.
9. Wynn *et al.*, op. cit.
10. Because EC is now available without a prescription in the United States, I will often refer to pharmacists' refusal to dispense legally available medications, as opposed to their refusal

to fill valid prescriptions. I do not think anything important turns on a legal drug's over-the-counter status, and I therefore believe that my conclusion in the EC case also generates implications for medications that require prescriptions.

11. James Trussell & Elizabeth G. Raymond, "Emergency contraception," http://ec.princeton.edu/questions/ec-review.pdf (May 2008), p. 5; Frank Davidoff & James Trussell, "Plan B and the politics of doubt," *Journal of the American Medical Association* 296, 14 (2006): 1775–1778, p. 1776.
12. Technically a zygote (fertilized egg) becomes a blastocyst in the days immediately preceding implantation. Assuming that the reader is more familiar with the term "zygote," I will continue to use it to refer to the product of fertilization that may or may not implant in the uterine wall.
13. M. Durand, M. Seppala, M. Cravioto, H. Koistinen, R. Koistinen, J. González-Macedo, & F. Larrea, "Late follicular phase administration of levonorgestrel as an emergency contraceptive," *Contraception* 71, 6 (2005): 451–457, p. 455.
14. Felicia H. Stewart, James Trussell, & Paul F.A. Van Look, "Emergency contraception," in R.A. Hatcher, *et al.* (eds) *Contraceptive Technologies* (New York: Ardent Media, 2004), pp. 279–303, p. 286.
15. Rebecca H. Allen & Alisa B. Goldberg, "Emergency contraception: A clinical review," *Clinical Obstetrics and Gynecology* 50,4 (2007): 927–936, at p. 930; Davidoff & Trussell, op. cit., p. 1775; Stewart, Trussell, & Van Look, op. cit., p. 287.
16. Eva LaFollette & Hugh LaFollette, "Private consciences, public acts," *Journal of Medical Ethics* 33 (2007): 249–254, p. 250.
17. LaFollette & LaFollette, op. cit., p. 249 (emphasis added).
18. LaFollette & LaFollette, op. cit., p. 250.
19. LaFollette & LaFollette, op. cit., p. 252.
20. LaFollette & LaFollette, op. cit., p. 251.
21. Card, op. cit., p. 9.
22. Card, op. cit.
23. Card, op. cit., p. 11; LaFollette & LaFollette, op. cit., p. 252.
24. Elizabeth Fenton & Loren Lomasky, "Dispensing with liberty: Conscientious refusal and the 'morning-after pill,'" *Journal of Medicine and Philosophy* 30 (2005): 579–592, p. 585.
25. Fenton & Lomasky, op. cit.
26. Fenton & Lomasky, op. cit., p. 586.
27. Fenton & Lomasky, op. cit., pp. 585, 586.
28. Fenton & Lomasky, op. cit., p. 588.
29. Fenton & Lomasky, op. cit., p. 580.
30. Fenton & Lomasky, op. cit., p. 589.
31. Fenton & Lomasky, op. cit., p. 583.
32. Kent Greenawalt, "Objections in conscience to medical procedures: Does religion make a difference?," *University of Illinois Law Review* 4 (2006): 799–825, p. 821.
33. Greenawalt, op. cit., p. 820.
34. Additionally, we do not think we must exempt objecting pharmacists from (any portion of) their tax liability on the ground that these monies are used to sustain a legal system that permits behavior they deem morally odious. Yet the imposition of tax liabilities is backed by the coercive apparatus of the state: those who do not pay may suffer serious penalties. Why, then, must the state exempt pharmacists from fulfilling an obligation they voluntarily incur through the free choice of their occupation, when it does not exempt them from an obligation they must discharge on pain of state coercion? If free exercise of religion and conscience is not threatened in the coercive context of taxation, why is it threatened in the voluntary occupational context?
35. Fenton & Lomasky, op. cit., p. 583. It is also interesting to note that while Fenton and Lomasky are quick to grant a *prima facie* right to pharmacists protecting them from being forced to dispense EC, they show much more reluctance in acknowledging that women who are refused EC and become pregnant are forced to incur an especially morally salient fate: "Note also that failure to receive emergency contraceptive services does not amount to infliction of mandatory motherhood; conception may not have occurred, and, whatever the wishes of the pharmacist, subsequent abortion is available if pregnancy does in fact eventuate" (p. 582).
36. For a persuasive argument against this conviction that in another context would call for a sustained response, see Don Marquis, "Why abortion is immoral," *The Journal of Philosophy* 86, 4 (1989): 183–202. As I go on to note, the specific mechanism of action of EC helps us to largely bypass critiques such as Marquis's "future like ours" account of moral status. For while it seems to make sense to say "I was once a zygote," it seems bizarre to say "I was once a gamete." So it is much less clear that even a successful sperm has "being a human" in its future. By blocking fertilization instead of implantation, EC helps us block the relevance

of arguments designed to show that an early zygote has the same moral status as a normal person. Still, the legitimate and powerful interests of women that I describe in the text would be eminently relevant to an argument claiming that pharmacists should be required to dispense EC even if it did work by blocking the implantation of a fertilized egg. Think here again of the risk of death we impose on others by driving our car. If the risk is small enough, and if the interests on the other side weighty enough, then there may well be nothing wrong with actions that carry a predictable risk of bad outcomes. (Here I'm assuming for the sake of argument that the destruction of a zygote is a bad outcome.) Since the pharmacist has a choice in whether or not she will (continue to) be materially involved in the events that create such risks, the arguments I present place the burden back on her to explain why she should not have to dispense EC as part of her voluntarily held job.

37. In the context of my broader argument, the fact of rape lends considerable support to a policy requiring all hospitals—including Catholic hospitals—to carry, offer, and dispense EC to all patients who show signs of sexual assault.
38. For very helpful comments on previous versions of this essay, I would like to thank Katrien Devolder, Elizabeth Fenton, Beth Jordan, Ann McCall, and Richard W. Miller.

J. Paul Kelleher is an associate professor in the Department of Medical History and Bioethics at the University of Wisconsin-Madison.

EXPLORING THE ISSUE

Should Pro-Life Health Providers Be Allowed to Deny Prescriptions on the Basis of Conscience?

Critical Thinking and Reflection

1. Why might refusal to dispense morning-after pills lead to a "slippery slope"?
2. Should health providers ever have the right to refuse to provide medical care or dispense medications they do not support?
3. What problems might develop if pharmacists have the right to refuse to fill all prescriptions?

Is There Common Ground?

In the years since Roe v. Wade, state and federal legislatures have seen a growth in conscience clauses. Many pro-choice advocates perceive these clauses as another way to limit a woman's right to choose. Within weeks of the *Roe* decision in the early 1970s, Congress adopted legislation that permitted individual health-care providers receiving Federal funding or working for organizations receiving such funding to refuse to perform or assist in performing abortions or sterilizations if these procedures violated their moral or religious beliefs. The provision also prohibited discrimination against these providers because of the refusal to perform abortions or sterilizations. Currently, 45 states allow health-care providers to refuse to be involved in abortions. Also, 12 states allow health-care providers to refuse to provide sterilization, while 13 states allow providers to refuse to provide contraceptive services or information related to contraception.

Pharmacists who refuse to fill prescriptions for birth control pills or emergency contraception largely believe that these medications are actually a method of abortion. In a paper published in the *Archives of Family Medicine* (2000), physicians Walter Larimore and Joseph B. Stanford stated that birth control pills have the potential of interrupting development of the fertilized egg after fertilization. Emergency contraception or the morning-after pill also has been seen as a means of abortion. It prevents pregnancy by either preventing fertilization or preventing implantation of a fertilized egg in the uterus. The morning-after pill is often confused with RU-486 which is clearly a method of abortion. Unlike RU-486, emergency contraception cannot disrupt an established pregnancy and cannot cause an abortion. Clearly, better education about the methods of action of these drugs would be valuable. Solutions have been proposed to enable patients to receive the drugs prescribed by their physicians. As a rule, it would make sense for pharmacists who will not dispense a drug to have an obligation to meet their customers' needs by referring them to other pharmacies. Pharmacists who object to filling prescriptions for birth control pills or emergency contraception might ensure that there is a pharmacist on duty who will fill the prescription or refer their customers elsewhere.

In some countries, customers can purchase the drug without a prescription. In the United States, a prescription can only be filled by a licensed pharmacist. As a result, pharmacists are the last link in the chain of delivery. The author believes it is not acceptable to allow refusals in urban areas where pharmacies are plentiful, but forbid them in rural settings, where pharmacies are scarce. Rather, there should be strong public policy requiring that all pharmacists dispense emergency contraception to customers who request it, regardless of pharmacists' moral or religious objections. In "Claims of Conscience: Setting the Ground Rules When Rights Collide," *Humanist*, September/October 2009 the author discusses right of conscience claims, which allow pharmacists to refuse to fill morning-after pill prescriptions. The author notes that these claims can be taken too far. It takes a results-oriented approach to the ethical argument so that if another pharmacist is available to fill the legal prescription, it would allow a conscience refusal but not otherwise. See also "*Pharmacist* conscience *clauses* and access to oral contraceptives," (*Journal of Medical Ethics,* July 2008). This paper examines the *pharmacists'* role and their professional and moral obligations to patients in the light of recent *refusals* by *pharmacists* to dispense oral contraceptives. This issue raises important questions about public health and individual rights. Should pharmacists have a right to reject prescriptions for birth control pills, emergency contraception, Viagara[Viagra], or any other drug which may be morally objectionable to them?

Additional Resources

Milosavljevic, J., Krajnovic, D., & Bogavac-Stanojevic, N. (2016). Predictors of pharmacists' provision of emergency contraceptive pills. *Health Care For Women International, 37*(10), 1170–1181.

Supreme Court Rejects Pharmacists' Refusal-to-Fill Appeal. (2016). *Pharmacy Times, 82*(8), 18.

Internet References . . .

American Pharmacists Association

www.aphanet.org/

National Right to Life

www.nrlc.org/

Pharmacists for Life International

www.pfli.org/

Selected, Edited, and with Issue Framing Material by:
Eileen L. Daniel, *SUNY College at Brockport*

ISSUE

Do the Benefits of the Cervical Cancer Vaccine Outweigh the Risks?

YES: Mark Donald White, from "Benefits of HPV Vaccination," *Translational Andrology and Urology* (2014)

NO: Mark Donald White, from "Cons of HPV Vaccine Administration," *Translational Andrology and Urology* (2014)

Learning Outcomes

After reading this issue, you will be able to:

- Discuss why many parents oppose having their daughters vaccinated against cervical cancer.
- Assess the risk associated with contracting the HPV virus.
- Identify the side effects associated with the vaccine.

ISSUE SUMMARY

YES: Physician Mark Donald White discusses the cervical cancer vaccine and asserts that it offers benefits to teens and is effective in preventing cervical cancer.

NO: Physician Mark Donald White points out that the cervical cancer vaccine comes with risks; various side effects including 32 reports of death.

A number of infectious diseases are almost completely preventable through childhood immunization. These include diphtheria, meningitis, pertussis (whooping cough), tetanus, polio, measles, mumps, and rubella (German measles). Largely as a result of widespread vaccination, these once common diseases have become relatively rare. Before the introduction of the polio vaccine in 1955, polio epidemics occurred each year. In 1952, a record of 20,000 cases were diagnosed, as compared to the last outbreak in 1979, when only 10 cases were identified.

While vaccination is a life saver, it may also be controversial. In June 2006, the U.S. Food and Drug Administration (FDA) approved a new immunization called Gardasil used to prevent diseases caused by the sexually transmitted human papillomavirus (HPV). The virus causes genital warts and cervical cancer. The Centers for Disease Control and Prevention (CDC) has determined that up to 50 percent of all sexually active men and women in the United States will be infected with HPV at some time in their life. The infection is especially common among women aged 20–24 years. Each year in the United States, 31,000 women and men are diagnosed with a cancer caused by HPV infection. Most of these cancers could have been prevented by the HPV vaccine plus the HPV vaccination prevents more than just cervical cancer. HPV vaccination can prevent uncomfortable testing and treatment even for cervical precancers. Three hundred thousand women each year in the United States endure invasive testing and treatment for lesions on the cervix that can develop into cancers. Testing and treatment for these "precancers" can have lasting physical effects. However, cervical cancer only accounts for one in three cancers caused by HPV infection. While there is screening for cervical cancer, there is no routine screening for the other cancers caused by HPV infections. Often these diseases such as cancers of the back of the throat and cancers of the anus/rectum aren't detected until later stages when they are more challenging to treat.

About 20 states are considering making the vaccination a requirement while Texas has already done so. Even after recommendations by the Advisory Committee on Immunization Practices (ACIP), school vaccination requirements are decided mostly by state legislatures. Some state legislatures have granted regulatory bodies such as the Health Department, the power to require vaccines, but they still need the legislature to provide funding. Many parents and lawmakers are opposed to the mandatory vaccination for a variety of reasons: the vaccine doesn't target all types of HPV, it doesn't prevent diseases caused by these other types, and while HPV affects both sexes, it's recommended only for girls and women. Other reasons for the opposition include the relatively high cost of the vaccine, the fact that many people don't understand that HPV causes cervical cancer and questions about its long term. Debate continues about whether or not to require girls *and* boys to be vaccinated against HPV, which causes virtually all cases of cervical cancer and genital warts. This state activity stems from the June 2006 recommendation by the national ACIP that routine vaccination is recommended for girls between ages 11 and 12 years, and it is now recommended for males as well.

The CDC supports getting as many girls vaccinated as early and as fast as possible. They believe this vaccination will reduce the incidence and prevalence of cervical cancer among older women and lessen the spread of this highly infectious disease. The American Cancer Society also supports early and widespread vaccination of young girls.

In the United States, it is believed that a valid way to lower the expense of the HPV vaccine and to educate the public on the advantages of vaccination is to make it compulsory for girls entering school. Mumps, measles, rubella, and hepatitis B (which is also sexually transmitted) are currently required. While there is value in preventing cervical cancer which is estimated to be the most common sexually transmitted infection in the United States, many parents have concerns over mandatory vaccination to prevent a sexually transmitted disease. Some parents believe that young girls should be encouraged to abstain from sexual relations rather than being forced to receive the vaccination. Each HPV vaccine went through years of extensive safety testing before they were licensed by the FDA. It was studied in clinical trials with more than 15,000 females and males. Research from before and after the vaccines were licensed shows that HPV vaccines are safe. As with all approved vaccines, CDC and the FDA closely monitor the safety of HPV vaccines after they are licensed. Any problems detected with these vaccines will be reported to health officials, health-care providers, and the public. Like any vaccine or medicine, HPV vaccines can cause side effects. The most common side effects are pain, redness, or swelling in the arm where the shot was given: dizziness, fainting, nausea, and headache. HPV vaccination is typically not associated with any serious side effects. The benefits of HPV vaccination appear to far outweigh any potential risk of side effects.

In the following selections, physician Mark Donald White asserts that the vaccine offers benefits to teens and is effective in preventing cervical cancer since virtually all cases of cervical cancer are linked to the HPV. He also points out that there are short- and long-term side effects to the vaccine including 32 reports of death.

YES 

Mark Donald White

Benefits of HPV Vaccination

Human papillomavirus (HPV) remains the most commonly sexually transmitted infection in both males and females. The current US estimate of new HPV infections is over 6.2 million cases each year (1,2). Many of these infections are asymptomatic and subclinical in nature, but certain viral serotypes have been implicated in causing cervical and penile carcinomas as well as anogenital, vulvar, vaginal, and oropharyngeal carcinomas. There are more than 150 documented HPV viruses with about 40 having potential transmission through sexual contact (3,4). Many infections are asymptomatic and cleared by the host immune system. The oncogenic viral types (HPV 16 and 18) and wart-causing viral types (HPV 6 and 11) are the targets for the quadrivalent vaccine (Gardasil®, Merck & Company, Whitehouse Station, NJ). A bivalent vaccine for HPV 16 and 18 has been marketed for female vaccine programs (Cervarix®, GSK, Research Triangle Park, NC) but has not been as widely marketed. In the European market, viral types 16 and 18 account for more than 70 percent of cervical cancers (5). The cancers caused by these viruses can have devastating consequences including high morbidity and mortality. Unfortunately, the incidence of all of these primary cancer cases appears to be increasing (6). Approximately 40 to 50 percent of all penile tumors are caused by HPV infection with HPV 16, 18, and 6 identified as the predominant viral types in 30.8 percent, 6.6 percent, and 6.7 percent, respectively. As noted by Backes, prophylactic vaccines targeting carcinogenic types HPV 16 and 18 could potentially reduce approximately 1/3 of incident squamous cell carcinomas of the penis (7,8). For genital warts in both males and females, HPV 6 and HPV 11 are the most common causative viral types. Despite wide adoption of Pap testing, almost 70 percent of cervical cancers are also associated with HPV 16 and 18 viral types. Male oropharyngeal cancers are highly associated with HPV 16 (9). Anal cancers are also highly associated with HPV 16 and 18 viral types. Two effective vaccines for the oncogenic HPV viral serotypes have been available for almost a decade after the initial administrative approval in June 2006. In 2011, the Centers for Disease Control and Prevention (CDC) extended the indications for universal use in male patients from ages 9 to 26 with additional regimens for catch-up dosing depending on age (10). In the United States, state-mandated immunization programs have increased the numbers of children vaccinated; however, there are states that do not mandate universal vaccination of school-age children for HPV. Only Virginia and the District of Columbia require HPV vaccination to attend school. Many other states (12) have adopted education programs and another eight provide funding for vaccination. The remaining 29 states do not have specific mandates regarding the vaccine, but many eligible dependent children are able to obtain the vaccines through linkage with Medicaid or other state insurance programs (11). Despite these programs that include financial coverage of the vaccine, only about 37.6 percent of female patients and 13.9 percent of male patients who start the vaccine series actually complete the three prescribed doses within the six-month time interval of administration as detailed from surveillance data from 2007 to 2013 (12). For females, the risk of cervical cancer and the potential for prevention of this devastating disease served as the impetus for widespread adoption of the vaccine. The increase in male genital lesions, penile cancer, as well as oropharyngeal and anogenital cancers helped extend the indications for this vaccine to both sexes up to the age of 26 years. There also documented benefits to male patients regarding a decrease in sexually transmitted lesions from female sexual partners who have been vaccinated. Hariri has summarized the early evidence of population impact of HPV vaccines with moderate reductions in HPV associated pathology in the vaccinated groups (13). Specifically, Markowitz details a nationally representative survey that documents a 50 percent decrease in viral prevalence from the prevaccine years [2003–2006] to the postvaccine era [2007–2010] (14). Many other studies detail the significant decline in the diagnosis of genital warts during this time frame as well. Preliminary data from Australia show that herd immunity may be an added benefit from the vaccine program (15). The ideal time to begin the vaccine series in both sexes is before the age of commencing sexual contact. In theory, this vaccination may help prevent the spread of genital warts in both sexes in addition to the cancer prevention rationale listed above. For some parents, this presents an ethical dilemma. The disease prevention benefits are easier to justify. For others, the vaccine is seen as a potential gateway to encouraging sexual contact at earlier ages or promoting higher risk sexual practices and, consequently, forms the basis of an argument to discourage the administration of the vaccine. For female patients, the argument that the vaccine will prevent cervical cancer appears far more persuasive than the counterargument of promoting earlier sexual activity and higher risk sexual practices. The most frequent parental reasons for not vaccinating teenage girls were summarized in the review by Darden et al. and stated the top reasons were that the girls with either not sexually active or a lack of knowledge about the vaccine (16). For parents of male patients, there also seems to be a relatively high rate of acceptance (by both parents and physicians) regarding the vaccine for male teenagers but with less emphasis than females (17).

There is ongoing, active scientific inquiry and clinical trials to extend the vaccine to include activity against more of the oncogenic viral subtypes for cancers invading the oropharyngeal and anogenital regions. Merck has a nine-valent vaccine (V503) including five additional cancer-causing subtypes to increase activity against these types of cancer (18). Sales for the Gardasil vaccine have increased over the past three years (19, Table 1). This measure serves as a surrogate for total vaccine doses produced by the pharmaceutical company. Numbers of patients actually vaccinated (either with a single initiation dose or complete series) are difficult to extrapolate. The current data regarding estimated HPV vaccination coverage among adolescent boys and girls aged 13–17 years details an increase in completed vaccine series from 5.9 percent in 2007 to 37.6 percent in 2013 for girls and 1.3 to 13.9 percent in boys from 2011 to 2013 (20).

Gardasil Sales

The Advisory Committee on Immunization Practices, in concert with other professional associations, recommends the administration schedule of vaccines (21). Despite the annual recommendations, there is no national governing body to implement these recommendations. In the United States, school vaccination requirements are generally decided by each state legislature. The CDC maintains federal Vaccines for Children in all 50 states and provides vaccine, and some state Medicaid programs also cover underinsured and uninsured children. Many states appear to endorse the administration of the vaccine but neither mandate universal compliance nor provide adequate funding for the vaccine administration (22).

Despite these objections, the public health benefits of the vaccine and cost-effectiveness have been validated in multiple studies. For female patients, the cervical cancer prevention with vaccine administration remains superior to cervical cancer screening programs employing Papanicolaou smears alone. In a systematic review of 29 studies by Seto and colleagues estimated that the addition of boys to the vaccination programs generally exceeds traditional cost-effectiveness thresholds (US$50,000 per QALY). They concluded that studies consistently show that the HPV vaccines can have a substantial impact on the epidemiology of HPV disease (23). Only longer observation of trends over time will validate these conclusions.

Conclusions

The goal of this article has been to review the benefits and risks of HPV vaccination in teenagers and preteenagers as well as a brief review of some of the more important ethical and practical issues that influence the widespread adoption of the vaccine. The overwhelming evidence favors administration of the vaccine to prevent the precancerous and malignant disease conditions caused by HPV infection. The risks of the vaccine are within the range of complications noted with other vaccination programs that have been maintained for decades. Only time will document whether inclusion of both males and females will induce additional herd immunity that ultimately protects a wider proportion of the population or not. Pediatric urologists and pediatricians remain on the "front lines" in informing patients and parents regarding the benefits of HPV vaccination and need to keep informed about the benefits of the vaccine. With better education, practicing urologists can help increase the numbers of children who complete the HPV vaccine and work to decrease the disease burden of HPV-related diseases.

References

1. Anic GM, Giuliano AR. Genital HPV infection and related lesions in men. *Prev Med* 2011;53 Suppl 1:S36–41. [PMC free article] [PubMed]
2. Smith JS, Gilbert PA, Melendy A, et al. Age-specific prevalence of human papillomavirus infection in males: A global review. *J Adolesc Health* 2011;48:540–52. [PubMed]

3. Low GM, Attiga YS, Garg G, et al. Can male vaccination reduce the burden of human papillomavirus-related disease in the United States? *Viral Immunol* 2012;25:174–86. [PubMed]
4. Gravitt PE. The known unknowns of HPV natural history. *J Clin Invest* 2011;121:4593–9. [PMC free article] [PubMed]
5. Muñoz N, Bosch FX, de Sanjosé S, et al. Epidemiologic classification of human papillomavirus types associated with cervical cancer. *N Engl J Med* 2003;348:518–27. [PubMed]
6. Moscicki AB, Palefsky JM. Human papillomavirus in men: An update. *J Low Genit Tract Dis* 2011;15: 231–4. [PMC free article] [PubMed]
7. Miralles-Guri C, Bruni L, Cubilla AL, et al. Human papillomavirus prevalence and type distribution in penile carcinoma. *J Clin Pathol* 2009;62:870–8. [PubMed]
8. Backes DM, Kurman RJ, Pimenta JM, et al. Systematic review of human papillomavirus prevalence in invasive penile cancer. *Cancer Causes Control* 2009;20:449–57. [PubMed]
9. van Monsjou HS, van Velthuysen ML, van den Brekel MW, et al. Human papillomavirus status in young patients with head and neck squamous cell carcinoma. *Int J Cancer* 2012;130:1806–12. [PubMed]
10. Recommendations on the Use of Quadrivalent Human Papillomavirus Vaccine in Males—Advisory Committee on Immunization Practices (ACIP), 2011. *Morbidity and Mortality Weekly Report* (MMWR) 2011;60;1705–8. Available online: http://www.cdc.gov/mmwr/preview/mmwrhtml/mm6050a3.htm [PubMed]
11. The HPV Vaccine: Access and Use in the U.S. Available online: http://kaiserfamilyfoundation.files.wordpress.com/2014/03/7602-04-the-hpv-vaccine-access-and-use-in-the-u-s.pdf
12. Centers for Disease Control and Prevention (CDC). National, state, and local area vaccination coverage among adolescents aged 13–17 years–United States, 2008. *MMWR Morb Mortal Wkly Rep* 2009;58: 997–1001. [PubMed]
13. Hariri S, Markowitz LE, Dunne EF, et al. Population impact of HPV vaccines: Summary of early evidence. *J Adolesc Health* 2013;53:679–82. [PubMed]
14. Markowitz LE, Hariri S, Lin C, et al. Reduction in human papillomavirus (HPV) prevalence among young women following HPV vaccine introduction in the United States, National Health and Nutrition Examination Surveys, 2003–2010. *J Infect Dis* 2013;208:385–93. [PubMed]
15. Moscicki AB, Palefsky JM. Human papillomavirus in men: An update. J Low Genit Tract Dis 2011; 15:231–4. [PMC free article] [PubMed]
16. Darden PM, Thompson DM, Roberts JR, et al. Reasons for not vaccinating adolescents: National Immunization Survey of Teens, 2008–2010. *Pediatrics* 2013;131:645–51. [PubMed]
17. Liddon N, Hood J, Wynn BA, et al. Acceptability of human papillomavirus vaccine for males: A review of the literature. *J Adolesc Health* 2010;46:113–23. [PubMed]
18. Merck & Company, 2013 Annual Report, page 9. Accessed online: merck.com/investor, July 17, 2014.
19. Merck & Company, 2013 Annual Report, page 42. Accessed online: merck.com/investor, July 17, 2014.
20. Stokley S, Jeyarajah J, Yankey D, et al. Human Papillomavirus Vaccination Coverage Among Adolescents, 2007–2013, and Postlicensure Vaccine Safety Monitoring, 2006–2014—United States. *Morbidity and Mortality Weekly Report* (MMWR) 2014;63; 620–4. [PubMed]
21. Centers for Disease Control and Prevention (CDC). Recommended childhood immunization schedule–United States, January–June 1996. *MMWR Morb Mortal Wkly Rep* 1996;44:940–3. [PubMed]
22. National Council of State Legislatures, chapter on HPV Vaccine. Available online: http://www.ncsl.org/research/health/hpv-vaccine-state-legislation-and-statutes.aspx, accessed May 14, 2014.
23. Seto K, Marra F, Raymakers A, et al. The cost effectiveness of human papillomavirus vaccines: a systematic review. *Drugs* 2012;72:715–43. [PubMed]

Mark Donald White is a physician in the Division of Urology, Albany Medical Center, Albany, NY, USA.

Mark Donald White

NO

Cons of HPV Vaccine Administration

. . . What are the risks and downsides to widespread adoption of the (human papillomavirus [HPV]) vaccination program? The Centers for Disease Control and Prevention published a summary document of adverse events reported in JAMA for vaccine administration from the time of approval in June 2006 to December 2008. The study also included patterns in adverse events reported to the Vaccine Adverse Event Reporting System (VAERS) and was the first nationwide published HPV post-licensure study. (The findings were similar to safety reviews of other vaccines recommended for a similar age group [9–26] and compared to such vaccines as meningitis and Tdap). Overall, the vaccine continues to be safe and effective and concluded that benefits continue to outweigh its risks. The main findings are summarized below as compiled from the reports with updated data to the July 2014 report (24).

I. More than 67 million doses were administered nationally since the HPV vaccine was licensed in June 2006 until March 2014. There were 25,176 reports to VAERS of adverse events.

II. About 92.4 percent of the adverse events were not serious. Adverse events are considered serious if it is life threatening, or results in death, permanent disability, abnormal conditions at birth, hospitalization, or prolonged administration.

III. The most common events reported (for both male and female patients) were

i. syncope (or fainting) common after needle injections, especially in preteens and teens,
ii. local reactions at the site of immunization (pain and redness),
iii. dizziness,
iv. nausea, and
v. headache.

IV. In the first report, there were 12,424 reports of adverse events 772 (6 percent of all reports) described serious adverse events including 32 reports of death. The most recent report from June 2006 to June 2013 reported 85 deaths after the vaccine. Upon further screening of the reported deaths, there were no common patterns to the deaths that would suggest that they were caused by the vaccine. Some of the deaths were attributable to diabetes, viral illness, illicit drug use, and heart failure.

V. There were two reports of unusual neurological illness that were variants of amyotrophic lateral sclerosis that resulted in the deaths of two young females. This finding is being evaluated by several highly regarded academic centers.

VI. There was increased reporting of syncope and pulmonary emboli compared to other vaccines given to females of the same age. Of the people who had blood clots, 90 percent had a known risk factor for blood clots, such as taking oral contraceptives. The VAERS reports cannot prove the vaccine caused the adverse event in women with these risk factors.

A follow-up report authored by Bednarczyk et al. reviewed the trends in HPV vaccination from the National Immunization Survey-Teen, 2008–2011 and concluded that minority and below-poverty adolescents consistently had higher series initiation than white and above-poverty adolescents. For the uptake of at least one dose of the vaccine, rates increased from 37.2 percent of adolescent females' ages 13–17 to 53 percent in 2011 with an average annual increase of 5.2 percent. Federally funded programs covering Medicaid beneficiaries most likely account for the increased coverage of the minority and below-poverty adolescents (25). Parental resistance to vaccination appears to be increasing with 44 percent of parents in 2010 said they did not intend to vaccinate their children (26). The resistance to vaccination appears to be related to the education of both health-care providers and parents regarding the side effects of the vaccination and the ethical issues relating to human sexuality. The top five reasons for parents not vaccinating adolescents with the HPV vaccine are lack of knowledge, not needed or necessary, safety concerns/side effects, not recommended, and not sexually active (27). Clearly, there is room for more education and counseling to improve the acceptance of the vaccine series.

Ethical and Practical Considerations

From the epidemiological perspective, widespread adoption of universal vaccination against HPV has strong supporting evidence. Worldwide, HPV infection is responsible for half a million cases of cancer and more than 250,000 deaths every year (28,29). The highest incidence of the virus occurs in developing countries that do not have resources to promote prevention or insure adequate treatment of the disease. The current worldwide scope of vaccination is greater than 120,000,000 people worldwide being vaccinated since the introduction of the vaccines in 2006. The relatively minor side effects of the vaccine seem to be worth the almost 100 percent effectiveness in preventing precancerous lesions caused by the HPV oncogenic viral subtypes (HPV-6, 11, 16, and 18). To date, none of the deaths that occurred after vaccine administration have been directly linked to the vaccine. In June 2013, Japan became the only country to cease the active promotion of the vaccine for patients until more studies related to the incidence of side effects could be completed (30).

Navarro-Illano and colleagues published a thought-provoking summary debate regarding the ethical considerations of universal vaccination against HPV in 2014 since the country of Spain was considering the adoption of an HPV vaccine program (31). Several ethical issues are highlighted in their analysis including whether to vaccinate people who have opted to abstain from sex and whether obtaining the vaccine increases the early onset of sexual relations (32). In the first instance, absolute sexual abstinence is a very difficult parameter to measure especially in the early age-group that has been targeted for the initial vaccination series. From a more scientific perspective, the antibody titer generated at the younger age appears to be highest between the ages of 9–14. Aside from the physical process of vaccination, the more important issues influencing the success of these programs are the educational components that counsel patients and parents regarding the initiation of sexual activity as well as the awareness of the serious health consequences of HPV infection (33). These programs are not successful in isolation and need the educational component to help decrease other higher risk sexual behaviors. Parents and physicians need to remain actively involved in the education process and continue to advocate for the children. Similarly, the parents ultimately retain the right to decide whether or not to vaccinate their children.

The ethical arguments also extend to the manufacturers of the HPV vaccines. The research costs for bringing a successful product to market are usually quite high. Successful programs require a balance such that commercial products are safe and effective and that continued research occurs to perpetuate the cycle of new viable products. Only continued time and monitoring will document the success of these programs worldwide. The practical aspects of recommending HPV vaccine to parents and patients are probably more important than the ethical issues with any type of vaccination program. As summarized by Holman, physicians and parents cite different barriers to the vaccine. Physicians cite financial concerns and parental attitudes and concerns, while most parents need more information about the vaccine before they will consent to administration (34). As with most other interventions, the parents look to the clinician for the ultimate recommendation to vaccinate.

Conclusions

The goal of this article has been to review the benefits and risks of HPV vaccination in teenagers and preteenagers as well as a brief review of some of the more important ethical and practical issues that influence the widespread adoption of the vaccine. The overwhelming evidence favors administration of the vaccine to prevent the precancerous and malignant disease conditions caused by HPV infection. The risks of the vaccine are within the range of complications noted with other vaccination programs that have been maintained for decades. Only time will document whether inclusion of both males and females will induce additional herd immunity that ultimately protects a wider proportion of the population or not. Pediatric urologists and pediatricians remain on the "front lines" in informing patients and parents regarding the benefits of HPV vaccination and need to keep informed about the benefits of the vaccine. With better education, practicing urologists can help increase the numbers of children who complete the HPV vaccine and work to decrease the disease burden of HPV-related diseases.

References

. . .

24. Human Papillomavirus (HPV) Vaccine. Available online: https: www.cdc.gov/vaccinesafety/Vaccines/HPV/jama.html. [accessed July 17, 2014].
25. Bednarczyk RA, Curran EA, Orenstein WA, et al. Health disparities in human papillomavirus vaccine coverage: Trends analysis from the National Immunization Survey-Teen, 2008–2011. *Clin Infect Dis* 2014;58:238–41. [PubMed]

26. Fiks AG, Grundmeier RW, Mayne S, et al. Effectiveness of decision support for families, clinicians, or both on HPV vaccine receipt. *Pediatrics* 2013;131:1114–24. [PMC free article] [PubMed]

27. Holman DM, Benard V, Roland KB, et al. Barriers to human papillomavirus vaccination among US adolescents: A systematic review of the literature. *JAMA Pediatr* 2014;168:76–82. [PMC free article] [PubMed]

28. Ferlay J, Bray F, Pisani P, et al. GLOBOCAN 2002. Cancer incidence, mortality and prevalence worldwide IARC CancerBase No. 5 [Internet]. Version 2.0. Lyon: IARC Press. 2004. Available online: http://www-dep.iarc.fr/

29. GLOBOCAN 2012, Cancer Incidence, Mortality, and Prevalence Worldwide in 2012, International Agency for Research on Cancer, World Health Organization. Accessed at globocan.iarc.fr/Pages/summary_table_site_sel.aspx. iarc.fr on July 17, 2014. Incidence of cervical cancer noted to be 527,624 cases reported worldwide.

30. Merck & Company, 2013 Annual Report, p. 48. Accessed online: merck.com/investor, July 17, 2014.

31. Navarro-Illana P, Aznar J, Díez-Domingo J. Ethical considerations of universal vaccination against human papilloma virus. *BMC Med Ethics* 2014;15:29. [PMC free article] [PubMed]

32. Charo RA. Politics, parents, and prophylaxis—mandating HPV vaccination in the United States. *N Engl J Med* 2007;356:1905–8. [PubMed]

33. Allison MA, Dunne EF, Markowitz LE, et al. HPV vaccination of boys in primary care practices. *Acad Pediatr* 2013;13:466–74. [PubMed]

34. Holman DM, Benard V, Roland KB, et al. Barriers to human papillomavirus vaccination among US adolescents: A systematic review of the literature. *JAMA Pediatr* 2014;168:76–82. [PMC free article] [PubMed]

Mark Donald White is a physician in the Division of Urology, Albany Medical Center, Albany, NY, USA.

EXPLORING THE ISSUE

Do the Benefits of the Cervical Cancer Vaccine Outweigh the Risks?

Critical Thinking and Reflection

1. Discuss why the vaccine is controversial.
2. What are the laws governing vaccinations for school children in the United States?
3. Why is it important to try to prevent and treat cervical cancer, especially among women?
4. Should boys as well as girls be vaccinated?

Is There Common Ground?

Currently, all 50 states require children to be vaccinated for a variety of illnesses, before enrolling in school. Exemptions apply for children whose parents' religious beliefs prohibit vaccinations. Some children are exempt for medical reasons, which must be certified by their doctors. However, almost all children are vaccinated by the time they enter school. The recent development of Gardasil could add another shot to the many children receive by age five. Should all states make it mandatory for school attendance?

There is considerable opposition to the HPV vaccination due partly to the increasing trend among some parents to refuse to have their children vaccinated. These parents believe, erroneously, that many vaccines are more dangerous than the diseases they prevent. The HPV vaccine adds the additional element of parents' beliefs that their children will remain abstinent until marriage. Abstinence provides effective and absolute protection against this sexually transmitted infection. Unfortunately, by age 19, nearly 70 percent of American girls are sexually active. Another concern among parents is that the vaccine will actually increase sexual activity among teens by removing the threat of HPV infection.

Some additional arguments against the HPV vaccine maintain that cervical cancer is different from measles or polio, diseases that are spread through casual contact. While cervical cancer kills approximately 3,700 women each year in the United States, and nearly 10,000 cases are diagnosed, the disease has a high survival rate though treatment can leave women infertile. In addition, cervical cancer deaths have dropped 75 percent from 1955 to 1992, and the numbers continue to decrease due to the widespread use of the Pap smear. Most women diagnosed with cervical cancer today either have never had a Pap smear or did not have one on a regular basis. Would it make more sense to use public funds to insure all women have access to Pap smears? Also, not all viral strains are prevented through use of the vaccine and women would still need to have routine Pap smears. Also, what if the vaccine causes health issues later in life? To determine the safety of Gardasil, researchers conducted a systematic review and meta-analysis to determine the effectiveness and safety of vaccines against cervical cancer. They concluded that the HPV vaccines are safe, well tolerated and highly effective in preventing infections and cervical diseases among young females. The authors determined, however, that long-term efficacy and safety need to be addressed in future trials. See "Efficacy and Safety of Prophylactic Vaccines against Cervical HPV Infection and Diseases among Women: A Systematic Review & Meta-Analysis"; *BMC Infectious Diseases*, 2011.

The American Cancer Society continues to endorse mandatory vaccination for HPV for all girls before entering school. They contend that since not all women get regular Pap smears, the vaccine would be a way to effectively prevent cervical cancer among American women. Physician Mark Donald White supports mandatory vaccination with Gardasil and is concerned that "cancer prevention has fallen victim to the culture wars."

Additional Resources

Angioli, R., Lopez, S., Aloisi, A., Terranova, C., De Cicco, C., Scaletta, G., et al. (2016). Ten years of HPV vaccines: State of art and controversies. *Critical Reviews In Oncology/Hematology*, 10265–72.

Dooren, J. (2012, October 2). Study finds HPV vaccine Gardasil safe. *Wall Street Journal—Eastern Edition*. p. D2.

Jenson, H.B. (2012). Community (herd) immunity follows HPV vaccination. (Cover story). *Infectious Disease Alert, 31*(12), 133–134.

Mahoney, D.J., Stojdl, D.F., & Laird, G. (2014). Virus therapy for cancer. *Scientific American, 311*(5), 54–59.

Tomljenovic, L., & Shaw, C.A. (2012). Too fast or not too fast: The FDA's approval of Merck's HPV vaccine Gardasil. *Journal of Law, Medicine & Ethics, 40*(3), 673–681.

Internet References . . .

American Cancer Society

www.cancer.org

HPV—Centers for Disease Control and Prevention

www.cdc.gov/vaccines/pubs/vis/downloads/vis-hpv-gardasil.pdf

U.S. National Institutes of Health (NIH)

www.nih.gov

U.S. National Library of Medicine

www.nlm.nih.gov

World Health Organization

www.who.int/en

Selected, Edited, and with Issue Framing Material by:
Eileen L. Daniel, *SUNY College at Brockport*

ISSUE

Does Watching Pornography Lead to Sexual Dysfunction?

YES: Philip Zimbardo, Gary Wilson, and Nikita Coulombe, from "How Porn Is Messing with Your Manhood," *Skeptic* (2016)

NO: Marty Klein, from "Skeptical of the Porn Skeptics," *Skeptic* (2016)

Learning Outcomes

After reading this issue, you will be able to:

- Understand the addictive nature of pornography.
- Discuss the potential role of pornography in sexual dysfunction.
- Understand the possible connection between watching pornography and sexual violence.

ISSUE SUMMARY

YES: Psychologist Philip Zimbardo and writers Gary Wilson and Nikita Coulombe argue that watching pornography, especially by young men, can lead to sexual dysfunction with a partner.

NO: Sex therapist Marty Klein counters that while young men may be getting some wrong ideas about sex from porn, they don't appear to suffer sexual dysfunction.

Recently, the Republican-led Utah House of Representatives became the first legislative body in the United States to pass a resolution declaring pornography "a public health hazard leading to a broad spectrum of individual and public health impacts and societal harms." There was backlash and criticism of the measure as some people argue that porn can actually enhance and improve sex lives, provide a safe sexual outlet, and possibly lower the incidence of sexual assault. Others, however, believe that it can ruin relationships, lead to sexual addiction or other unhealthy activities, and increase sexually aggressive behaviors. Whatever one's views are on the subject, pornography is widely available, especially online, and has been extensively studied. After many years of peer-reviewed investigations, researchers contend that pornography influences how we think about gender, sexuality, relationships, intimacy, sexual violence, and gender equality often, but not always, in a negative way. Utah's resolution to take a health-focused view of porn and recognizing its increasing impact not only on consumers but also on society at large reflects both the research and the increase in availability of Internet pornography.

Access to online porn has definitely increased. A 2013 article in the *Huffington Post* indicated that "Porn Sites Get More Visitors Each Month than Netflix, Amazon, and Twitter Combined." Various international studies have put porn consumption rates at 50 percent to 99 percent among men and 30 percent to 86 percent among women. Extensive scientific research reveals that this high volume exposure to Internet pornography may harm the social, emotional, and physical health of individuals, families, and communities and highlights the degree to which porn may be considered a public health crisis rather than a private matter. Due to the availability of porn on digital devices, often for free, the average age of first viewing porn is estimated by some researchers to be as young as 11 years. In the absence of a comprehensive sex education curriculum in many states and school districts, pornography has become de facto sex education for youth. And the porn, free and widely available, is often violent, degrading, and extreme.

However, there are also people viewing porn who don't appear to have problems with it though there appears to be a gender difference. In a 2013 study, researchers at Brigham Young University and the University of Missouri surveyed heterosexual couples who were married or living together and found that men's use of porn was associated with lower sexual quality for both men and their partners. Female use of porn, however, was associated with improved sexual quality for women. This may because men tend to be solo viewers while women are more likely to watch it with their partners in a shared experience. Other research indicates that men who are frequent porn viewers tend to develop sexual dysfunction when they're with a partner since it appears that for some men, watching and responding to porn is more exciting than the real thing.

In 2007, Kinsey Institute researchers were among the first to report sexual dysfunction including pornography-induced erectile-dysfunction and pornography-induced abnormally low libido. Half of those studied, recruited from bars and bathhouses where video pornography was common, were unable to achieve erections in the laboratory in response to video porn. In talking to the subjects, researchers discovered that high exposure to pornography videos apparently resulted in lower responsivity and an increased need for more extreme, specialized, or "kinky" material to become aroused. The researchers actually redesigned their study materials to include more varied clips and permit some self-selection. A quarter of the participants' bodies still did not respond normally. Since that study, there has been evidence that online porn may be an issue in the increasing rates of sexual dysfunction especially among young men. Close to 60 percent of visitors seeking help for sexual dysfunction on an online medical forum were younger than age 25 years. A 2015 study of high school seniors found that online porn use was often correlated with low sexual desire. Of those who viewed online pornography more than once per week, about one in six reported a low sex drive compared with 0 percent of nonviewers.

Researchers now believe that one of the most important factors related to problematic sexual behavior is the frequent viewing of Internet pornography. This type of sexual behavior is an abnormal stimulus since online porn tends to be more sexually arousing than other forms of pornography or fantasy. Frequent viewing, in addition to sexual dysfunction, can also lead to addictive behaviors. Finnish researchers found "adult entertainment" to be the most common reason for compulsive Internet use and a one-year longitudinal study of Internet applications revealed that Internet pornography may have the highest potential for addiction with Internet gaming a close second in both studies. A 2015 study reported that, compared to healthy controls, compulsive online porn users had an increased need for novel sexual images, a risk associated with a greater chance for several types of addiction.

As the rate of sexual dysfunctions and low sexual desires among young men rises, there is a need to better understand the relationship between these problems and frequent viewing of Internet pornography. Internet pornography's unique properties including unlimited novelty and the potential for viewers to move on to more extreme material may be strong enough to condition sexual arousal to Internet pornography but not real-life partners. This can mean that sex with desired partners may not register as meeting expectations and arousal declines. Psychologist Philip Zimbardo and writers Gary Wilson and Nikita Coulombe argue that watching pornography, especially by young men, can lead to sexual dysfunction with an actual partner. Sex therapist Marty Klein argues that while young men may be getting some wrong ideas about sex from Internet porn, they don't appear to suffer sexual dysfunction.

YES

Philip Zimbardo, Gary Wilson, and Nikita Coulombe

How Porn Is Messing with Your Manhood

Finding a needle in a haystack would be easier than finding an adolescent male who hasn't seen online porn. Surveys indicate the average boy watches roughly two hours of porn every week with porn viewing becoming common by age 15 years [1].

The most popular porn site—PornHub—reported that the average Millennial porn session lasts nine minutes [2], while the average age young people have sex for the first time is 17 years [3]. This means the average boy has had about 1,400 porn sessions prior to having real-life sex. So why aren't more people asking what kind of effects porn is having on these young viewers?

Almost all people can recall the first erotic image they saw; like a flashbulb memory, it is forever emblazoned in our minds. There appears to be a special window of time when visual sexual interests form most readily: adolescence [4]. When this critical period gets hijacked by watching copious amounts of online porn [5], it seems some men can suffer from what one Italian urology survey called "sexual anorexia," or difficulty having sex with a real partner [6]. Many of the young Italians in the 28,000-person survey started "excessive consumption" of porn sites as early as 14 years old and later, when in their mid-20s, they became inured to "even the most violent images." Professor Carlo Foresta, head of the Italian Society of Andrology and Sexual Medicine, explained that the problem worsens when young men's sexuality develops independently from real-life sexual relationships. First, he said, viewers become less responsive to porn sites, then their libido drops, and finally, it becomes difficult to get an erection.

In a 2014 study, Dr. Foresta found that 16 percent of high school seniors who used online porn more than once a week reported abnormally low sexual desire, while none of those who didn't use it reported abnormally low sexual desire [7]. Could the advent of high-speed Internet porn, especially porn-tube sites at the end of 2006, explain the tremendous increase in erectile dysfunction (ED) and low sexual desire in men under 40? Studies published in the last six years report ED rates ranging from 27 to 33 percent, while rates for low libido (hyposexuality) ranged from 16 to 37 percent. The lower ranges are taken from studies involving teens and men 25 years and under, while the higher ranges are from studies involving men 40 years and under [8]. Traditionally, ED rates have been negligible in young men, usually around 2 to 3 percent [9].

In the first comprehensive study of male sexual behavior in the United States, which was conducted by Alfred Kinsey in 1948 and published in the book Sexual Behavior in the Human Male, just 1 percent of men under 30 years old and 3 percent of men between 30 and 45 years old reported impotence [10]. What variable has changed in this time that could possibly explain a 1,000 percent increase in youthful ED? Unlimited access to high-speed, streaming Internet porn.

Not surprisingly, a number of recent studies have found relationships between online porn use in young men and ED, anorgasmia, low sexual desire, delayed ejaculation, and lower brain activation to sexual images [11]. Many of the young men who participated in the 20,000-person survey conducted by myself (Phil) and my coauthor Nikita Coulombe for our book, Man Interrupted [12], said that porn distorted their idea of a healthy sexual relationship and that "the script" of porn was always playing in the back of their minds when they were with a real partner.

Other male survey participants claimed they were able to watch porn occasionally and not suffer significant side effects. But they were in the minority. It was clear that plenty of young men out there, including teens and preteens with highly plastic brains, find they are compulsively using online porn with their porn tastes slipping out of sync with their real-life sexuality.

Porn on the Brain

In Man Interrupted, we dubbed the need for novel online stimulation arousal addiction. Unlike alcohol or drug addiction, where someone wants more of the same alcohol or drug, a person who exhibits addictive behavior with arousing activities such as porn craves material that is constantly changing. Simply put, it is like saying, "give me the same but different." I (Gary) ascribe this phenomenon in my book, Your Brain on Porn [13], to the human brain's natural propensity to find novelty arousing, corresponding with spurts of dopamine. Dopamine is a neurotransmitter associated with activation of the brain's reward system. Its presence helps initiate feelings of wanting, desire, and even cravings. Experiences such as eating, taking drugs, and having sex release dopamine into two main brain regions: the striatum and the frontal cortex.

However, as a person slips into addiction, more lasting changes take place [14]. This very specific constellation of brain changes manifests as the signs, symptoms, and behaviors we recognize as addiction. Neutral stimuli and events that are associated with an addictive substance or its process, such as gambling or drug-taking sequences, can also become conditioned to generate further arousal and add to the body's chemical response [15]. This is known as sensitization, which is at the core of all addictions. For a recovered alcoholic, a sensitized cue could be walking by his favorite bar, which elicits an overwhelming desire to drink. Cues for a porn addict might be turning on the computer, seeing a sexy pop-up, or simply being alone.

In porn addiction, these deeply etched Pavlovian memories cause events to become cues for diving back into a behavior. These cues trigger intense, hard to ignore cravings for porn use. In the last few years, 15 studies have reported sensitization in porn users (see 1–15) [16]. Critics of porn addiction posit that excessive porn use simply reflects a high libido, often referencing a single 2013 EEC study [17]. It actually reported greater cue reactivity to porn correlating with less desire for sex with a partner. In short, those with more brain activation and cravings for porn would rather masturbate to porn than have sex with a real person. This is most assuredly not an indication of high sexual desire. Various recent studies refute the "sex/porn addiction = high libido" hypothesis [18].

If an image or scene is no longer stimulating enough for today's porn users they will look for variety, surprise factor in the content, more hard-core and stranger material, anything they haven't seen in order to attain a sexual climax. One result is that some brains on porn are being "digitally rewired" in a totally new way to demand change, excitement, and constant stimulation [19]. Each dose of dopamine is a brain-training experience [20]. It communicates, "This experience is important to our survival and should be remembered."

Less stimulating pursuits, on the other hand, may be forgotten. The subtle and not so subtle effects of excessive online porn use can negatively affect any parts of a person's life that are analog, static, involve planning, delaying gratification, and long-term goal setting. With porn, there is a "cognitive absorption" effect where the complete involvement in porn excites cognitive, sensory, and imaginative curiosity to the point where a boy loses track of time and other demands on attention, such as homework and socializing, become inferior. Using the excitation transfer model and sexual behavior sequence of psychologists Dolf Zillmann and Donn Byrne, respectively, Belgian researchers have recently suggested that the high states of arousal achieved in porn stimulated impulsive and "restless" behavior that may impair actions that require long periods of constant focus [21].

Sensitization and Sexual Conditioning

At the same time, everything associated with a young man's porn/masturbation session is imprinted upon his neural circuits, such as a voyeur's perspective, clicking from video to video, constant novelty, switching to new porn genres, and searching for the perfect scene to finish. Though the impact of chronic overstimulation on the brain and behavior varies from individual to individual, it is worth examining the potential physiological, mental, and emotional effects of watching too much porn, because few people consider how it may be affecting their brains and their ability to become aroused in real-life sexual encounters.

Initially, online porn had to be downloaded prior to watching. That took a long time and variety was limited. At the end of 2006, however, streaming porn that no longer had to be downloaded started showing up in every genre imaginable. Using these sites, users now effortlessly click from scene to scene and genre to genre to boost their arousal. Sites allow viewers to control their dopamine drip with a click of mouse. The change means the user can—and many do—condition their arousal patterns to ongoing, escalating, and ever changing novelty. Today's porn users can also learn to associate their sexual response with shock, surprise, or anxiety—all of which increase dopamine and sexual arousal. Thus, users are conditioning their sexual arousal template to everything associated with their porn use, not just "watching a lot." Their brains then expect these things during sexual arousal. Yet none of these attributes of online porn match sex with a real person who cannot compete with the buffet provided by porn no matter how attractive they are. When arousal expectations are unmet, dopamine drops, and so do erections and orgasms during intercourse.

In relationships, it's not uncommon for young men to find themselves aroused at first because of a partner's newness, yet after several months of being intimate with the same person, find that partner no longer turns them on. Not suspecting the true cause of their problems, many young men are baffled when they experience lack of desire for real partners, unreliable erections when using condoms, or difficulty climaxing or sustaining erections with partners. After all, they may have no problem climaxing while viewing porn. People we've spoken with who demonstrated signs of arousal addiction often feel very anxious in social situations in general, have less motivation to set and complete goals, feel out of control, and even discuss suicide.

Guys themselves are not only starting to talk about how porn has personally affected them, but, more important, about the benefits when they stop using it, such as clearer thinking and better memory, more motivation, increased charisma, deeper relationships, and better real-life sex.

New Brain Research

Supports the Porn Addiction Model

Researchers have finally begun to investigate the effects of online porn on heavy users' brains in order to figure out what's going on. A number of these studies have uncovered evidence of brain alterations and behaviors that are also seen in other kinds of addicts [22]. In the first-ever brain-scan study of online porn users, conducted at the Max Planck Institute for Human Development in Berlin, researchers found that the hours and years of porn use were correlated with decreased gray matter in regions of the brain associated with reward sensitivity, as well as reduced responsiveness to erotic still photos [23]. Less gray matter in this region translates into a decline in dopamine signaling. The lead researcher, Simone Kühn, hypothesized that "regular consumption of pornography more or less wears out your reward system" [24]. This can be thought of as densitization or a numbed pleasure response.

This addiction-related brain change leaves the individual less sensitive to pleasure [25] and often manifests as the need for greater and greater stimulation to achieve the same buzz (tolerance). In the past year, two more brain studies have reported desensitization in compulsive porn users [26]. While sensitization makes your brain hyperreactive to anything associated with your porn addiction, densitization numbs you to everyday pleasures. Over time, this dual-edged mechanism can have your reward circuitry buzzing at the hint of porn use but less than enthused when presented with the real deal [27]. If these two neuroplastic changes could speak, desensitization would be saying, "I can't get no satisfaction" (low dopamine signaling), while sensitization would be saying, "Hey buddy, I got just what you need," which happens to be me very thing that caused the desensitization. A numbed pleasure response (desensitization), combined with a deep brain pathway leading to cravings and short-term relief (sensitization), is what powers most addictions.

Another German study showed users' problems correlated most closely with the number of browser tabs open and degree of arousal [28]. This helps explain why some users become dependent on new, surprising, or more extreme, porn. They need more and more stimulation to become aroused, get an erection, and reach climax. In further support of the hypothesis that online porn's novelty contributes to its risk, a 2015 brain-scan study led by researchers at the University of Cambridge found that men who demonstrate compulsive sexual behavior require more novel sexual images than their peers because they habituate to what they are seeing faster than their peers do [29]. Study spokesperson Valerie Voon said that "Our findings are particularly relevant in the context of online pornography" and "It's not clear what triggers sex addiction in the first place and it is likely that some people are more predisposed to the addiction than others, but the seemingly endless supply of novel sexual images available online helps feed their addiction, making it more and more difficult to escape" [30].

A 2014 brain-scan study from the University of Cambridge by Voon and colleagues found that young porn addicts exhibit brain responses that are comparable to drug addicts [31] and results that have been replicated repeatedly [32]. A 2016 Belgian study has found that problematic Internet porn use is associated with reduced erectile function and reduced sexual satisfaction as well as escalation to porn material subjects previously found uninteresting or disgusting. Voon also reported that over 50 percent of the subjects (average age 25 years) had difficulty achieving erections with real partners, yet could achieve erections with porn. This could be interpreted as an overt physical sign of brain desensitization. Finally, Voon found that younger subjects had enhanced reward circuit activity when exposed to porn cues. Higher dopamine spikes and greater reward sensitivity are major factors in adolescents being more vulnerable to addiction and sexual conditioning [33]. It may be no coincidence, then, that solo male porn users report altered sexual tastes [34], less satisfaction in their relationships, and real-life intimacy and attachment problems [35].

Just prior to the arrival of porn-tube sites, research published in 2005 indicated that young people who consume online porn were more likely to exhibit clinical symptoms of depression and lesser degrees of bonding with caregivers than those who consumed porn through other means, such as magazines [36]. Online sexual activities were also already beginning to displace normal relationship development, learned courtship, and romantic behaviors in college students [37]. In the intervening decade, almost all porn users have shifted to online streaming porn. Understandably, researchers have focused increasingly on the effects of its use on aggression, risky sexual behavior, sexual attitudes, and so forth. This has left the adverse effects on users themselves underresearched.

Levels of narcissism are higher in online porn users [38], while excessive porn users also have reduced ability to monitor their own consumption [39]. A longitudinal study showed that academic performance declines with porn use [40]. Men who cut out porn often report improvements in mental clarity and ability to focus. Is this because online porn interferes with working memory during and after its use? [41]. In undergraduate college males, depression, anxiety, stress, and social functioning were significantly related to online porn use, and more viewing was related to greater problems [42]. Also, the more young men use online porn and masturbate, the more shyness they reported [43]. They were also more dissatisfied with their sexual performance and body image [44]. Many users then do not engage in real-life sexual activity, perhaps due to severe social anxiety.

In case you're wondering which way causation runs, there is evidence that social anxiety, depression, and compulsivity are related to how intensely arousing users find the material, rather than personality traits [45]. In fact, some of the most common improvements mentioned by recovering users in the online forums are reduced social anxiety, improved concentration and memory, and increased motivation and charisma after quitting online porn use. This highlights a significant deficiency with nearly every study trying to assess porn's effect on the user: researchers don't ask study participants to abstain from porn use. While recovery forums contain thousands of stories involving remission or improvement of myriad conditions and symptoms, only two studies had participants attempt to eliminate porn use. It was for only three weeks, yet both studies reported significant differences between abstainers and controls. In a 2015 study where participants reduced or eliminated porn use for three weeks, researchers found that reducing porn viewing significantly improved participants ability to delay gratification in pursuit of more valuable future rewards [46]. The second study, employing a similar three-week procedure, found that subjects who continued using pornography reported lower levels of relationship commitment [47]. In a third "case study," a compulsive porn user, whose tastes had escalated to extreme hardcore pornography, sought help for low sexual desire during sex [48]. Eight months after stopping all pornography, the patient reported experiencing successful orgasm and ejaculation and finally enjoying good sexual relations.

Light at the End of the Tunnel

Ultimately, more research needs to be conducted in order to provide clarity on both the causes of porn addiction and the stages of recovery. To porn users, we're not saying there's something wrong with wanting to look at the images of naked hotties. And static photos pose less risk than videos. High-speed, streaming Internet porn is simply more than some brains can handle. Healthy young men should not have any trouble getting or maintaining a full erection and then masturbating to orgasm regardless of whether they are watching porn or not. (Just a note: if you have a strong erection and can orgasm while masturbating without porn, but have trouble with a real-life partner, your sexual dysfunctions could be anxiety-related.) Viagra or Cialis may, or may not, help, but they won't solve the underlying problem in instances of porn-induced sexual dysfunctions. Such drugs only dilate the blood vessels to sustain an erection. You still need genuine desire to initiate one. Without arousal, nothing can happen.

So, if you watch porn, ask yourself how much of what you're attracted to has been influenced by porn. Young men today are forming their sexual attitudes and arousal templates around having access to dozens of sexual partners in a single masturbatory session—in other words, having more partners in less than 10 min than our ancestors would have had in an entire lifetime. Watching porn that is out of sync with your sexuality doesn't necessarily mean your sexuality is changing; it may mean you simply need more stimulation. Sometimes you just have to hit the "reset" button and stop using porn completely for a few months. In fact, even if you're not struggling, you might experiment with a break from porn, just to see if there are any hidden powers you never knew you had.

References

1. http://bit.ly/lswD7qO.
2. http://bit.ly/lgxjBnG.
3. http://bit.ly/lr4xclq.
4. http://Lusa.gov/lYAppNi.
5. http://bit.ly/lWDoApl.

6. http://bit.ly/lR7moyl.
7. http://l.usa.gov/lsp7ZZD.
8. http://l.usa.gov/lTYhW9x, http://l.usa.gov/lTYi8Wd, http://l.usa.gov/lsp7ZZD, http://l.usa.gov/lTmyTfb, http://bit.ly/lHm93Cc.
9. http://bit.ly/10Elu09.
10. http://l.usa.gov/lTmzf5o.
11. http://bit.ly/lXI5Slt, http://l.usa.gov/lswFzOA, http://l.usa.gov/lTWZawq, http://bit.ly/lWDoRZm, http://l.usa.gov/lsp7ZZD, http://l.usa.gov/22fFJoR, http://bit.ly/lkZjb42.
12. http://amzn.to/lspa3Rr.
13. http://amzn.to/27xUmM.
14. http://bit.ly/20ngQuc.
15. http://l.usa.gov/lTYjf8k.
16. http://bit.ly/lXI5Slt, http://l.usa.gov/lWC14K3, http://bit.ly/lTGTAyv, http://bit.ly/lXympmn, http://bit.ly/lR7qabl, http://l.usa.gov/24Ypfml.
17. http://bit.ly/lBg5G9K.
18. http://l.usa.gov/lspgcx5, http://l.usa.gov/lR7ql7a, http://l.usa.gov/lTmD3Um, http://l.usa.gov/lTmD3Um, http://bit.ly/lXI5Slt.
19. http://bit.ly/lXlalF0.
20. http://l.usa.gov/lWlmdwx.
21. http://bit.ly/lWC0J9X.
22. http://bit.ly/lXlalF0.
23. http://bit.ly/lkZjb42.
24. http://bit.ly/lTiSo4M.
25. http://bit.ly/lTXlVhn.
26. http://l.usa.gov/lTYkQLs, http://bit.ly/lR7oxtT.
27. http://l.usa.gov/lXI9sMe.
28. http://l.usa.gov/24Ypfml.
29. http://l.usa.gov/lTeODTp.
30. http://bit.ly/lspedst.
31. http://bit.ly/lXI5Slt.
32. https://www.researchgate.net/publication/286882727%5FOnline%5Fsexual%5Factivities%5FAn%5Fexploratory%5Fstudy%5Fofproblematic"and%5Fnon-problematic%5Fusage%5Fpatterns%5Fin%5Fa%5Fsample%5Fof%5Fmen.
33. http://bit.ly/24Yq534, http://bit.ly/10yHSnT.
34. http://l.usa.gov/lspdjwi.
35. http://bit.ly/lTmBNAz, http://bit.ly/lXI7wUe.
36. http://l.usa.gov/lWBZFTI.
37. http://l.usa.gov/lNxzCcW.
38. http://l.usa.gov/10yHgi3.
39. http://l.usa.gov/lXI78VI.
40. http://bit.ly/lTeNVWl.
41. http://l.usa.gov/2030gc0.
42. http://bit.ly/lXyk3Ee.
43. http://bit.ly/lWBZzvi.
44. http://bit.ly/lXI7wUe.
45. http://l.usa.gov/24Ypfml.
46. http://l.usa.gov/lXI6JT0.
47. http://l.usa.gov/lXI6JT0.
48. http://l.usa.gov/lTWZawq.

Philip Zimbardo is a psychologist and a professor emeritus at Stanford University.

Gary Wilson is the author of *Your Brain on Porn: Internet Pornography and the Emerging Science of Addiction.*

Nikita Coulombe is a writer and blogger.

Marty Klein

NO

Skeptical of the Porn Skeptics

Philip Zimbardo and Gary Wilson have outlined the many ways that they believe "porn is messing with your manhood." I personally know Phil Zimbardo to be a compassionate and energetic man who is generally positive about sexuality (I don't know his coauthor Gary Wilson). And everyone knows that Dr. Zimbardo is a world-famous social scientist. But in my opinion, this article is short on facts that are reliable and relevant. Before we get to that, however, we do agree on several things. Yes, a majority of adolescent American males look at pornography. Yes, some of them report sexual difficulties. And yes, some of them report a compulsive quality to their attachment to porn viewing. Finally, there's plenty to be concerned about when an entire generation of young men get a substantial amount of their sex education from Internet porn.

However, Zimbardo and Wilson hypothesize effects of porn that science does not support empirically. They describe epidemics that really affect only a small number of people; they blame these alleged epidemics on neurological processes that haven't really been shown to exist; and they stitch together a few isolated studies to conclude that porn viewing is undermining a generation's ability to relate to real sex.

One of the key foundations of Zimbardo and Wilson's article is that high school and college students report a lack of "normal" sexual functioning. They cite studies of young guys reporting "low sexual desire" and "erection difficulties," who blame their "condition" on porn. But obsession with "normal" sex is a hallmark of adolescence and young adulthood [1]. Exactly what baseline are these 17-year-olds using to decide that their desire isn't "normal"? Which 19-year-old actually understands enough about sexuality to gauge how much his peers desire sex, how much they enjoy it, how reliable their erections are, and how often they have sex? [2].

For example, it is well-known that most adolescents (and adults, for that matter) overestimate the amount of sex everyone else has. Sociologist Michael Kimmel found that a sample of male undergraduates thought 80 percent of their classmates were having sex every weekend [3]. Kathleen Bogle found the same distorted estimates in her interviews with students [4]. So adolescent concerns about the normality of their sexual function are not a good measure of their sexual function. But it does explain the popularity of online forums like NoFap—where young people enjoy the sense of community, somewhere they can talk about sex and masturbating without fear of humiliation.

One reason some physicians mistakenly think they are seeing more erectile dysfunction (ED) in young men is because some want erection drugs for performance enhancement rather than real ED, and they know what to say to get them. This is similar to the documented ways that students have learned to fake the symptoms of ADHD to get prescriptions for Adderall to help them study [5].

Zimbardo and Wilson cite many studies purporting to show that neuroscience now proves that porn erodes young brains. They don't mention the tiny sample sizes of these studies—literally 10 or 15 people, in some cases. Nor do they mention the most common caveat of these studies' authors, also routinely omitted by the popular media. For example, Zimbardo and Wilson approvingly quote neuroscientist Valerie Voon discussing the results of two different studies. But contrary to how they interpret her words, she says quite clearly that "inferences about causality cannot be made" [6]. Of a study, she coauthored on compulsive sexual behavior, she says "significant gaps in understanding continue to complicate classification of CSB as an addiction" [7].

Most people, of course, are unable to read an MRI scan or evaluate claims about what neuroscience demonstrates. When Zimbardo and Wilson state that "young porn addicts exhibit brain responses that are comparable to drug addicts," many lay people think that proves the existence of porn addiction. But this reasoning by analogy means nothing. What does the similarity in brain responses mean? Scientists themselves say they aren't sure. Besides, our brains respond in this same observable way when we cuddle a grandchild or enjoy a sunset.

Thousands of miles apart, peer-reviewed studies challenge the idea that porn use leads to addiction, or sexual dysfunction, or worrisome brain changes. North

American neuroscientists Prause and Pfaus recently published a study in which pornography use was related to greater sexual desire for one's partner, not to ED or lower desire [8]. An ocean away, European researchers Landripet and Stulhofer found that neither frequency of porn viewing nor changes in the frequency of use were related to erectile problems [9]. Both published in a high-prestige medical journal, these two studies refute claims that watching porn desensitizes erectile function, which supposedly leads to decreased desire and arousal for partner sex.

Further, according to Rory C. Reid, a research psychologist at UCLA's Neuropsychiatric Institute who is also an expert in hypersexual behavior, "Watching the NCAA playoffs is going to change your brain, eating chocolate—any time you have any kind of experience, it's going to change your brain." And Reid is hardly pro-porn: "Philosophically, I've got all sorts of problems with porn." But as a scientist, he says, "this idea that consumption of pornography causes cortical atrophy that leads to negative consequences? We haven't seen that" [10].

Even stronger in his conviction is Bruce Carpenter, a researcher at Brigham Young University who is morally opposed to pornography because he suspects that "pornography has larger deleterious effects upon individuals, family, and society." Nevertheless, he admits: "Now to the evidence, there is none. There is not a single study of pornography use showing brain damage or even brain changes" [11].

Dr. Barry Komisaruk, a Rutgers University psychologist who has done groundbreaking neuroscience research on the brain during orgasm, also says that there are no studies demonstrating that porn's effect on the brain resembles addiction [12].

For an article about the use and impacts of pornography, there is, oddly, very little mention of masturbation—which of course accompanies most porn watching. The authors don't seem to consider that an increase in the number of times per week, or minutes per week, spent masturbating can account for some of the changes they allege—particularly dissatisfaction (or dysfunction) with partner sex. Many sex therapists are currently discussing the possibility that young men may becoming increasingly accustomed to the special (and rather strong) grip of their own hand, making a partner's vagina, mouth, or hand less enjoyable in comparison. This would be true, of course, whether masturbation involves porn, mental fantasy, or watching the Food Network.

When men give up pornography for a period of time (say, as part of the NoFap movement), the positive effects they describe are generally attributed to the lack of porn. They could just as easily be attributed to the lack of masturbation. Certainly, when a young man has trouble not looking at porn for a month, the reason his resolve may weaken is the yearning to masturbate or ejaculate far more than the desire to look at sexy videos.

Zimbardo and Wilson's article does note that porn users may experience decreased participation in offline life. In fact, it says that by 2005 "online sexual activities were also already beginning to displace normal relationship development, learned courtship, and romantic behaviors in college students." I agree and have been asked about this across the country when I lecture. While the authors describe this watershed as resulting from enhanced speed (and therefore availability) of porn, I propose a different explanation: widespread use of then-new smartphones (the term "CrackBerry" became popular in 2006), and the cultural norms that have placed them in the center of our lives. This is one of the most important recent developments in American society; porn is only part of this bigger story.

As a sex therapist, I am very concerned by how much trouble young people of both genders are having enjoying sex. Because of the new digital ways of relating—constantly multitasking, not learning to listen as carefully, not expecting as much engagement from others, diminished experiential learning about nonverbal cues—they're not as emotionally present during two-person interactions, which makes sex hard to enjoy at any age. Given the choice of texting, young people even find the real-time give-and-take of a telephone conversation too taxing. The performative culture of selfies, sexting, Instagram, and live-Tweeting encourages people to think of sex as one more performance, undermining authentic self-expression.

It isn't simply that real sex can't compete with porn; real sex can't compete with the novelty and stimulation-on-demand (and mutual emotional separation) that smartphones and the Internet provide. Most young people don't date and practice relationship skills, they "hang out" and text their respective friends while sitting near each other.

I agree with the article's concern about "arousal addiction" (although I think that wording is unhelpful); I just think that Zimbardo and Wilson have placed its locus incorrectly. It isn't porn; it's the Internet/smartphone/asynchronous communication nexus.

It's easy for everyone—young people, researchers, critics—to blame porn, because virtually every young person having trouble with courtship looks at porn, or is involved with someone who does. But they also all own smartphones and occupy huge amounts of their time on them, spending less time learning to relate to others in ways that would eventually facilitate sexual connection.

They spend less time making out ("French kissing"); instead, things go rather quickly to fellatio (often joyless for both parties), which typically doesn't lead to closeness or erotic self-confidence for either party.

Putting aside the rare instances of people watching three hours of porn every night (a clearly self-destructive behavior that's often more about the Internet than about porn), there are reasonable concerns about young people marinating in Internet porn. For starters, most porn leaves out most of what makes sex worthwhile (kissing, laughing, caressing, and feeling connected). Porn rarely shows all the off-camera preparation that makes certain depicted activities possible. It devotes a lot of attention to activities that people rarely do in real life. And it shows women as wildly orgasmic from intercourse, which most women aren't.

Porn consumers (of all ages) need to remember that they're watching fiction, not a documentary. Real sex does not look like the sex in porn; indeed, real sex usually doesn't feel like the sex in porn seems to feel (that's what actors do—they portray feelings). Attempting to recreate what's seen in porn with a live partner generally leads to dissatisfaction for both.

That said, many of the problems young people face in launching their sexual lives are not unique to the 21st century: as in the 20th century (and before that), young people actually don't know what's sexually "normal," but fear they're not; young people want to feel desired and special, even though sexual experimentation increasingly takes place in anonymous settings (fueled by alcohol); young people want to feel sexually competent but lack the communication skills (and often the motivation) to learn about their partners' sexual interests and subjective experience.

So we don't need to imagine porn-induced neurological changes or sexual dysfunction in order to be concerned about young men watching a lot of porn. And we don't need to imagine that they have to abstain in order to "recover" from these allegedly profound effects. Finally, we shouldn't imagine that without porn, young men will go back to some mythical pre-Internet time when their ideas about sex were realistic, their erections were always firm, and their desire always high. I was a teen way before the Internet, and life wasn't like that at all: teen boys had distorted ideas about sex, many were terrified of "impotence," and desire was, for a substantial minority, contingent or sporadic. Back then, these young men were called "shy" or "late bloomers."

One further way Zimbardo and Wilson shortchange us in their discussion: talking about the detrimental effects of porn without talking about sex education or parental involvement is as shortsighted as talking about reducing abortion without talking about birth control. The state of Utah has recently declared pornography a public health crisis [13]. They also recently voted down science-based school sex education [14]. This shows they're more interested in condemning porn than in supporting the healthy sexuality of their young people. It also helps explain why Utah has the highest per capita use of porn in the country and one of the highest rates of unwanted pregnancy.

That said, most nonviolent porn (i.e., the vast majority of it) also shows sex as being about pleasure, and it shows women as having desire, even if it's depicted unrealistically ("Thanks for delivering the pizza, Joe—how about sex?"). It frequently shows the importance of the clitoris as a sex organ, and more often than not it shows that both men and women can touch their own genitalia during partner sex. It's dishonest to talk about porn without acknowledging all of this.

And what exactly are people watching when they watch porn? According to PornHub, the largest porn aggregator site on the Internet, the most common search terms are quite consistent across age and geography: "Lesbian" is the runaway favorite, followed by "teen," "stepsister," and "ebony." Topics suggested by dystopian antiporn activists like Gail Dines—"torture," "humiliation," "female pain," and "misogyny"—don't even come close [15]. And, contrary to the ugly, manipulative myths driven by activists like Pamela Paul, Rebecca Whisnant, and Melissa Farley, the rate of sexual violence in the United States has steadily decreased since broadband Internet started saturating the country in 2000 [16, 17]. So the idea that porn consumption leads to rape is flatly refuted by federal statistics [18].

Young men may be getting some wrong ideas about sex from porn, but they're not seeking out images that reflect hatred of women or lead to hatred of women. That, in addition to the lack of evidence that porn changes brains, should hearten policy makers and concerned citizens everywhere.

References

1. Boyd, Dana. 2014. *It's Complicated: The Social Lives of Networked Teens*. New Haven: Yale University Press.
2. http://bit.ly/lc9adDV.
3. Kimmel, Michael. 2009. *Guy-land: The Perilous World in Which Boys Become Men*. New York: Harper Perennial.
4. Bogle, Kathleen. 2008. *Hooking Up: Sex, Dating, and Relationships on Campus*. New York: NYU Press.

5. Sollman, M. 2010. "Detection of Feigned ADHD in College Students," *Psychological Assessment, 22*(2), 325–335.
6. Voon, Mole, Banca, et al. 2014. "Neural Correlates of Sexual Cue Reactivity In Individuals with and without Compulsive Sexual Behaviors." *PLoS One,* 9(7), 1–10.
7. Kraus, Shane W., Valerie Voon, and Marc N. Potenza. 2016. "Should compulsive sexual behavior be considered an addiction?" Addiction, February 18. doi:10.1111/add.13297.
8. Prause, N. and J. Pfaus. 2015. "Viewing sexual stimuli associated with greater sexual responsiveness, not erectile dysfunction." *J Sex Med.* doi:10.1002/sm2.58.
9. Landripet I. and A. Stulhofer A. 2015. "Is pornography use associated with sexual difficulties and dysfunctions among younger heterosexual men?" *J Sex Med.* 12, 1136–9.
10. http://bit.ly/lNkmXtw.
11. http://bit.ly/lNkmXtw.
12. http://bit.ly/lNkmXtw.
13. http://bit.ly/lVgGJca.
14. http://bit.ly/lTBaqSH.
15. http://bit.ly/lTFZ0C5.
16. http://l.usa.gov/lqWtUqE.
17. http://l.usa.gov/lLCBEDE.
18. Rape, of course, is an underreported crime. Not only are there no data suggesting it is more underreported now than before 2000, if anything it is less underreported now—that is, more accurately reported now than 20 years ago. This makes the decline in reported rape even more impressive.

Marty Klein is a licensed marriage and family therapist.

EXPLORING THE ISSUE

Does Watching Pornography Lead to Sexual Dysfunction?

Critical Thinking and Reflection

1. Why do so many men become addicted to Internet porn?
2. What are some of the social downsides to frequent pornography viewing?
3. What physical effects can occur from accessing porn?

Is There Common Ground?

There is a growing number of young men who are certain that their sexual responses have been damaged because their brains were saturated in pornography during their adolescence. That generation has viewed large quantities and varieties of explicit content not available in the past, delivered on electronic devices designed to provide content quickly and privately. In addition, a range of other means, such as social media and smart phones, enable porn addiction by providing an outlet to view pornography anywhere and at any time. For young men, this occurs early in life when their brains are more prone to permanent change than in later years. These young men are taking part in an unmonitored decade-long experiment in unprecedented sexual behaviors. Many are now beginning to create smart phone apps, online blogs, and other means to help other men stop viewing pornography and kick their addiction.

While porn viewing is linked to sexual dysfunction, it also has other downsides including the potential for addiction. Pornography addiction is a type of compulsive sexual behavior in spite of negative consequences to the viewer's mental, social, physical, or financial well-being. Viewing pornography at work can often have disastrous consequences though research has shown that approximately 20 percent of men and 13 percent of women admit accessing pornography while on the job though this may be a conservative estimate. These men and women often face sanctions or loss of their jobs if discovered.

Additional Resources

Landripet, I., & Štulhofer, A. (2015). Is Pornography Use Associated with Sexual Difficulties and Dysfunctions among Younger Heterosexual Men? *Journal of Sexual Medicine, 12*(5), 1136–1139.

Luscombe, B. (2016). Porn and the threat to virility. *Time, 187*(13), 40–47.

Park, B.Y. et al., (2016). Is Internet porn causing sexual dysfunctions? A review with clinical reports. *Behavioral Sciences, 6*, 1–25.

Vaillancourt-Morel, M., Blais-Lecours, S., Labadie, C., Sabourin, S., Bergeron, S., & Godbout, N. (2017). Profiles of cyberpornography use and sexual well-being in adults. *Journal of Sexual Medicine, 14*(1), 78–85.

Internet References . . .

National Institute of Mental Health

www.nimh.nih.gov

Porn Free

https://www.reddit.com/r/NoFap/

SIECUS: Sexuality Information and Education Council of the United States

www.siecus.org/

Unit 5

UNIT

Public Health Issues

There are many health issues that concern the public and are affected by public policy and public health laws. The focus of public health intervention is to improve the health and quality of life of populations. This is accomplished through the prevention and treatment of disease and other physical and mental health conditions, surveillance of disease cases, enactment of public health laws (i.e., smoking bans in public), environmental policy, and the promotion of healthy behaviors. An important component of public health policy is the balance between protecting public health and the maintenance of individual freedoms.

Selected, Edited, and with Issue Framing Material by:
Eileen L. Daniel, *SUNY College at Brockport*

ISSUE

Should Vaccines Be Mandatory?

YES: Ronald Bailey, from "Refusing Vaccination Puts Others at Risk," *Reason* (2014)

NO: Jeffrey A. Singer, from "Vaccination and Free Will," *Reason* (2014)

Learning Outcomes

After reading this issue, you will be able to:

- Discuss the risk factors associated with opting out of vaccinations.
- Understand the reasons some parents refuse to have their children vaccinated.
- Discuss the concept of herd immunity.

ISSUE SUMMARY

YES: Senior correspondent and author Ronald Bailey argues that the popularization of invalid anti-immunization reporting has resulted in many parents opting out of vaccinating their children resulting in serious health problems.

NO: Physician Jeffrey A. Singer counters that parents and their choices to vaccinate or not should be respected and preserved.

Vaccination against infectious diseases such as measles, polio, and mumps has been a very successful preventive agent. However, because of this success, many people have forgotten how dreadful these diseases were and can be and may focus not on the danger of contracting the disease but on the small but possible risk associated with the vaccine itself. Like any medication, vaccines can cause side effects though the most common are mild. The side effects associated with getting vaccines are almost always minor (such as redness and swelling where the shot was given) and go away within a few days. Serious side effects following vaccination, such as severe allergic reaction, pneumonia, and inflammation of the stomach or intestines, are very rare. In many cases, it is not always clear if the mild or more serious side effects were caused by the vaccine or occurred after vaccination by chance or coincidence.

Most of the concerns about the safety of vaccines have focused on the measles, mumps, and rubella (MMR) and on thiomersal, the mercury-based preservative used in some vaccines before 2001. In 1998, researcher Andrew Wakefield published a paper in the British medical journal, *Lancet.* It reported on 12 children who had autism spectrum disorder as well as bowel symptoms. In eight of these children, the parents or the child's doctor linked the MMR vaccination with the onset of the behavioral symptoms. The paper was seized upon by the media and parents groups creating a furor that led to a significant drop in the number of British children who were vaccinated, leading to a return of mumps and measles cases in England. Interestingly, in February 2009, a special federal court ruled that there was no proven link between certain early childhood vaccines such as MMR and autism that developed in three children.

There is a difference between federal vaccine policies and state vaccine laws. Federal public health officials at the Centers for Disease Control and Prevention (CDC) make national vaccine policy recommendations for children and adults. With the approval of state legislatures, public health officials in state health departments make and enforce vaccine mandates. That is why vaccine laws and legal exemptions to vaccination vary from state to state. The first vaccine mandated in the United States was smallpox vaccine. By 1922, some states had passed laws requiring that children show proof they were vaccinated for smallpox in order to attend school. By the early 1980s, the CDC recommended and most states mandated that children get 23 doses of seven vaccines (polio, diphtheria, tetanus, pertussis, and MMR) to attend kindergarten. By 2014, the CDC recommended that children get 69 doses of 16 vaccines between day of birth and age 18. Most states mandate that children get 29 doses of nine vaccines to attend kindergarten and children enrolled in daycare in many states are required to get multiple doses of 13 vaccines.

While vaccine policymakers in the American Academy of Pediatrics and the CDC make vaccine recommendations for children and adults, the bottom line is not all states may not require all federally recommended vaccines as a condition of employment, and school or day care attendance.

In addition to health concerns, there are many people who oppose mandatory vaccination policies because they believe that governments should not encroach on an individual's autonomy to choose medical treatment even if that choice increases the risk of disease to themselves and others. If a vaccination program successfully lessens the threat of disease, it may lower the perceived risk of disease as collective memories of the effects of that disease fade away. At this point, some parents may consider that they have nothing to lose by refusing vaccinations for their children. They don't remember much if anything about diseases such as whooping cough so believe that refusing vaccination may prevent their child from complications of the vaccine. If enough people hope to gain the benefits of herd immunity without vaccination, vaccination levels could drop to a point where herd immunity ceases to be effective.

Compulsory vaccination laws in the United States provoke negative reactions from members of antigovernment factions, who profess concern for what they view as the meeting or union of the public and private sectors. They point to possible conflicts of interest due to vaccine research funding and misinformation that fuel debate on both sides. Others argue that for mandatory immunizations to effectively and broadly prevent disease, there must be not only available vaccines and a population willing to immunize but also sufficient ability to decline vaccination on grounds of personal belief. There are still others who oppose vaccination on religious grounds and opt out.

Immunization creates ethical concerns beyond the normal issues of a parent deciding on medical care for their children, as unvaccinated but asymptomatic or weakly infected individuals may spread disease to people (especially babies, children, and the elderly) with weaker immune systems and to individuals for whom the vaccine has not been effective. For this reason, even where not required by law, some schools and doctors' offices have prohibited parents with unvaccinated children from attending. A further complication arises in emergency room and urgent care facilities, particularly those geared toward treating children as an unvaccinated child is often brought to these facilities after acquiring the disease and showing symptoms. Other children that are in the facility with compromised immune systems are then exposed to the disease with potential dire consequences. In the following selections, journalist Ronald Bailey believes there is much invalid reporting about the so-called dangers of immunization. This has resulted in parents opting out of vaccinating their children resulting in the potential for serious health problems. Physician Jeffrey A. Singer disagrees and counters that parents and their choices to vaccinate or not should be respected and preserved.

Ronald Bailey

Refusing Vaccination Puts Others at Risk

Millions of Americans believe it is perfectly all right to put other people at risk of death and misery. These people are your friends, neighbors, and fellow citizens who refuse to have themselves or their children vaccinated against preventable infectious diseases.

Aside from the issue of child neglect, there would be no argument against allowing people to refuse government-required vaccination if they and their families were the only ones who suffered the consequences of their foolhardiness. But that is not the case in the real world. Let's first take a look at how vaccines have improved health, then consider the role of the state in promoting immunization.

Vaccines are among the most effective health care innovations ever devised. A November 2013 *New England Journal of Medicine* article, drawing on the University of Pittsburgh's Project Tycho database of infectious disease statistics since 1888, concluded that vaccinations since 1924 have prevented 103 million cases of polio, measles, rubella, mumps, hepatitis A, diphtheria, and pertussis. They have played a substantial role in greatly reducing death and hospitalization rates, as well as the sheer unpleasantness of being hobbled by disease.

A 2007 article in the *Journal of the American Medical Association* compared the annual average number of cases and resulting deaths of various diseases before the advent of vaccines to those occurring in 2006. Before an effective diphtheria vaccine was developed in the 1930s, for example, the disease infected about 21,000 people in the United States each year, killing 1,800. By 2006, both numbers were zero. Polio, too, went from deadly (16,000 cases, 1,900 deaths) to nonexistent after vaccines were rolled out in the 1950s and 1960s. Chickenpox used to infect four million kids a year, hospitalize 11,000, and kill 105; within a decade of a vaccine being rolled out in the mid-1990s, infections had dropped to 600,000, resulting in 1,276 hospitalizations and 19 deaths. Similar dramatic results can be found with whooping cough, measles, rubella, and more.

And deaths don't tell the whole story. In the case of rubella, which went from infecting 48,000 people and killing 17 per year, to infecting just 17 and killing zero, there were damaging pass-on effects that no longer exist. Some 2,160 infants born to mothers infected by others were afflicted with congenital rubella syndrome-causing deafness, cloudy corneas, damaged hearts, and stunted intellects—as late as 1965. In 2006, that number was one.

It is certainly true that much of the decline in infectious disease mortality has occurred as a result of improved sanitation and water chlorination. A 2004 study by the Harvard University economist David Cutler and the National Bureau of Economic Research economist Grant Miller estimated that the provision of clean water "was responsible for nearly half of the total mortality reduction in major cities, three-quarters of the infant mortality reduction, and nearly ⊠ of the child mortality reduction." Providing clean water and pasteurized milk resulted in a steep decline in deadly waterborne infectious diseases. Improved nutrition also reduced mortality rates, enabling infants, children, and adults to fight off diseases that would have more likely killed their malnourished ancestors. But it is a simple fact that vaccines are the most effective tool yet devised for preventing contagious airborne diseases.

Vaccines do not always produce immunity, so a percentage of those who took the responsibility to be vaccinated remain vulnerable. Other defenseless people include infants who are too young to be vaccinated and individuals whose immune systems are compromised. In America today, it is estimated that about 10 million people are immuno-compromised through no fault of their own.

This brings us to the important issue of "herd immunity." Herd immunity works when most people in a community are immunized against an illness, greatly reducing the chances that an infected person can pass his microbes along to other susceptible people.

People who refuse vaccination for themselves and their children are free riding off of herd immunity. Even while receiving this benefit, the unvaccinated inflict the negative externality of being possible vectors of disease, threatening those 10 million most vulnerable to contagion.

Vaccines are like fences. Fences keep your neighbor's livestock out of your pastures and yours out of his. Similarly, vaccines separate people's microbes. Antivaccination folks are taking advantage of the fact that most people around them have chosen differently, thus acting as a firewall protecting them from disease. But if enough people refuse, that firewall comes down, and innocent people get hurt.

Oliver Wendell Holmes articulated a good libertarian principle when he said, "The right to swing my fist ends where the other man's nose begins." Holmes' observation is particularly salient in the case of whooping cough shots.

Infants cannot be vaccinated against whooping cough (pertussis), so their protection against this dangerous disease depends upon the fact that most of the rest of us are immunized. Unfortunately, as immunization refusals have increased in recent years, so have whooping cough infections. The annual number of pertussis cases fell from 200,000 prevaccine to a low of 1,010 in 1976. Last year, the number of reported cases rose to 48,277, the highest since 1955. Eighteen infants died of the disease in 2012, up from just four in 1976.

The trend is affecting other diseases as well. In 2005, an intentionally unvaccinated 17-year-old Indiana girl brought measles back with her from a visit to Romania and ended up infecting 34 people. Most of them were also intentionally unvaccinated, but a medical technician who had been vaccinated caught the disease as well, and was hospitalized.

Another intentionally unvaccinated seven-year-old boy in San Diego sparked an outbreak of measles in 2008. The kid, who caught the disease in Switzerland, ended up spreading his illness to 11 other children, all of whom were also unvaccinated, putting one infant in the hospital. Forty-eight other children younger than vaccination age had to be quarantined.

Some people object to applying Holmes' aphorism by arguing that aggression can only occur when someone intends to hit someone else; microbes just happen. However, being intentionally unvaccinated against highly contagious airborne diseases is, to extend the metaphor, like walking down a street randomly swinging your fists without warning. You may not hit an innocent bystander, but you've substantially increased the chances. Those harmed by the irresponsibility of the unvaccinated are not being accorded the inherent equal dignity and rights every individual possesses. The autonomy of the unvaccinated is trumping the autonomy of those they put at risk.

As central to libertarian thinking as the nonaggression principle is, there are other tenets that also inform the philosophy. One such is the harm principle, as outlined by John Stuart Mill. In On Liberty, Mill argued that "the only purpose for which power can be rightfully exercised over any member of a civilized community, against his will, is to prevent harm to others." Vaccination clearly prevents harm to others.

So what are the best methods for increasing vaccination? Education and the incentives of the market have encouraged many Americans to get themselves and their children immunized, and surely, those avenues of persuasion can and should be used more. Perhaps schools and daycare centers and pediatric clinics could attract clients by advertising their refusal to admit unvaccinated kids. Or social pressure might be exercised by parents who insist on assurances from other parents that their children are vaccinated before agreeing to playdates.

But it would be naive not to acknowledge the central role of government mandates in spreading immunization. By requiring that children entering school be vaccinated against many highly contagious diseases, states have greatly benefited the vast majority of Americans.

For the sake of social peace, vaccine opt-out loopholes based on religious and philosophical objections should be maintained. States should, however, amend their vaccine exemption laws to require that people who take advantage of them acknowledge in writing that they know their actions are considered by the medical community to be putting others at risk. This could potentially expose vaccine objectors to legal liability, should their decisions lead to infections that could have been prevented.

In terms of net human freedom, the tradeoff is clear: in exchange for punishment-free government requirements that contain opt-out loopholes, humans have freed themselves from hundreds of millions of infections from diseases that maimed and often killed people in recent memory. People who refuse vaccination are asserting that they have a right to "swing" their microbes at other people. That is wrong.

Being intentionally unvaccinated against highly contagious airborne diseases is like walking down a street randomly swinging your fists without warning.

Ronald Bailey is a senior correspondent and author.

Jeffrey A. Singer

NO

Vaccination and Free Will

In Steven Spielberg's 2002 sci-fi film Minority Report, a special police agency called PreCrime nabs suspects before they ever commit an offense. No trial is necessary because the crime is seen as an infallible prediction of the future and thus a matter of fact. The movie challenges viewers to consider the tension between technological determinism and free will, between the rights of an individual and the health of a community. It's a useful metaphor for the argument against coercive vaccination.

Some argue that mandatory mass vaccination is an act of communal self-defense and thus completely compatible with the principles underpinning a free society. Unless people are forcibly immunized, they will endanger the life and health of innocent bystanders, goes the argument. But such a position requires a level of precognition we haven't yet attained.

Not everyone who is vaccinated against a microbe develops immunity to that microbe. Conversely, some unvaccinated people never become infected. Some people have inborn "natural" immunity against certain viruses and other microorganisms. Central Africans born with the sickle-cell trait provide a classic example of such inborn immunity: their sickle-shaped red blood cells are inhospitable to the mosquito-borne parasite that causes malaria. Other people are just lucky and never get exposed to a contagious microbe.

Just like not every pregnant woman who drinks alcohol or smokes tobacco passes on a malady or disability to her newborn baby, not every pregnant woman infected with a virus or other microbe passes on the infection to her fetus—nor are all such babies born with birth defects.

A free society demands adherence to the nonaggression principle. No person should initiate force against another and should only use force in retaliation or self-defense. Forcibly injecting substances—attenuated microbes or otherwise—into someone else's body cannot be justified as an act of self-defense, because there is no way to determine with certainty that the person will ever be responsible for disease transmission.

Ronald Bailey suggests that the choice to remain unvaccinated is analogous to "walking down a street randomly swinging your fists without warning." But this is a poor analogy. Such a person is engaging in a deliberate action, as opposed to choosing inaction. And, unlike those prevented from opting out of vaccination, the fist-swinger incurs no threat to life or limb when prohibited from throwing his punches.

If someone chooses the inaction of nonvaccination based upon the belief—right or wrong—that the vaccination is harmful or even life threatening, then coercive vaccination in this context is clearly a case of aggression. For it to be otherwise requires certainty that those beliefs are wrong. And certainty in this case is not possible. How can you be sure, for example, that a child won't have an adverse or even fatal reaction to a vaccine? And how can defending forced immunization as self-defense be justified when it can never be shown with certainty that the nonvaccinated person would have been responsible for another person's harm?

Then, there is the matter of "herd immunity." The phenomenon of herd immunity allows many unvaccinated people to avoid disease because they free ride off the significant portion of the population that is immunized. Economists point out that free riding is an unavoidable fact of life: people free ride when they purchase a new, improved, and cheaper product that was "pretested" on more affluent people who wanted to be the first to own it; people free ride when they use word-of-mouth reviews to decide whether to buy goods or services, or to see a film; those who choose not to carry concealed weapons free ride a degree of personal safety off the small percentage of the public that does.

So here is a way of dunking about it: as long as the person who is being free-ridden is still getting desired value for an acceptable price and is not being harmed by the free riding, it really shouldn't matter. Achieving a society without free riders is not only unnecessary, it is impossible.

Perhaps allowing a certain number of free riders could mitigate the disruption to liberty caused by mandatory vaccination programs. But then, how many free riders should be allowed? I don't think that question can be answered with any degree of certainty. And what criteria would be used to decide who gets to ride free? An objective answer to this question appears equally elusive. Finally, how can the population be monitored to make sure the proportion of free riders is maintained at the right level without unreasonably infringing on civil liberties and privacy rights ? The task would be titanic. I think the only practical solution—and the solution that is in the best interest of liberty—is to just accept the free riding of the current regime as a fact of reality, and focus instead on persuading people about the benefits of vaccination.

Most states coax, but don't coerce, vaccination of children in the public school system. Two of the 50 states, Mississippi and West Virginia, are indeed coercive. But the remaining 48 allow parents to opt out for religious reasons, and 19 allow for some kind of philosophical objection. Some states require parents to read about the risks of opting out before exempting their children. Some require them to acknowledge in writing that, in the event of a major school outbreak of a contagious disease for which their child has not received immunization, he or she will be held out of school until the outbreak clears.

Private schools requiring vaccination of children as a precondition for admission is not coercive, since private education is a voluntary transaction. But even with the government school monopoly in existence today, immunization policy in at least 19 states is compatible with the nonaggression principle.

As a medical doctor, I am a strong advocate of vaccination against communicable and infectious diseases. I am irritated by the hysteria and pseudoscience behind much of the antivaccination literature and rhetoric. In my perfect world, everyone would agree with me and voluntarily get vaccinated against the gamut of nasty diseases for which we have vaccines. (In my perfect world, pregnant women also wouldn't smoke tobacco or drink alcohol until after delivery.)

But free societies are sometimes messy. To live in a free society, one must be willing to tolerate people who make bad decisions and bad choices, as long as they don't directly infringe on the rights of others.

A strong argument can be made that it is self-defense to quarantine people who are infected with a disease-producing organism and are objectively threatening the contamination of others. But in such a case, the use of force against the disease carrier is based upon evidence that the carrier is contagious and may infect others.

Any mass immunization program that uses compulsion rather than persuasion will, on balance, do more harm to the well-being of a free people than any good it was intended to convey.

. . .

Jeffrey A. Singer is a physician.

EXPLORING THE ISSUE

Should Vaccines Be Mandatory?

Critical Thinking and Reflection

1. Why do some parents opt out of vaccinating their children?
2. Why do some doctors refuse to treat unvaccinated children?
3. What are the differences between federal and statewide vaccination laws?
4. What is herd immunity and how is it being threatened?

Is There Common Ground?

Nine-year-old Hannah Poling had an uneventful birth and appeared to be developing normally. And then, right after receiving several routine vaccines, she became ill. Hannah recovered from her acute illness but lost her speech and eye contact and, in a matter of months, began displaying the repetitive behaviors and social withdrawal that indicate autism. Her parents reported that after her vaccinations, she just deteriorated and never came back. "Parents of children with autism have been blaming vaccines—and, especially, the mercury-based vaccine preservative thimerosal as a cause of autism for over a decade, but researchers have repeatedly failed to identify a connection."

What is unusual about Hannah's case is that for the first time, federal authorities have agreed there is a connection between her autistic symptoms and the vaccines she received, though the relationship is by no means clear. A panel of medical evaluators at the Department of Health and Human Services determined that Hannah had been injured by vaccines and recommended that her family be compensated for the injuries. The panel said that Hannah had an underlying cellular disorder that was aggravated by the vaccines, causing brain damage with features of autism spectrum disorder.

The Poling case is also causing concern among public health officials, who are anxious to reassure parents that immunizations are safe and valuable. In a recent public statement, Dr. Julie Gerberding, director of the Centers for Disease Control and Prevention (CDC), insisted that "the government has made absolutely no statement about indicating that vaccines are the cause of autism, as this would be a complete mischaracterization of any of the science that we have at our disposal today." Dr. Gerberding and other health authorities point out that the benefits of vaccines far exceed their risks. They also note that thimerosal was eliminated from routinely administered childhood vaccines manufactured after 2001, and yet autism rates have not dropped. The current CDC estimate is that 1 of the 150 American children has an autism spectrum disorder.

Additional Resources

Buck, G., & Gatehouse, J. (2015). The real vaccine scandal. *Maclean's, 128*(7), 28–35.

Holton, A., Weberling, B., Clarke, C. E., & Smith, M. J. (2012). The blame frame: Media attribution of culpability about the MMR–autism vaccination scare. *Health Communication, 27*(7), 690–701.

Hotez, Peter J. 2017. "How the Anti-Vaxxers Are Winning." *New York Times*, February 08. A25.

Johnstone, M. (2017). Ethics, evidence and the anti-vaccination debate. *Australian Nursing & Midwifery Journal, 24*, 27.

Offit, P. A. (2008, May 15). Vaccines and autism revisited—The Hannah Poling case. *New England Journal of Medicine*, 2089–2091.

Internet References . . .

American Academy of Pediatrics

https://www.aap.org/en-us/Pages/Default.aspx

Autism Society

http://www.autism-society.org/

Centers for Disease Control and Behaviors/ Vaccines: Home page for Vaccines and Immunizations Site

www.cdc.gov/vaccines/

Selected, Edited, and with Issue Framing Material by:
Eileen L. Daniel, *SUNY College at Brockport*

ISSUE

Will Hydraulic Fracturing (Fracking) Negatively Affect Human Health and the Environment?

YES: **John Rumpler**, from "Fracking: Pro and Con," *Tufts Now* (2013)

NO: **Bruce McKenzie Everett**, from "Fracking: Pro and Con," *Tufts Now* (2013)

Learning Outcomes

After reading this issue, you will be able to:

- Understand the environmental impact of fracking.
- Discuss the health concerns of fracking.
- Discuss the impact that fracking has on the economy and oil dependence.

ISSUE SUMMARY

YES: Environmentalist and senior attorney for Environment America John Rumpler argues that fracking is not worth the damage to health and the environment.

NO: Energy researcher and Adjunct Professor Bruce McKenzie Everett claims fracking provides substantial economic benefits and its health and environmental problems are relatively small.

Hydraulic fracturing, or fracking, is a process that extracts natural gas from rock beneath the earth's surface. Many rocks such as shale, sandstones, and limestone deep in the ground contain natural gas, which was formed as dead organisms in the rock decomposed. This gas can be released and captured at the surface for energy use when the rocks in which it is trapped are drilled. To enhance the flow of released gas, the rocks are broken apart, or fractured. In the past, drillers often detonated small explosions in the wells to increase flow. Starting about 70 years ago, oil and gas drilling companies began fracking rock by pumping pressurized water into it.

Since the 1940s, about 1 million American wells have been fracked. The majority of these are vertical wells that tap into porous sandstone or limestone. During the past 20 years, however, energy companies have had the ability to capture the gas still stuck in the original shale source. Fracking shale is achieved by drilling level wells that expand from their vertical well shafts along thin, horizontal shale layers. Drilling of this nature has allowed engineers to insert millions of gallons of high-pressure water directly into layers of shale to generate the fractures that release the gas. Chemicals added to the water dissolve minerals, destroy bacteria that might block the well, and add sand to hold open the fractures.

While the process offers inexpensive energy options, there are many opponents of the process. The majority of these opponents concentrate on possible local environmental outcomes. Some of these consequences are specific to the more recent fracking technology, while others are more relevant to the overall processes of natural gas extraction. The mixture of chemicals used in fracking processes includes acids, detergents, and toxins that are not controlled by federal laws but can cause problems if they leak into drinking water. Since the 1990s, the fracking process has employed increased amounts of chemical-laden water, injected at higher pressures. This causes the escape of methane gas into the environment out of gas wells, producing the real, though slight, chance of hazardous explosions. In general, water from all gas wells often returns to the surface' containing very low but measurable concentrations of radioactive elements and large salt concentration. Salts or brine can be harmful if not treated properly. Small earthquakes have been triggered in rare instances after the introduction of brine into deep wells.

Along with these regional consequences, natural gas extraction has worldwide environmental impacts, because both the methane gas that is retrieved through extraction and the carbon dioxide liberated during methane burning are greenhouse gases that add to global climate change. Recent fracking technologies foster the extraction of higher quantities of gas, which adds more to climate change than former natural gas extraction processes.

In Pennsylvania, there has been rapid development of the Marcellus Shale, a geological formation that could contain nearly 500 trillion cubic feet of gas. This amount of natural gas is considered enough to power all U.S. residences for 50 years at current rates of usage. The experience in Pennsylvania with water and soil contamination, however, is of concern. Shale gas in Pennsylvania is accessed at depths of thousands of feet, while water for drinking is removed from depths of only hundreds of feet. Nowhere in the state have fracking chemicals injected at depth been shown to contaminate drinking water. In a research study of 200 private drinking water wells in Pennsylvania fracking regions, water quality was the same before and shortly after drilling in all wells except one. Unfortunately, however, trucking and storage accidents have spilled fracking chemicals and brines, leading to contamination of water and soils that required decontamination. Also, many gas companies do not consistently reveal the composition of all fracking and drilling compounds, which makes it challenging to check for injected chemicals in surface and groundwater.

Instances of methane leaking into aquifers in regions where shale-gas drilling is ongoing have also occurred in Pennsylvania. A portion of this gas is "drift gas" that forms naturally in deposits left behind by the most recent glaciers. But occasionally methane seeps out of gas wells because linings are not structurally sound, which occurs in about 1–2 percent of the wells. The linings can be repaired to address these slight leaks, and the risk of such methane leaks could further decrease if linings were designed specifically for each geological area.

The disposal of shale gas salt/brine was originally addressed in Pennsylvania by permitting the gas industry to use municipal water treatment plants that were not equipped to manage the toxic substances. In 2011 new regulations were enacted and Pennsylvania energy companies now recycle 90 percent of the salty water by using it to frack more shale.

Overall, the experience of fracking in Pennsylvania has led to industry changes that alleviate the impact of drilling and fracking on the local environment. Though the natural gas produced by fracking does increase greenhouse gases in the atmosphere through leakage during gas extraction and carbon dioxide emitted during burning, it does hold an important environmental benefit over coal mining. Gases released from shale contain 50 percent of the carbon dioxide per unit of energy as does coal, and coal burning also releases metals such as mercury into the atmosphere that ultimately settle back into water and soil.

In Europe, there is currently an increase in reliance on coal while discouraging or restricting fracking. If Americans are going to get our energy needs mostly from fossil fuels, banning fracking while mining and burning coal appears to be a negative environmental trade-off. The question is: Should Europe and the United States support fracking or prohibit it? Many regional effects of fracking and drilling have received a lot of press but actually generated a small amount of problems, while others are more serious. Economic interests in the short term favor fracking. The Pennsylvania experience caused natural gas prices to fall and jobs were created both directly in the gas industry and indirectly as local and national economies benefit from reduced energy costs. If, however, fracked gas shifts efforts to develop cleaner energy sources without decreasing reliance on coal, the consequences of accelerated global climate change will occur.

Overall, there are both advantages and disadvantages to hydraulic fracturing. The environmental impact could be lessened as well as the risk to human health via water contamination and the increase in greenhouse gases by utilizing lessons learned from Pennsylvania. In the YES and NO selections, John Rumpler argues that we are making a mistake in thinking that fracking is worth the damage to the environment. Bruce McKenzie Everett disagrees and claims that fracking offers substantial economic benefits and its problems are relatively minor compared to the advantages.

YES

John Rumpler

Fracking: Pro and Con

For some Americans, it is our energy dreams come true. To others, it is an environmental nightmare. Ever since a new drilling technology, called hydraulic fracturing or fracking, made it possible to extract natural gas from shale deposits about a mile underground, a new gold rush has been under way.

While fracking has created jobs and contributed to record-low natural gas prices, it comes with another kind of potential cost: risks to our environment and health that some say are far too high.

The fracking process begins with a bore hole drilled some 6,000 feet below ground, cutting through many geological layers and aquifers, which tend to be no more than a few hundred feet below the surface. The shaft is then lined with steel and cement casing. Monitors above ground signal when drilling should shift horizontally, boring sideways to pierce long running sections of shale bedrock.

Millions of gallons of water mixed with sand and chemicals are then blasted into the bedrock, the pressure creating cracks that release trapped natural gas from the shale. The gas and water mixture then flows back up to the surface, where the gas is separated from the water. While most of the water stays in the well bore, up to 20 percent is either reused for more fracking or injected into disposal wells thousands of feet underground.

The wellpad and related infrastructure take up to eight to nine acres of land, according to the Nature Conservancy. Fracking is currently occurring in Texas and Pennsylvania, the two largest gas-producing states, as well as in North Dakota, Arkansas, California, Colorado and New Mexico. And the oil and gas industry is eager to expand its fracking operations into New York, North Carolina, Maryland and Illinois. . . .

John Rumpler . . . argues that we are making a mistake in thinking that fracking is worth the damage to the environment. He is a senior attorney at Environment America, which is leading a national effort to restrict, regulate and ultimately end the practice of fracking. He has fought for clean air in Ohio and advocated to protect the Great Lakes and the Chesapeake Bay. This fall he is teaching the Experimental College course Fracked Out: Understanding the New Gas Rush.

Tufts Now: Is Fracking Safe?

. . .

John Rumpler: Fracking presents a staggering array of threats to our environment and our health. These range from contaminating drinking water and making families living near well sites sick to turning pristine landscapes into industrial wastelands. There are air pollution problems and earthquakes from the deep-well injections of the wastewater into the gas-producing shale, as well as significant global warming emissions.

When the industry says there has not been a single case of groundwater contamination, they mean there is not a verified instance of the fracking fluid traveling up through a mile of bedrock into the water table. What they cannot dispute is that fluid and chemicals have leached into groundwater at 421 fracking waste pits in New Mexico. What they cannot dispute is that a peer-reviewed study by Duke University linked methane in people's drinking water wells to gas-drilling operations in surrounding areas. What they cannot dispute is a University of Colorado study published earlier this year documenting that people living within a half mile of fracking and other gas-drilling operations have an increased risk of health problems, including cancer from benzene emissions.

Are There Sufficient Regulations Now in Place to Ensure Safety?

Rumpler: Is it conceivable to imagine regulatory fixes for all the various problems caused by fracking? Theoretically, perhaps. But imagine trying to implement the hundreds of different rules and regulations at thousands of oil- and gas-drilling sites across the country, and you realize there is no practical likelihood that fracking will ever be made safe.

And there are consequences that we don't even know how to regulate yet. Geologists are just beginning to think about the long-term implications of drilling down a mile and then drilling horizontally through shale rock for another mile. We don't know what happens to the structural integrity of that bedrock once you withdraw all of the gas and liquid from it. No one has the definitive answer. There's been some recent modeling that indicates a loss of stability that goes all the way up to the water table. The U.S. Geological Survey took a look at some earthquakes that occurred in the vicinity of Youngstown, Ohio, in proximity to deep-well fracking. They found that the seismic activity was most certainly manmade—and there was no manmade activity in the area except fracking.

So when you look at the whole picture—from contaminated wells to health problems to earthquakes—[you quickly come] to see that the best defense against fracking is no fracking at all.

As for the current state of regulations, it is worth noting that fracking is exempt from key provisions of our nation's environmental laws, including the Safe Drinking Water Act, the Clean Air Act, the Clean Water Act, and the Resource Conservation Recovery Act. The reason we have national environmental laws is to prevent states from "racing to the bottom of the barrel" to appease powerful industries. . . .

What Are the Economic Benefits of Fracking?

. . .

Rumpler: First of all, any discussion of economics needs to deal with costs as well as benefits. This fall, our *Costs of Fracking* report detailed the dollars drained by dirty drilling—from property damage to health-care costs to roads ruined by heavy machinery. In Pennsylvania's last extractive boom, the state was stuck with a $5 billion bill to clean up pollution from abandoned mines. What happens when the fracking boom is long gone and communities are stuck with the bill?

In contrast, energy efficiency, wind and solar all provide great economic benefits with no hidden costs. But the oversupply of cheap gas is driving wind and solar out of the market. It's long been fashionable to say that natural gas can be a bridge to clean energy, but in fact it's become a wall to clean energy, because investors don't want to put money into wind and solar when gas is so cheap.

What Danger to the Environment or the Economy Is Caused by the Billions of Gallons of Fresh Water Each Year That Are "Consumed" by Fracking Operations? How Might This Affect the Economic Benefits or Environmental Concerns?

. . .

Rumpler: Each fracking well uses millions of gallons of water. And that water mostly winds up either staying down in the well or being injected deep into the earth as wastewater. So unlike other sectors that use much more water by volume, including agriculture and residential, the water used for fracking is mostly consumed, gone to us for ever.

Does the Current Low Price of Natural Gas Affect Fracking or Conventional Gas Production?

Rumpler: Take a look at Chesapeake Energy, which is one of the biggest fracking operators out there. By the accounts of some analysts, they are massively overextended, with too much land and too many drilling leases. With the price at $2 per million BTU, there was some risk that Chesapeake could at some point lose enough money to risk bankruptcy—and then what would happen to these communities where fracking has taken place? If not Chesapeake, it will be another driller—probably one of the smaller ones—that goes under, and the communities will be left holding the bag. And gas companies don't tell landowners leasing property that oil and gas operations are violations of most standard mortgage agreements, because that is not a risk that the lender is willing to take. Likewise, homeowners' insurance may not cover damages from fracking. Nationwide insurance announced just this summer that their standard policy does not cover damage from fracking. That tells you something. The risk analysts who did the math figured out this is not a safety winner for them. . . .

What If We Halted All Fracking Right Now?

. . .

Rumpler: There's a difference between not starting fracking in new areas and halting it everywhere immediately. If we don't open new places to fracking in New York, Pennsylvania and Texas—just stop where we are now—the impact would be minimal. As Bruce notes, there is so much gas being produced right now that some gas companies are aggressively seeking export licenses, because they want to get rid of the excess and earn a profit. We don't need it to fill energy needs.

In North Dakota they are flaring off the gas, just wasting it into the air. If we need this gas to meet our energy needs, then they should make gas flaring a federal crime and should immediately ban any and all exports of natural gas. The industry would fight tooth and nail against this.

Until we know more, the risks to our health and environment far outweigh any possible benefit to our economy or energy future.

John Rumpler is an environmentalist and attorney.

Bruce McKenzie Everett

NO

Fracking: Pro and Con

For some Americans, it is our energy dreams come true. To others, it is an environmental nightmare. Ever since a new drilling technology, called hydraulic fracturing or fracking, made it possible to extract natural gas from shale deposits about a mile underground, a new gold rush has been under way. . . .

The fracking process begins with a bore hole drilled some 6,000 feet below ground, cutting through many geological layers and aquifers, which tend to be no more than a few hundred feet below the surface. The shaft is then lined with steel and cement casing. Monitors above ground signal when drilling should shift horizontally, boring sideways to pierce long running sections of shale bedrock.

Millions of gallons of water mixed with sand and chemicals are then blasted into the bedrock, the pressure creating cracks that release trapped natural gas from the shale. The gas and water mixture then flows back up to the surface, where the gas is separated from the water. While most of the water stays in the well bore, up to 20 percent is either reused for more fracking or injected into disposal wells thousands of feet underground. . . .

Bruce McKenzie Everett, F70, F72, F80, an adjunct associate professor of international business at the Fletcher School, says fracking provides substantial economic benefits and its problems are relatively small compared to those benefits. He worked at the U.S. Department of Energy from 1974 to 1980 before beginning a 20-year career with ExxonMobil, working in Hong Kong, the Middle East, Africa and Latin America. His research has included gas-to-liquid conversion technology as well as the economics of oil, gas and coal production and use. . . .

Tufts Now: Is Fracking Safe?

Bruce McKenzie Everett: Nothing in the world is entirely safe, but by the standards of industrial activity in the United States, fracking is very, very safe. Think about the airline industry. Lots of things can go wrong with airplanes, but we work very hard to make sure they don't, and as a result, flying is one of the safest activities we've got. Now, that does not mean that things can't happen. It just means that with proper attention, mistakes can be kept to an extremely low level.

The question about fracking that gets the most attention is contamination of drinking water. Aquifers, the underground rivers that provide our drinking water, are about 100 to 200 feet below the surface. The gas-producing shale rock formations tend to be 5,000 to 6,000 feet below the surface. So you need to make sure that the well you drill to pump the water and chemicals through the shale to fracture it and release the gas is sealed properly, and that's not a hard thing to do. . . .

Are There Sufficient Regulations Now in Place to Ensure Safety?

. . .

Everett: There are a lot of regulations currently in place. The question is whether they should be done at the federal or state level. For example, the state government of Pennsylvania understood that the economic activity from fracking could be very, very positive for the state. So they worked with the fracking industry and enacted numerous regulations to try to make sure that two things happened: that they eliminated the dangers to the extent that you can, but that they allowed fracking sites to go forward because the jobs and tax revenue were so positive.

In New York State, they've put a moratorium on fracking, basically saying, "I don't know what to do, so I'll study it and see what happens." I think that's unfortunate, because most of New York is quite economically depressed, and they are denying people economic opportunities.

I have taken a very strong position that it's a bad idea to federalize regulations. If you leave it at the state level, local governments will tend to strike a balance between the economic benefits and the environmental safety issues. If it is left to the federal government, you'll have the same problem you had with the Keystone oil pipeline: people who are not impacted, who will not enjoy the economic benefits, will be allowed to come in and say they don't like it.

What Are the Economic Benefits of Fracking?

Everett: It creates jobs, but that's not the most important way to measure its economic effect. The cost of everything we purchase has an energy component to it, either in its manufacture or its shipping or its packaging. So it is very important to the economy to have energy prices that are relatively low.

Natural gas has become incredibly inexpensive, way beyond what we ever thought possible. We're talking about prices going from $10 or $11 per thousand cubic feet 10 years ago down to $3.77 now, because the supply that has been released by this innovative fracking production technique is just so large. It is a simple consequence of supply and demand. These natural gas prices are the equivalent of oil prices falling to $21 per barrel from their current $86 per-barrel price. . . .

What Danger to the Environment or the Economy Is Caused by the Billions of Gallons of Fresh Water Each Year That Are "Consumed" By Fracking Operations? How Might This Affect the Economic Benefits or Environmental Concerns?

Everett: The water from fracking can be handled in one of several ways: storing, reinjecting and recycling. The real problem we have is that water is not properly priced. As a landowner, you are entitled to draw water from underground aquifers at whatever rate you wish, even if that water is only flowing through your land. We therefore tend to treat water as a free good. Putting a price on it or, alternatively, finding a way to assign property rights would probably fix this problem. As a third alternative, government could regulate it. In any case, it's a solvable problem. . . .

Does the Current Low Price of Natural Gas Affect Fracking or Conventional Gas Production?

. . .

Everett: The price of natural gas has now gotten so low that some are saying they can't produce it economically—but this is a *good* thing for all of us, because it will force them to explore new markets and uses. The United States has an open economy and is a large global trading player. Americans pay the global price for the many things we buy and sell, and energy is one. There are several directions that natural gas production, both fracking and conventional, can take.

One is that people just stop producing it at the current rates, and the price returns to a more stable level and just stays there, likely at the $10-to-$12-dollar level of a decade ago. We could also start exporting. The world price for natural gas is $15 to $16 per thousand cubic feet. By selling it on the global market, that money would come into the U.S. economy. It would require some expensive infrastructure to support it, but the profit margin is so huge, some $12 per thousand cubic feet, that it would be well worth it and a positive impact on our economy.

We could also begin to shut down older coal-fired power plants and replace them with cleaner natural gas plants, and natural gas could find its way into the transportation sector. With engine modifications, it could be used as fuel for cars, or it could be used to produce the battery power for electric cars.

What If We Halted All Fracking Right Now?

Everett: If we stopped right now, or placed a moratorium on new fracking, the price of natural gas would go up to the previous $10 to $11, or worse case, to the global price of $15 to $16. This means electricity prices would go up, heating prices would go up, and we'd lose the economic activity the industry is generating through jobs and lower prices. Basically we would be giving up an opportunity.

Hazards can be controlled through solid regulations that include monitoring and quick responses to problems that arise. Any risks are outweighed by economic benefits. It's not even a close call. . . .

Bruce McKenzie Everett is an energy researcher and adjunct professor.

EXPLORING THE ISSUE

Will Hydraulic Fracturing (Fracking) Negatively Affect Human Health and the Environment?

Critical Thinking and Reflection

1. What are the major economic advantages to fracking?
2. What impact will fracking have on the quality of drinking water?
3. What effect will increased fracking have on the incentive to develop other cleaner energy sources including renewable?
4. What are the health implications of fracking?

Is There Common Ground?

In the spring of 2008, filmmaker Josh Fox received an offer from a natural gas company to lease his family's land in Milanville, Pennsylvania, for $100,000 to drill for gas. Fox then set out to see how communities are being affected in the West where a natural gas drilling boom has been underway for the last 10 years. He spent time with people in their homes and on their land as they relayed their stories of natural gas drilling in Colorado, Wyoming, Utah, and Texas. Fox spoke with residents who experienced a variety of chronic health problems they claim were directly traceable to contamination of their air, of their water wells, or of surface water. In some cases, the residents report that they obtained a court injunction or settlement monies from gas companies to replace the affected water supplies with drinkable water.

The result of Fox's research was the documentary film *Gasland*. During the making of the film, Fox connected with scientists, politicians, and gas industry executives and ultimately found himself in Washington as a subcommittee was discussing the Fracturing Responsibility and Awareness of Chemicals Act, a proposed exemption for hydraulic fracturing from the Safe Drinking Water Act. While the film has both supporters and critics, it did bring publicity to the issues surrounding fracking and raised the question: Is the process safe for the environment and human health and do the economic benefits outweigh any actual or potential problems?

As the United States and Europe seek ways to reduce energy costs and reliance on imported fuels, fracking may be an opportunity to achieve these goals. It's a domestic resource that can be extracted around the country and offers jobs and cheaper energy. On the other hand, there are concerns that the fracking processes needed to extract gas may contaminate ground and surface water with toxic chemicals that could impact health and the environment.

Additional Resources

Grealy, N. (2013). Fracking is one of the best things to happen to onshore gas exploration for a century. *Engineering & Technology (17509637), 8*(1), 24.

Herman, A. (2015). The liberal war on American energy independence. *Commentary*, 17–24.

Pierre-Louis, K. (2017). What the frack. *Popular Science*, 12.

Ratcliffe, I. (2013). Fracking is dangerous to environment and throws good energy after bad. *Engineering & Technology (17509637), 8*(1), 25.

Vogel, L. (2017). Fracking tied to cancer-causing chemicals. *CMAJ: Canadian Medical Association Journal, 189*(2), E94–E95.

Internet References . . .

Environmental Protection Agency

www.epa.gov

Natural Gas.org

www.naturalgas.org

Hydraulic Fracturing—AmericanRivers.org

www.americanrivers.org/fracking

Selected, Edited, and with Issue Framing Material by:
Eileen L. Daniel, *SUNY College at Brockport*

ISSUE

Is There a Valid Link Between Saturated Fat and Heart Disease?

YES: Henry Blackburn, from "In Defense of U Research: The Ancel Keys Legacy," *Star Tribune* (2014)

NO: Jon White, from "Fat or Fiction?" *New Scientist* (2014)

Learning Outcomes

After reading this issue, you will be able to:

- Understand the different types of fat in the diet.
- Discuss the relationship between saturated fat and heart disease researched by Dr. Ancel Keys and his team.
- Understand the possible link between refined carbohydrates and heart disease.

ISSUE SUMMARY

YES: Professor emeritus and researcher Henry Blackburn contends that valid research by Dr. Ancel Keys and his team established a strong link between saturated fat and heart disease.

NO: Opinion editor at *New Scientist* magazine Jon White argues that the science behind the saturated fat–heart disease link was flawed and that carbohydrates, not fats, are the real culprits.

Eating foods that contain saturated fats has long been thought to raise the blood levels of cholesterol, a risk factor for heart disease and stroke. From a chemical standpoint, saturated fats are fat molecules that have no double bonds between carbon molecules because they are saturated with hydrogen molecules. Saturated fats are typically solid at room temperature and occur naturally in many foods. The majority are found in animal products such as beef, lamb, pork, butter, cheese, and other dairy products which contain fat. In addition, many baked goods and fried foods can contain high levels of saturated fats from plant-based oils such as palm oil, palm kernel oil, and coconut oil. Most mainstream organizations including the American Heart Association maintain that eating these foods that contain saturated fats raises the level of serum cholesterol, a risk for cardiovascular disease (CVD).

However, recent research published in respectable medical journals seems to contradict the advice to eat less saturated fat and replace it with unsaturated oils. A 2014 article published in the *Annals of Internal Medicine* concluded that "Current evidence does not clearly support cardiovascular guidelines that encourage high consumption of polyunsaturated fatty acids and low consumption of total saturated fats." Consumers have long been warned of the link between saturated fat and heart disease. But this large and exhaustive new analysis by a team of international scientists found no evidence that eating saturated fat increased heart attacks and other cardiac events. The new findings are part of a growing body of research that has challenged the accepted wisdom that saturated fat is inherently bad for you and will continue the debate about what foods are best to eat. But the new research did not find that individuals who ate higher levels of saturated fat had more heart disease than those who ate less. Nor did it find less disease in those eating higher amounts of unsaturated fat, including monounsaturated fat such as olive oil or corn oil or other polyunsaturated fats.

Scientists claim that looking at individual fats and other nutrient groups in isolation could be misleading, because when people cut down on fats they tend to eat more bread, cold cereal, and other refined carbohydrates that can also be bad for cardiovascular health. Consumers would likely be better off to eat foods that are typical of the Mediterranean diet, like nuts, fish, avocado, high-fiber grains, and olive oil. A recent study showed that a Mediterranean diet with more nuts and extra virgin olive oil reduced heart attacks and strokes when compared with a lower fat diet with more starches.

In the new research, researchers reviewed and evaluated the most relevant evidence to date from 80 studies involving more than a half million people. They looked not only at what people reportedly ate, but also at the composition of fatty acids in their bloodstreams and in their fat tissue. The scientists also reviewed evidence from 27 randomized controlled trials—the gold standard in scientific research—that assessed whether taking polyunsaturated fat supplements such as fish oil promoted heart health. They did determine there was a link between trans fats, partially hydrogenated oils that had long been added to processed foods, and heart disease. But they found no evidence of dangers from saturated fat, or benefits from other kinds of fats.

The primary reason saturated fat has historically had a bad reputation is that it increases low-density lipoprotein cholesterol, or LDL, which raises the risk for heart attacks. But the relationship between saturated fat and LDL is complex. In addition to raising LDL cholesterol, saturated fat also increases high-density lipoprotein, or HDL, the so-called good cholesterol. And the LDL that it raises is a subtype of big, fluffy particles that are generally benign. Doctors refer to a preponderance of these particles as LDL pattern A. The smallest and densest form of LDL is more dangerous. These particles are easily oxidized and are more likely to set off inflammation and contribute to the buildup of artery-narrowing plaque. An LDL profile that consists mostly of these particles, known as pattern B, usually coincides with high triglycerides and low levels of HDL, both risk factors for heart attacks and stroke. The smaller, more artery-clogging particles are increased not by saturated fat, but by sugary foods and an excess of carbohydrates. It appears that a high carbohydrate or sugary diet should be the focus of dietary guidelines.

Although the new research showed no relationship overall between saturated or polyunsaturated fat intake and cardiac events, there are numerous unique fatty acids within these two groups, and there was some indication that they are not all equal. When the researchers looked at fatty acids in the bloodstream, for example, they found that a type of saturated fat found in milk and dairy products was associated with lower cardiovascular risk. Two types of polyunsaturated fats found in fish also appeared protective. But a number of fatty acids commonly found in vegetable oils and processed foods may pose risks, the findings suggested.

The researchers then looked at data from the randomized trials to see if taking supplements like fish oil produced any cardiovascular benefits. It did not. An explanation for this discrepancy might be that the studies involved people who had preexisting heart disease or were at high risk of developing it, while the other studies involved generally healthy populations. So it is possible that the benefits of eating fish or taking fish oils lie in preventing heart disease, rather than treating or reversing it. At least two large clinical trials designed to see if this is the case are currently underway.

While the evidence against restricting saturated fats seems clear, Professor Walter Willett, chair of the Department of Nutrition at Harvard School of Public Health, is concerned that the conclusions may be misleading. A recent World Health Organization (WHO) and Food and Agricultural Organization (FAO) expert consultation report concluded that "intake of saturated fatty acids is directly related to cardiovascular risk. The traditional target is to restrict the intake of saturated fatty acids to less than 10% of daily energy intake and less than 7% for high-risk groups." The Dietary Guidelines for Americans, 2010 produced by the United States Department of Agriculture (USDA) indicates that the human body makes more than enough saturated fats to meet its needs and does not require more from dietary sources. Higher levels of saturated fats are associated with higher levels of total cholesterol and low-density lipoprotein "bad" cholesterol and recommends reduced saturated fat intake. While many other organizations support this, others disagree.

YES

Henry Blackburn

In Defense of U Research: The Ancel Keys Legacy

Recently, a number of writers identifying themselves as "health-science journalists" have been calling on Americans to "end the war on fat" as they promote a high-fat, low-carbohydrate diet ("Chocolate milk in the schools and other products of expert opinion," June 22). What's puzzling is that they draw attention to their arguments by using personal attacks on one of Minnesota's premier scientists, Ancel Keys.

Keys was a University of Minnesota physiologist who spent most of his career conducting wide-ranging studies on the relationship of lifestyle—especially the foods we eat—to heart disease. He worked at the university from the late 1930s until his death at age 100 in 2004, and he carried out classic experiments of diet effects on blood-cholesterol levels in the laboratory and of diet associations with heart attacks among cultures with contrasting traditional eating patterns. "Contrasting" is the operative word here.

Keys' most influential work is the Seven Countries Study. Begun in 1958 and still in progress, it compares diet, risk factors, and rates of heart attack and stroke among regions of Greece, Italy, the former Yugoslavia, the Netherlands, Finland, the United States and Japan. Some recent (nonscientist) interpreters of the study have accused Keys of "cherry-picking" the countries with "preconceived" ideas about what he would find. Demonstrating a lack of understanding of how scientists approach new questions, they suggest he should have chosen specific other countries or should have chosen his sites "randomly." Any savvy scientist at an early phase of questioning knows to look first not randomly but across wide variations of the cause under consideration, in this case diet.

Keys chose the study areas because of their apparent differences in traditional diet, between the extremes of the rice- and vegetable-based diets of Japanese farmers and fishermen and the fatty meat, cheese and butter lunches of Finnish loggers. Another criterion was the availability of collaborators who understood the cultures and could provide logistical support and access to communities.

After years of observations among these regions, Keys and colleagues found major, five- to tenfold differences in heart-attack rates in relation to diet, an association compatible with the hypothesis that diet influences heart-attack risk and one congruent with their findings in feeding experiments back home. They also showed that the lowest heart-attack rates and longest survival occurred in both Japan, with its low-fat diet, and Greece, where the diet was relatively high in fat, mostly from olive oil. Their common factor was not the amount of fat people ate but the type of fat, with both areas consuming very little saturated fat.

The critics also accuse Keys of suppressing evidence collected during the studies in Crete. They claim that he rejected the results of hundreds of individual diet questionnaires and that his characterization of the diet was inaccurate because it was based on a survey that took place during Lent. Both charges are false and misleading.

Keys determined early that occasional questionnaires about foods we eat were unreliable, useful only for detecting significant departures from a population's typical eating habits. Although individual questionnaires were recorded, the study did not rely on them for the regional comparisons. Instead, Keys collected actual foods eaten for a full week among randomly selected families and chemically analyzed their nutrient content in the standardized laboratory in Minnesota. Repeat food collections were scheduled in different seasons during different years to provide a valid estimate of the nutrients consumed by an entire population. Events such as religious holidays and crop failures have an effect on what people eat at a given time and are part of the bigger picture of a community's eating pattern. Avoiding variations in eating at different parts of the yearly cycle would have been the real "cherry-picking."

The eating pattern that came out of these international comparisons is being referred to by critics as "low-fat" or "extreme low-fat," even though it includes leaner meats and lower-fat dairy foods as well as many types of vegetable oils. In fact, only Keys' saturated-fat recommendation—less than 10 percent of calories—might be considered "low." In the popular cookbooks written with his wife, Margaret, Keys called the pattern "eating well" and, later, "eating well the Mediterranean way."

In the most bizarre accusation of all, several writers are laying the blame on Keys for our modern epidemics of obesity and diabetes. It all started in the 1950s, they say, with Keys' undue influence on the American Heart Association and the later U.S. government dietary guidelines. The idea that one person could hold such sway for years over these notoriously skeptical bodies strains credulity. It was the strength of the evidence, plus a pragmatic decision how best to reduce saturated-fat consumption, not Keys' "force of will," that inspired the dietary policies.

In the meantime, social and cultural changes already underway truly did set the nation on the path to obesity. Restaurants increased portion sizes and people consumed more calories. Suburbs were built without sidewalks, and schools installed pop machines and served fast food. The food industry, already expert at marketing high-fat packaged foods, saw a new marketing opportunity and developed companion product lines in which fats were replaced by sugar and other simple carbohydrates or substitutes—something Keys never advised nor supported. Industry and advertisers, not Keys, led shoppers to believe that these "reduced-fat" foods were the healthier choices.

In addition to finding—and exploiting for profit—a common villain in Keys, these writers use a number of devices to promote what Nina Teicholz, author of "The Big Fat Surprise," advocates as a return to "tallow and lard." Innuendo, distortions and accusations may be good for media attention and book sales, but they can do real damage—not only to the reputation of a pioneering researcher, but to public understanding of the scientific method and the evolving science of nutrition. It's time to end the war on Ancel Keys.

Henry Blackburn is a physician and professor emeritus of epidemiology at the University of Minnesota School of Public Health.

Jon White

Fat or Fiction?

Can decades of health warnings about steak, butter and cream really be wrong?

There's a famous scene in Woody Allen's film *Sleeper* in which two scientists in the year 2173 are discussing the dietary advice of the late 20th century.

"You mean there was no deep fat, no steak or cream pies or hot fudge?" asks one, incredulous. "Those were thought to be unhealthy," replies the other. "Precisely the opposite of what we now know to be true."

We're not quite in Woody Allen territory yet, but steak and cream pies are starting to look a lot less unhealthy than they once did. After 35 years as dietary gospel, the idea that saturated fat is bad for your heart appears to be melting away like a lump of butter in a hot pan.

So is it OK to eat more red meat and cheese? Will the current advice to limit saturated fat be overturned? If it is, how did we get it so wrong for so long?

The answers matter. According to the World Health Organization, cardiovascular disease is the world's leading cause of death, killing more than 17 million people annually, about a third of all deaths. It predicts that by 2030, 23 million will succumb each year. In the US, an estimated 81 million people are living with cardiovascular disease. The healthcare bill is a small fortune.

The idea that eating saturated fat—found in high levels in animal products such as meat and dairy—directly raises the risk of a heart attack has been a mainstay of nutrition science since the 1970s. Instead, we are urged to favour the "healthy" fats found in vegetable oils and foods such as fish, nuts and seeds.

In the US the official guidance for adults is that no more than 30 per cent of total calories should come from fat, and no more than 10 per cent from saturated fat. UK advice is roughly the same. That is by no means an unattainable target: an average man could eat a whole 12-inch pepperoni pizza and still have room for an ice cream before busting the limit. Nonetheless, adults in the UK and US manage to eat more saturated fat than recommended.

We used to eat even more. From the 1950s to the late 1970s, fat accounted for more than 40 per cent of dietary calories in the UK. It was a similar story in the US. But as warnings began to circulate, people trimmed back on foods such as butter and beef. The food industry responded, filling the shelves with low-fat cookies, cakes and spreads.

So the message got through, at least partially. Deaths from heart disease have gone down in Western nations. In the UK in 1961 more than half of all deaths were from coronary heart disease; in 2009 less than a third were. But medical treatment and prevention have improved so dramatically it's impossible to tell what role, if any, changes in diet played. And even though fat consumption has gone down, obesity and its associated diseases have not.

To appreciate how saturated fat in food affects our health we need to understand how it is handled by the body, and how it differs from other types of fat.

When you eat fat, it travels to the small intestine where it is broken down into its constituent parts—fatty acids and glycerol and absorbed into cells lining the gut. There they are packaged up with cholesterol and proteins and posted into the bloodstream. These small, spherical packages are called lipoproteins, and they are what allow water-insoluble fats and cholesterol (together known as lipids) to get to where they are needed.

The more fat you eat, the higher the levels of lipoprotein in your blood. And that, according to conventional wisdom, is where the health problems begin.

Good and Bad Cholesterol

Lipoproteins come in two main types, high density and low density. Low-density lipoproteins (LDLs) are often simply known as "bad cholesterol" despite the fact that they contain more than just cholesterol. LDLs are bad because they can stick to the insides of artery walls, resulting in deposits called plaques that narrow and harden the vessels, raising the risk that a blood clot could cause a blockage. Of all types of fat in the diet, saturated fats have been shown to raise bad cholesterol levels the most. (Consuming cholesterol has surprisingly little influence: the reason it has a bad name is that it is found in animal foods that also tend to be high in saturated fat.)

High-density lipoproteins (HDLs), or "good cholesterol," on the other hand, help guard against arterial plaques. Conventional wisdom has it that HDL is raised by eating foods rich in unsaturated fats or soluble fibre such as whole grains, fruits and vegetables. This, in a nutshell, is the lipid hypothesis, possibly the most influential idea in the history of human nutrition.

The hypothesis traces its origins back to the 1940s when a rising tide of heart attacks among middle-aged men was spreading alarm in the US. At the time this was explained as a consequence of ageing. But Ancel Keys, a physiologist at the University of Minnesota, had other ideas.

Keys noted that heart attacks were rare in some Mediterranean countries and in Japan, where people ate a diet lower in fat. Convinced that there was a causal link, he launched the pioneering Seven Countries Study in 1958. In all, he recruited 12,763 men aged 40 to 59 in the US, Finland, The Netherlands, Italy, Yugoslavia, Greece and Japan. The participants' diet and heart health were checked five and 10 years after enrolling.

Keys concluded that there was a correlation between saturated fat in food, raised levels of blood lipids and the risk of heart attacks and strokes. The lipid hypothesis was born.

The finding was supported by other research, notably the Framingham Heart Study, which tracked diet and heart health in a town in Massachusetts. In light of this research and the rising toll—by the 1980s nearly a million Americans a year were dying from heart attacks—health authorities decided to officially push for a reduction in fat, and saturated fat in particular. Official guidelines first appeared in 1980 in the US and 1991 in the UK, and have stood firm ever since.

Yet the voices of doubt have been growing for some time. In 2010, scientists pooled the results of 21 studies that had followed 348,000 people for many years. This meta-analysis found "no significant evidence" in support of the idea that saturated fat raises the risk of heart disease (*American Journal of Clinical Nutrition*, vol. 91, p. 535).

The doubters were given a further boost by another meta-analysis published in March (*Annals of Internal Medicine*, vol. 160, p. 398). It revisited the results of 72 studies involving 640,000 people in 18 countries.

To the surprise of many, it did not find backing for the existing dietary advice. "Current evidence does not clearly support guidelines that encourage high consumption of polyunsaturated fatty acids and low consumption of total saturated fats," it concluded. "Nutritional guidelines may require reappraisal."

In essence, the study found that people at the extreme ends of the spectrum—that is, those who ate the most or least saturated fat—had the same chance of developing heart disease. High consumption of unsaturated fat seemed to offer no protection.

The analysis has been strongly criticised for containing methodological errors and omitting studies that should have been included. But the authors stand by their general conclusions and say the paper has already had the intended effect of breaking the taboo around saturated fat.

Green Light

Outside of academia, its conclusion was greeted with gusto. Many commentators interpreted it as a green light to resume eating saturated fat. But is it? Did Keys really get it wrong? Or is there some other explanation for the conflict between his work and the many studies that supported it, and the two recent meta-analyses?

Even as Keys's research was starting to influence health advice, critics were pointing out flaws in it. One common complaint was that he cherry-picked data to support his hypothesis, ignoring countries such as France which had high-fat diets but low rates of heart disease. The strongest evidence in favour of a low-fat diet came from Crete, but it transpired that Keys had recorded some food intake data there during Lent, a time when Greek people traditionally avoid meat and cheese, so he may have underestimated their normal fat intake.

The Framingham research, too, has its detractors. Critics say that it followed an unrepresentative group of predominantly white men and women who were at high risk for heart disease for non-dietary reasons such as smoking.

More recently, it has also become clear that the impact of saturated fat is more complex than was understood back then.

Ronald Krauss of the University of California, San Francisco, has long researched the links between lipoprotein and heart disease. He was involved in the 2010 meta-analysis and is convinced there is room for at least a partial rethink of the lipid hypothesis.

He points to studies suggesting that not all LDL is the same, and that casting it all as bad was wrong. It is now widely accepted that LDL comes in two types—big, fluffy particles and smaller, compact ones. It is the latter, Krauss says, that are strongly linked to heart-disease risk, while the fluffy ones appear a lot less risky. Crucially, Krauss says, eating saturated fat boosts fluffy LDL. What's more, there is some research suggesting small LDL gets a boost from a low-fat, high-carbohydrate diet, especially one rich in sugars.

Why might smaller LDL particles be riskier?

In their journey around the bloodstream, LDL particles bind to cells and are pulled out of circulation. Krauss says smaller LDLs don't bind as easily, so remain in the blood for longer—and the longer they are there, the greater their chance of causing damage. They are also more easily converted into an oxidised form that is considered more damaging. Finally, there are simply more of them for the same overall cholesterol level. And more LDLs equate to greater risk of arterial damage, Krauss says. He thinks that the evidence is strong enough for the health advice to change.

But Susan Jebb, professor of diet and population health at the University of Oxford, says it is too early to buy into this alternative model of LDLs and health. "The jury has to be out because relatively few of the studies have subdivided LDL. It may well be worth exploring, but right now I am not persuaded."

Jeremy Pearson, a vascular biologist and associate medical director at the British Heart Foundation, which part-funded the 2014 meta-analysis, agrees. He says the original idea that a diet high in saturated fat raises the risk of heart disease remains persuasive, and that there are other meta-analyses that support this. He also points to hard evidence from studies in animals, where dietary control is possible to a degree that it is not in people. They repeatedly show high saturated fat leads to high LDL and hardened arteries, he says.

So how does he explain the meta-analyses that cast doubt on the orthodoxy? "I guess what that means is that in free living humans there are other things that are usually more important regarding whether you have a heart attack or not than the balance of saturated and unsaturated fat in your diet," Pearson says. Factors such as lack of exercise, alcohol intake and body weight may simply overshadow the impact of fat.

Certainly, the debate cannot be divorced from the issue of overall calorie intake, which rose in the three decades from the 1970s in the US and many other countries. The result was rising numbers of overweight people. And being overweight or obese raises the risk of heart disease.

Another key factor might be what people now eat instead of saturated fat. "The effect of reducing saturated fat depends on what replaces it," says Walter Willett of the Harvard School of Public Health. "We consciously or unconsciously replace a large reduction in calories with something else."

The problem, as some see it, is that the something else is usually refined carbohydrates, especially sugars, added to foods to take the place of fat. A review in 2009 showed that if carbohydrates were raised while saturated fat cut, the outcome was a raised heart-disease risk. This plays to the emerging idea that sugar is the real villain.

Then there are trans fats. Created by food chemists to replace animal fats such as lard, they are made by chemically modifying vegetable oils to make them solid. Because they are unsaturated, and so "healthy" the food industry piled them into products such as cakes and spreads. But it later turned out that trans fats cause heart disease. All told, it is possible that the meta-analyses simply show that the benefits of switching away from saturated fat were cancelled out by replacing them with sugar and trans fats.

Meanwhile, science continues to unravel some intricacies of fat metabolism which could also help to account for the confusing results. One promising avenue is that not all types of saturated fat are the same. The 2014 meta-analysis, for example, found clear indications that different saturated fatty acids in blood are associated with different coronary risk. Some saturated fats appear to lower the risk; some unsaturated ones increase it.

Meat vs. Dairy

Although further big studies are needed to confirm these findings, lead author Rajiv Chowdhury, an epidemiologist at the University of Cambridge, says this is an avenue that might be worth exploring.

There is other evidence that not all saturated fats are the same. A study from 2012 found that while eating lots of saturated fat from meat increased the risk of heart disease, equivalent amounts from dairy actually reduced it. The researchers calculated that cutting calories from meaty saturated fat by just 2 per cent and replacing them with saturated fat from dairy reduces the risk of a heart attack or stroke by 25 per cent.

Krauss also cites studies showing that eating cheese does not raise bad cholesterol as much as eating butter, even when both have identical levels of saturated fat.

So could future advice say that saturated fat from dairy sources is less risky than that from meat, for example? Or urge us to favour cheese over butter? It's too early to say. Jebb is aware that the idea that some saturated fatty acids may be worse than others is gaining credence, but says it is far from being ready to guide eating habits.

Nonetheless, there is a growing feeling that we need to reappraise our thinking on fat.

Marion Nestle, professor of nutrition at New York University, says that studies of single nutrients have a fundamental flaw. "People do not eat saturated fat," she says. "They eat foods containing fats and oils that are mixtures of saturated, unsaturated and polyunsaturated fats, and many other nutrients that affect health and also vary in calories. So teasing saturated fat out of all that is not simple."

The only way to rigorously test the various hypotheses would be to put some people on one kind of diet and others on another for 20 years or more. "Doable? Fundable? I don't think so," says Nestle.

So where does that leave us? Is it time to reverse 35 years of dietary advice and stop worrying about fuzzing up our arteries?

Some nutritionists say yes. Krauss advocates a rethink of guidelines on saturated fat when a new version of the Dietary Guidelines for Americans is put together next year. He certainly believes that the even stricter limit on saturated fat recommended by the American Heart Association—that it constitute no more than 7 per cent of daily calorie intake—should be relaxed.

Others, though, strike a note of caution. Nestle says that the answer depends on context. "If calories are balanced and diets contain plenty of vegetables, foods richer in saturated fat should not be a problem. But that's not how most people eat," she says.

Jebb and Pearson see no reason to shift the guidance just yet, although Jebb says it may be time for a review of fat by the UK's Scientific Advisory Committee on Nutrition, which last visited the issue in 1991.

So while dietary libertarians may be gleefully slapping a big fat steak on the griddle and lining up a cream pie with hot fudge for dessert, the dietary advice of the 1970s still stands—for now. In other words, steak and butter can be part of a healthy diet. Just don't overdo them.

Jon White is opinion editor of *New Scientist* magazine.

EXPLORING THE ISSUE

Is There a Valid Link Between Saturated Fat and Heart Disease?

Critical Thinking and Reflection

1. Is it better to eat more carbohydrates and less fat? Explain.
2. Why do so many organizations support restricting saturated fats?
3. Why has saturated fat traditionally had a bad reputation?

Is There Common Ground?

In 1955 Dr. Ancel Keys began research that came to be known as the Seven Countries Study. His interest in diet and cardiovascular disease (CVD) was based on seemingly paradoxical data. Well nourished American business executives had high rates of heart disease, while in Europe after World War II, CVD rates had decreased sharply despite limited food supplies. Dr. Keys hypothesized there was a correlation between cholesterol levels and CVD and began a study of Minnesota businessmen. At a 1955 expert meeting at the World Health Organization in Geneva, Keys presented his diet–lipid–heart disease hypothesis.

Following that presentation, Dr. Keys observed that southern Italy had the highest rate of centenarians in the world and theorized that a Mediterranean-style diet low in animal fat protected against heart disease while a high-fat diet increased the risk. The results of what later became known as the Seven Countries Study seemed to indicate that serum cholesterol was strongly correlated to coronary heart disease mortality at both the population and individual levels. Following this, the American Heart Association and the U.S. government began educating the public that a diet which included large amounts of butter, lard, eggs, and beef would lead to coronary heart disease and that these foods should be replaced by fish, oils, and fat-free dairy products.

The conclusion Keys reached was that saturated fats have negative effects as opposed to the beneficial impact of unsaturated fats. For the next 20-year period all dietary fats were considered unhealthy, driven by the hypothesis that all dietary fats cause obesity and cancer. Recent studies question cardiovascular guidelines that encourage high consumption of polyunsaturated fatty acids and low consumption of total saturated fats. Overall, it appears that researchers are questioning Dr. Keys' research, though no final conclusions have been drawn.

Additional Resources

Chowdhury, R., Warnakula, S., Kunutsor, S., Crowe, F., Ward, H. A., Johnson, L.,. . . Di Angelantonio, E. (2014). Association of dietary, circulating, and supplement fatty acids with coronary risk. *Annals of Internal Medicine, 160*(6), 398–407.

Myers, E. F. (2015). New insights or confusion—is butter really back? *Nutrition Today, 50*(1), 12–27.

Harvard researchers renew warnings about saturated fat and heart disease (2017). *Harvard Health Letter, 42*(4), 8.

Walsh, B. (2014). Don't blame fat. *Time, 183*(24), 28–35.

Internet References . . .

Academy of Nutrition and Dietetics

www.eatright.org

American Heart Association

www.heart.org

Center for Science in the Public Interest

www.cspinet.org

Selected, Edited, and with Issue Framing Material by:
Eileen L. Daniel, *SUNY College at Brockport*

ISSUE

Are Restrictions on Sugar and Sugary Beverages Justified?

YES: Gary Taubes and Cristin Kearns Couzens, from "Sweet Little Lies," *Mother Jones* (2012)

NO: Kenneth W. Krause, from "Saving Us from Sweets: This Is Science and Government on Sugar," *Skeptical Inquirer* (2012)

Learning Outcomes

After reading this issue, you will be able to:

- Discuss the nutritional risk factors associated with the consumption of sugar and sugary beverages.
- Understand the role sugar and sugary beverages may play in the current obesity epidemic.
- Assess the need for government restrictions on the sale of sugary and sugar beverages.

ISSUE SUMMARY

YES: Writers Gary Taubes and Cristin Kearns Couzens maintain that added sugars and sweeteners pose dangers to health and that the sugar industry continually campaigns to enhance its image.

NO: Journalist Kenneth W. Krause argues that individuals have the ability to make decisions about sugar consumption themselves and that government should not restrict our access to sugar and sugar-containing food products.

The per capita consumption of refined sugar in the United States has varied between 60 and 100 pounds in the last 40 years. In 2008, American per capita total consumption of sugar and sweeteners, exclusive of artificial sweeteners, equaled 136 pounds per year. This consisted of 65.4 pounds of refined sugar and 68.3 pounds of corn-derived sweeteners per person. Granulated sugars are used at the table to sprinkle on foods and to sweeten hot drinks and in home baking to add sweetness and texture to cooked products. From a dietary perspective, the top five contributors to added sugars in our food supply are sugar-sweetened sodas, grain-based desserts and snacks such as cakes and cookies, fruit drinks, dairy-based desserts including ice cream, and puddings and candy.

There are numerous studies linking sugar to a variety of health concerns including diabetes and obesity. Studies on the relationship between sugars and diabetes are inconsistent since some propose that consuming large quantities of sugar does not directly increase the risk of diabetes. The extra calories, however, from eating excessive amounts of sugar can lead to obesity, which may itself increase the risk of developing diabetes. Other studies show a relationship between refined sugar consumption and the onset of diabetes. These included a 2010 analysis of 11 studies involving over 300,000 participants. Researchers found that sugar-sweetened beverages may increase the risk of developing type 2 diabetes through obesity and other metabolic abnormalities linked to sugar consumption.

To address the increasing rates of obesity and its link to diabetes and other diseases, the New York City Board of Health approved a ban on the sale of large sodas and other sugary drinks at restaurants, street carts, and movie theaters, the first restriction of its kind in the country, in the fall of 2012. The measure, promoted by Mayor Michael

R. Bloomberg, is likely to strengthen a growing national debate about soft drinks and obesity, and it could prompt other cities to follow suit, despite the fact that many New Yorkers appear uncomfortable with the ban. The measure, which bars the sale of many sweetened drinks in containers larger than 16 ounces, was to take effect in March 2013. The vote by the Board of Health was the only regulatory approval needed to make the ban binding in the city, but the American soft drink industry has campaigned strongly against the measure and promised to fight it through other means, possibly in the courts. The soft drink industry argued that to single out one food item and claim it is the cause of obesity is inappropriate. While a state judge blocked the law in March 2013, the mayor vowed to continue his fight against mounting obesity by encouraging a ban on super large sized soft drinks.

Soft drink and other food manufacturers, like all companies, advertise and promote their products in order to maximize sales. Many non-nutritious foods are presented to the public in a misleading way for that purpose. For instance, low fiber, high sugar breakfast cereals may be sprinkled with vitamins and marketed as a low fat, nutritious breakfast. Some school districts, working with food manufacturers and producers, sell fast food items in school cafeterias. Soft drink companies have provided monies and other support to schools who promote their products. Non-nutritious foods including sugary breakfast cereals, fast food, and candy are heavily advertised on television shows catering to children.

Ethical and legal standards for the food industry, mandated by the government, could address some of these concerns. For instance, clearer food labels, which allow consumers to better understand what they're eating, might help reduce excessive consumption of calories, fat, and sugar. Many non-nutritious food labels seem to have incredibly small or unrealistic serving sizes. A more accurate serving size might be beneficial to consumers. A ban on the advertising of junk foods in public schools, specifically soft drinks, candy, and other items with high sugar content, could also be enacted as well as increased taxes on these foods. Alcohol and tobacco advertisements are not allowed on children's television, so it would seem reasonable to ban the promotion of foods that encourage overeating and obesity. In addition, non-nutritious foods could have health warnings similar to the warnings on cigarette packs or bottles of alcoholic beverages.

On the other hand, the proposed ban on the sale of large containers of soft drinks, while well intentioned, is controversial as some consumers wonder just how far the government should go to protect us from ourselves. To promote public health, New York City currently restricts smoking in public parks and bans trans fats from food served in restaurants. But Mayor Bloomberg's proposal raises questions about government's role in shaping and restricting individual choices. If government officials can limit the size of sodas, next it could decide to restrict portion sizes of restaurant food or the size of pre-made meals sold at supermarkets. If government is within its rights to restrict behavior to protect health, many other limits could be imposed in the name of health promotion. As many ponder the role of government in restricting the individual freedom to eat what one wants in whatever quantity, the rate of obesity in this country remains a serious health issue.

In addressing the question of whether or not restrictions on sugar and sugary beverages are justified, Gary Taubes and Cristin Kearns Couzens believe that added sugars and sweeteners pose a threat to health by increasing the risk for diabetes and heart disease. Kenneth W. Krause argues that individuals have the ability to make decisions about sugar consumption themselves and that government should not restrict our access to sugar or sugar-containing foods.

YES

Gary Taubes and Cristin Kearns Couzens

Sweet Little Lies

Inside an industry's campaign to frost its image, hold regulators at bay, and keep scientists from asking: **Does sugar kill?**

On a brisk spring Tuesday in 1976, a pair of executives from the Sugar Association stepped up to the podium of a Chicago ballroom to accept the Oscar of the public relations world, the Silver Anvil award for excellence in "the forging of public opinion." The trade group had recently pulled off one of the greatest turnarounds in PR history. For nearly a decade, the sugar industry had been buffeted by crisis after crisis as the media and the public soured on sugar and scientists began to view it as a likely cause of obesity, diabetes, and heart disease. Industry ads claiming that eating sugar helped you lose weight had been called out by the Federal Trade Commission, and the Food and Drug Administration had launched a review of whether sugar was even safe to eat. Consumption had declined 12 percent in just two years, and producers could see where that trend might lead. As John "JW" Tatem Jr. and Jack O'Connell Jr., the Sugar Association's president and director of public relations, posed that day with their trophies, their smiles only hinted at the coup they'd just pulled off.

Their winning campaign, crafted with the help of the prestigious public relations firm Carl Byoir & Associates, had been prompted by a poll showing that consumers had come to see sugar as fattening, and that most doctors suspected it might exacerbate, if not cause, heart disease and diabetes. With an initial annual budget of nearly $800,000 ($3.4 million today) collected from the makers of Dixie Crystals, Domino, C&H, Great Western, and other sugar brands, the association recruited a stable of medical and nutritional professionals to allay the public's fears, brought snack and beverage companies into the fold, and bankrolled scientific papers that contributed to a "highly supportive" FDA ruling, which, the Silver Anvil application boasted, made it "unlikely that sugar will be subject to legislative restriction in coming years."

The story of sugar, as Tatem told it, was one of a harmless product under attack by "opportunists dedicated to exploiting the consuming public." Over the subsequent decades, it would be transformed from what the *New York Times* in 1977 had deemed "a villain in disguise" into a nutrient so seemingly innocuous that even the American Heart Association and the American Diabetes Association approved it as part of a healthy diet. Research on the suspected links between sugar and chronic disease largely ground to a halt by the late 1980s, and scientists came to view such pursuits as a career dead end. So effective were the Sugar Association's efforts that, to this day, no consensus exists about sugar's potential dangers. The industry's PR campaign corresponded roughly with a significant rise in Americans' consumption of "caloric sweeteners," including table sugar (sucrose) and high-fructose corn syrup (HFCS). This increase was accompanied, in turn, by a surge in the chronic diseases increasingly linked to sugar. (See chart below.) Since 1970, obesity rates in the United States have more than doubled, while the incidence of diabetes has more than tripled.

Precisely how did the sugar industry engineer its turnaround? The answer is found in more than 1,500 pages of internal memos, letters, and company board reports we discovered buried in the archives of now-defunct sugar companies as well as in the recently released papers of deceased researchers and consultants who played key roles in the industry's strategy. They show how Big Sugar used Big Tobacco-style tactics to ensure that government agencies would dismiss troubling health claims against their products. Compared to the tobacco companies, which knew for a fact that their wares were deadly and spent billions of dollars trying to cover up that reality, the sugar industry had a relatively easy task. With the jury still out on sugar's health effects, producers simply needed to make sure that the uncertainty lingered. But the goal was the same: to safeguard sales by creating a body of evidence companies could deploy to counter any unfavorable research.

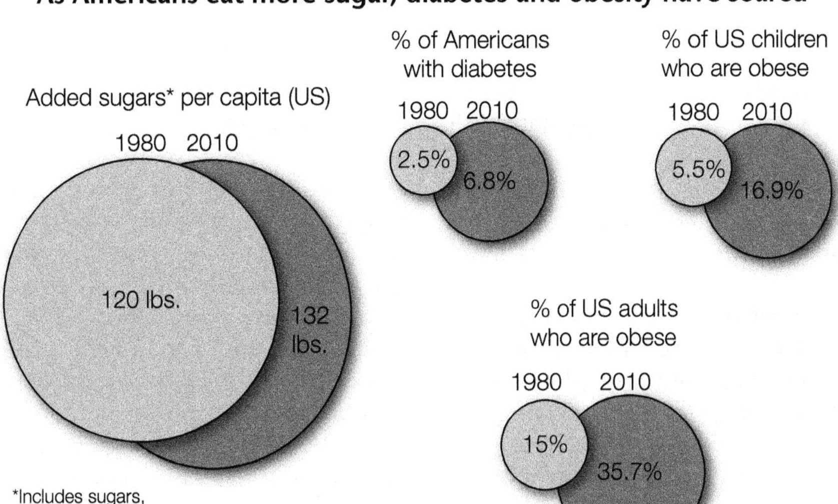

Sources: USDA, CDC, US Census Bureau

This decades-long effort to stack the scientific deck is why, today, the USDA's dietary guidelines only speak of sugar in vague generalities. ("Reduce the intake of calories from solid fats and added sugars.") It's why the FDA insists that sugar is "generally recognized as safe" despite considerable evidence suggesting otherwise. It's why some scientists' urgent calls for regulation of sugary products have been dead on arrival, and it's why—absent any federal leadership—New York City Mayor Michael Bloomberg felt compelled to propose a ban on oversized sugary drinks that passed in September.

In fact, a growing body of research suggests that sugar and its nearly chemically identical cousin, HFCS, may very well cause diseases that kill hundreds of thousands of Americans every year, and that these chronic conditions would be far less prevalent if we significantly dialed back our consumption of added sugars. Robert Lustig, a leading authority on pediatric obesity at the University of California-San Francisco (whose arguments Gary explored in a 2011 *New York Times Magazine* cover story), made this case last February in the prestigious journal *Nature*. In an article titled "The Toxic Truth About Sugar," Lustig and two colleagues observed that sucrose and HFCS are addictive in much the same way as cigarettes and alcohol, and that overconsumption of them is driving worldwide epidemics of obesity and type 2 diabetes (the type associated with obesity). Sugar-related diseases are costing America around $150 billion a year, the authors estimated, so federal health officials need to step up and consider regulating the stuff.

The Sugar Association dusted off what has become its stock response: The Lustig paper, it said, "lacks the scientific evidence or consensus" to support its claims, and its authors were irresponsible not to point out that the full body of science "is inconclusive at best." This inconclusiveness, of course, is precisely what the Sugar Association has worked so assiduously to maintain. "In confronting our critics," Tatem explained to his board of directors back in 1976, "we try never to lose sight of the fact that no confirmed scientific evidence links sugar to the death-dealing diseases. This crucial point is the lifeblood of the association."

The Sugar Association's earliest incarnation dates back to 1943, when growers and refiners created the Sugar Research Foundation to counter World War II sugar-rationing propaganda—"How Much Sugar Do You Need? None!" declared one government pamphlet. In 1947, producers rechristened their group the Sugar Association and launched a new PR division, Sugar Information Inc., which before long was touting sugar as a "sensible new approach to weight control." In 1968, in the hope of enlisting foreign sugar companies to help defray costs, the Sugar Association spun off its research division as the International Sugar Research Foundation. "Misconceptions concerning the causes of tooth decay, diabetes, and heart problems exist on a worldwide basis," explained a 1969 ISRF recruiting brochure.

As early as 1962, internal Sugar Association memos had acknowledged the potential links between sugar and chronic diseases, but at the time sugar executives had a more pressing problem: Weight-conscious Americans were switching in droves to diet sodas—particularly Diet Rite and Tab—sweetened with cyclamate and saccharin. From 1963 through 1968, diet soda's share of the soft-drink market shot from 4 percent to 15 percent. "A dollar's worth of sugar," ISRF vice president and research director John Hickson warned in an internal review, "could be replaced with a dime's worth" of sugar alternatives. "If anyone can undersell you nine cents out of 10," Hickson told the *New York Times* in 1969, "you'd better find some brickbat you can throw at him."

By then, the sugar industry had doled out more than $600,000 (about $4 million today) to study every conceivable harmful effect of cyclamate sweeteners, which are still sold around the world under names like Sugar Twin and Sucaryl. In 1969, the FDA banned cyclamates in the United States based on a study suggesting they could cause bladder cancer in rats. Not long after, Hickson left the ISRF to work for the Cigar Research Council. He was described in a confidential tobacco industry memo as a "supreme scientific politician who had been successful in condemning cyclamates, on behalf of the [sugar industry], on somewhat shaky evidence." It later emerged that the evidence suggesting that cyclamates caused cancer in rodents was not relevant to humans, but by then the case was officially closed. In 1977, saccharin, too, was nearly banned on the basis of animal results that would turn out to be meaningless in people.

Meanwhile, researchers had been reporting that blood lipids—cholesterol and triglycerides in particular—were a risk factor in heart disease. Some people had high cholesterol but normal triglycerides, prompting health experts to recommend that they avoid animal fats. Other people were deemed "carbohydrate sensitive," with normal cholesterol but markedly increased triglyceride levels. In these individuals, even moderate sugar consumption could cause a spike in triglycerides. John Yudkin, the United Kingdom's leading nutritionist, was making headlines with claims that sugar, not fat, was the primary cause of heart disease.

In 1967, the Sugar Association's research division began considering "the rising tide of implications of sucrose in atherosclerosis." Before long, according to a confidential 1970 review of industry-funded studies, the newly formed ISRF was spending 10 percent of its research budget on the link between diet and heart disease. Hickson, the ISRF's vice president, urged his member corporations to keep the results of the review under wraps. Of particular concern was the work of a University of Pennsylvania researcher on "sucrose sensitivity," which sugar executives feared was "likely to reveal evidence of harmful effects." One ISRF consultant recommended that sugar companies get to the truth of the matter by sponsoring a full-on study. In what would become a pattern, the ISRF opted not to follow his advice. Another ISRF-sponsored study, by biochemist Walter Pover of the University of Birmingham, in England, had uncovered a possible mechanism to explain how sugar raises triglyceride levels. Pover believed he was on the verge of demonstrating this mechanism "conclusively" and that 18 more weeks of work would nail it down. But instead of providing the funds, the ISRF nixed the project, assessing its value as "nil."

The industry followed a similar strategy when it came to diabetes. By 1973, links between sugar, diabetes, and heart disease were sufficiently troubling that Sen. George McGovern of South Dakota convened a hearing of his Select Committee on Nutrition and Human Needs to address the issue. An international panel of experts—including Yudkin and Walter Mertz, head of the Human Nutrition Institute at the Department of Agriculture—testified that variations in sugar consumption were the best explanation for the differences in diabetes rates between populations, and that research by the USDA and others supported the notion that eating too much sugar promotes dramatic population-wide increases in the disease. One panelist, South African diabetes specialist George Campbell, suggested that anything more than 70 pounds per person per year—about half of what is sold in America today—would spark epidemics.

In the face of such hostile news from independent scientists, the ISRF hosted its own conference the following March, focusing exclusively on the work of researchers who were skeptical of a sugar/diabetes connection. "All those present agreed that a large amount of research is still necessary before a firm conclusion can be arrived at," according to a conference review published in a prominent diabetes journal. In 1975, the foundation reconvened in Montreal to discuss research priorities with its consulting scientists. Sales were sinking, Tatem reminded the gathered sugar execs, and a major factor was "the impact of consumer advocates who link sugar consumption with certain diseases."

Following the Montreal conference, the ISRF disseminated a memo quoting Errol Marliss, a University of

Toronto diabetes specialist, recommending that the industry pursue "well-designed research programs" to establish sugar's role in the course of diabetes and other diseases. "Such research programs *might* produce an answer that sucrose is bad in certain individuals," he warned. But the studies "should be undertaken in a sufficiently comprehensive way as to produce results. A gesture rather than full support is unlikely to produce the sought-after answers."

A gesture, however, is what the industry would offer. Rather than approve a serious investigation of the purported links between sucrose and disease, American sugar companies quit supporting the ISRF's research projects. Instead, via the Sugar Association proper, they would spend roughly $655,000 between 1975 and 1980 on 17 studies designed, as internal documents put it, "to maintain research as a main prop of the industry's defense." Each proposal was vetted by a panel of industry-friendly scientists and a second committee staffed by representatives from sugar companies and "contributing research members" such as Coca-Cola, Hershey's, General Mills, and Nabisco. Most of the cash was awarded to researchers whose studies seemed explicitly designed to exonerate sugar. One even proposed to explore whether sugar could be shown to boost serotonin levels in rats' brains, and thus "prove of therapeutic value, as in the relief of depression," an internal document noted.

At best, the studies seemed a token effort. Harvard Medical School professor Ron Arky, for example, received money from the Sugar Association to determine whether sucrose has a different effect on blood sugar and other diabetes indicators if eaten alongside complex carbohydrates like pectin and psyllium. The project went nowhere, Arky told us recently. But the Sugar Association "didn't care."

In short, rather than do definitive research to learn the truth about its product, good or bad, the association stuck to a PR scheme designed to "establish with the broadest possible audience—virtually everyone is a consumer—the safety of sugar as a food." One of its first acts was to establish a Food & Nutrition Advisory Council consisting of a half-dozen physicians and two dentists willing to defend sugar's place in a healthy diet, and set aside roughly $60,000 per year (more than $220,000 today) to cover its cost.

Working to the industry's recruiting advantage was the rising notion that cholesterol and dietary fat—especially saturated fat—were the likely causes of heart disease. (Tatem even suggested, in a letter to the *Times Magazine,* that some "sugar critics" were motivated merely by wanting "to keep the heat off saturated fats.") This was the brainchild of nutritionist Ancel Keys, whose University of Minnesota laboratory had received financial support from the sugar industry as early as 1944. From the 1950s through the 1980s, Keys remained the most outspoken proponent of the fat hypothesis, often clashing publicly with Yudkin, the most vocal supporter of the sugar hypothesis—the two men "shared a good deal of loathing," recalled one of Yudkin's colleagues.

So when the Sugar Association needed a heart disease expert for its Food & Nutrition Advisory Council, it approached Francisco Grande, one of Keys' closest colleagues. Another panelist was University of Oregon nutritionist William Connor, the leading purveyor of the notion that it is dietary cholesterol that causes heart disease. As its top diabetes expert, the industry recruited Edwin Bierman of the University of Washington, who believed that diabetics need not pay strict attention to their sugar intake so long as they maintained a healthy weight by burning off the calories they consumed. Bierman also professed an apparently unconditional faith that it was dietary fat (and *being* fat) that caused heart disease, with sugar having no meaningful effect.

It is hard to overestimate Bierman's role in shifting the diabetes conversation away from sugar. It was primarily Bierman who convinced the American Diabetes Association to liberalize the amount of carbohydrates (including sugar) it recommended in the diets of diabetics, and focus more on urging diabetics to lower their fat intake, since diabetics are particularly likely to die from heart disease. Bierman also presented industry-funded studies when he coauthored a section on potential causes for a National Commission on Diabetes report in 1976; the document influences the federal diabetes research agenda to this day. Some researchers, he acknowledged, had "argued eloquently" that consumption of refined carbohydrates (such as sugar) is a precipitating factor in diabetes. But then Bierman cited five studies—two of them bankrolled by the ISRF—that were "inconsistent" with that hypothesis. "A review of all available laboratory and epidemiologic evidence," he concluded, "suggests that the most important dietary factor in increasing the risk of diabetes is total calorie intake, irrespective of source."

The point man on the industry's food and nutrition panel was Frederick Stare, founder and chairman of the department of nutrition at the Harvard School of Public Health. Stare and his department had a long history of ties to Big Sugar. An ISRF internal research review credited the sugar industry with funding some 30 papers in his department from 1952 through 1956 alone. In 1960, the department broke ground on a new $5 million building funded largely by private donations, including a $1 million gift from General Foods, the maker of Kool-Aid and Tang.

By the early 1970s, Stare ranked among the industry's most reliable advocates, testifying in Congress about the wholesomeness of sugar even as his department kept raking in funding from sugar producers and food and beverage giants such as Carnation, Coca-Cola, Gerber, Kellogg, and Oscar Mayer. His name also appears in tobacco documents, which show that he procured industry funding for a study aimed at exonerating cigarettes as a cause of heart disease.

The first act of the Food & Nutrition Advisory Council was to compile "Sugar in the Diet of Man," an 88-page white paper edited by Stare and published in 1975 to "organize existing scientific facts concerning sugar." It was a compilation of historical evidence and arguments that sugar companies could use to counter the claims of Yudkin, Stare's Harvard colleague Jean Mayer, and other researchers whom Tatem called "enemies of sugar." The document was sent to reporters—the Sugar Association circulated 25,000 copies—along with a press release headlined "Scientists dispel sugar fears." The report neglected to mention that it was funded by the sugar industry, but internal documents confirm that it was.

The Sugar Association also relied on Stare to take its message to the people: "Place Dr. Stare on the AM America Show" and "Do a 3½ minute interview with Dr. Stare for 200 radio stations," note the association's meeting minutes. Using Stare as a proxy, internal documents explained, would help the association "make friends with the networks" and "keep the sugar industry in the background." By the time Stare's copious conflicts of interest were finally revealed—in "Professors on the Take," a 1976 exposé by the Center for Science in the Public Interest—Big Sugar no longer needed his assistance. The industry could turn to an FDA document to continue where he'd left off.

While Stare and his colleagues had been drafting "Sugar in the Diet of Man," the FDA was launching its first review of whether sugar was, in the official jargon, generally recognized as safe (GRAS), part of a series of food-additive reviews the Nixon administration had requested of the agency. The FDA subcontracted the task to the Federation of American Societies of Experimental Biology, which created an 11-member committee to vet hundreds of food additives from acacia to zinc sulfate. While the mission of the GRAS committee was to conduct unbiased reviews of the existing science for each additive, it was led by biochemist George W. Irving Jr., who had previously served two years as chairman of the scientific advisory board of the International Sugar Research Foundation. Industry documents show that another committee member, Samuel Fomon, had received sugar-industry funding for three of the five years prior to the sugar review.

The FDA's instructions were clear: To label a substance as a potential health hazard, there had to be "credible evidence of, or reasonable grounds to suspect, adverse biological effects"—which certainly existed for sugar at the time. But the GRAS committee's review would depend heavily on "Sugar in the Diet of Man" and other work by its authors. In the section on heart disease, committee members cited 14 studies whose results were "conflicting," but 6 of those bore industry fingerprints, including Francisco Grande's chapter from "Sugar in the Diet of Man" and 5 others that came from Grande's lab or were otherwise funded by the sugar industry.

The diabetes chapter of the review acknowledged studies suggesting that "long term consumption of sucrose can result in a functional change in the capacity to metabolize carbohydrates and thus lead to diabetes mellitus," but it went on to cite five reports contradicting that notion. All had industry ties, and three were authored by Ed Bierman, including his chapter in "Sugar in the Diet of Man."

In January 1976, the GRAS committee published its preliminary conclusions, noting that while sugar probably contributed to tooth decay, it was not a "hazard to the public." The draft review dismissed the diabetes link as "circumstantial" and called the connection to cardiovascular disease "less than clear," with fat playing a greater role. The only cautionary note, besides cavities, was that all bets were off if sugar consumption were to increase significantly. The committee then thanked the Sugar Association for contributing "information and data." (Tatem would later remark that while he was "proud of the credit line . . . we would probably be better off without it.")

The committee's perspective was shared by many researchers, but certainly not all. For a public hearing on the draft review, scientists from the USDA's Carbohydrate Nutrition Laboratory submitted what they considered "abundant evidence that sucrose is one of the dietary factors responsible for obesity, diabetes, and heart disease." As they later explained in the *American Journal of Clinical Nutrition,* some portion of the public—perhaps 15 million Americans at that time—clearly could not tolerate a diet rich in sugar and other carbohydrates. Sugar consumption, they said, should come down by "a minimum of 60 percent," and the government should launch a national campaign "to inform the populace of the hazards of excessive sugar consumption." But the committee stood by its conclusions in the final version of its report presented to the FDA in October 1976.

For the sugar industry, the report was gospel. The findings "should be memorized" by the staff of every company associated with the sugar industry, Tatem told his membership. "In the long run," he said, the document "cannot be sidetracked, and you may be sure we will push its exposure to all comers of the country."

The association promptly produced an ad for newspapers and magazines exclaiming "Sugar is Safe!" It "does not cause death-dealing diseases," the ad declared, and "there is no substantiated scientific evidence indicating that sugar causes diabetes, heart disease or any other malady. . . . The next time you hear a promoter attacking sugar, beware the ripoff. Remember he can't substantiate his charges. Ask yourself what he's promoting or what he is seeking to cover up. If you get a chance, ask him about the GRAS Review Report. Odds are you won't get an answer. Nothing stings a nutritional liar like scientific facts."

The Sugar Association would soon get its chance to put the committee's sugar review to the test. In 1977, McGovern's select committee—the one that had held the 1973 hearings on sugar and diabetes—blindsided the industry with a report titled "Dietary Goals for the United States," recommending that Americans lower their sugar intake by 40 percent. The association "hammered away" at the McGovern report using the GRAS review "as our scientific Bible," Tatem told sugar executives.

McGovern held fast, but Big Sugar would prevail in the end. In 1980, when the USDA first published its own set of dietary guidelines, it relied heavily on a review written for the American Society of Clinical Nutrition by none other than Bierman, who used the GRAS committee's findings to bolster his own. "Contrary to widespread opinion, too much sugar does not seem to cause diabetes," the USDA guidelines concluded. They went on to counsel that people should "avoid too much sugar," without bothering to explain what that meant.

In 1982, the FDA once again took up the GRAS committee's conclusion that sugar was safe, proposing to make it official. The announcement resulted in a swarm of public criticism, prompting the agency to reopen its case. Four years later, an agency task force concluded, again leaning on industry-sponsored studies, that "there is no conclusive evidence . . . that demonstrates a hazard to the general public when sugars are consumed at the levels that are now current." (Walter Glinsmann, the task force's lead administrator, would later become a consultant to the Corn Refiners Association, which represents producers of high-fructose corn syrup.)

The USDA, meanwhile, had updated its own dietary guidelines. With Fred Stare now on the advisory committee, the 1985 guidelines retained the previous edition's vague recommendation to "avoid too much" sugar but stated unambiguously that "too much sugar in your diet does not cause diabetes." At the time, the USDA's own Carbohydrate Nutrition Laboratory was still generating evidence to the contrary and supporting the notion that "even low sucrose intake" might be contributing to heart disease in 10 percent of Americans.

By the early 1990s, the USDA's research into sugar's health effects had ceased, and the FDA's take on sugar had become conventional wisdom, influencing a generation's worth of key publications on diet and health. Reports from the surgeon general and the National Academy of Sciences repeated the mantra that the evidence linking sugar to chronic disease was inconclusive, and then went on to equate "inconclusive" with "nonexistent." They also ignored a crucial caveat: The FDA reviewers had deemed added sugars—those in excess of what occurs naturally in our diets—safe at "current" 1986 consumption levels. But the FDA's consumption estimate was 43 percent lower than that of its sister agency, the USDA. By 1999, the average American would be eating more than double the amount the FDA had deemed safe—although we have cut back by 13 percent since then.

Asked to comment on some of the documents described in this article, a Sugar Association spokeswoman responded that they are "at this point historical in nature and do not necessarily reflect the current mission or function" of the association. But it is clear enough that the industry still operates behind the scenes to make sure regulators never officially set a limit on the amount of sugar Americans can safely consume. The authors of the 2010 USDA dietary guidelines, for instance, cited two scientific reviews as evidence that sugary drinks don't make adults fat. The first was written by Sigrid Gibson, a nutrition consultant whose clients included the Sugar Bureau (England's version of the Sugar Association) and the World Sugar Research Organization (formerly the ISRF). The second review was authored by Carrie Ruxton, who served as research manager of the Sugar Bureau from 1995 to 2000.

The Sugar Association has also worked its connections to assure that the government panels making dietary recommendations—the USDA's Dietary Guidelines Advisory Committee, for instance—include researchers sympathetic to its position. One internal newsletter boasted in 2003 that for the USDA panel, the association had "worked diligently to achieve the nomination of another expert wholly through third-party endorsements."

In the few instances when governmental authorities have sought to reduce people's sugar consumption, the industry has attacked openly. In 2003, after an expert panel convened by the World Health Organization recommended that no more than 10 percent of all calories in people's diets should come from added sugars—nearly 40 percent less than the USDA's estimate for the average American—current Sugar Association president Andrew Briscoe wrote the WHO's director general warning that the association would "exercise every avenue available to expose the dubious nature" of the report and urge "congressional appropriators to challenge future funding" for the WHO. Larry Craig (R-Idaho, sugar beets) and John Breaux (D-La., sugarcane), then co-chairs of the Senate Sweetener Caucus, wrote a letter to Secretary of Health and Human Services Tommy Thompson, urging his "prompt and favorable attention" to prevent the report from becoming official WHO policy. (Craig had received more than $36,000 in sugar industry contributions in the previous election cycle.) Thompson's people responded with a 28-page letter detailing "where the US Government's policy recommendations and interpretation of the science differ" with the WHO report. Not surprisingly, the organization left its experts' recommendation on sugar intake out of its official dietary strategy.

In recent years, the scientific tide has begun to turn against sugar. Despite the industry's best efforts, researchers and public health authorities have come to accept that the primary risk factor for both heart disease and type 2 diabetes is a condition called metabolic syndrome, which now affects more than 75 million Americans, according to the Centers for Disease Control and Prevention. Metabolic syndrome is characterized by a cluster of abnormalities—some of which Yudkin and others associated with sugar almost 50 years ago—including weight gain, increased insulin levels, and elevated triglycerides. It also has been linked to cancer and Alzheimer's disease. "Scientists have now established causation," Lustig said recently. "Sugar causes metabolic syndrome."

Newer studies from the University of California-Davis have even reported that LDL cholesterol, the classic risk factor for heart disease, can be raised significantly in just *two weeks* by drinking sugary beverages at a rate well within the upper range of what Americans consume—four 12-ounce glasses a day of beverages like soda, Snapple, or Red Bull. The result is a new wave of researchers coming out publicly against Big Sugar.

During the battle over the 2005 USDA guidelines, an internal Sugar Association newsletter described its strategy toward anyone who had the temerity to link sugar consumption with chronic disease and premature death: "Any disparagement of sugar," it read, "will be met with forceful, strategic public comments and the supporting science." But since the latest science is anything but supportive of the industry, what happens next?

"At present," Lustig ventures, "they have absolutely no reason to alter any of their practices. The science is in—the medical and economic problems with excessive sugar consumption are clear. But the industry is going to fight tooth and nail to prevent that science from translating into public policy."

Like the tobacco industry before it, the sugar industry may be facing the inexorable exposure of its product as a killer—science will ultimately settle the matter one way or the other—but as Big Tobacco learned a long time ago, even the inexorable can be held up for a very long time.

Gary Taubes is a science writer and journalist.

Cristin Kearns Couzens is a senior consultant at the University of Colorado Center for Health Administration and an acting instructor at the University of Washington School of Dentistry.

Kenneth W. Krause

Saving Us from Sweets: This Is Science and Government on Sugar

I've carried an intense personal grudge against "sugar" for decades. No, not the mostly benign, unrefined types packed into blueberries, green beans, and pumpernickels, for example. And no, not *only* the sickly sweet stuff shamelessly dumped into sodas, pastries, and swirling coffee froths either. I truly despise every pale-ish, pure and innocent looking slice of bread, wedge of potato, and grain of rice, and, I promise you, no pasta noodle, cracker, or corn flake will ever again bamboozle its way into my ever-shriveling food pantry.

At emotionally critical moments, my well-intentioned mother told me I was "husky" or "big-boned," which, by the way, is never true if it needs to be said. I was just plain F-A-T—obese, actually, just like more than a third of Americans today—until my junior year of high school. At that fateful point, I got fed up and decided to take matters into my own ignorant yet determined hands. Thanks to vigorous exercise and a dramatically reformed diet, I dropped seventy pounds in about three months. From then on, my world just got bigger and brighter.

Even now, at age forty-seven, I can relish every exhilaration my aging body will tolerate. In fact, I've recently given up weight lifting and jogging for power lifting, plyometrics, and high-intensity intervals. Last month, I look up mountain biking (the initial wounds should heal well before publication) because road cycling just wasn't exciting enough anymore.

I'm not bragging. Truth he told, I'm not particularly good at any of it. The point, rather, is that I love it all, and that I should have enjoyed an even richer physical life as a kid. In some tragic measure, I squandered the most dynamic years of my life guzzling and gobbling the same general strain of refuse that farmers use every day to fatten their cattle for slaughter. Yes, I'm a little bitter about sugar.

And I'm clearly not alone. "Clean-eating" advocates now dominate the nutrition world, and most of us agree generally with food guru Michael Pollan that we should eat less and that our diets should consist of mostly plants. Nevertheless, others in our ranks have lately embraced a more militant and less scientifically defensible approach to the problem.

Take, for example, Robert Lustig, Laura Schmidt, and Claire Brindis, three public health experts from the University or California, San Francisco. In a recent issue of *Nature*, they compared the "deadly effect" of added sugars (high-fructose corn syrup and sucrose) to that of alcohol. When consumed to excess, they observe, both substances cause a host of dreadful maladies, including hypertension, myocardial infarction, dyslipidemia, pancreatitis, obesity, malnutrition, hepatic dysfunction, and habituation (if not addiction).[1]

Far from mere "empty calories," they add, sugar is potentially "toxic." It alters metabolism, raises blood pressure, causes hormonal chaos, and damages our livers. Like both tobacco and alcohol (a distillation of sugar), it affects our brains, encouraging us to increase consumption. Indeed, they say, worldwide sugar consumption has tripled in the last fifty years.

Thus, Lustig et al. infer that sugar is at least partly responsible tor thirty-five million deaths every year from chronic, non-communicable diseases, which according to the United Nations now pose a greater health risk worldwide than their infectious counterparts. The authors also point out that Americans waste $65 billion in lost productivity and $150 billion on health-care related resources annually vis-à-vis illnesses linked to sugar-induced metabolic syndrome.

At the risk of piling on, I should emphasise that 17 percent of U.S. children are now obese too, and that the average American consumes more than forty pounds of high-fructose corn syrup per year. Recent investigations suggest that sugar might also impair our cognition. For example, in a new study from the University of California, Los Angeles, physiologist Fernando Gomez-Pinilla concludes that dicts consistently high in fructose can slow brain functions and weaken memory and learning in rats.

All of this reinforces my already firm personal resolve. But apparently many accomplished scientists lack not only confidence in our abilities as individuals to educate or control ourselves, but also respect for our rights to disagree or to make informed but less than perfectly rational decisions regarding our private consumption habits. As such, Lustig et al. urge Americans especially to support restrictions on their own liberty in the form of government-imposed regulation of sugar.

To support their cause, Lustig et al. rely on four criteria, "now largely accepted by the public health community," originally offered by social psychologist Thomas Babor in 2003 to justify the regulation of alcohol. The target substance must be toxic and unavoidable (or pervasive), and it must have a negative impact on society and a potential for abuse. Sugar satisfies each requirement, they contend, and is thus analogous to alcohol in terms of demanding bureaucratic imposition.

In a letter to me, Gomez-Pinilla echoed their concerns. Diabetes and obesity, he specified, come with greatly increased risks of several neurological and psychiatric disorders. In light of both the human and economic costs, he opined broadly, "it is in the general public concern to regulate high-sugar products as well as other unhealthy aspects of diet and lifestyle."

Unsurprisingly, the *Nature* paper inspired a flurry of defiant correspondences. Observers close to the sugar industry quickly took issue with both the researchers' facts and their logic. Richard Cottrell from the World Sugar Research Organisation in London first disputed the San Franciscans' calculation of worldwide sugar consumption. Because global population has more than doubled since 1960, he corrected, intake has increased only by 60 percent, not 300 percent. Moreover, he added, consumption in the United States, the United Kingdom, and Canada has risen only marginally as a proportion of total food-energy intake.

Judging metabolic syndrome a "controversial concept" in itself, Cottrell then cited analyses from the United Nations, the United States, and Europe that found no evidence of typical sugar consumption's contribution to any non-dental disease. On the other hand, he chided, "Overconsumption of anything is harmful, including water and air."

Ron Boswell, a senator from Queensland, Australia, noted that while the overweight population in his country has doubled and the incidence of diabetes has tripled since 1980, sugar consumption has actually dropped 23 percent during the same period. To describe sugar as "toxic," he continued, "is extreme, as is its ludicrous comparison with alcohol." The senator then scolded Lustig et al. for risking "damage to the livelihoods of thousands of people working in the sugar industry worldwide."

Other writers were no less reproachful. Christiani Jeyakumar Henry, a nutrition researcher in Singapore, criticized the *Nature* piece for its exclusive emphasis on sugar. Several foods with high glycemic indices, he noted, including wheat, rice, and potatoes, also contribute to both obesity and diabetes. Finally, writing from the University of Vermont, Burlington, Saleem Ali criticized the San Franciscans' "misleading" comparison of sugar to alcohol and tobacco, the former of which causes neither behavioral intoxication nor second-hand contamination.

But David Katz, MD, renowned nutritionist and founding director of the Yale University Prevention Research Center, has long contested Lustig's claims. Last spring, for example, Katz characterized the researcher's dualistic, good vs. evil attacks on sugar as fanatical "humbug." "It is the overall quality and quantity of our diet that matters," be reasoned, "not just one villainous or virtuous nutrient du jour."

Refreshingly, Katz reassessed the subject from a broader, more reliable perspective based on evolutionary science. "We like sweet," he appreciated, "because mammals who like sweet are more apt to survive than mammals who don't. Period." Why should it shock and abhor so many of us that sugar is addictive? The real surprise, Katz answered, is not that high-energy food is habit-forming, "but rather that anything else is."

Katz's subsequent response to the *Nature* article, however, sends a frustratingly abstruse and well-mixed message. On the one hand, he recognizes that "Regulating nutrients, *per se*, is a slippery slope." Good intentions, he wisely if somewhat vaguely counsels, "could bog us down in conflict that forestalls all progress, distort the relative importance of just one nutrient relative to overall nutrition," and lead us to "unintended consequences."

On the other hand, Katz expressly defends some of Lustig et al.'s proposed governmental intrusions, Most reasonably, he favors restrictions on the sale of sugary products to kids where their attendance is officially compelled. "There is no reason," he argues, "why schools should be propagating the consumption of solid or liquid candy by students." Many locales have already seen fit to install such policies.

Far less noble, however, is the good doctor's support for punitive taxes on sugary drinks. "There is no inalienable right to afford soda in the Constitution," he observes. Those of lesser means, Katz resolves, "should perhaps consider that they can't afford to squander such limited funds on the empty calories of soda." Indeed they should, but Katz never explains how people can make decisions already made on their behalf.

But—in the name of science, most regrettably—Lustig et al. advocate considerably more intrusive schemes decorously styled "gentle, supply-side" controls.

Unsatisfied with a soda tax, they favor a similar penalty on "processed foods that contain any form of added sugars." That means ketchup, salsa, jam, deli meat, frozen fruit, many breads, and chocolate milk (now highly rated as a recovery drink following intense exercise). Ideally, the trio adds, such tariffs would be accompanied by an outright "ban" on television advertisements.

The San Franciscans would like to "limit availability" as well, by "reducing the hours that retailers are open, controlling the location and density of retail markets and limiting who can legally purchase the products." Alluding to a cadre of parents in South Philadelphia who recently blocked children from entering nearby convenience stores for snacks, Lustig et al. inquired, "Why couldn't a public health directive do the same?"

In late May of this year, New York City Mayor Michael Bloomberg announced the first plan in U.S. history to outlaw the sale of large sugary drinks—anything over sixteen fluid ounces—in all restaurants, movie theaters, sports arenas, and even from street carts. If approved by the Bloomberg-appointed Board of Health, the ban could take effect next March.

Sugar can be bad; most of us get that. But even the most impassioned personal grudge against potentially harmful food is just that—personal. Science, like government, is valued beyond calculation insofar as it expands personal choice. But the appropriate boundaries of science are almost always exceeded when it attempts to join with government to first judge the masses incompetent and then restrict their personal choices.

I grow particularly nervous when even the most distinguished researchers transcend their callings to campaign for product taxes and bans or, most egregiously, to vaguely advocate for the regulation of "unhealthy aspects of diet and lifestyle." Science's time-tested authority springs vibrantly from its practitioners' exacting and impartial roles as explorers, skeptics, and even teachers. But never has it spawned from the deluded cravings of some to act as our parents or priests.

Notes

1. The authors dispute the common assertion that these diseases are caused by obesity. Rather, they argue, obesity is merely "a marker for metabolic dysfunction, which is even more prevalent." In support, they cite statistics showing that 20 percent of obese people have normal metabolism and that 40 percent of normal-weight people develop metabolic syndrome.
2. Neither "inalienable" nor "unalienable" rights are listed in the Constitution, of course. But three of the latter—life, liberty, and the pursuit of happiness—are enshrined in the Declaration of Independence. Katz and others might wish to reexamine their historical and philosophical significance.

Kenneth W. Krause is a contributing editor, book editor, and "The Good Book" columnist for *The Humanist* and a contributing editor and columnist for *Skeptical Inquirer*.

EXPLORING THE ISSUE

Are Restrictions on Sugar and Sugary Beverages Justified?

Critical Thinking and Reflection

1. What impact would restriction of sugar and sugary beverages have on our right to make individual choices?
2. Do the health risks of sugar warrant bans on the sale of large sized sugary beverages?
3. Describe the role government should play in regard to prevention of obesity.

Is There Common Ground?

Jacob Sullum, in "The War on Fat: Is the Size of Your Butt the Government's Business?" (*Reason*, August/September 2004), grants that while obesity is a health problem, it should not be a government issue. Despite Sullum's views, Americans have been steadily gaining weight over the past 30 years. Children, in particular, have grown heavier for a variety of reasons including less physical activity, more eating away from home, and increased portion sizes. Food manufacturers advertise an increasing array of non-nutritious foods to children while schools offer these foods in the cafeteria. With the success of the antismoking forces, some nutritionists see the government as the answer to the obesity problem. Increased taxes on junk food, warning labels on non-nutritious food packages, and restrictions on advertising have all been discussed as a means of improving the nation's nutritional status. In "The Perils of Ignoring History: Big Tobacco Played Dirty and Millions Died. How Similar Is Big Food?" (*Milbank Quarterly*, March 2009), the authors discussed how in 1954 the tobacco industry paid to publish the "Frank Statement to Cigarette Smokers" in hundreds of U.S. newspapers. It stated that the public's health was the industry's concern above all others and promised a variety of good-faith changes. What followed were years of lies and actions that cost countless lives. The tobacco industry had a script that focused on personal responsibility, paying scientists who delivered research that instilled doubt, criticizing the "junk" science that found risks associated with smoking, making self-regulatory pledges, lobbying with massive resources to stifle government action, introducing "safer" products, and simultaneously manipulating and denying both the addictive nature of their products and their marketing to children. The script of the food industry is both similar to and different from the tobacco industry script. Food is quite different from tobacco, and the food industry differs from tobacco companies in other ways, but there are also major similarities in the actions that these two industries have taken in response to concern that their products cause disease. Because obesity is now a major global problem, the world cannot afford a repeat of the tobacco history. If sugary food advertisements were banned from children's television, less might be consumed.

Other proposals to improve Americans' diets include levying a tax on sugary foods such as soft drinks, candy, and sugared cereals and the ban on trans fats in New York City. While many states already tax these items if purchased in a restaurant or grocery store, proponents argue that these foods should be taxed regardless of where purchased. While this may seem to be a reasonable approach to address the problem, it is not approved by all. The food industry, understandably, is not in favor of any of these measures.

Additional Resources

Jacobson, M. E., & Lusk, J. L. (2014). At issue: Should the government tax sugary soda? *CQ Researcher, 24*(35), 833.

Jacobson, M. F. (2014). Time to rein in "big soda." *Nutrition Action Health Letter, 41*(5), 2.

Sanders, T. (2016). Much fizz, little pop. *New Scientist, 229*(3056), 26–27.

Sullum, J. (2012). Bloomberg's big beverage ban. *Reason, 44*(5), 8.

Tax Linked to Drop in Soda Consumption. (2017). *USA Today Magazine, 145*(2861), 15.

Internet References . . .

The American Dietetic Association

www.eatright.org

Center for Science in the Public Interest (CSPI)

www.cspinet.org

Food and Nutrition Information Center

www.nalusda.gov/fnic/index.html

The Sugar Association, Inc.

www.sugar.org

Unit 6

UNIT

Consumer Health

A shift is occurring in medical care toward informed self-care. People are starting to reclaim their autonomy, and the relationship between doctor and patient is changing. Many patients are asking more questions of their physicians, considering a wider range of medical options, accessing medical information online, focusing on prevention, and in general, becoming more educated about what determines their health. They are also concerned about the quality of numerous consumer health products, drugs, and services available to them. This section addresses consumer issues and initiatives that empower consumers to make decisions and take actions that improve personal, family, and community health.

Selected, Edited, and with Issue Framing Material by:
Eileen L. Daniel, *SUNY College at Brockport*

ISSUE

Is Weight-Loss Maintenance Possible?

YES: Barbara Berkeley, from "The Fat Trap: My Response," *refusetoregain.com* (2011)

NO: Tara Parker-Pope, from "The Fat Trap," *The New York Times Magazine* (2011)

Learning Outcomes

After reading this issue, you will be able to:

- Discuss why it is so difficult for many people to maintain weight loss.
- Discuss the argument that weight-loss maintenance is not possible for most people.
- Discuss the risk factors associated with obesity and overweight.

ISSUE SUMMARY

YES: Physician Barbara Berkeley believes that weight maintenance is not easy but possible as long as people separate themselves from the world of typical American eating. She also claims that some individuals are heavy because they are susceptible to the modern diet or because they use food for comfort.

NO: Journalist Tara Parker-Pope disagrees and maintains that there are biological imperatives that cause people to regain all the weight they lose and for those genetically inclined to obesity, it's almost impossible to maintain weight loss.

While the number of Americans who diet varies, depending on the source, the Boston Medical Center indicates that approximately 45 million Americans diet each year and spend $33 billion on weight-loss products in their pursuit of a trimmer, fitter body. Currently, about two-thirds of American adults are overweight including more than one-third who are classified as obese. This is almost 20 percent more than 20 years ago. Obesity can double mortality and can reduce life expectancy by 10–20 years. If current trends continue, the average American's life expectancy will actually begin to decline by 5 years. Obesity is linked to unhealthy blood fat levels including cholesterol and heart disease. Other health risks associated with obesity include high blood pressure, some cancers, diabetes, gallbladder and kidney disease, sleep disorders, arthritis, and other bone and joint disorders. Obesity is also linked to complications of pregnancy, stress incontinence, and elevated surgical risk. The risks from obesity rise with its severity, and they are much more likely to occur among people more than double their recommended body weight. Obesity can impact psychological as well as physical well-being. Being obese can contribute to psychological problems including depression, anxiety, and low self-esteem.

Since 1990, the prevalence of overweight and obesity has been rising in the United States. Despite public health campaigns, the trend shows little sign of changing. A 2006 campaign conducted by Ogden et al. ("Prevalence of Overweight and Obesity in the US 1999–2004," *JAMA*, vol. 295, 2006) reported that during the 6-year period from 1999 to 2004, the prevalence of overweight in children and adolescents increased significantly, as did the prevalence of obesity in men. Along with these rising rates of obesity come increased rates of obesity-related health issues. There has been a 60 percent rise in type 2 diabetes since 1990. Inactivity and overweight may be responsible for as many as 112,000 premature deaths each year in the United States, second only to smoking-related deaths.

According to the U.S. Department of Agriculture (USDA), the average American has increased his/her caloric intake by more than 500 calories per day while levels of physical activity have decreased. This is related to more meals eaten away from the home, which typically are higher in calories, fat, sugar, and salt. Restaurants also tend to serve larger portions than home-cooked meals. Many Americans are also sleep deprived. Lack of sleep appears to trigger weight gain. Finally, Americans are more engaged in sedentary activities and less likely to engage in physical activity on a regular basis. Whatever the cause of obesity, its incidence and prevalence appear to be rising and it is linked to multiple health concerns.

Because of health and appearance concerns, many Americans attempt to lose weight by dieting and/or exercise. Types of weight-loss diets typically include reduced calories or a reduction of a major nutrient such as fat or carbohydrates. Interestingly, most studies find no difference between the main diet types and subsequent weight loss. However, long-term studies of dieting indicate that the majority of individuals who lose weight regain virtually all of the weight that was lost after dieting, regardless of whether they maintain their diet or exercise program.

A new study, however, suggests that specific strategies could modestly slow the rate of weight regain in obese adults who have lost weight. These strategies include planning for situations which could cause backsliding and daily weighing in. In the study, utilizing these strategies increased the proportion of adults who stayed at or lowered their weight after initial weight loss by around 14%. However, more research is needed to determine which specific strategies offered the best benefit.

The YES and NO selections address whether it is possible to diet, lose weight, and actually maintain that weight loss. Barbara Berkeley maintains that while it's not easy to maintain lost pounds, it is certainly possible. Tara Parker-Pope disagrees and believes that our biological makeup causes us to regain weight and for most people, it's almost impossible to maintain a weight loss.

YES 

Barbara Berkeley

The Fat Trap: My Response

Once a month, in a small room off the lobby of Lake West Hospital in Willoughby, Ohio, a special group convenes. For someone observing the group and unaware of its purpose, it might appear to be a simple mix of everyday people . . . young, old, racially diverse. The members would seem to be old friends but with a particular seriousness of purpose, perhaps a community group attending a lecture or learning some new skill together. What a casual observer would not guess is that each of these people was once obese, some having weighed over 100 pounds more than they do today.

Our Refuse to Regain group is an experiment, a safe haven for maintainers who have lost weight in many different ways and now face the reality of reconstructing their lives. We've had people from Weight Watchers, people who've undergone bariatric surgery, people I've treated in my practice and others who simply did it on their own. A weight loss diet is no different than emptying the trash. It doesn't matter which technique you use to toss out the garbage. But learning how to avoid the reaccumulation of unwanted junk is a completely different skill. There are many basics in this process that will be the same for everyone. There are also many specifics that will vary from person to person and which must be individually discovered.

Here's some of what we've learned so far:

1. Weight maintenance is possible. There is nothing in our group experience (or in my personal clinical experience) to suggest that the body "forces" one to regain.
2. Weight maintenance requires a separation from the world of "normal" American eating . . . which is not normal at all.
3. Some people are heavy simply because they are susceptible to the modern diet, no more no less. Others are heavy because they use food for soothing or sedation. Most people are a mix of both. If psychological issues are a *major* part of weight gain—significantly beyond the common enjoyment of food for pleasure, they need to be addressed during the maintenance phase.
4. Weight maintainers are special people who live on a kind of food island. It's really nice to know that the island is inhabited, often with fascinating, determined people just like you. Rarely do maintainers get to meet and talk with one another.

This week, I gave my group a reading assignment. That was a first. I asked everyone to read Tara Parker Pope's article on weight maintenance called *The Fat Trap*. This article is currently online and will appear in Sunday's *New York Times Magazine*. Our group will be discussing it at our January meeting, but I'll give you a preview of my reaction here. Many of you may be reading our blog because you read "The Fat Trap" and discovered Lynn Haraldson, my blogging partner on this site. The fact that you got here likely means that you are interested in knowing whether we are bound to regain the weight we lose, so please, read on . . . leave comments and join the discussion.

For those of you who are new to this blog, you should know that I am a physician who has specialized in weight management since the late 1980s. This is the only thing I do and that's unusual. Why? Because most doctors are not particularly interested in obesity, and certainly weren't back in the 80s. Over the past twenty years, a continuing source of frustration for me has been the willingness of doctors and the general public to accept "truths" about weight loss that are the beliefs of everyone *except* those who actually work with overweight people.

Scientific research needs to square with what we see in clinical practice. If it doesn't, we should question its validity. "The Fat Trap" is an article that starts with a single, small research study and builds around it. Its point? That there are inevitable biological imperatives that cause people to regain all the weight they lose.

I don't buy it.

Here is the opening paragraph of Ms. Parker Pope's article:

> For 15 years, Joseph Proietto has been helping people lose weight. When these obese patients arrive at his weight-loss clinic in Australia, they are determined to slim down. And most of the time, he says, they do just that, sticking to the clinic's program and dropping excess pounds. But then, almost without exception, the weight begins to creep back. In a matter of months or years, the entire effort has come undone, and the patient is fat again.

At one time, this was my experience too. But things have changed. After years of focusing my practice much more on weight maintenance, writing a book about it, and trying to figure out how to teach and encourage it, I no longer see patients with an "entire effort come undone." Instead, I see more and more people learning how to become successfully anchored at their new weight. And these POWs (previous overweight people) are not from my practice alone. They are people like Lynn Haraldson and her friends "The Maintaining Divas." They are the long term POWs who write to me via this blog, on Facebook and on Twitter. They are the people I hear about with increasing frequency every day.

I admire Ms. Parker Pope for acknowledging her own struggles with weight, but as someone who has not yet solved the maintenance problem I would submit that she is not the best person to rationally evaluate evidence that says that regain is inevitable. After talking to a number of scientists who believe that the body fights weight loss, her concluding paragraph says:

> For me, understanding the science of weight loss has helped make sense of my own struggles to lose weight, as well as my mother's endless cycle of dieting, weight gain and despair. I wish she were still here so I could persuade her to finally forgive herself for her dieting failures. While I do, ultimately, blame myself for allowing my weight to get out of control, it has been somewhat liberating to learn that there are factors other than my character at work when it comes to gaining and losing weight.

Those of us who come from families which struggle with obesity can believe one of two things. We can believe that biological and metabolic factors doom us to fatness or we can believe that we come from families who are very sensitive to the current food environment and perhaps need to live in a new and more creative way. It has been my experience that all successful maintainers have learned how to live a life that exists outside the current food norms. For some, this is a daily and difficult challenge and for others it becomes a simple and treasured way of life, but either way, it is not about some inevitable biological destiny. Rather, these maintainers have come to terms with the fact that they are ancient bodies and souls living in a modern environment and that our food culture is capable of killing them. Controlling that environment is their choice and their challenge.

Where I do agree with "The Fat Trap" is in its assertion that obesity is much more difficult to deal with once it is established. We would do well to focus intense and constant attention on healthful nutrition during pregnancy and in childhood. I believe that we can do this much more easily than we believe, if we would only adopt the idea that we should eat more like we did originally as hunter-gatherers. It has been my clinical experience that elimination (or major curtailment) of starches and sugars (including whole grains and the things that come from them, by the way) simply works. And this clinical observation makes sense, since the ancestors whose genes we carry were not exposed to the large amounts of starch and sugar we now eat. Along with consumption of real food . . . not things in boxes, cans, or packages . . . this easy concept can change lives. We could make things so much easier by teaching this lesson to kids rather than endlessly focusing them on percents of fat, protein and carbs and on counting calories.

But such approaches to weight maintenance are not easily sold. It's far simpler to believe that weight must be regained. I'm fond of using this example for patients: If you were to tell your friends that you are becoming vegetarian and that you will no longer touch a drop of red meat, fish, or poultry, no one would blink an eye. You'd probably be encouraged and congratulated. If, on the other hand, you announced that you were giving up sugar and grain, the same friends would be horrified. "You mean you're never going to have another piece of bread???"

I believe that the resistance to finding the maintenance solution comes from the addictive nature of starch and sugar foods. I also believe that most of America and other SAD (standard American diet) countries are operating "under the influence" of addictive carbs. Life without them, or even with LESS of them, is too awful to contemplate.

But I digress. To return to my original point, I want to forcefully say that we must stop finding reasons we can't maintain and start getting much, much better at teaching people how to do it. Support networks, communication between maintainers, and many more books, advocates, and techniques that focus on maintenance are key.

I believe I may scream if I see yet another book with a catchy title that touts yet another weight loss approach without ever talking about what happens in the after-diet world. January is the month for those glossy little productions.

Time to get serious. Maintenance can be done, and if you want to meet the people who are doing it, hang around this blog.

Barbara Berkeley is a physician and diplomate of the American Board of Internal Medicine and the American Board of Obesity Medicine. She has specialized in the care of overweight and obese patients since 1988.

Tara Parker-Pope

NO

The Fat Trap

For 15 years, Joseph Proietto has been helping people lose weight. When these obese patients arrive at his weight-loss clinic in Australia, they are determined to slim down. And most of the time, he says, they do just that, sticking to the clinic's program and dropping excess pounds. But then, almost without exception, the weight begins to creep back. In a matter of months or years, the entire effort has come undone, and the patient is fat again. "It has always seemed strange to me," says Proietto, who is a physician at the University of Melbourne. "These are people who are very motivated to lose weight, who achieve weight loss most of the time without too much trouble and yet, inevitably, gradually, they regain the weight."

Anyone who has ever dieted knows that lost pounds often return, and most of us assume the reason is a lack of discipline or a failure of willpower. But Proietto suspected that there was more to it, and he decided to take a closer look at the biological state of the body after weight loss.

Beginning in 2009, he and his team recruited 50 obese men and women. The men weighed an average of 233 pounds; the women weighed about 200 pounds. Although some people dropped out of the study, most of the patients stuck with the extreme low-calorie diet, which consisted of special shakes called Optifast and two cups of low-starch vegetables, totaling just 500 to 550 calories a day for eight weeks. Ten weeks in, the dieters lost an average of 30 pounds.

At that point, the 34 patients who remained stopped dieting and began working to maintain the new lower weight. Nutritionists counseled them in person and by phone, promoting regular exercise and urging them to eat more vegetables and less fat. But despite the effort, they slowly began to put on weight. After a year, the patients already had regained an average of 11 of the pounds they struggled so hard to lose. They also reported feeling far more hungry and preoccupied with food than before they lost the weight.

While researchers have known for decades that the body undergoes various metabolic and hormonal changes while it's losing weight, the Australian team detected something new. A full year after significant weight loss, these men and women remained in what could be described as a biologically altered state. Their still-plump bodies were acting as if they were starving and were working overtime to regain the pounds they lost. For instance, a gastric hormone called ghrelin, often dubbed the "hunger hormone," was about 20 percent higher than at the start of the study. Another hormone associated with suppressing hunger, peptide YY, was also abnormally low. Levels of leptin, a hormone that suppresses hunger and increases metabolism, also remained lower than expected. A cocktail of other hormones associated with hunger and metabolism all remained significantly changed compared to pre-dieting levels. It was almost as if weight loss had put their bodies into a unique metabolic state, a sort of post-dieting syndrome that set them apart from people who hadn't tried to lose weight in the first place. "What we see here is a coordinated defense mechanism with multiple components all directed toward making us put on weight," Proietto says. "This, I think, explains the high failure rate in obesity treatment."

While the findings from Proietto and colleagues, published this fall in *The New England Journal of Medicine,* are not conclusive—the study was small and the findings need to be replicated—the research has nonetheless caused a stir in the weight-loss community, adding to a growing body of evidence that challenges conventional thinking about obesity, weight loss and willpower. For years, the advice to the overweight and obese has been that we simply need to eat less and exercise more. While there is truth to this guidance, it fails to take into account that the human body continues to fight against weight loss long after dieting has stopped. This translates into a sobering reality: once we become fat, most of us, despite our best efforts, will probably stay fat.

I have always felt perplexed about my inability to keep weight off. I know the medical benefits of weight loss, and I don't drink sugary sodas or eat fast food. I exercise regularly—a few years ago, I even completed a marathon. Yet during the 23 years since graduating from college, I've lost 10 or 20 pounds at a time, maintained it for a little while and then gained it all back and more, to the point where I am now easily 60 pounds overweight.

I wasn't overweight as a child, but I can't remember a time when my mother, whose weight probably fluctuated between 150 and 250 pounds, wasn't either on a diet or, in her words, cheating on her diet. Sometimes we ate healthful, balanced meals; on other days dinner consisted of a bucket of Kentucky Fried Chicken. As a high-school cross-country runner, I never worried about weight, but in college, when my regular training runs were squeezed out by studying and socializing, the numbers on the scale slowly began to move up. As adults, my three sisters and I all struggle with weight, as do many members of my extended family. My mother died of esophageal cancer six years ago. It was her great regret that in the days before she died, the closest medical school turned down her offer to donate her body because she was obese.

It's possible that the biological cards were stacked against me from the start. Researchers know that obesity tends to run in families, and recent science suggests that even the desire to eat higher-calorie foods may be influenced by heredity. But untangling how much is genetic and how much is learned through family eating habits is difficult. What is clear is that some people appear to be prone to accumulating extra fat while others seem to be protected against it.

In a seminal series of experiments published in the 1990s, the Canadian researchers Claude Bouchard and Angelo Tremblay studied 31 pairs of male twins ranging in age from 17 to 29, who were sometimes overfed and sometimes put on diets. (None of the twin pairs were at risk for obesity based on their body mass or their family history.) In one study, 12 sets of the twins were put under 24-hour supervision in a college dormitory. Six days a week they ate 1,000 extra calories a day, and one day they were allowed to eat normally. They could read, play video games, play cards and watch television, but exercise was limited to one 30-minute daily walk. Over the course of the 120-day study, the twins consumed 84,000 extra calories beyond their basic needs.

That experimental binge should have translated into a weight gain of roughly 24 pounds (based on 3,500 calories to a pound). But some gained less than 10 pounds, while others gained as much as 29 pounds. The amount of weight gained and how the fat was distributed around the body closely matched among brothers, but varied considerably among the different sets of twins. Some brothers gained three times as much fat around their abdomens as others, for instance. When the researchers conducted similar exercise studies with the twins, they saw the patterns in reverse, with some twin sets losing more pounds than others on the same exercise regimen. The findings, the researchers wrote, suggest a form of "biological determinism" that can make a person susceptible to weight gain or loss.

But while there is widespread agreement that at least some risk for obesity is inherited, identifying a specific genetic cause has been a challenge. In October 2010, the journal *Nature Genetics* reported that researchers have so far confirmed 32 distinct genetic variations associated with obesity or body-mass index. One of the most common of these variations was identified in April 2007 by a British team studying the genetics of Type 2 diabetes. According to Timothy Frayling at the Institute of Biomedical and Clinical Science at the University of Exeter, people who carried a variant known as FTO faced a much higher risk of obesity—30 percent higher if they had one copy of the variant; 60 percent if they had two.

This FTO variant is surprisingly common; about 65 percent of people of European or African descent and an estimated 27 to 44 percent of Asians are believed to carry at least one copy of it. Scientists don't understand how the FTO variation influences weight gain, but studies in children suggest the trait plays a role in eating habits. In one 2008 study led by Colin Palmer of the University of Dundee in Scotland, Scottish schoolchildren were given snacks of orange drinks and muffins and then allowed to graze on a buffet of grapes, celery, potato chips and chocolate buttons. All the food was carefully monitored so the researchers knew exactly what was consumed. Although all the children ate about the same amount of food, as weighed in grams, children with the FTO variant were more likely to eat foods with higher fat and calorie content. They weren't gorging themselves, but they consumed, on average, about 100 calories more than children who didn't carry the gene. Those who had the gene variant had about four pounds more body fat than noncarriers.

I have been tempted to send in my own saliva sample for a DNA test to find out if my family carries a genetic predisposition for obesity. But even if the test came back negative, it would only mean that my family doesn't carry a known, testable genetic risk for obesity. Recently the British television show "Embarrassing Fat Bodies" asked Frayling's lab to test for fat-promoting genes, and the results showed one very overweight family had a lower-than-average risk for obesity.

A positive result, telling people they are genetically inclined to stay fat, might be self-fulfilling. In February, *The New England Journal of Medicine* published a report on how genetic testing for a variety of diseases affected a person's mood and health habits. Overall, the researchers found no effect from disease-risk testing, but there was a suggestion, though it didn't reach statistical significance, that after testing positive for fat-promoting genes, some people were more likely to eat fatty foods, presumably because they thought being fat was their genetic destiny and saw no sense in fighting it.

While knowing my genetic risk might satisfy my curiosity, I also know that heredity, at best, would explain only part of why I became overweight. I'm much more interested in figuring out what I can do about it now.

The National Weight Control Registry tracks 10,000 people who have lost weight and have kept it off. "We set it up in response to comments that nobody ever succeeds at weight loss," says Rena Wing, a professor of psychiatry and human behavior at Brown University's Alpert Medical School, who helped create the registry with James O. Hill, director of the Center for Human Nutrition at the University of Colorado at Denver. "We had two goals: to prove there were people who did, and to try to learn from them about what they do to achieve this long-term weight loss." Anyone who has lost 30 pounds and kept it off for at least a year is eligible to join the study, though the average member has lost 70 pounds and remained at that weight for six years.

Wing says that she agrees that physiological changes probably do occur that make permanent weight loss difficult, but she says the larger problem is environmental, and that people struggle to keep weight off because they are surrounded by food, inundated with food messages and constantly presented with opportunities to eat. "We live in an environment with food cues all the time," Wing says. "We've taught ourselves over the years that one of the ways to reward yourself is with food. It's hard to change the environment and the behavior."

There is no consistent pattern to how people in the registry lost weight—some did it on Weight Watchers, others with Jenny Craig, some by cutting carbs on the Atkins diet and a very small number lost weight through surgery. But their eating and exercise habits appear to reflect what researchers find in the lab: to lose weight and keep it off, a person must eat fewer calories and exercise far more than a person who maintains the same weight naturally. Registry members exercise about an hour or more each day—the average weight-loser puts in the equivalent of a four-mile daily walk, seven days a week. They get on a scale every day in order to keep their weight within a narrow range. They eat breakfast regularly. Most watch less than half as much television as the overall population. They eat the same foods and in the same patterns consistently each day and don't "cheat" on weekends or holidays. They also appear to eat less than most people, with estimates ranging from 50 to 300 fewer daily calories.

Kelly Brownell, director of the Rudd Center for Food Policy and Obesity at Yale University, says that while the 10,000 people tracked in the registry are a useful resource, they also represent a tiny percentage of the tens of millions of people who have tried unsuccessfully to lose weight. "All it means is that there are rare individuals who do manage to keep it off," Brownell says. "You find these people are incredibly vigilant about maintaining their weight. Years later they are paying attention to every calorie, spending an hour a day on exercise. They never don't think about their weight."

Janice Bridge, a registry member who has successfully maintained a 135-pound weight loss for about five years, is a perfect example. "It's one of the hardest things there is," she says. "It's something that has to be focused on every minute. I'm not always thinking about food, but I am always aware of food." Bridge, who is 66 and lives in Davis, Calif., was overweight as a child and remembers going on her first diet of 1,400 calories a day at 14. At the time, her slow pace of weight loss prompted her doctor to accuse her of cheating. Friends told her she must not be paying attention to what she was eating. "No one would believe me that I was doing everything I was told," she says. "You can imagine how tremendously depressing it was and what a feeling of rebellion and anger was building up."

After peaking at 330 pounds in 2004, she tried again to lose weight. She managed to drop 30 pounds, but then her weight loss stalled. In 2006, at age 60, she joined a medically supervised weight-loss program with her husband, Adam, who weighed 310 pounds. After nine months on an 800-calorie diet, she slimmed down to 165 pounds. Adam lost about 110 pounds and now weighs about 200.

During the first years after her weight loss, Bridge tried to test the limits of how much she could eat. She used exercise to justify eating more. The death of her mother in 2009 consumed her attention; she lost focus and slowly regained 30 pounds. She has decided to try to maintain this higher weight of 195, which is still 135 pounds [less] than her heaviest weight.

"It doesn't take a lot of variance from my current maintenance for me to pop on another two or three pounds," she says. "It's been a real struggle to stay at this weight, but it's worth it, it's good for me, it makes me feel better. But my body would put on weight almost instantaneously if I ever let up."

So she never lets up. Since October 2006 she has weighed herself every morning and recorded the result in a weight diary. She even carries a scale with her when she travels. In the past six years, she made only one exception to this routine: a two-week, no-weigh vacation in Hawaii.

She also weighs everything in the kitchen. She knows that lettuce is about 5 calories a cup, while flour is about 400. If she goes out to dinner, she conducts a Web search first to look at the menu and calculate calories to help her decide what to order. She avoids anything with sugar or white flour, which she calls her "gateway drugs" for cravings and overeating. She has also found that drinking copious amounts of water seems to help; she carries a 20-ounce water bottle and fills it five times a day. She writes down everything she eats. At night, she transfers all the information to an electronic record. Adam also keeps track but prefers to keep his record with pencil and paper.

"That transfer process is really important; it's my accountability," she says. "It comes up with the total number of calories I've eaten today and the amount of protein. I do a little bit of self-analysis every night."

Bridge and her husband each sought the help of therapists, and in her sessions, Janice learned that she had a tendency to eat when she was bored or stressed. "We are very much aware of how our culture taught us to use food for all kinds of reasons that aren't related to its nutritive value," Bridge says. Bridge supports her careful diet with an equally rigorous regimen of physical activity. She exercises from 100 to 120 minutes a day, six or seven days a week, often by riding her bicycle to the gym, where she takes a water-aerobics class. She also works out on an elliptical trainer at home and uses a recumbent bike to "walk" the dog, who loves to run alongside the low, three-wheeled machine. She enjoys gardening as a hobby but allows herself to count it as exercise on only those occasions when she needs to "garden vigorously." Adam is also a committed exerciser, riding his bike at least two hours a day, five days a week.

Janice Bridge has used years of her exercise and diet data to calculate her own personal fuel efficiency. She knows that her body burns about three calories a minute during gardening, about four calories a minute on the recumbent bike and during water aerobics and about five a minute when she zips around town on her regular bike.

"Practically anyone will tell you someone biking is going to burn 11 calories a minute," she says. "That's not my body. I know it because of the statistics I've kept."

Based on metabolism data she collected from the weight-loss clinic and her own calculations, she has discovered that to keep her current weight of 195 pounds, she can eat 2,000 calories a day as long as she burns 500 calories in exercise. She avoids junk food, bread and pasta and many dairy products and tries to make sure nearly a third of her calories come from protein. The Bridges will occasionally share a dessert, or eat an individual portion of Ben and Jerry's ice cream, so they know exactly how many calories they are ingesting. Because she knows errors can creep in, either because a rainy day cuts exercise short or a mismeasured snack portion adds hidden calories, she allows herself only 1,800 daily calories of food. (The average estimate for a similarly active woman of her age and size is about 2,300 calories.)

Just talking to Bridge about the effort required to maintain her weight is exhausting. I find her story inspiring, but it also makes me wonder whether I have what it takes to be thin. I have tried on several occasions (and as recently as a couple weeks ago) to keep a daily diary of my eating and exercise habits, but it's easy to let it slide. I can't quite imagine how I would ever make time to weigh and measure food when some days it's all I can do to get dinner on the table between finishing my work and carting my daughter to dance class or volleyball practice. And while I enjoy exercising for 30- or 40-minute stretches, I also learned from six months of marathon training that devoting one to two hours a day to exercise takes an impossible toll on my family life.

Bridge concedes that having grown children and being retired make it easier to focus on her weight. "I don't know if I could have done this when I had three kids living at home," she says. "We know how unusual we are. It's pretty easy to get angry with the amount of work and dedication it takes to keep this weight off. But the alternative is to not keep the weight off."

"I think many people who are anxious to lose weight don't fully understand what the consequences are going to be, nor does the medical community fully explain this to people," Rudolph Leibel, an obesity researcher at Columbia University in New York, says. "We don't want to make them feel hopeless, but we do want to make them understand that they are trying to buck a biological system that is going to try to make it hard for them."

Leibel and his colleague Michael Rosenbaum have pioneered much of what we know about the body's response to weight loss. For 25 years, they have meticulously tracked about 130 individuals for six months or longer at a stretch. The subjects reside at their research clinic where every aspect of their bodies is measured. Body fat is determined by bone-scan machines. A special hood monitors oxygen consumption and carbon-dioxide output to precisely measure metabolism. Calories burned during digestion are tracked. Exercise tests measure maximum heart rate, while blood tests measure hormones and brain chemicals. Muscle biopsies are taken to analyze their metabolic efficiency. (Early in the research, even stool samples were collected and tested to make sure no calories went unaccounted for.) For their trouble, participants are paid $5,000 to $8,000.

Eventually, the Columbia subjects are placed on liquid diets of 800 calories a day until they lose 10 percent of their body weight. Once they reach the goal, they are subjected to another round of intensive testing as they try to maintain the new weight. The data generated by these experiments suggest that once a person loses about 10 percent of body weight, he or she is metabolically different than a similar-size person who is naturally the same weight.

The research shows that the changes that occur after weight loss translate to a huge caloric disadvantage of about 250 to 400 calories. For instance, one woman who entered the Columbia studies at 230 pounds was eating about 3,000 calories to maintain that weight. Once she dropped to 190 pounds, losing 17 percent of her body weight, metabolic studies determined that she needed about 2,300 daily calories to maintain the new lower weight. That may sound like plenty, but the typical 30-year-old 190-pound woman can consume about 2,600 calories to maintain her weight—300 more calories than the woman who dieted to get there.

Scientists are still learning why a weight-reduced body behaves so differently from a similar-size body that has not dieted. Muscle biopsies taken before, during and after weight loss show that once a person drops weight, their muscle fibers undergo a transformation, making them more like highly efficient "slow twitch" muscle fibers. A result is that after losing weight, your muscles burn 20 to 25 percent fewer calories during everyday activity and moderate aerobic exercise than those of a person who is naturally at the same weight. That means a dieter who thinks she is burning 200 calories during a brisk half-hour walk is probably using closer to 150 to 160 calories.

Another way that the body seems to fight weight loss is by altering the way the brain responds to food. Rosenbaum and his colleague Joy Hirsch, a neuroscientist also at Columbia, used functional magnetic resonance imaging to track the brain patterns of people before and after weight loss while they looked at objects like grapes, Gummi Bears, chocolate, broccoli, cellphones and yo-yos. After weight loss, when the dieter looked at food, the scans showed a bigger response in the parts of the brain associated with reward and a lower response in the areas associated with control. This suggests that the body, in order to get back to its pre-diet weight, induces cravings by making the person feel more excited about food and giving him or her less willpower to resist a high-calorie treat.

"After you've lost weight, your brain has a greater emotional response to food," Rosenbaum says. "You want it more, but the areas of the brain involved in restraint are less active." Combine that with a body that is now burning fewer calories than expected, he says, "and you've created the perfect storm for weight regain." How long this state lasts isn't known, but preliminary research at Columbia suggests that for as many as six years after weight loss, the body continues to defend the old, higher weight by burning off far fewer calories than would be expected. The problem could persist indefinitely. (The same phenomenon occurs when a thin person tries to drop about 10 percent of his or her body weight—the body defends the higher weight.) This doesn't mean it's impossible to lose weight and keep it off; it just means it's really, really difficult.

Lynn Haraldson, a 48-year-old woman who lives in Pittsburgh, reached 300 pounds in 2000. She joined Weight Watchers and managed to take her 5-foot-5 body down to 125 pounds for a brief time. Today, she's a member of the National Weight Control Registry and maintains about 140 pounds by devoting her life to weight maintenance. She became a vegetarian, writes down what she eats every day, exercises at least five days a week and blogs about the challenges of weight maintenance. A former journalist and antiques dealer, she returned to school for a two-year program on nutrition and health; she plans to become a dietary counselor. She has also come to accept that she can never stop being "hypervigilant" about what she eats. "Everything has to change," she says. "I've been up and down the scale so many times, always thinking I can go back to 'normal,' but I had to establish a new normal. People don't like hearing that it's not easy."

What's not clear from the research is whether there is a window during which we can gain weight and then lose it without creating biological backlash. Many people experience transient weight gain, putting on a few extra pounds during the holidays or gaining 10 or 20 pounds during the first years of college that they lose again. The actor Robert De Niro lost weight after bulking up for his performance in "Raging Bull." The filmmaker Morgan Spurlock also lost the weight he gained during the making of "Super Size Me." Leibel says that whether these temporary pounds became permanent probably depends on a person's genetic risk for obesity and, perhaps, the length of time a person carried the extra weight before trying to lose it. But researchers don't know how long it takes for the body to reset itself permanently to a higher weight. The good news is that it doesn't seem to happen overnight.

"For a mouse, I know the time period is somewhere around eight months," Leibel says. "Before that time, a fat mouse can come back to being a skinny mouse again without too much adjustment. For a human we don't know, but I'm pretty sure it's not measured in months, but in years."

Nobody wants to be fat. In most modern cultures, even if you are healthy—in my case, my cholesterol and blood pressure are low and I have an extraordinarily healthy heart—to be fat is to be perceived as weak-willed and lazy. It's also just embarrassing. Once, at a party, I met a well-respected writer who knew my work as a health writer. "You're not at all what I expected," she said, eyes widening. The man I was dating, perhaps trying to help, finished the thought. "You thought she'd be thinner, right?" he said. I wanted to disappear, but the woman was gracious. "No," she said, casting a glare at the man and reaching to warmly shake my hand. "I thought you'd be older."

If anything, the emerging science of weight loss teaches us that perhaps we should rethink our biases about people who are overweight. It is true that people who are overweight, including myself, get that way because they eat too many calories relative to what their bodies need. But a number of biological and genetic factors can play a role in determining exactly how much food is too much for any given individual. Clearly, weight loss is an intense struggle, one in which we are not fighting simply hunger or cravings for sweets, but our own bodies.

While the public discussion about weight loss tends to come down to which diet works best (Atkins? Jenny Craig? Plant-based? Mediterranean?), those who have tried and failed at all of these diets know there is no simple answer. Fat, sugar and carbohydrates in processed foods may very well be culprits in the nation's obesity problem. But there is tremendous variation in an individual's response.

The view of obesity as primarily a biological, rather than psychological, disease could also lead to changes in the way we approach its treatment. Scientists at Columbia have conducted several small studies looking at whether injecting people with leptin, the hormone made by body fat, can override the body's resistance to weight loss and help maintain a lower weight. In a few small studies, leptin injections appear to trick the body into thinking it's still fat. After leptin replacement, study subjects burned more calories during activity. And in brain-scan studies, leptin injections appeared to change how the brain responded to food, making it seem less enticing. But such treatments are still years away from commercial development. For now, those of us who want to lose weight and keep it off are on our own.

One question many researchers think about is whether losing weight more slowly would make it more sustainable than the fast weight loss often used in scientific studies. Leibel says the pace of weight loss is unlikely to make a difference, because the body's warning system is based solely on how much fat a person loses, not how quickly he or she loses it. Even so, Proietto is now conducting a study using a slower weight-loss method and following dieters for three years instead of one.

Given how hard it is to lose weight, it's clear, from a public-health standpoint, that resources would best be focused on preventing weight gain. The research underscores the urgency of national efforts to get children to exercise and eat healthful foods.

But with a third of the U.S. adult population classified as obese, nobody is saying people who already are very overweight should give up on weight loss. Instead, the solution may be to preach a more realistic goal. Studies suggest that even a 5 percent weight loss can lower a person's risk for diabetes, heart disease and other health problems associated with obesity. There is also speculation that the body is more willing to accept small amounts of weight loss.

But an obese person who loses just 5 percent of her body weight will still very likely be obese. For a 250-pound woman, a 5 percent weight loss of about 12 pounds probably won't even change her clothing size. Losing a few pounds may be good for the body, but it does very little for the spirit and is unlikely to change how fat people feel about themselves or how others perceive them.

So where does that leave a person who wants to lose a sizable amount of weight? Weight-loss scientists say they believe that once more people understand the genetic and biological challenges of keeping weight off, doctors and patients will approach weight loss more realistically and more compassionately. At the very least, the science may compel people who are already overweight to work harder to make sure they don't put on additional pounds. Some people, upon learning how hard permanent weight loss can be, may give up entirely and return to overeating. Others may decide to accept themselves at their current weight and try to boost their fitness and overall health rather than changing the number on the scale.

For me, understanding the science of weight loss has helped make sense of my own struggles to lose weight, as well as my mother's endless cycle of dieting, weight gain and despair. I wish she were still here so I could persuade her to finally forgive herself for her dieting failures. While

I do, ultimately, blame myself for allowing my weight to get out of control, it has been somewhat liberating to learn that there are factors other than my character at work when it comes to gaining and losing weight. And even though all the evidence suggests that it's going to be very, very difficult for me to reduce my weight permanently, I'm surprisingly optimistic. I may not be ready to fight this battle this month or even this year. But at least I know what I'm up against.

Tara Parker-Pope is an author of books on health topics and a columnist for *The New York Times,* where she edits the Well blog.

EXPLORING THE ISSUE

Is Weight-Loss Maintenance Possible?

Critical Thinking and Reflection

1. Why is it so difficult for most people to maintain their weight loss?
2. What role does the typical American diet play in overweight and obesity?
3. Describe the biological mechanisms that make weight-loss maintenance so challenging.
4. What role does genetics play in the onset of obesity?

Is There Common Ground?

Although genetics and metabolism may elevate the risk for overweight and obesity, they don't explain the rising rate of obesity seen in the United States. Our genetic background has not changed significantly in the past 40 years, during which time the rate of obesity among Americans has more than doubled. The causes can be linked to changing eating habits and a decline in physical activity.

While dieting is a common means of losing weight, there is an overall belief that even if one loses weight, virtually no one succeeds in long-term maintenance of weight loss. However, research has shown that approximately 20 percent of overweight people are successful at long-term weight loss (defined as losing at least 10 percent of initial body weight and maintaining the loss for at least 1 year). The National Weight Control Registry provides information about the approaches used by successful weight-loss maintainers to attain and sustain long-term weight loss. To maintain their weight loss, the successful report high levels of physical activity, eating a low-calorie, low-fat diet, eating breakfast regularly, self-monitoring weight, and maintaining a consistent eating pattern across weekdays and weekends. In addition, weight-loss maintenance may get less challenging over time. After individuals have successfully maintained their weight loss for over 2 years, the chance of longer-term success greatly increases. Continuing to diet and exercise is also associated with long-term success. National Weight Control Registry members provide evidence that long-term weight-loss maintenance is possible and helps identify the specific approaches associated with long-term success (Wing and Phelan, 2005).

The same tactics that help people lose weight don't necessarily help them keep it off. A recent study, which appears in the August 2011 issue of the *American Journal of Preventive Medicine,* suggests that successful losers need to rethink their eating and exercise practices to maintain their weight loss. Researchers interviewed nearly 1,200 adults about 36 specific behaviors to find out which of these practices were associated with weight loss and, more important, weight-loss maintenance.

From the study results, it appears that different skill sets and behaviors are involved with weight loss and weight maintenance. Participating in a weight-loss program, restricting sugar, eating healthy snacks, and not skipping meals may help people initially lose weight, but these practices don't appear to be effective in maintaining the loss.

Eating low-fat sources of protein, following a consistent exercise routine, and using rewards for maintaining these behaviors were linked to maintaining weight loss.

Additional Resources

Derbyshire, D., Weir, K., Gunther, M., & Weeks, J. (2015). Thinking big about obesity. *Food Technology, 69*(3), 20–31.

Galchen, R. (2016). Keeping it off. *New Yorker, 92*(30), 32–37.

Santos, I., Sniehotta, F. F., Marques, M. M., Carraça, E. V., & Teixeira, P. J. (2017). Prevalence of personal weight control attempts in adults: A systematic review and meta-analysis. *Obesity Reviews, 18*(1), 32–50.

Sherwood, N. E., Crain, A., Martinson, B. C., Anderson, C. P., Hayes, M. G., Anderson, J. D., & Jeffery, R. W. (2013). Enhancing long-term weight loss maintenance: 2-Year results from the Keep It Off randomized controlled trial. *Preventive Medicine, 56*(3/4), 171–177.

Stubbs, R. J., & Lavin, J. H. (2013). The challenges of implementing behavior changes that lead to sustained weight management. *Nutrition Bulletin, 38*(1), 5–22.

Internet References . . .

The American Dietetic Association

www.eatright.org

Center for Science in the Public Interest (CSPI)

www.cspinet.org

Food and Nutrition Information Center

www.nalusda.gov/fnic/index.html

National Weight Control Registry

www.nwcr.ws

Shape Up America!

www.shapeup.org

Selected, Edited, and with Issue Framing Material by:
Eileen L. Daniel, *SUNY College at Brockport*

ISSUE

Does Obesity Increase the Risk of Premature Death?

YES: Harvard School of Public Health, from "As Overweight and Obesity Increase, So Does Risk of Dying Prematurely," *Harvard School of Public Health* (2016)

NO: Harriet Brown, from "The Weight of the Evidence," *Medical Examiner* (2015)

Learning Outcomes

After reading this issue, you will be able to:

- Understand the difference between obesity and overweight.
- Explain the types of illnesses associated with being overweight and obese.
- Discuss the relationship between obesity and premature death.

ISSUE SUMMARY

YES: The editors of the Harvard School of Public Health argue that being overweight or obese is clearly associated with a higher risk of dying prematurely than being normal weight.

NO: Writer Harriet Brown maintains that obese individuals with chronic diseases fare better and live longer than those of normal weight.

In 1960, approximately 10 percent of adult males and 15 percent of adult females in the United States were obese. Fifty years later, those numbers had risen to 32.2 and 35.5 percent, respectively. The same pattern has occurred in most other developed nations, but it has generally been less pronounced than in the United States. The rates of obesity in the United States during the late 1970s were already higher than the rates in most of the other high-income countries today. Obesity and overweight are assessed using body mass index (BMI), a height-weight ratio. BMI is used as a screening tool to determine underweight, healthy weight, overweight, and obesity. For example, a 5′9″ person is considered at a healthy weight at 125–168 pounds, overweight at 169–202 pounds, and obese if greater than 203 pounds.

Obesity is linked to various diseases, it leads to different types of disability, and it shortens lives. The most common effects of obesity include diabetes; high blood pressure; heart disease; gallstones; and certain cancers, such as colorectal cancer, breast cancer in women, endometrial cancer, and cancers of the kidney, pancreas, liver, and gallbladder. Type 2 diabetes, most typically adult-onset, is particularly sensitive to body weight, is uncommon in people of normal weight, and the risk for developing it increases rapidly with increasing weight. The risks of developing high blood pressure, coronary heart disease, and gallstones also grow as obesity increases, as do the risks for the various obesity-related cancers, but none of these conditions are as sensitive to body weight as diabetes. Worldwide, the countries with the highest rates of obesity were those hardest hit by diabetes and heart disease in older adults.

Among older adults, obesity is also correlated with various types of disabilities. Excess weight can make it difficult to engage in certain activities, such as climbing stairs or walking for long distances, and it frequently leads to joint problems. These limitations are often worsened by the various chronic diseases associated with obesity which can also cause disabilities.

The effect of being overweight or obese on the risk of dying has been an area of rather contentious debate. A recent study reviewed the mortality risk and years of life lost due to different levels of obesity, breaking the numbers down by age, gender, race, and smoking status and found in general, that being *overweight* does not increase mortality risk and sometimes decreases it, although the effect usually is not statistically significant either way. Obesity, however, has a greater effect on years of life lost for men than for women and for Whites than for African Americans, and its effects are similar for smokers and nonsmokers, with smoking adding greatly to the mortality risk for all groups.

Since obesity increases mortality in at least some groups, it's unclear whether this obesity–mortality connection combined with the higher rates of obesity in the United States might explain at least part of this country's lower-than-expected life expectancy. Since life expectancy at age 50 in the United States would increase significantly more than in other countries through the hypothetical elimination of obesity, the U.S. longevity shortfall would be reduced and in some cases eliminated.

It is well known that Americans have, on average, higher weight for a particular height than people in other developed countries. It is also well known that obesity is associated with a variety of negative health effects, such as diabetes, heart disease, high blood pressure, and certain types of cancer. So it is natural to ask whether the higher rates of obesity in the United States may help explain the divergence in life expectancy trends that has been observed over the past quarter of a century. It may seem obvious that the heavier one is, the greater likelihood of a shorter life expectancy, however, the data can be confusing and not always clear. Complicating the discussion of weight and mortality is the fact that as weight decreases *below* normal range, mortality increases. However, the relationship between weight and mortality may vary depending on the people examined and how other variables are taken into account. Smoking is an example of another health behavior that is related to obesity. It is usually related to lower weight, and giving up smoking can produce weight gain. In addition, people who have been overweight or obese at any time during their lives may be more likely to die prematurely, even if they lose weight later.

The obesity paradox is a medical hypothesis which states that obesity may actually protect from disease and increase longevity especially among the very old and among people with certain chronic diseases. The paradox further assumes that normal to low BMI may actually be harmful and linked to higher death rates among individuals without disease symptoms. The paradox was first described in 1999 based on the studies of overweight and obese people with kidney failure. Later studies found the same paradox among those with heart failure and chronic obstructive pulmonary disease. In people with heart disease, those with a BMI in the obese range had lower death rates than those at a healthy weight. This was later attributed to the fact that people lose weight as they become sicker and sicker. The paradox has been criticized on poor study design as well as BMI may not be a valid measure of health and weight.

The editors of the Harvard School of Public Health argue that being overweight or obese is clearly associated with a higher risk of dying prematurely than being at a healthy weight. Writer Harriet Brown disagrees and maintains that obese individuals with chronic diseases fare better and live longer than those of a healthy weight.

Harvard School of Public Health

As Overweight and Obesity Increase, So Does Risk of Dying Prematurely

New Study Provides Strong Evidence on Dangers of Excess Weight

Being overweight or obese is associated with a higher risk of dying prematurely than being normal weight—and the risk increases with additional pounds, according to a large international collaborative study led by researchers at the Harvard T.H. Chan School of Public Health and the University of Cambridge, UK. The findings contradict recent reports that suggest a survival advantage to being overweight—the so-called "obesity paradox."

The study was published online on July 13, 2016, in *The Lancet.*

The deleterious effects of excess body weight on chronic disease have been well documented. Recent studies suggesting otherwise have resulted in confusion among the public about what is a healthy weight. According to the authors of the new study, those prior studies had serious methodological limitations. One common problem is called reverse causation, in which a low body weight is the result of underlying or preclinical illness rather than the cause. Another problem is confounding by smoking because smokers tend to weigh less than nonsmokers but have much higher mortality rates.

"To obtain an unbiased relationship between body mass index (BMI) and mortality, it is essential to analyze individuals who never smoked and had no existing chronic diseases at the start of the study," said Frank Hu, a professor of nutrition and epidemiology at Harvard Chan School and a coleader of the collaboration. Hu stressed that doctors should continue to counsel patients regarding the deleterious effects of excess body weight, which include a higher risk of diabetes, cardiovascular disease, and cancer.

In order to provide more definitive evidence for the association of excess body weight with premature mortality, researchers joined forces in 2013 to establish the Global BMI Mortality Collaboration, which involves over 500 investigators from over 300 global institutions.

"This international collaboration represents the largest and most rigorous effort so far to resolve the controversy regarding BMI and mortality," said Shilpa Bhupathiraju, research scientist in the Department of Nutrition at Harvard Chan School and colead author of the study.

For the new study, consortium researchers looked at data from more than 10.6 million participants from 239 large studies, conducted between 1970 and 2015, in 32 countries. A combined 1.6 million deaths were recorded across these studies, in which participants were followed for an average of 14 years. For the primary analyses, to address potential biases caused by smoking and preexisting diseases, the researchers excluded participants who were current or former smokers, those who had chronic diseases at the beginning of the study, and any who died in the first five years of follow-up, so that the group they analyzed included 4 million adults. They looked at participants' BMI—an indicator of body fat calculated by dividing a person's weight in kilograms by their height in meters squared (kg/m^2).

The results showed that participants with BMI of 22.5 to <25 kg/m^2 (considered a healthy weight range) had the lowest mortality risk during the time they were followed. The risk of mortality increased significantly throughout the overweight range: a BMI of 25 to <27.5 kg/m^2 was associated with a 7 percent higher risk of mortality, a BMI of 27.5 to <30 kg/m^2 was associated with a 20 percent higher risk, a BMI of 30.0 to <35.0 kg/m^2 was associated with a 45 percent higher risk, a BMI of 35.0 to <40.0 kg/m^2 was associated with a 94 percent higher risk, and a BMI of 40.0 to <60.0 kg/m^2 was associated with a nearly three-fold risk. Every five units higher BMI above 25 kg/m^2 was associated with about 31 percent higher risk of premature death. Participants who were underweight also had a higher mortality risk.

Looking at specific causes of death, the study found that, for each five-unit increase in BMI above 25 kg/m^2, the corresponding increases in risk were 49 percent for cardiovascular mortality, 38 percent for respiratory disease mortality, and 19 percent for cancer mortality. Researchers also found that the hazards of excess body weight were greater in younger than in older people and in men than in women.

The Harvard T.H. Chan School of Public Health (formerly **Harvard School of Public Health**) is the public health graduate school of Harvard University, located in Boston, MA.

Harriet Brown

NO

The Weight of the Evidence

It's Time to Stop Telling Fat People to Become Thin

If you're one of the 45 million Americans who plan to go on a diet this year, I've got one word of advice for you: Don't.

You'll likely lose weight in the short term, but your chance of keeping if off for five years or more is about the same as your chance of surviving metastatic lung cancer: 5 percent. And when you do gain back the weight, everyone will blame *you*. Including you.

This isn't breaking news; doctors know the holy trinity of obesity treatments—diet, exercise, and medication—don't work. They know yo-yo dieting is linked to heart disease, insulin resistance, higher blood pressure, inflammation, and, ironically, long-term weight gain. Still, they push the same ineffective treatments, insisting they'll make you not just thinner but healthier.

In reality, 97 percent of dieters regain everything they lost and then some within three years. Obesity research fails to reflect this truth because it rarely follows people for more than 18 months. This makes most weight-loss studies disingenuous at best and downright deceptive at worst.

One of the principles driving the $61 billion weight-loss industries is the notion that fat is inherently unhealthy and that it's better, healthwise, to be thin, no matter what you have to do to get there. But a growing body of research is beginning to question this paradigm. Does obesity *cause* ill health, *result* from it, both, or neither? Does weight loss lead to a longer, healthier life for most people?

Studies from the Centers for Disease Control and Prevention repeatedly find the lowest mortality rates among people whose body mass index (BMI) puts them in the "overweight" and "mildly obese" categories. And recent research suggests that losing weight doesn't actually improve health biomarkers such as blood pressure, fasting glucose, or triglyceride levels for most people.

So why, then, are we so deeply invested in treatments that not only fail to do what they're supposed to—make people thinner and healthier—but often actively makes people fatter, sicker, and more miserable?

Weight inched its way into the American consciousness around the turn of the 20th century. "I would sooner die than be fat," declared Amelia Summerville, author of the 1916 volume *Why Be Fat? Rules for Weight-Reduction and the Preservation of Youth and Health.* (She also wrote, with a giddy glee that likely derived from malnutrition, "I possibly eat more lettuce and pineapple than any other woman on earth!") As scales became more accurate and affordable, doctors began routinely recording patients' height and weight at every visit. Weight-loss drugs hit the mainstream in the 1920s, when doctors started prescribing thyroid medications to healthy people to make them slimmer. In the 1930s, 2,4-dinitrophenol came along, sold as DNP, followed by amphetamines, diuretics, laxatives, and diet pills like fen-phen, all of which caused side effects ranging from the annoying to the fatal.

The national obsession with weight got a boost in 1942, when the Metropolitan Life Insurance Company crunched age, weight, and mortality numbers from policyholders to create "desirable" height and weight charts. For the first time, people (and their doctors) could compare themselves to a standardized notion of what they "should" weigh. And compare they did, in language that shifted from words like *chubby* and *plump* to the more clinical-sounding *adipose, overweight*, and *obese*. The word *overweight*, for example, suggests you're over the "right" weight. The word *obese*, from the Latin *obesus*, or "having eaten until fat," conveys both a clinical and a moral judgment.

In 1949, a small group of doctors created the National Obesity Society, the first of many professional associations meant to take obesity treatment from the margins to the mainstream. They believed that "any level of thinness was healthier than being fat, and the thinner a person was, the healthier she or he was," writes Nita Mary McKinley, a psychologist at the University of Washington Tacoma. This attitude inspired a number of new and terrible treatments for obesity, including jaw wiring and stereotactic brain surgery that burned lesions into the hypothalamus.

Bariatric surgery is the latest of these. In 2000, about 37,000 bariatric surgeries were performed in the United States; by 2013, the number had risen to 220,000. The best estimates suggest that about half of those who have surgery regain some or all of the weight they lose. While such surgeries are safer now than they were 10 years ago, they still lead to complications for many, including long-term malnutrition, intestinal blockages, disordered eating, and death. "Bariatric surgery is barbaric, but it's the best we have," says David B. Allison, a biostatistician at the University of Alabama at Birmingham (UAB).

Reading the research on obesity treatments sometimes feels like getting stuck in an M.C. Escher's illustration, where walls turn into ceilings and water flows upward. You can find studies that "prove" the merit of high-fat/low-carb diets and low-fat/high-carb diets, and either 30 min of daily aerobic exercise or 90 min. You'll read that fen-phen is safe (even though the drug damaged heart valves in a third of those who took it). Studies say that orlistat (which causes liver damage and "uncontrollable" bowel movements) and sibutramine (which ups the risk of heart attacks and strokes) are effective. After reading literally more than a thousand studies, each of them claiming some nucleus of truth, the only thing I know for sure is that we really don't know weight and health at all.

"We make all these recommendations, with all this apparent scientific precision, but when it comes down to it we don't know, say, how much fat someone should have in their diet," says Asheley Skinner, a pediatrician at the University of North Carolina at Chapel Hill School of Medicine. "We argue like we know what we're talking about, but we don't."

For instance, much of the research assumes that when fat people lose weight, they become "healthy" in the same ways as a thinner person is healthy. The evidence says otherwise. "Even if someone loses weight, they will always need fewer calories and need to exercise more," says Skinner. "So we're putting people through something we know will probably not be successful anyway. Who knows what we're doing to their metabolisms."

Debra Sapp-Yarwood, a fiftysomething from Kansas City, Missouri, who's studying to be a hospital chaplain, is one of the three percenters, the select few who have lost a chunk of weight and kept it off. She dropped 55 pounds 11 years ago and maintains her new weight with a diet and exercise routine most people would find unsustainable: she eats 1,800 calories a day—no more than 200 in carbs—and has learned to put up with what she describes as "intrusive thoughts and food preoccupations." She used to run for an hour a day, but after foot surgery, she switched to her current routine: a 50-min exercise video performed at twice the speed of the instructor, while wearing ankle weights and a weighted vest that add between 25 and 30 pounds to her small frame.

"Maintaining weight loss is not a lifestyle," she says. "It's a job." It's a job that requires not just time, self-discipline, and energy—it also takes up a lot of mental real estate. People who maintain weight loss over the long term typically make it their top priority in life. Which is not always possible or desirable.

While concerns over appearance motivate a lot of would-be dieters, concerns about health fuel the national conversation about the "obesity epidemic." So how bad is it, healthwise, to be overweight or obese? The answer depends in part on what you mean by "health." Right now, we know obesity is *linked* with certain diseases, most strongly type 2 diabetes, but as scientists are fond of saying, correlation does not equal causation. Maybe weight gain is an early symptom of type 2 diabetes. Maybe some underlying mechanism causes both weight gain and diabetes. Maybe weight gain causes diabetes in some people but not others. People who lose weight often see their blood sugar improve, but that's likely an effect of calorie reduction rather than weight loss. Type 2 diabetics who have bariatric surgery go into complete remission after only seven days, long before they lose much weight, because they're eating only a few hundred calories a day.

Disease is also attributed to what we eat (or don't), and here, too, the connections are often assumed to relate to weight. For instance, eating fast food once a week has been linked to high blood pressure, especially for teens. And eating fruits and vegetables every day is associated with lower risk of heart disease. But it's a mistake to simply assume weight is the mechanism linking food and disease. We have yet to fully untangle the relationship.

Higher BMIs have been linked to a higher risk of developing type 2 diabetes, heart disease, and certain cancers, especially esophageal, pancreatic, and breast cancers. But weight loss is not necessarily linked to lower levels of disease. The only study to follow subjects for more than five years, the 2013 Look AHEAD study, found that people with type 2 diabetes who lost weight had just as many heart attacks, strokes, and deaths as those who didn't.

Not only that, since 2002, study after study has turned up what researchers call the "obesity paradox":

Obese patients with heart disease, heart failure, diabetes, kidney disease, pneumonia, and many other chronic diseases fare better and live longer than those of normal weight.

Likewise, we don't fully understand the relationship between weight and overall mortality. Many of us assume it's a linear relationship, meaning the higher your BMI, the higher your risk of early death. But Katherine Flegal, an epidemiologist with the CDC, has consistently found a J-shaped curve, with the highest death rates among those at either end of the BMI spectrum and the *lowest* rates in the overweight and mildly obese categories.

Study after study has turned up the "obesity paradox": obese patients with disease live longer than those of normal weight.

None of this stops doctors and researchers from recommending weight loss for health reasons. Donna Ryan, professor emeritus at the Pennington Biomedical Research Center in Baton Rouge, co-chaired the National Institutes of Health panel that recently developed new guidelines for treating obesity, including calorie-restricted diets and commercial diet programs. "Those who have a BMI of 30 and up need treatment, no questions asked," they wrote. I asked Ryan why, given that so few people keep weight off and given the risks of yo-yo dieting, the committee backed the same old ineffective treatments. "I'm not familiar with any of the research that says yo-yoing is bad for you," Ryan told me. "I'm not convinced there's any harm whatsoever in losing and regaining weight."

Why do doctors keep prescribing treatments that don't work for a condition that's often benign? I suspect one reason lies in the fanaticism that often seems to drive the public debate around weight. Last January, for instance, when Flegal's meta-analysis showing a low risk of death for overweight people hit the news, one of its most vocal critics was Walter Willett, an epidemiologist at the Harvard School of Public Health. He told a reporter from NPR, "This study is really a pile of rubbish, and no one should waste their time reading it." A month later, Willett organized a symposium at Harvard *just to attack Flegal's findings*.

Willett's career, like countless others', has been built on the obesity-will-kill-you paradigm. Tam Fry, a spokesperson for the National Obesity Forum in the U.K., also dissed Flegal's work. "This is a horrific message to put out," he told the BBC. "We shouldn't take it for granted that we can cancel the gym, that we can eat ourselves to death with black forest gateaux."

Actually, Flegal's findings suggest nothing of the kind. But Willett, Fry, and others seem to see them as a dangerous challenge to a fundamental truth. UCLA sociologist Abigail Saguy, author of *What's Wrong With Fat?*, says people are often invested in their own thin privilege. "They want to think they've earned it by working hard and counting calories, and they cling to it," she says.

There's a lot of money at stake in treating obesity. The American Medical Association—against the recommendations of its own Committee on Science and Public Health—recently classified obesity as a disease, and doctors hope insurers will start covering more treatments for obesity. If Medicare goes along with the AMA and designates obesity as a disease, doctors who discuss weight with their patients will be able to add that diagnosis code to their bill and charge more for the visit.

Obesity researchers and doctors also defend what appear to be financial conflicts of interest. In 2013, the *New England Journal of Medicine* published "Myths, Presumptions, and Facts About Obesity." The authors dismissed the often-observed link between weight cycling and mortality, saying it was "probably due to confounding by health status" (code for "We just can't believe this could be true") and went on to plug meal replacements like Jenny Craig, medications, and bariatric surgery.

Five of the 20 authors disclosed financial support from sponsors in related industries, including UAB's David Allison. I asked him how he would respond to allegations of financial self-interest. "It would be no different than anybody saying about any other person who puts forth an idea, 'I want to comment that you have this background or personality, this sexual orientation, weight, gender, or race,'" he argued. "These conflicts were disclosed, we didn't hide them, we weren't ashamed of them. And what's your point?"

Another layer to the onion may lie in our deeply held cultural assumptions around weight. "People, journalists, and researchers live in a world where it's taken for granted that fat is bad and thin is good," says Saguy.

Doctors buy into those assumptions and biases even more heavily than the rest of us, which may explain in part why they continue to blame patients who can't keep weight off. Joseph Majdan, a cardiologist who teaches at Jefferson Medical College in Philadelphia, has lost and regained the same 100 or so pounds more times than he can count. Some of the meanest comments Majdan has heard about his weight have come from other doctors, like the med-school classmate who asked if she could project slides onto a pair of his white intern's pants for a skit. Or the colleague who asked him, "Aren't you disgusted with yourself?"

"When a person has recurrent cancer, the physician is so empathetic," says Majdan. "But when a person regains weight, there's disgust. And that is morally and professionally abhorrent."

The idea that obesity is a choice, that people who are obese lack self-discipline or are gluttonous or lazy, is deeply ingrained in our public psyche. And there are other costs to this kind of judgmentalism. Research done by Lenny Vartanian, a psychologist at the University of New South Wales, suggests that people who believe they're worthless because they're not thin, who have tried and failed to maintain weight loss, are less likely to exercise than fat people who haven't strongly internalized weight stigma.

It's hard to think of any other disease—if you want to call it that—where treatment rarely works and most people are blamed for not "recovering."

Over the years, Robin Flamm, a full-time parent from Portland, Oregon, has bounced in and out of Weight Watchers and Overeaters Anonymous, gone paleo, done Medifast. Everything worked—for a while. She'd lose 30 pounds and gain back 35, lose 35, and regain 40. She thought she needed to exercise more, eat less, and work harder. Like most of us, she blamed herself.

At age 48, she decided she'd spent enough time hating her body, wishing herself different, feeling like a failure. She started seeing a therapist who offers an approach called Health at Every Size, although she was skeptical at first. In the current "obesity epidemic" climate, the idea of pursuing health separate from weight, of accepting that people come in many shapes and sizes, feels radical.

It's hard to think of any other disease where treatment rarely works and most people are blamed for not "recovering."

She felt both terrified and relieved to put away her scale, delete her calorie-counting app, and start to rethink her beliefs around food and health. While most obesity docs insist that restrained eating—counting calories or points or exchanges—is necessary for good health, not everyone agrees. About 10 years ago, Ellyn Satter, a dietitian and therapist in Madison, Wisconsin, developed a concept she calls eating competence, which encourages internal self-regulation about what and how much to eat rather than relying on calorie counts or lists of "good" and "bad" foods. Competent eaters, says Satter, enjoy food; they're not afraid of it. And there's solid evidence that competent eaters score better on cardiovascular risk markers like total cholesterol, blood pressure, and triglycerides than noncompetent eaters.

Not that abiding by competent eating, which fits the Health at Every Size paradigm, is easy; Robin Flamm would tell you that when her clothes started to feel a little tighter, she panicked. Her first impulse was to head back to Weight Watchers. Instead, she says, she asked herself if she was eating mindfully, if she was exercising in a way that gave her pleasure, if she, maybe, needed to buy new clothes. "It's really hard to let go of results," she says. "It's like free falling. And even though there's no safety net ever, really, this time it's knowing there's no safety net."

One day she was craving a hamburger, a food she wouldn't typically have eaten. But that day, she ate a hamburger and fries for lunch. "And I was done. End of story," she says, with a hint of wonder in her voice. No cravings, no obsessing over calories, no weeklong binge-and-restrict, no "feeling fat," and staying away from exercise. She ate a hamburger and fries, and nothing terrible happened. "I just wish more people would get it," she says.

Harriet Brown is a writer and the author of "Body of Truth: How Weight-and What We Can Do About it."

EXPLORING THE ISSUE

Does Obesity Increase the Risk of Premature Death?

Critical Thinking and Reflection

1. Why is there an increased risk of premature death among the obese?
2. What are some explanations for the obesity paradox?
3. Why is body mass index not always a valid measurement of weight and health?

Is There Common Ground?

Carrying too many pounds is a clear indication of current or future health problems for most people but not for everyone. Some overweight or obese individuals seem to avoid the typical hazards associated with their weight and are often referred to as the metabolically healthy obesity. However, most people who are overweight or obese have changes in their metabolism which leads to risks such as high blood pressure, or elevated cholesterol, which can damage arteries in the heart and in other parts of the body. In addition, other changes include resistance to insulin which leads to elevated blood sugar. As a result of these changes, overweight or obese individuals are usually at a high risk of developing heart disease, stroke, or type 2 diabetes. The metabolically healthy person can often manage to avoid these physical changes and the diseases associated with them. Genes may play a role in how a person's body and metabolism respond to their body weight and may offer protection from developing insulin resistance and other changes while others are genetically programmed to store fat is less harmful parts of the body such as hips or thighs which are less a risk than storing fat around the abdomen.

Metabolically healthy obesity is rare, and researchers believe it doesn't offer lifelong protection from the hazards of obesity. Scientists believe that with aging, a reduction in exercise, or other changes, metabolically healthy obesity can change into unhealthy obesity. In addition, obesity can harm more than just metabolism. Excess weight can damage knee and hip joints, leads to sleep apnea and respiratory problems, and contributes to the development of cancer including breast, uterine, and colon. Overall, while some overweight or obese individuals may appear to be metabolically healthy, that may not be permanent and other health issues can occur.

Additional Resources

Haomiao, J., Zack, M. M., Thompson, W. W. (2016). Population-based estimates of decreases in quality-adjusted life expectancy associated with unhealthy body mass index. *Public Health Reports,* 131, 177–184.

Wilson, C. (2016, June 11). Fat lot of good. *New Scientist,* 230, 28–32.

Bariatric Times (2017, January). Obesity and cardiovascular health. *Bariatric Times,* 14, 16.

Internet References . . .

Academy of Nutrition and Dietetics

www.eatright.org/

American Heart Association

www.aha.org

Centers for Disease Control and Prevention

www.cdc.gov

Selected, Edited, and with Issue Framing Material by:
Eileen L. Daniel, *SUNY College at Brockport*

ISSUE

Are Energy Drinks with Alcohol Dangerous Enough to Ban?

YES: Don Troop, from "Four Loko Does Its Job with Efficiency and Economy, Students Say," *The Chronicle of Higher Education* (2010)

NO: Jacob Sullum, from "Loco over Four Loko," *Reason* (2011)

Learning Outcomes

After reading this issue, you will be able to:

- Discuss the health implications of energy drinks.
- Discuss the argument that energy drinks should be banned from sale and distribution.
- Assess the reasons for the drink's popularity among college students.

ISSUE SUMMARY

YES: *Chronicle of Higher Education* journalist Don Troop argues that the combination of caffeine and alcohol is extremely dangerous and should not be sold or marketed to college students and young people.

NO: Journalist and editor of *Reason* magazine Jacob Sullum disagrees and claims that alcoholic energy drinks should not have been targeted and banned since many other products are far more dangerous.

Energy drinks such as Four Loko are alcoholic beverages that originally also contained caffeine and other stimulants. These products have been the object of legal, ethical, and health concerns related to companies supposedly marketing them to underaged consumers and the alleged danger of combining alcohol and caffeine. After the beverage was banned in several states, a product reintroduction in December 2010 removed caffeine and the malt beverage is no longer marketed as an energy drink.

In 2009, companies that produced and sold caffeinated alcohol beverages were investigated, on the grounds that their products were being inappropriately advertised to an underage audience and that the drinks had possible health risks by masking feelings of intoxication due to the caffeine content. Energy drinks came under major fire in 2010, as colleges and universities across the United States began to see injuries and blackouts related to the drink's consumption. Colleges such as the University of Rhode Island banned this product from their campus that year. The state of Washington banned Four Loko after nine university students, all under 20, from Central Washington University became ill after consuming the beverage at a nearby house party. The Central Washington college students were hospitalized and one student, with extremely high blood alcohol content, nearly died.

While experts believe it's safe for most healthy adults to consume up to 400 milligrams of caffeine a day, about the equivalent of one venti 20-ounce Starbucks coffee or two shots of 5-Hour Energy, the Center for Science in the Public Interest reports, drinking multiple energy drinks daily could quickly put someone over that limit, increasing their risk for headaches as well as elevate blood pressure and heart rate or worse.

Following the hospitalization of 17 students and 6 visitors in 2010, Ramapo College of New Jersey banned the possession and consumption of Four Loko on its campus. Several other colleges also prohibited the sale of the beverages. Many colleges and universities sent out notices informing their students to avoid the drinks because of the risk associated with their consumption.

Other efforts to control the use of energy drinks have been under way. The Pennsylvania Liquor Control Board sent letters to all liquor stores urging distributors to discontinue the sale of the drink. The PLCB also sent letters to all colleges and universities warning them of the dangers of the product. While the board has stopped short of a ban, it has asked retailers to stop selling the drink until U.S. Food and Drug Administration (FDA) findings prove the products are safe. Several grocery chains have voluntarily removed energy beverages from their stores. In Oregon, the sale of the restricted products carried a penalty of 30-day suspension of one's liquor license.

The U.S. FDA issued a warning letter in 2010 to four manufacturers of caffeinated alcohol beverages stating that the caffeine added to their malt alcoholic beverages is an "unsafe food additive" and said that further action, including seizure of their products, may occur under federal law. The FDA determined that beverages that combine caffeine with alcohol, such as Four Loco energy drinks, are a "public health concern" and couldn't stay on the market in their current form. The FDA also stated that concerns have been raised that caffeine can mask some of the sensory cues individuals might normally rely on to determine their level of intoxication. Warning letters were issued to each of the four companies requiring them to provide to the FDA in writing within 15 days of the specific steps the firms will be taking. Prior to the FDA ruling, many consumers bought and hoarded large quantities of the beverage. This buying frenzy created a black market for energy drinks, with some sellers charging inflated prices. A reformulated version of the drink was put on shelves in late 2010. The new product had exactly the same design as the original, but the caffeine had been removed.

Effective February 2013, cans of Four Loko carry an "Alcohol Facts" label. The label change is part of a final settlement between the Federal Trade Commission and Phusion Projects, the manufacturer of Four Loko. The company still disagrees with the commission's allegations, but said in a statement that the agreement provides a practical way for the company to move ahead. The FTC claimed that ads for Four Loko inaccurately claimed that a 23.5-ounce can contain the alcohol equivalent of one to two cans of beer. In fact, the FTC says, it's more like four to five beers. In the YES and NO selections, Don Troop argues that the combination of caffeine and alcohol is extremely dangerous and should not be sold or marketed to college students and young people. Journalist and editor of *Reason Magazine* Jacob Sullum disagrees and claims that alcoholic energy drinks should not have been targeted and banned since many other products are far more dangerous.

YES 

Don Troop

Four Loko Does Its Job with Efficiency and Economy, Students Say

It's Friday night in this steep-hilled college town, and if anyone needs an excuse to party, here are two: In 30 minutes the Mountaineers football team will kick off against the UConn Huskies in East Hartford, Conn., and tonight begins the three-day Halloween weekend.

A few blocks from the West Virginia University campus, young people crowd the aisles of Ashebrooke Liquor Outlet, an airy shop that is popular among students. One rack in the chilled-beverage cooler is nearly empty, the one that is usually filled with 23.5-ounce cans of Four Loko, a fruity malt beverage that combines the caffeine of two cups of coffee with the buzz factor of four to six beers.

"That's what everyone's buying these days," says a liquor store employee, "Loko and Burnett's vodka," a line of distilled spirits that are commonly mixed with nonalcoholic energy drinks like Red Bull and Monster to create fruity cocktails with a stimulating kick.

Four Loko's name comes from its four primary ingredients—alcohol (12 percent by volume), caffeine, taurine, and guarana. Although it is among dozens of caffeinated alcoholic drinks on the market, Four Loko has come to symbolize the dangers of such beverages because of its role in binge-drinking incidents this fall involving students at New Jersey's Ramapo College and at Central Washington University. Ramapo and Central Washington have banned Four Loko from their campuses, and several other colleges have sent urgent e-mail messages advising students not to drink it. But whether Four Loko is really "blackout in a can" or just the highest-profile social lubricant of the moment is unclear.

Just uphill from Ashebrooke Liquor Outlet, four young men stand on a porch sipping cans of Four Loko—fruit punch and cranberry-lemonade. All are upperclassmen except for one, Philip Donnachie, who graduated in May. He says most Four Loko drinkers he knows like to guzzle a can of it at home before meeting up with friends, a custom that researchers in the field call "predrinking."

"Everyone that's going to go out for the night, they're going to start with a Four Loko first," Mr. Donnachie says, adding that he generally switches to beer.

A student named Tony says he paid $5.28 at Ashebrooke for two Lokos—a bargain whether the goal is to get tipsy or flat-out drunk. Before the drink became infamous, he says, he would see students bring cans of it into classrooms. "The teachers didn't know what it was," Tony says, and if they asked, the student would casually reply, "It's an energy drink."

Farther uphill, on the sidewalk along Grant Avenue, the Tin Man from *The Wizard of Oz* carries a Loko—watermelon flavor, judging by its color. Down the block a keg party spills out onto the front porch, where guests sprawl on a sofa and flick cigarette ashes over the railing. No one here is drinking Four Loko, but most are eager to talk about the product because they've heard that it could be banned by the federal government as a result of the student illnesses.

Research Gap

That's not likely to happen anytime soon, according to the Food and Drug Administration.

"The FDA's decision regarding the regulatory status of caffeine added to various alcoholic beverages will be a high priority for the agency," Michael L. Herndon, an FDA spokesman, wrote in an e-mail message. "However, a decision regarding the use of caffeine in alcoholic beverages could take some time." The FDA does not consider such drinks to be "generally recognized as safe." A year ago the agency gave 27 manufacturers 30 days to provide evidence to the contrary, if it existed. Only 19 of the companies have responded.

Dennis L. Thombs is chairman of the Department of Social and Behavioral Sciences at the University of North Texas Health Science Center, in Fort Worth. He knows a great deal about the drinking habits of young people.

Last year he was the lead author on a paper submitted to the journal *Addictive Behaviors* that described his team's study of bar patrons' consumption of energy drinks and alcohol in the college town of Gainesville, Fla. After interviewing 802 patrons and testing their blood-alcohol content, Mr. Thombs and his fellow researchers concluded that energy drinks' labels should clearly describe the ingredients, their amounts, and the potential risks involved in using the products.

But Mr. Thombs says the government should have more data before it decides what to do about alcoholic energy drinks.

"There's still a big gap in this research," he says. "We need to get better pharmacological measures in natural drinking environments" like bars.

He says he has submitted a grant application to the National Institutes of Health in hopes of doing just that.

"Liquid Crack"

Back at the keg party in Morgantown, a student wearing Freddy Krueger's brown fedora and razor-blade glove calls Four Loko "liquid crack" and says he prefers not to buy it for his underage friends. "I'll buy them something else," he says, "but not Four Loko."

Dipsy from the *Teletubbies* says the people abusing Four Loko are younger students, mostly 17- and 18-year-olds. He calls the students who became ill at Ramapo and Central Washington "a bunch of kids that don't know how to drink."

Two freshmen at the party, Gabrielle and Meredith, appear to confirm that assertion.

"I like Four Loko because it's cheap and it gets me drunk," says Gabrielle, 19, who seems well on her way to getting drunk tonight, Four Loko or not. "Especially for concerts. I drink two Four Lokos before going, and then I don't have to spend $14 on a couple drinks at the stadium."

Meredith, 18 and equally intoxicated, says that although she drinks Four Loko, she favors a ban. "They're 600 calories, and they're gross."

An interview with Alex, a 19-year-old student at a religiously affiliated college in the Pacific Northwest, suggests one reason that the drink might be popular among a younger crowd. In his state and many others, the laws that govern the sale of Four Loko and beer are less stringent than those for hard liquor.

That eases the hassle for older friends who buy for Alex. These days that's not a concern, though. He stopped drinking Four Loko because of how it made him feel the next day.

"Every time I drank it I got, like, a blackout," says Alex. "Now I usually just drink beer."

Don Troop is a senior editor of the *Chronicles of Higher Education,* which covers state policy, as well as economic development, town-and-gown relations, fund raising and endowments, and other financial issues at the campus level.

Jacob Sullum

Loco over Four Loko: How a Fruity, Brightly Colored Malt Beverage Drove Politicians to Madness in Two Short Years

In a column at the end of October, *The New York Times* restaurant critic Frank Bruni looked down his nose at Four Loko, a fruity, bubbly, brightly colored malt beverage with a lower alcohol content than Chardonnay and less caffeine per ounce than Red Bull. "It's a malt liquor in confectionery drag," Bruni wrote, "not only raising questions about the marketing strategy behind it but also serving as the clearest possible reminder that many drinkers aren't seeking any particular culinary or aesthetic enjoyment. They're taking a drug. The more festively it's dressed and the more vacuously it goes down, the better."

Less than two weeks after Bruni panned Four Loko and its déclassé drinkers, he wrote admiringly of the "ambition and thought" reflected in hoity-toity coffee cocktails offered by the Randolph at Broome, a boutique bar in downtown Manhattan. He conceded that "there is a long if not entirely glorious history of caffeine and alcohol joining forces, of whiskey or liqueurs poured into after-dinner coffee by adults looking for the same sort of effect that Four Loko fans seek: an extension of the night without a surrender of the buzz."

Like Bruni's distaste for Four Loko, the moral panic that led the Food and Drug Administration (FDA) to ban the beverage and others like it in November, just two years after it was introduced, cannot be explained in pharmacological terms. As Brum admitted and as the drink's Chicago-based manufacturer, Phusion Projects, kept pointing out to no avail, there is nothing new about mixing alcohol with caffeine. What made this particular formulation intolerable—indeed "adulterated," according to the FDA—was not its chemical composition but its class connotations: the wild and crazy name, the garish packaging, the low cost, the eight color-coded flavors, and the drink's popularity among young partiers who see "blackout in a can" as a recommendation. Those attributes made Four Loko offensive to the guardians of public health and morals in a way that Irish coffee, rum and cola, and even Red Bull and vodka never were.

The FDA itself conceded that the combination of alcohol and caffeine, a feature of many drinks, that remain legal, was not the real issue. Rather, the agency complained that "the marketing of the caffeinated versions of this class of alcoholic beverage appears to be specifically directed to young adults," who are "especially vulnerable" to "combined ingestion of caffeine and alcohol."

Because Four Loko was presumed to be unacceptably hazardous, the FDA did not feel a need to present much in the way of scientific evidence. A grand total of two studies have found that college students who drink alcoholic beverages containing caffeine (typically bar or home-mixed cocktails unaffected by the FDA's ban) tend to drink more and are more prone to risky behavior than college students who drink alcohol by itself. Neither study clarified whether the differences were due to the psychoactive effects of caffeine or to the predispositions of hearty partiers attracted to drinks they believe will help keep them going all night. But that distinction did not matter to panic-promoting politicians and their publicists in the press, who breathlessly advertised Four Loko while marveling at its rising popularity.

This dual function of publicity about an officially condemned intoxicant is familiar to anyone who has witnessed or read about previous scare campaigns against stigmatized substances, ranging from absinthe to *Salvia divinorum*. So is the evidentiary standard employed by Four Loko alarmists: If something bad happens and Four Loko is anywhere in the vicinity, blame Four Loko.

The National Highway Traffic Safety Administration counted 13,800 alcohol-related fatalities in 2008. It did not place crashes involving Four Loko drinkers in a special category. But news organizations around the country, primed to perceive the drink as unusually dangerous, routinely did. Three days before the FDA declared Four Loko illegal, a 14-year-old stole his parents' SUV and crashed it into a guardrail on Interstate 35 in Denton, Texas. His girlfriend, who was not wearing a seat belt, was ejected from the car and killed. Police, who said they found a 12-pack of beer and five cans of Four Loko in the SUV, charged the boy with intoxication manslaughter. Here is how the local Fox station headlined its story: "'Four Loko' Found in Deadly Teen Crash."

Likewise, college students were getting sick after drinking too much long before Four Loko was introduced in August 2008. According to the federal government's Drug Abuse Warning Network, more than 100,000 18-to-20-year-olds make alcohol-related visits to American emergency rooms every year. Yet 15 students at two colleges who were treated for alcohol poisoning after consuming excessive amounts of Four Loko were repeatedly held up as examples of the drink's unique dangers.

If all alcoholic beverages had to satisfy the reckless college student test, all of them would be banned. In a sense, then, we should be grateful for the government's inconsistency. With Four Loko, as with other taboo tipples and illegal drugs, there is little logic to the process by which the scapegoat is selected, but there are noticeable patterns. Once an intoxicant has been identified with a disfavored group—in this case, heedless, hedonistic "young adults"—everything about it is viewed in that light. Soon the wildest charges seem plausible: Four Loko is "a recipe for disaster," "a death wish disguised as an energy drink," a "witch's brew" that drives you mad, makes you shoot yourself in the head, and compels you to steal vehicles and crash them into things.

The timeline that follows shows how quickly a legal product can be transformed into contraband once it becomes the target of such over-the-top opprobrium. Although it's too late for Four Loko, lessons gleaned from the story of its demise could help prevent the next panicky prohibition by scaremongers who criminalize first and ask questions later.

June 2008: Anheuser-Busch, under pressure from 11 attorneys general who are investigating the brewing giant for selling the caffeinated malt beverages Tilt and Bud Extra, agrees to decaffeinate the drinks. "Drinking is not a sport, a race, or an endurance test," says New York Attorney General Andrew Cuomo, who will later be elected governor. "Adding alcohol to energy drinks sends exactly the wrong message about responsible drinking, most especially to young people."

August 2008: Phusion Projects, a Chicago company founded in 2005 by three recent graduates of Ohio State University, introduces Four Loko, which has an alcohol content of up to 12 percent (depending on state regulations); comes in brightly colored, 23.5-ounce cans; contains the familiar energy-drink ingredients caffeine, guarana, and taurine; and is eventually available in eight fruity, neon-hued varieties.

September 2008: The Center for Science in the Public Interest (CSPI), a pro-regulation group that is proud of being known as "the food police," sues MillerCoors Brewing Company over its malt beverage Sparks, arguing that the caffeine and guarana in the drink are additives that have not been approved by the FDA. "Mix alcohol and stimulants with a young person's sense of invincibility," says CSPI's George Hacker, "and you have a recipe for disaster. Sparks is a drink designed to mask feelings of drunkenness and to encourage people to keep drinking past the point at which they otherwise would have stopped. The end result is more drunk driving, more injuries, and more sexual assaults."

December 2008: In a deal with 13 attorneys general and the city of San Francisco, MillerCoors agrees to reformulate Sparks, removing the caffeine, guarana, taurine, and ginseng. Cuomo says caffeinated alcoholic beverages are "fundamentally dangerous and put drinkers of all ages at risk."

July 2009: *The Wall Street Journal* reports that Cuomo, Connecticut Attorney General Richard Blumenthal (now a U.S. senator), California Attorney General Jerry Brown (now governor), and their counterparts in several other states are investigating Four Loko and Joose, a close competitor. The National Association of Convenience Stores says the two brands are growing fast now that Tilt and Sparks have left the caffeinated malt beverage market.

August 2009: To demonstrate the threat that Four Loko poses to the youth of America, Blumenthal cites an online testimonial from a fan of the drink: "You just gotta drink it and drink it and drink it and drink it and not even worry about it because it's awesome and you're just partying and having fun and getting wild and drinking it." *The Chicago Tribune* cannot locate that particular comment on Phusion Projects' website, but it does find this: "I'm having a weird reaction to Four that makes me want to dance in my bra and panties. Please advise."

September 2009: Eighteen attorneys general ask the FDA to investigate the safety of alcoholic beverages containing caffeine.

November 2009: The FDA sends letters to 27 companies known to sell caffeinated alcoholic beverages, warning them that the combination has never been officially approved and asking them to submit evidence that it is "generally recognized as safe," as required by the Food, Drug, and Cosmetic Act. In addition to Phusion Projects, the recipients include Joose's manufacturer, United Brands;

Charge Beverages, which sells similar products; the PINK Spirits Company, which makes caffeinated vodka, rum, gin, whiskey, and sake; and even the Ithaca Beer Company, which at one point made a special-edition stout brewed with coffee. "I continue to be very concerned that these drinks are extremely dangerous," says Illinois Attorney General Lisa Madigan, "especially in the hands of young people."

February 2010: In a feature story carried by several newspapers under headlines such as "Alcopops Only Look Innocent and Can Hook Kids," Kim Hone-McMahan of the *Akron Beacon Journal* outlines one scenario in which these extremely dangerous drinks might end up in tiny hands: "Intentionally or by accident, a child could grab an alcoholic beverage that looks like an energy drink, and hand it to Mom to pay for at the register. Without taking a closer look at the label, Mom may think it's just another brand of nonalcoholic energy beverage." It does seem like the sort of mistake that Hone-McMahan, who confuses fermented malt beverages with distilled spirits and warns parents about an alcoholic energy drink that was never actually introduced, might make. She explains that the combination of alcohol and caffeine "can confuse the nervous system," producing "wired, wide-awake drunks."

July 12, 2010: Sen. Charles Schumer (D-N.Y.) urges the Federal Trade Commission to investigate Four Loko and products like it. "It is my understanding that caffeine-infused, flavored malt beverages are becoming increasingly popular among teenagers," he writes. "The style and promotion of these products is extremely troubling." Schumer complains that the packaging of Joose and Four Loko is "designed to appear hip with flashy colors and funky designs that could appeal to younger consumers."

July 29, 2010: Schumer, joined by Sens. Dianne Feinstein (D-Calif.), Amy Klobuchar (D-Minn.), and Jeff Merkley (D-Ore.), urges the FDA to complete its investigation. "The FDA needs to determine once and for all if these drinks are safe, and if they're not, they ought to be banned," says Schumer, right before telling the FDA the conclusion it should reach: "Caffeine and alcohol are a dangerous mix, especially for young people."

August 1, 2010: After a crash in St. Petersburg, Florida, that kills four visitors from Orlando, police arrest 20-year-old Demetrius Jordan and charge him with drunk driving and manslaughter. The *St. Petersburg Times* reports that Jordan, who "had been drinking liquor and a caffeinated alcoholic beverage and smoking marijuana prior to the crash," "may have been going in excess of 80 mph when he crashed into the other vehicle." It notes that a "can of Four Loko was found on the floor of the back seat."

August 5, 2010: In a follow-up story, the *St. Petersburg Times* reports that "Four Loko, the caffeine-fueled malt liquor that police say Demetrius Jordan downed before he was accused of driving drunk and killing four people, is part of a new breed of beverages stirring controversy across the country." It quotes Bruce Goldberger, a toxicologist at the University of Florida, who declares, "I don't think there's a place for these beverages in the marketplace." The headline: "Alcohol, Caffeine: A Deadly Combo?"

August 12, 2010: The *Orlando Sentinel*, catching up with the *St. Petersburg Times*, shows it can quote Goldberger too. "It's a very bad combination having alcohol, plus caffeine, plus the brain of a young person," he says. "It's like a perfect storm." The headline: "Did High-Octane Drink Fuel Deadly Crash?"

September 2010: Peter Mercer, president of Ramapo College in Mahwah, New Jersey, bans Four Loko and other caffeinated malt beverages from campus after several incidents in which a total of 23 students were hospitalized for alcohol poisoning. Just six of the students were drinking Four Loko. Mercer later tells the Associated Press, "There's no redeeming social purpose to be served by having the beverage."

October 9, 2010: In a story about nine gang members who tied up and tortured a gay man after luring him to an abandoned building in the Bronx by telling him they were having a party, the *New York Daily News* plays up the detail that they "forced him to guzzle four cans" of the Four Loko he had brought with him. "The sodomized man couldn't give police a clear account of what he'd gone through," the paper reports, "possibly because of the Four Loko he was forced to drink."

October 10, 2010: In a follow-up story, the *Daily News* reports that Four Loko, a "wild drink full of caffeine and booze," "is causing controversy from coast to coast," citing the deadly crash in St. Petersburg.

October 13, 2010: Police in New Port Richey, Florida, arrest Justin Barker, 21, after he breaks into an old woman's home, trashes the place, strips naked, defecates on the floor, and then breaks into another house, where he falls asleep on the couch. Barker says Four Loko made him do it.

October 15, 2010: Calling Four Loko "a quick and intense high that has been dubbed 'blackout in a can,'" the Passaic County, New Jersey, *Herald News* notes the Ramapo College ban and quotes Mahwah Police Chief James Batelli. "The bottom line on the product is it gets you very drunk, very quick," he says. "To me, Four Loko is just a dangerous substance." The "blackout in a can" sobriquet, obviously hyperbolic when applied to a beverage that contains less alcohol per container than a bottle of wine, originated with Four Loko fans who considered it high praise; one of their Facebook pages is titled "four lokos are blackouts in a can and the end of my morals."

October 19, 2010: Bruce Goldberger, who co-authored one of the two studies linking caffeinated alcohol to risky behavior, tells the *Pittsburgh Post-Gazette* "the science is clear that consumption of alcohol with caffeine leads to risky behaviors." Mary Claire O'Brien, the Wake Forest University researcher who co-authored the other study, expresses her anger at the FDA. "I'm mad as a hornet that they didn't do something in the first place," she says, "and I'm mad as a hornet that they haven't done anything yet."

October 20, 2010: Based on a single case of a 19-year-old who came to Temple University Hospital in Philadelphia with chest pains after drinking Four Loko, ABC News warns that the stuff, which contains about one-third as much caffeine per ounce as coffee, can cause fatal heart attacks in perfectly healthy people. "That was the only explanation we had," says the doctor who treated the 19-year-old, before extrapolating further from his sample of one: "This is a dangerous product from what we've seen. It doesn't have to be chronic use. I think it could happen to somebody on a first-time use."

October 25, 2010: Citing the hospitalization of nine Central Washington University students for alcohol poisoning following an October 8 party in Roslyn where they drank Four Loko along with beer, rum, and vodka, Washington Attorney General Rob McKenna calls for a ban on caffeinated malt liquor. "The wide availability of the alcoholic energy drinks means that a single mistake can be deadly," he says. "They're marketed to kids by using fruit flavors that mask the taste of alcohol, and they have such high levels of stimulants that people have no idea how inebriated they really are." McKenna's office cites Ken Briggs, chairman of the university's physical education department, who says Four Loko is known as "liquid cocaine" as well as "blackout in a can," and with good reason, since it is "a binge drinker's dream."

October 26, 2010: McKenna's reaction to college students who drank too much Four Loko, like Peter Mercer's at Ramapo, attracts national attention. A Pennsylvania E.R. doctor quoted by *The New York Times* calls Four Loko "a recipe for disaster" and "one of the most dangerous new alcohol concoctions I have ever seen."

November 1, 2010: The Pennsylvania Liquor Control Board asks retailers to stop selling Four Loko, which is produced at the former Rolling Rock brewery in Latrobe, because it may "pose a significant threat to the health of all Pennsylvanians." State Rep. Robert Donatucci (D-Philadelphia) says "there is overriding circumstantial evidence that this combination may be very dangerous," and "until we can determine its effect on people and what kind of danger it may present, it should be yanked from the shelves."

November 3, 2010: Two Chicago aldermen propose an ordinance that would ban Four Loko from the city where its manufacturer is based. "I think it is completely irresponsible," says one, "to manufacture and market a product that can make young people so intoxicated so fast."

November 4, 2010: The Michigan Liquor Control Commission bans 55 "alcohol energy drinks," including Four Loko, Joose, a "hard" iced tea that no longer exists, a cola-flavored variety of Jack Daniel's Country Cocktails, and an India pale ale brewed with yerba mate. "With all the things that are happening, it's very alarming," explains commission chairwoman Nida Samona. "It's more serious than any of us ever imagined."

November 8, 2010: Oklahoma's Alcoholic Beverage Laws Enforcement Commission bans Four Loko from the state "in light of the growing scientific evidence against alcohol energy drinks, and the October 8th incident involving Four Loko in Roslyn, Washington."

November 9, 2010: NPR quotes Washington State University student Jarod Franklin as an authority on Four Loko's effects. "We would start to lose those inhibitions," he says, "and then [it would be like], 'How did you get a broken knuckle?' 'Oh, I punched through a three-inch layer of ice [because] you bet me I couldn't.'"

November 10, 2010: The Washington State Liquor Control Board bans beverages that "combine beer, strong beer, or malt liquor with caffeine, guarana, taurine, or other similar substances." Gov. Christine Gregoire, who recommended the ban, explains her reasoning: "I was particularly concerned that these drinks tend to target young people. Reports of inexperienced or underage drinkers consuming them in reckless amounts have given us cause for concern. . . . By taking these drinks off the shelves we are saying 'no' to irresponsible drinking and taking steps to prevent incidents like the one that made these college students so ill."

Sen. Schumer urges the New York State Liquor Authority to "immediately ban caffeinated alcoholic beverages." He says drinks like Four Loko "are a toxic, dangerous mix of caffeine and alcohol, and they are spreading like a plague across the country." Schumer claims "studies have shown that caffeinated alcoholic beverages raise unique and disturbing safety concerns, especially for younger drinkers."

While they "can be extremely hazardous for teens and adults alike," he says, they "pose a unique danger because they target young people" with their "vibrantly colored aluminum can colors and funky designs."

November 12, 2010: A CBS station in Baltimore reports that two cans of Four Loko caused a 21-year-old Maryland woman to "lose her mind," steal a friend's pickup truck, and crash it into a telephone pole, killing herself.

A CBS station in Philadelphia reports that a middle-aged suburban dad "spiraled into a hallucinogenic frenzy" featuring "nightmarish delusions" after drinking a can and a half of Four Loko. "It was like he was stuck inside a horror movie and he couldn't get out and I couldn't get him out," the man's wife says. "In his mind, he had harmed all of our kids and he had to kill me and kill himself so that we could go to heaven to take care of them. Next thing I know, he was having convulsions [and] making gurgling sounds as if someone were choking him, and then he stopped breathing."

Connecticut Attorney General Blumenthal urges the FDA to "impose a nationwide ban on these dangerous and potentially deadly drinks."

November 14, 2010: Under pressure from Gov. David Paterson and the state liquor authority, Phusion Projects agrees to stop shipping Four Loko to New York. "We have an obligation to keep products that are potentially hazardous off the shelves," says the liquor authority's chairman.

Bruce Goldberger tells the *New Haven Register* Four Loko is "a very significant problem" for the "instant gratification generation." The kids today, he says, "text, they have iPhones, and they can access the Internet any minute of their life. And now, they can get drunk for literally less than $5, and they can get drunk very rapidly."

November 15, 2010: WBZ, the CBS affiliate in Boston, reports that the Massachusetts Alcoholic Beverages Control Commission plans to ban Four Loko. According to WBZ, commission officials say the drink—a fermented malt beverage with an alcohol content of 12 percent, compared to 40 percent or more for distilled spirits—"is really not a malt liquor, but a much more potent form of hard liquor, like vodka." The commission's chairman explains that the ban is aimed at protecting consumers who cannot read: "We are concerned that people who are drinking these alcoholic beverages are not aware of the ingredients which are contained in them."

The New York Times reports that Four Loko "has been blamed for several deaths over the last several months," including that of a 20-year-old sophomore at Florida State University in Tallahassee who "started playing with a gun and fatally shot himself after drinking several cans of Four Loko over a number of hours." Richard Blumenthal tells the *Times* "there's just no excuse for the delay in applying standards that clearly should bar this kind of witch's brew." Mary Claire O'Brien argues that Four Loko is guilty until proven innocent: "The addition of the caffeine impairs the ability of the drinker to tell when they're drunk. What is the level at which it becomes dangerous? We don't know that, and until we can figure it out, the answer is that no level is safe."

November 16, 2010: Phusion Projects says it will reformulate Four Loko, removing the caffeine, guarana, and taurine. "We have repeatedly contended—and still believe, as do many people throughout the country—that the combination of alcohol and caffeine is safe," the company's founders say. "We are taking this step after trying—unsuccessfully—to navigate a difficult and politically charged regulatory environment at both the state and federal levels."

The Arizona Republic reports that an "extremely intoxicated" 18-year-old from Mesa crashed her SUV into a tree after "playing 'beer pong' with the controversial caffeinated alcoholic beverage Four Loko." The headline: "Caffeine, Alcohol Drink Tied to Crash."

Reporting on a lawsuit against Phusion Projects by the parents of the FSU student who shot himself after drinking Four Loko, ABC News quotes Schumer, who avers, "It's almost a death wish disguised as an energy drink."

November 17, 2010: The FDA and the Federal Trade Commission send warning letters to Phusion Projects, United Brands, Charge Beverages, and New Century Brewing Company, which makes a caffeinated lager called Moonshot. The agency says their products are "adulterated," and therefore illegal under the Food, Drug, and Cosmetic Act, because they contain an additive, caffeine, that is not generally recognized as safe in this context. But the FDA does not conclude that all beverages combining alcohol and caffeine are inherently unsafe. It focuses on these particular companies because they "seemingly target the young adult user." Federal drug czar Gil Kerlikowske approves the FDA's marketing-based definition of adulteration, saying "these products are designed, branded, and promoted to encourage binge drinking."

NPR correspondent Tovia Smith reports that "many college students say they agree with the FDA that alcoholic energy drinks do result in more risky behavior, like drunk driving or sexual assaults." Smith presents one such student, Ali Burak of Boston College, who says "it seems like every time someone wakes up in the morning and regrets the night before it's usually because they had Four Loko."

November 20, 2010: In a *Huffington Post* essay, David Katz, director of Yale University's Prevention Research Center, explains why "anyone who is for sanity and safety in marketing" should welcome the FDA's ban. "Combining alcohol and caffeine is—in one word—crazy," he writes. "Don't do it! It has an excellent chance of hurting you, and a fairly good chance of killing you." His evidence: the Maryland car crash in which a woman who had been drinking Four Loko died after colliding with a telephone pole. "It's hard to imagine any argument for such products," Katz concludes. "It's also hard to imagine anyone objecting to a ban of such products."

Jacob Sullum is a journalist and editor of *Reason* magazine.

EXPLORING THE ISSUE

Are Energy Drinks with Alcohol Dangerous Enough to Ban?

Critical Thinking and Reflection

1. Why were energy drinks with caffeine banned?
2. Why are caffeinated energy drinks so popular among college students?
3. Describe why the drinks are dangerous and how they contributed to deaths among some college students.

Is There Common Ground?

Four Loko and other energy drinks provide the effects of caffeine and sugar, but there is little or no evidence that a wide variety of other ingredients have any impact on the body. A variety of physiological and psychological effects, however, have been blamed on energy drinks and their components. Excess use of energy drinks may produce mild to moderate euphoria primarily due to the stimulant properties of caffeine. The drinks may also cause agitation, anxiety, irritability, and sleeplessness.

Ingestion of a single energy drink will not lead to excessive caffeine intake, but consumption of two or more drinks over the course of a day can. Ginseng, guarana, and other stimulants are often added to energy drinks and may bolster the effects of caffeine. Negative effects associated with caffeine consumption in amounts greater than 400 mg include nervousness, irritability, sleeplessness, increased urination, abnormal heart rhythms, and upset stomach. By comparison, a cup of drip coffee contains about 150 mg of caffeine. Caffeine in energy drinks can cause the excretion of water from the body to dilute high concentrations of sugar entering the blood stream, leading to dehydration.

In the United States, energy drinks have been linked with reports of emergency room visits due to heart palpitations and anxiety. The beverages have been associated with seizures due to the crash following the high energy that occurs after ingestion. In the United States, caffeine dosage is not required to be on the product label for food, unlike drugs, but some advocates are urging the FDA to change this practice.

Drinking one 24-ounce can of Four Loko provides the alcoholic kick of four beers and the caffeine buzz of a strong cup of coffee. Drinking one quickly makes someone pretty drunk and reasonably awake, and able to drink more. As a result, college students seem particularly drawn to it, which has landed some in hospitals. But should Four Loko be banned state-by-state as a result? Banning Four Loko might prevent some people, especially some college students, from hurting themselves or others. But does it improve people's judgment or otherwise empower them to protect themselves?

Additional Resources

Esser, M. B., & Siegel, M. (2014). Alcohol facts labels on Four Loko: Will the Federal Trade Commission's order be effective in reducing hazardous drinking among underage youth? *American Journal of Drug & Alcohol Abuse, 40*(6), 424–427.

R., B. (2016). Energy drinks: Ban the can? *University Business, 19*(4), 16.

Siegel, S. (2011). The Four-Loko effect. *Perspectives on Psychological Science, 6*(4), 357–362.

Stoll, J. D., Esterl, M., Robinson, F., Houston-Waesch, M., & Bomsdorf, C. (2014, May 16). Energy drink ban takes bull by horns. *Wall Street Journal—Eastern Edition.* pp. B1–B2.

Wood, D. B. (2010, November 19). Four Loko: Does FDA's caffeinated alcoholic beverage ban go too far? *Christian Science Monitor*, p. N.PAG.

Internet References . . .

Energy Drinks—American Association of Poison Control Centers

www.aapcc.org/alerts/energy-drinks

Food and Drug Administration

www.fda.gov

National Institute on Drug Abuse (NIDA)

www.nida.nih.gov

Selected, Edited, and with Issue Framing Material by:
Eileen L. Daniel, *SUNY College at Brockport*

ISSUE

Do Diet Sodas Aid in Weight Loss?

YES: William Hudson, from "Diet Soda Helps Weight Loss, Industry-funded Study Finds," *CNN* (2014)

NO: Stephanie Bucklin, from "Why Diet Soda Could Actually Prevent You from Losing Weight," *The Huffington Post* (2016)

Learning Outcomes

After reading this issue, you will be able to:

- Discuss the role of diet soda in weight loss.
- Address the risks versus benefits of drinking diet soda.

ISSUE SUMMARY

YES: CNN Medical Producer William Hudson reports that studies show that diet soda drinkers are likely to lose more weight than water drinkers.

NO: Writer Stephanie Bucklin argues that research indicates that diet soda may actually hinder weight loss efforts.

According to a study by the *National Center for Health Statistics*, approximately 20 percent of Americans ages two years and over consumed diet soft drinks on a given day in 2009–2010, and 11 percent consumed 16 fluid oz. of diet drinks or more. Overall, the percentage drinking diet soft drinks was greater among females compared with males. The percentage consuming diet drinks was similar for females and males at all ages except among 12- to 19-year-olds, where a higher percentage of females than males consumed diet drinks. A higher percentage of non-Hispanic white persons consumed diet drinks compared with non-Hispanic black and Hispanic persons. The study included calorie-free and low-calorie versions of soft drinks, fruit drinks, energy drinks, sports drinks, and carbonated water. Many of those consuming diet drinks do so to lose weight or avoid gaining. However, several studies have indicated that using diet drinks does not necessarily cause weight loss and may even contribute to weight gain.

Research published in the May 2016 edition of the journal *JAMA Pediatrics*, investigated over 3,000 pregnant women and their infants. The study found that mothers that frequently consumed diet beverages sweetened artificially were two times more likely to have babies who were overweight or obese at one year after birth compared to women who consumed fewer artificially sweetened drinks. While the results don't necessarily prove that diet drinks and artificial sweeteners *cause* weight gain, it certainly raises questions about the perceived benefits of diet soft drinks.

Another 2015 study published in the *Journal of the American Geriatrics Society* found that people who drank diet soda gained almost triple the abdominal fat over nine years as those who didn't drink diet soda. The study analyzed data from 749 people ages 65 and older who were asked, every couple of years, how many cans of soda they drank a day, and how many of those sodas were diet or regular. Those responses ended up being especially predictive of abdominal-fat gain, even after the investigators adjusted for issues such as smoking, diabetes, and intensity of physical activity. Individuals who didn't consume diet soda gained approximately 0.8 inches around their waists over the study period, but people who drank diet soda daily gained about 3.2 inches. Those who fell in the middle, occasional drinkers of diet soda, gained about 1.8 inches. The increase in waist circumference is of particular concern because it highlights an unfortunate fact about weight distribution: the abdomen, or visceral fat, is a risky place to store extra pounds since it's linked to an increase risk of heart disease, inflammation, and type 2 diabetes. These results contribute to the growing concerns that diet sodas with artificial sweeteners may contribute to health issues.

While it's not clear the exact mechanisms by which these sweeteners in diet soda cause weight gain and abdominal fat deposits, there is some evidence as to how. Artificial sweeteners may activate receptors in the brain which cause the body to ready itself for an intake of calories. Since diet sodas have no calories, the body still craves them and that may motivate people to eventually consume more overall calories increasing the risk for weight gain. Regular sugar has about 50 calories per tablespoon and those calories can generate a feeling of satisfaction. Our bodies have become accustomed to associating sweet tastes with eating calories. The artificial sweeteners in diet soda tend to obscure this reaction and alter the connection in our brains between calories and a sweet taste which may lead to weight gain and cravings for sugary foods. In addition, other variables may be of concern. A recent research study involving rodents showed that artificial sweeteners actually altered the gut bacteria of mice in ways that made them susceptible to insulin resistance and glucose intolerance which can both lead to weight gain. And other research with mice implies that artificial sweeteners are associated with a drop in the appetite-regulating hormone leptin which inhibits hunger.

In addition to research questioning the relationship between diet drinks and weight loss, there are also concerns over the potential health risks associated with these products. Many consumers are concerned about possible health effects of artificial sweeteners. Altering caloric intake from one food will not necessarily change a person's overall caloric intake or cause a person to lose weight. In an independent study by researchers with the Framingham Heart Study in Massachusetts, consumption of any kind of soft drink correlated with increased incidence of metabolic syndrome. Of the 9,000 males and females studied, these drinkers were at 48 percent higher risk for metabolic syndrome, which involves weight gain and elevated blood glucose. No significant difference in these findings was observed between sugary and diet soft drinks. The researchers surmised that diet drinkers were less likely to consume healthy foods and that drinking diet beverages flavored with artificial sweeteners more than likely increases cravings for sugar-flavored sweets. There have also been concerns over the possible connection between artificial sweeteners and cancer. Questions about artificial sweeteners and cancer arose when early studies showed that the artificial sweetener cyclamate in combination with saccharin caused bladder cancer in laboratory animals. However, results from subsequent studies that examined whether these substances can cause cancer have not provided clear evidence of an association with cancer in humans. Similarly, studies of other FDA-approved sweeteners have not demonstrated clear evidence of an association with cancer in humans.

While the research isn't clear as to whether or not diet soft drinks affect body weight, there are other benefits associated with their use. Artificial sweeteners don't contribute to tooth decay and cavities and may also be a good alternative for individuals with diabetes.

YES 

William Hudson

Diet Soda Helps Weight Loss, Industry-funded Study Finds

Most people choose artificially sweetened soda over regular soda to avoid packing on extra pounds. But what if you already choose diet? Would it be helpful to quit that too?

Dr. Jim Hill says he gets this question all the time from patients in his weight loss program at the University of Colorado's Anschutz Health and Wellness Center.

With funding from the American Beverage Association, Hill helped design a study that divided approximately 300 adults into two groups: one group would continue drinking diet, and the other group—referred to in the study as the "water group"—would go cold turkey. The study was published in the journal Obesity.

Both participant groups received intensive coaching on successful techniques for weight loss, including regular feedback on the meals they logged in journals. Participants weighed, on average, just over 200 pounds at the start of the study.

"The results, to us, were not at all surprising," says Hill.

While the typical participant banned from drinking diet sodas lost 9 pounds over 12 weeks, those allowed to continue drinking diet soda lost, on average, 13 pounds in the same time period. That's a 4-pound difference.

Hill says that in his clinical experience, many people who have successfully lost significant weight "are heavy users of noncaloric sweeteners."

But why was the diet soda group more successful? The most likely reason is that this group had the easier task.

Cutting calories and boosting exercise takes a lot of willpower. Trying to simultaneously give up something else you regularly enjoy—such as diet soda—taxes your ability to stay the course. Most psychologists agree that our willpower is a limited resource.

So while this study did not track calorie consumption, the group blocked from drinking diet sodas most likely ate (or drank) more calories over the course of the 12-week diet.

Since the study lasted just 12 weeks, it remains to be seen whether artificial sweeteners are beneficial in the long term, says Susan Swithers, a professor of Behavioral Neuroscience at Purdue University. Swithers authored a report last year that found that diet soda drinkers have the same health issues as those who drink regular soda. It found that people who drink diet soda may be "at increased risk of excessive weight gain, metabolic syndrome, type 2 diabetes, and cardiovascular disease," according to the study.

"What the prospective studies actually suggest is that if you go out 7 years, 10 years, 15 years, 20 years, the cohorts of individuals who are consuming diet sodas have much worse health outcomes," says Swithers.

Those studies show a correlation and are not designed to show causation. But some researchers like Swithers suspect artificial sweeteners ultimately increase the desire for sweets.

"Doing these short-term studies that look at weight can't really tell us anything about whether or not these products are contributing to these increased risks," says Swithers. "And it's really hard to look at the (long-term) data and come up with any argument that they're helping."

Hill, who along with four other researchers, designed the study, which was selected for funding by the American Beverage Association from among multiple competing proposals. The American Beverage Association's membership includes numerous Coca-Cola and Pepsi-Cola bottling companies.

"It makes sense that it would have been harder for the water group to adhere to the overall diet than the (artificially sweetened beverage) group," says Hill.

He added, "The most likely explanation was that having access to drinks with sweet taste helps the (artificially sweetened beverage) group to adhere better to the behavioral change program."In short, this study addresses the question of whether a regular diet soda drinker should attempt to kick his or her habit while also attempting to lose weight, not whether we should all drink more diet soda in order to lose weight.

Artificially sweetened beverages "are not weight-loss enhancers, so it's not anything in the compounds themselves that are promoting weight loss," says Hill.

Kristi Norton, a regular diet soda drinker before the study began, was assigned to the group that required her to kick the habit. At the time of her CNN interview, she was not aware of the study's findings.

She says she lost 12 pounds during the course of the study, but the real difference is in how she feels.

"I feel like I could 1000 percent tell the benefit of drinking water only. I felt better, I had more energy, I felt healthier, I just generally felt way better," says Norton. "And I can feel the difference now when I drink a diet drink, I can feel this 'heaviness.'"

William Hudson is a medical producer at CNN.

Stephanie Bucklin

NO

Why Diet Soda Could Actually Prevent You from Losing Weight

Aspartame May Interfere with an Important Enzyme Responsible for Breaking Down Fat

Reaching for a diet soda may actually hinder weight loss efforts, a new study done in mice suggests.

In experiments, researchers found that the artificial sweetener aspartame, which is found in some diet drinks, may contribute to the development of a condition called "metabolic syndrome," which involves a cluster of symptoms, including high blood pressure, high cholesterol levels, and a large waist size. People with metabolic syndrome face an increased risk of heart disease, stroke, and diabetes.

The researchers found how aspartame could be linked with metabolic syndrome: aspartame may stop a key gut enzyme from performing its work in breaking down fat during digestion.

"This is the novel mechanistic insight," and it may explain why diet drinks can be ineffective at helping people to lose weight, Dr. Richard Hodin, senior author of the study and a professor of surgery at Harvard Medical School, told Live Science.

The study included three separate experiments. In the first, researchers added the gut enzyme to solutions of diet soda and regular soda. They found that the activity of the enzyme was significantly lower in the solutions of diet soda as compared to the solutions of regular soda.

Normally, the enzyme—intestinal alkaline phosphatase or IAP—works in the intestines to break down cholesterol and fatty acids. Previous studies by the researchers showed that the levels of IAP may be linked with people's risk of obesity, diabetes, and metabolic syndrome.

In the second experiment, researchers looked at the effects of aspartame in the small intestines of male mice. They injected either a solution containing aspartame or a placebo solution of salt water into the small intestines of the mice and then measured the same gut enzyme's activity. They found that three hours later, the enzyme's activity was 50 percent lower in mice that were injected with the aspartame solution as compared to the mice injected with the salt water.

In the final experiment, the researchers looked at four groups of male mice over a period of 18 weeks: the mice were all allowed to eat as much food as they wanted, but two groups were given normal food and two groups were given high-fat food. Within each division, one group received water to drink that contained aspartame, while the other received regular water to drink. [Five Experts Answer: Is Diet Soda Bad for You? http://www.livescience.com/35534-is-diet-soda-bad-for-you.html]

At the end of this experiment, the researchers found that the mice given the high-fat food and the aspartame-infused water gained more weight than the mice fed a high-fat food and the regular water.

However, the aspartame did not seem to make a difference for the mice on the normal diet: there was no difference in weight gain between the group given aspartame water and the group given regular water.

In addition to the difference in weight gain among the mice on the high-fat diet, the researchers also found that the mice on both diets that drank the aspartame-infused water had significantly higher levels of glucose intolerance than mice that drank the regular water. Glucose intolerance is a condition in which the body has trouble using the glucose in the bloodstream, leading to higher levels of glucose in the blood, and which may lead to diabetes.

Also, both of the groups of mice that drank the aspartame-infused water showed increased markers of inflammation, which previously has been linked to the development of the metabolic syndrome, the researchers said.

Bucklin, Stephanie. "Why Diet Soda Could Actually Prevent You From Losing Weight," *Huffington Post*, December 2016, as adapted from Bucklin, Stephanie. "Why Aspartame May Prevent Weight Loss," *LiveScience.com*, December 2, 2016.

The new results should be confirmed in experiments with a larger sample size, the researchers said. In addition, only male mice were used in the experiment, which is significant because male and female mice tend to react differently to dietary changes; for example, male mice tend to have higher levels of diet-induced inflammation, and female mice have better insulin sensitivity.

It remains unclear whether the findings may apply to people.

The effects of aspartame may be more complicated in humans, due to a "number of factors related to human behavior," Hodin told Live Science. However, he said, all else being equal, "diet drinks are probably not a great alternative to sugary sodas. Water is probably better."

Stephanie Bucklin is a freelance writer.

EXPLORING THE ISSUE

Do Diet Sodas Aid in Weight Loss?

Critical Thinking and Reflection

1. What role does diet soda plays in weight loss?
2. What are the benefits of diet versus sugar containing soft drinks?
3. What risks are associated with consuming artificial sweeteners?

Is There Common Ground?

A recently published study in the American Heart Association journal *Stroke* determined that a daily diet soft drink puts a person at three times the risk of dementia and stroke compared to someone who drinks less than one a week. Researchers found that consuming regular soft drinks with sugar or fruit juice doesn't elevate a person's risk of stroke and dementia.

Over seven years, researchers studied thousands of people over the age of 45 from the area of Framingham, MA, on their drinking and eating habits. Researchers followed up a decade later to see who had experienced a stroke or dementia. The data were adjusted for a number of factors, including age, gender, and caloric intake. Overall, the results were mixed. There was consistency when it came to sugary drinks since none of the tests showed a statistically significant association with either dementia or stroke. But it was a different with diet soft drinks. Recent intake of artificially sweetened sodas was associated with strokes, although there was no dose effect, and cumulative intake dropped below statistical significance. For ischemic strokes which occur when a blood vessel supplying blood to the brain is blocked, the association was consistent across all groups. Since ischemic strokes account for over 85 percent of all cases, this could be significant.

On the dementia side, things were less complicated. While some associations were statistically significant among the heavier diet soda drinkers, they were eliminated when all the health indicators were taken into account. The study only tracked the trend between artificial sweetener consumers, dementia, and stroke but was unable to prove that drinking artificial drinks was the cause of the diseases.

Additional Resources

Choose Water Over Diet Drinks For Weight Loss. (2017). *Environmental Nutrition, 40*(3), 1.

Fake sugar, hungry flies. (2016). *Prevention, 68*(12), 17.

Jiantao, M., McKeown, N. M., Shih-Jen, H., Hoffmann, U., Jacques, P. F., Fox, C. S., & Hwang, S. (2016). Sugar-sweetened beverage consumption is associated with change of visceral adipose tissue over 6 years of follow-up. *Circulation, 133*(4), 370–377.

Sylvetsky, A. C., & Rother, K. I. (2016). Trends in the consumption of low-calorie sweeteners. *Physiology & Behavior, 164*, 446–450.

Internet References . . .

Academy of Nutrition and Dietetics

www.eatright.org

Center for Science in the Public Interest

www.cspi.org

Sugar Association

https://www.sugar.org/

Selected, Edited, and with Issue Framing Material by:
Eileen L. Daniel, *SUNY College at Brockport*

ISSUE

Do the Benefits of Statin Drugs Outweigh the Risks?

YES: Jo Willey, from "The Benefits of Statins 'Greatly Outweigh' Small Risks Say Experts," *express.co.uk* (2014)

NO: Martha Rosenberg, from "Do You Really Need That Statin?" *huffingtonpost.com* (2012)

Learning Outcomes

After reading this issue, you will be able to:

- Assess the overall benefits of statin drugs for patients without symptoms of heart disease.
- Understand the risk factors associated with heart disease.
- Understand the side effects of statin drugs.

ISSUE SUMMARY

YES: Journalist Jo Willey reports that statins' ability to prevent heart attacks and stroke outweighed any risks and that tens of thousands of deaths from cardiovascular disease could be prevented if all eligible adults took the drugs.

NO: Investigative reporter Martha Rosenberg interviewed physician Barbara Roberts, who claims that statins treat high cholesterol, which is a weak risk factor for heart disease, and that the side effects of the drugs negate any benefits, especially when taken by otherwise healthy adults with high cholesterol.

About 610,000 people die of cardiovascular disease (CVD) in the United States every year, which represents one in every four deaths. CVD is the leading cause of death for both men and women though more than half of the deaths due to heart disease in 2009 were in men. Coronary heart disease is the most common type of heart disease, killing over 370,000 people annually. There are a number of risk factors linked to heart disease including age, smoking, diet, and elevated serum cholesterol. Statins are a category of drugs prescribed to reduce serum cholesterol levels by blocking a liver enzyme that plays a central role in the production of cholesterol. The majority of cholesterol in the blood stream is manufactured by the body, primarily in the liver. Elevated cholesterol levels have been linked to cardiovascular disease (CVD) including heart disease and stroke. Statins have been found to reduce the risk of cardiovascular disease and mortality especially among individuals at high risk. The evidence is strong that statins are effective for treating CVD in the early stages of the disease and potentially in those at elevated risk but without CVD. As a result, statin drugs are among the most widely prescribed drugs on the market, with one in four Americans over 45 taking them. While the drug has some important benefits, it also has side effects, which include muscle pain, increased risk of diabetes mellitus, and abnormalities in liver enzyme tests. In addition, the drugs have rare but severe adverse effects, particularly muscle damage. Some research suggests statins help with asthma symptoms, but a 2011 study found that some individuals with asthma who took statins had more symptoms and worse lung function than asthma patients who didn't take them.

While there are side effects associated with statins, the drugs are also considered by many to be one of the greatest public health triumphs of the past quarter century. During that time period, the death rate from heart disease in the United States fell by half, resulting in close to 350,000 fewer Americans dying from heart disease each year. Though the data are fairly spectacular, there is a debate over whether statins actually reduce death from heart disease among asymptomatic patients with no known heart disease. Statins have been proven effective for individuals who have already suffered a heart attack or stroke. The data on healthy adults is not as clear, though the drug is prescribed for both patients who have had a heart attack and those who are healthy but have high cholesterol, particularly high levels of low-density lipoproteins. Interestingly, serum cholesterol levels are as not strongly predictive of heart disease as once thought and most current research indicates that these levels are actually a fairly weak predictor of who will have a heart attack.

There is another possibility that statins might provide benefits unrelated to cholesterol reduction. There is some evidence that they also decrease inflammation which, when it occurs in the arteries, is thought to increase the risk of heart disease. A 2008 study called the JUPITER trial tested statins in about 18,000 people with normal high-density lipoproteins but with an elevated marker for inflammation. Statins reduced the risks of heart attack and stroke among this group, leading proponents to conclude that by working through an additional mechanism, lowering inflammation, not just low-density lipoproteins, statins were beneficial to people with normal cholesterol levels.

New American Heart Association guidelines released in 2014 expanded the criteria for statin use. Under these new guidelines, nearly 13 million more Americans, mostly over 60, will be eligible to take statin drugs. The American Heart Association guidelines expanded the criteria for statin use to include people with an increased risk of developing heart disease over a 10-year period.

In this study, researchers used data from more than 3,700 Americans, aged 40 to 75, to determine how the new guidelines would affect the number of people who use the drugs. A large increase in usage would occur among people older than 60, with 77 percent eligible for statins under the new guidelines compared to 48 percent under the previous standards. The use of statins among people aged 40 to 60 would increase only from 27 percent to 30 percent, the researchers said. Men aged 60 to 75 who are not taking statins and do not have heart disease would be most affected by the new recommendations, with the number who are eligible increasing from about 30 percent to 87 percent, according to the study, which was published in 2014 in the *New England Journal of Medicine*. The use of statins among healthy women in this age group would rise from 21 percent to 53 percent. On the other hand, the researchers also found that about 1.6 million adults who were previously eligible for statins would no longer be candidates for the drugs. Most of these people are young adults who have elevated cholesterol but a low 10-year risk of heart disease.

It has been standard practice among doctors for the last 50 years at least to treat serum cholesterol levels as a risk factor for heart disease, and to assume that there is a causal connection. Half of Americans over 65 are taking prescription statin drugs (and one-sixth of people between 45 and 65). It's clear that statins lower serum cholesterol, but whether the drugs lower risk of heart disease is less clear, and there may be no benefit at all for overall mortality rate.

The above questions are difficult to answer because there is such a deep division of opinion in the medical community. The mainstream view, which has the best data and the best studies behind it, has been funded by the pharmaceutical industry, and statin drugs are a $35 billion dollar industry in America, growing rapidly. It may ultimately be determined that the drugs are not effective for healthy people despite their ability to lower cholesterol.

YES

Jo Willey

The Benefits of Statins "Greatly Outweigh" Small Risks Say Experts

The pills taken by 8 million people in the UK have been given a clean bill of health by British researchers despite raising the risk of diabetes.

They found the pills may cause small increases in weight gain and blood sugar which in turn raises a person's chances of Type 2 diabetes.

But they said that statins' ability to prevent heart attack and stroke negated this danger—and that simple lifestyle changes could be used to balance out any problems.

Professor Colin Baigent, from the University of Oxford, said: "The magnitude of the benefits of statins arising from the prevention of heart attacks and strokes greatly outweighs any small risks of diabetes, so the current recommendations for statin use remain appropriate."

The backing came after researchers from University College London and the University of Glasgow discovered how statins increase the risk of diabetes and stroke.

They found that taking statins was associated with an around 240g—or half a pound—weight gain and a 12 per cent increased risk of developing type 2 diabetes over four years.

In a separate comment on the research, Professor Baigent added: "Statins have previously been shown to cause a small increase in the risk of developing diabetes, and this study provides some clues about the biological mechanism by which this occurs.

"But although it is helpful to understand mechanisms, this research does not change our assessment of the safety of statins."

Statins work by reducing the efficiency of a liver enzyme involved in cholesterol production, which causes liver cells to trap more "bad" low-density lipoprotein (LDL) cholesterol from the blood and lower levels.

This is why the drugs are credited with dramatically lowering the risk of suffering a heart attack or stroke.

The research published in *The Lancet* looked at data on nearly 130,000 people from clinical trials that previously tested the effect of statins on heart disease and stroke.

It found those given statins vs placebo, or higher vs lower doses of statins, had a small increase in risk of developing Type 2 diabetes of about 12 per cent over a four-year period, and also to gain 240g in weight.

Co-lead author Dr David Preiss of the University of Glasgow Institute of Cardiovascular and Medical Sciences, said: "Weight gain is a risk factor for diabetes which might help explain the small increased risk of diabetes observed in people taking statins."

The researchers found that commonly occurring genetic variants were also associated with a higher weight and marginally higher type 2 diabetes risk.

The effects were much smaller than from statin treatment, but enabled the researchers to conclude that the weight gain and diabetes risk found in the analysis from trials were related to the known mechanism of action of statins rather than some other unintended effect.

Co-senior author Professor Naveed Sattar of the University of Glasgow, added: "Previous analyses have indicated that the cardiovascular benefits of statin treatment greatly outweigh the risk of new-onset type 2 diabetes.

"Nevertheless, many patients eligible for statin treatment would also benefit from lifestyle changes including increased physical activity, eating more healthily and stopping smoking. The modest increases in weight and diabetes risk seen in this study could easily be mitigated by adopting healthier diets and lifestyles.

"Reinforcing the importance of lifestyle changes when discussing these issues with patients would further enhance the benefit of statin treatment in preventing heart attacks and strokes."

Professor Jeremy Pearson, associate medical director at the British Heart Foundation, which helped fund the study, said: "Statins offer substantial protection from coronary heart disease. This rigorous and extensive study looked at why people taking them have a small increased risk of diabetes.

"The researchers found a direct relationship between how statins reduce cholesterol production and small increases in weight gain and blood sugar. This could explain the slightly increased risk of diabetes—a risk that could be reduced through lifestyle changes.

"This study should reassure people that the benefits of taking statins far outweigh the small effect on diabetes risk. But the results also reinforce that, alongside prescribed medication, taking steps to maintain a healthy weight is essential to stay heart healthy."

Professor Tom Sanders, honorary nutritional director of HEART UK, said: "Statin treatment seems to result in a small weight gain and increase blood glucose resulting in an increased diagnosis of type 2 diabetes.

"Advice to maintain a healthy weight and physical activity, which are key to preventing type 2 diabetes, should accompany the prescription of statins."

The new research comes after Britain's leading heart doctors joined forces to state "the jury is no longer out" on whether the benefits of statins outweigh the risks, confirming that quarter of a century of research has provided clear and definitive evidence to back the use of the cholesterol-lowering drugs.

The heart pills have been mired in controversy after scare stories about their dangers which were later retracted.

In May, researchers were forced to withdraw "misleading" claims about statins published in the respected *British Medical Journal* which overestimated side effects 20-fold.

They later accepted the research, which claimed the drugs caused higher rates of diabetes, tiredness and muscle pain than had previously been scientifically proven, was incorrect.

At the time, medics warned that thousands of people could be needlessly putting their lives at risk if they stopped taking the life-saving pills because of the false claim that statins had severe side effects in a fifth of patients.

Although six leading scientists joined forces to declare the evidence is "substantial" that the pills are safe, they said people should not rely on the medication as a "quick fix" but be encouraged to adopt healthier lifestyles to lower heart attack and stroke risk and make an informed choice with a doctor about statins.

Statins are already used by eight million people in the UK.

In July, updated guidance from the National Institute for Health and Care Excellence said statins could soon be taken by as many as 17 million adults in a bid to prevent heart problems.

The pills are currently offered to people who have a 20 per cent risk of developing cardiovascular disease within 10 years.

But the NHS will now lower this threshold to include people with just a 10 per cent risk.

This could see an additional 4.5 million patients offered the drugs, bringing the total of all eligible people to 17 million—around 40 per cent of the adult population of England.

If everyone eligible took the drugs, Nice estimates that between 20,000 and 50,000 deaths could be prevented every year.

Jo Willey is a journalist specializing in health and medical issues.

Martha Rosenberg

NO

Do You Really Need That Statin? This Expert Says No

This is an interview with Barbara H. Roberts, M.D., author of The Truth About Statins: Risks and Alternatives to Cholesterol-Lowering Drugs.

Statins are medications that lower cholesterol by inhibiting an enzyme involved in its production by the liver and other organs. First approved by the FDA in 1987, statins are arguably the most widely-prescribed medicine in the industrialized world today—and the most profitable, representing billions a year in profits to the drug industry. In fact, Lipitor was the world's best-selling drug until its patent expired recently. Yet most trials that prove statins' effectiveness in preventing cardiac events and death have been funded by companies and principle investigators who stand to benefit from their wide use. In February, the FDA warned that statins can increase users' risk of Type 2 diabetes and memory loss, confusion and other cognition problems.

Barbara H. Roberts, M.D., is director of the Women's Cardiac Center at the Miriam Hospital in Providence, R.I. and associate clinical professor of medicine at the Alpert Medical School of Brown University. She spent two years at the National Heart, Lung and Blood Institute of the National Institutes of Health (NIH), where she was involved in the first clinical trial that demonstrated a beneficial effect of lowering cholesterol on the incidence of heart disease. In addition to *The Truth About Statins: Risks and Alternatives to Cholesterol-Lowering Drugs*, she is also author of *How to Keep from Breaking Your Heart: What Every Woman Needs to Know About Cardiovascular Disease.*

Martha Rosenberg: Statins have become so popular with adults middle-aged and older in industrialized countries, they are almost a pharmaceutical rite of passage. Yet you write in your new book there is little evidence they are effective in many groups and no evidence they are effective in one group: women without heart disease. Worse, you provide evidence, including stories from your own patients, that they are doing serious harm.

Barbara Roberts: Yes. Every week in my practice I see patients with serious side effects to statins, and many did not need to be treated with statins in the first place. These side effects range from debilitating muscle and joint pain to transient global amnesia, neuropathy, cognitive dysfunction, fatigue and muscle weakness. Most of these symptoms subside or improve when they are taken off statins. There is even growing evidence of a statin link to Lou Gehrig's disease.

Martha Rosenberg: One patient you write about caused a fire in her home by forgetting that the stove was on. Another was a professor who experienced such memory loss on a statin he could no longer teach; others ended up in wheelchairs. The only thing more shocking than the side effects you write about is the apparent blindness of the medical establishment to them. Until half a year ago, there were practically no warnings at all.

Barbara Roberts: There is no question that many doctors have swallowed the Kool-Aid. Big Pharma has consistently exaggerated the benefits of statins and some physicians used scare tactics so that patients are afraid that if they go off the statins, they will have a heart attack immediately. Yet high cholesterol, which the statins address, is a relatively weak risk factor for developing atherosclerosis. For example, diabetes and smoking are far more potent when it comes to increasing risk.

Martha Rosenberg: One group you say should not be given statins at all because there is no benefit and significant risk is women who have no heart disease.

Barbara Roberts: In three major studies [1–3] of women without diagnosed heart disease, but who were at high risk (in one of these studies, each participant had to have high blood pressure and three other risk factors), 40 women out of 4,904 on statins had either a heart attack or cardiac death, compared to 44 women out of 4,836 on placebo.

That is not a statistically significant difference. Since the likelihood of experiencing a statin side effect is about 20 to 25 percent, the risk of putting a healthy woman on a statin far outweighs the benefit. Still, statins are routinely given to this group because the guidelines are shaped by Big Pharma. The guidelines are not supported by the evidence, and in the case of healthy women I don't follow them.

Martha Rosenberg: You give a story in your book about your 92-year-old patient who had a total cholesterol of 266, triglycerides of 169, HDL cholesterol of 66, and LDL cholesterol of 165. Her primary care doctor wanted her to take a statin, but you did not feel she needed to because she had no evidence of heart disease, had never smoked, did not have high blood pressure and was not diabetic.

Barbara Roberts: Yes and today she is 103.5—and doing fine, never having taken a statin.

Martha Rosenberg: In *The Truth About Statins* you explain pretty clearly how studies have made statins look more effective and safer than they are. How has this been done?

Barbara Roberts: First of all, the studies are of short duration, and some of them even have a "run in" phase during which people are given the drug to see if they tolerate it. If not, they are not enrolled in the study. Secondly, study subjects are cherry-picked to exclude the very elderly, people with liver or kidney disease or those with any chronic illness that might "muddy" the results.

Martha Rosenberg: In other words, the very people who will be taking them?

Barbara Roberts: Yes, and of course patients will also be staying on the drugs for life unlike trial subjects. Then, the data from the studies are usually given in terms of relative rather than absolute risk. The absolute risk of a cardiac event is only reduced by a few percentage points by statins and in some patients, like the women without heart disease we just talked about, the reduction is not even statistically significant. In some studies surrogate end points like inflammation or artery thickness are used but a favorable change in surrogate markers does not always translate into clinical benefit. In addition, many studies use composite end points, which include not only "hard" end points like heart attack or death (which are pretty hard to misdiagnose) but also "softer" end points like the "need" for revascularization or the occurrence of acute coronary syndromes. For example, studies may be performed in many countries with very different rates of revascularization procedures, making use of this as an end point very problematic.

Martha Rosenberg: This brings to mind the JUPITER trial, which enrolled people without heart disease, with normal levels (less than 130) of LDL or bad cholesterol, but evidence of increased inflammation as measured by the hsCRP test and treated them with placebo or rosuvastatin. JUPITER stood for "Justification for the Use of Statins in Prevention," and both the study and its principle investigator were funded by AstraZeneca, who makes the statin Crestor. The principal investigator also holds the patent for the hsCRP blood test. Why was JUPITER regarded as medical science and not marketing?

Barbara Roberts: Actually, the JUPITER study was criticized to some extent. But you have to remember that medical journals depend upon Big Pharma for their ads and reprint orders just as medical centers and medical professionals rely on Big Pharma for funding. It is a round robin situation that probably won't change until the patients, doctors and the public demand change. As for CRP, it can also rise if a patient has a cold, bronchitis or is taking post-menopausal hormones.

Martha Rosenberg: You are very outspoken about the problem of industry shaping and influencing medical practice, yet you also admit that you accepted Big Pharma money yourself.

Barbara Roberts: In 2004, Pfizer asked me to become a speaker, specifically on Lipitor. I told the drug rep who invited me to be a speaker that I would be interested in giving talks on gender-specific aspects of cardiac disease, but not in just talking about their statin, and I gave lectures in restaurants and hospitals. Despite the fact that Pfizer was sponsoring my talks, I never failed to point out that there was no evidence that Lipitor—or any statin—prevented cardiac events in women who did not have established cardiovascular disease. They tolerated this until one day a regional manager came to one of my talks, and then I was disinvited. I was on the speaker's bureau for another company, Abbott, but when they began to insist that I use their slides rather than my own, I gave up being on any Big Pharma speaker's bureaus. I write in my book that even though my interactions with drug and device companies complied with ethical guidelines it does not mean I was not influenced.

Martha Rosenberg: In journalism, when a reporter takes money from someone she is writing about, she is regarded as no longer a reporter but a publicist. Yet doctors who consult to Pharma are not judged as harshly and most contend they are not influenced by industry money . . .

Barbara Roberts: They are wrong. An article in the *American Journal of Bioethics* in 2003 found that gifts bestow a sense of indebtedness and influence behavior whether or not the recipient is directly conscious of it. More recently, research presented at a symposium at Houston's Baylor College of Medicine called the Scientific Basis of Influence and Reciprocity mapped actual changes in the brain when gifts are received.

Martha Rosenberg: I was surprised to find recipes in your book and even more surprised by some of your dietary recommendations, such as avoiding a low-fat diet and eating a lot of olive oil. A lot of experts have recommended a low-fat diet.

Barbara Roberts: The first thing I prescribe to my patients who have low levels of the "good" or HDL cholesterol is two to three tablespoons of olive oil a day, and in every case the HDL increases. Olive oil is rich in polyphenols, which have anti-inflammatory and antioxidant effects. Several studies [4, 5] have shown that the Mediterranean diet reduces total mortality and especially death from cardiovascular disease, yet it gets little media attention. The Mediterranean diet is a plant-based diet that includes colorful vegetables, fruits, whole grains, beans, cheese, nuts, olive oil, seafood, red wine with meals, and very little meat.

Martha Rosenberg: You indict professional medical associations like the American Heat Association (AHA) for profiteering at the public's expense by calling harmful foods healthful in exchange for corporate money.

Barbara Roberts: For years, the AHA preached the gospel of the low-fat diet, calling it the "cornerstone" of its dietary recommendations though there was, and is, no evidence of its benefit. The AHA rakes in millions from food corporations for the use of its "heart-check mark." Some of the so-called heart-healthy foods it has endorsed include Boar's Head All Natural Ham, which contains 340 milligrams of sodium in a two-ounce serving, and Boar's Head EverRoast Oven Roasted Chicken Breast, which contains 440 milligrams of sodium in a two-ounce serving. High sodium intake raises blood pressure, which increases the risk of cardiovascular disease. In addition, studies have shown that eating processed meat increases the risk of diabetes and atherosclerosis.

Martha Rosenberg: You are not afraid to express strong opinions. You say that the AHA has "sold its soul," that medical centers conducting drug trials for Big Pharma have become "hired hands" and that one university medical center is Big Pharma's "lapdog." Are you afraid of retaliation from Big Pharma, medical centers or the colleagues you work with?

Barbara Roberts: I haven't received any communiqués from Big Pharma. A few colleagues have expressed dismay, but I am thick-skinned and hard-headed and don't care what they say. My main concern is the health and safety of my patients.

References

1. http://circ.ahajournals.org/content/121/9/1069.short
2. http://www.thelancet.com/journals/lancet/article/PIIS0140-6736(03)12948-0/abstract
3. http://fundacionconfiar.com.ar/capacitacion/Clase_5/Levels%20Results%20of%20AFCAPSTexCAPS.pdf
4. http://www.ncbi.nlm.nih.gov/pubmed/9989963
5. http://www.ncbi.nlm.nih.gov/pubmed/18071168

Martha Rosenberg is an investigative health reporter.

EXPLORING THE ISSUE

Do the Benefits of Statin Drugs Outweigh the Risks?

Critical Thinking and Reflection

1. Do the benefits of statins outweigh the risks?
2. What are the alternatives to statin drugs?
3. Who would most benefit from statins and why?

Is There Common Ground?

Cholesterol-lowering statin drugs are ubiquitous these days, with more and more being prescribed each year. But questions remain about their safety and effectiveness. While the medical literature does show that statins may help people with a history of a heart attack, stroke, or current signs and symptoms of existing cardiovascular disease (CVD), studies have found that people without a history of heart attack or stroke who take statin drugs do not live any longer than the people who take a placebo. This is particularly true for women, who have not been well represented in clinical research studies.

In a review of statin data published in the *British Medical Journal,* lead author John Abramson of Harvard Medical School says that people who take statins to prevent a first heart event don't lower their risk of dying from any cause, or from heart disease over 10 years. Not only do statins *not* lower the risk of dying early, but they also don't lower the chances of being hospitalized for a heart problem or other serious heart-related illness. The medication can lower—very slightly—the risk of having a heart attack or stroke. But that benefit is offset by the drugs' side effects. "For people with a less than 20% risk of having a heart event in 10 years, which is the vast majority for whom the statins would be prescribed under the new 2014 guidelines, we are not seeing a net benefit," Abramson says.

And while they're generally considered safe, statins have a variety of side effects, including decreased liver function, interference with the manufacture of coenzyme Q10 (CoQ10), rhabdomyolysis (the breaking down of muscle tissue), nerve damage, impaired mental function with prolonged use, possible increased risk of cancer and heart failure with long-term use, fatigue, diabetes, and weight gain. Fortunately, there are safe and effective lifestyle changes which can help lower cholesterol and reduce the risk of cardiovascular disease. These include weight loss, exercise, smoking cessation, blood pressure control, and eating a diet high in fruits and vegetables, especially the Mediterranean diet.

Additional Resources

Brooks, M. (2017). Cholesterol wars. *New Scientist, 244*(31), 28–32.

Four myths about statins. (2015). *Harvard Heart Letter, 25*(6), 1–7.

Benefits strongly outweigh risks associated with statins. (2014). *Reactions Weekly, 1503*(1), 2.

Mlodinow, S. G., Onysko, M. K., Vandiver, J. W., Hunter, M. L., & Mahvan, T. D. (2014). Statin adverse effects. *Clinician Reviews, 24*(11), 41–50.

Internet References . . .

American Heart Association

www.heart.org

Food and Drug Administration

www.fda.gov/Drugs

National Institutes of Health

www.nlm.nih.gov/medlineplus/heartdiseases.html